THE HISTORY

OF

THE HOLY, MILITARY, SOVEREIGN ORDER

OF

ST. JOHN OF JERUSALEM.

THE HISTORY

OF

THE HOLY, MILITARY, SOVEREIGN ORDER

OF

ST. JOHN OF JERUSALEM;

OR,

KNIGHTS HOSPITALLERS, KNIGHTS TEMPLARS,
KNIGHTS OF RHODES, KNIGHTS OF MALTA.

By JOHN TAAFFE

KNIGHT COMMANDER OF THE ORDER, AND AUTHOR OF
"ADELAIS."

IN FOUR VOLUMES.
VOL. I.

The Naval & Military Press Ltd

Published by

The Naval & Military Press Ltd
Unit 5 Riverside, Brambleside
Bellbrook Industrial Estate
Uckfield, East Sussex
TN22 1QQ England

Tel: +44 (0)1825 749494

www.naval-military-press.com
www.nmarchive.com

In reprinting in facsimile from the original, any imperfections are inevitably reproduced and the quality may fall short of modern type and cartographic standards.

It is requested that before reading these Volumes, the Errata be neatly corrected.

ERRATA, VOL. I.

Page.
150, Note 3, for XLIII, read XLIV.
ib., Note 4, for XLII, read XLIII.
190, line 15, for 119, read 183.
216. Note 1, for XIV, cap. XVI, read XXIII, cap III, and XXV, cap. X.
218, Note 2, for XXXVII, read XXXVI.
219, Note 4, for VI, read VIII.
323, Note 2, for XXIV, read XXXIV.
338, Note 1, after Tyronem, dele the stop.

THE HISTORY

OF THE ORDER OF

ST. JOHN OF JERUSALEM.

BOOK I.

CHAPTER I.

THE order of St. John of Jerusalem was created in 1099. That I undertake its history is neither quite my choice, nor quite superfluous; for it is a subject on which I *ought* to be well informed; and many discoveries have been made since its other historians in any language. Those early times were confused. In battles, retreats, conflagrations, papers and parchments were soon lost or burned. So to make up for them, writers employed their imaginations, with a sort of foundation in the chronicler William of Tyre, who was no contemporary of what he relates, but was himself one of those fabulists, and either from not knowing, or not wishing to know the real state of the case, was misinformed and misinformed others. But of late several of those long-lost documents (or original duplicates) found in the Vatican and other dusty archives show things in a totally different light; and enable a modern to reveal many secrets and render clear what before had been so obscure that it appeared a kind of neutral ground where everybody might fearlessly erect their castles. But are there not too many books already? Yes, with exceptions; and this is one, for it makes what is remote, new; not by any process of fancy, but by relating the plain facts. This removes one considerable difficulty; for otherwise I should not like to be involved in clouds at such a distance behind. Not for the sake of what may be rancid; but truth —sacred truth which is of all times, and the best at all times.

Yet, as vantage ground, it is requisite to take a view of our part of the globe in ages immediately preceding those to be soon treated of; and, to do so intelligibly, it will be convenient to consider the public condition somewhat earlier also, in a few of the principal countries as a fair sample of the remainder; it appearing to me hard, in any other way, to account for the universal ferment which had kept on increasing little by little—a feeling of disquietude preparing Christendom for some great change, it knew not what, nor perhaps cared; but everywhere was it held certain that some important event, some radical cure was coming. Therefore these two first chapters shall be confined to such preliminary matters—not to alter, but to refresh readers' minds; nor will notes be necessary, as repeating what is general; but very different forwards, beginning with the third chapter, where my authorities for each iota shall be distinctly cited, to be occasionally consulted or not.

And first, concerning that noble and high-minded nation who usually take the lead wherever there is anything of great or good to be undertaken. As far back as Charlemagne, he wept at observing some Norman vessels off the French coasts; for he foresaw what ruin they would one day bring on France. Danes or Normans are either precisely a single people; or, at most, varieties of one race in different places or periods; since some of that same fleet putting into an English harbour, were there called *Danes*.

At one time we are told of a Danish pirate who, conducting his armada up the Seine, and plundering both its banks, took Paris for awhile and sacked it; and of another who, after being repulsed from England by Alfred, assailed France, and settled a Danish colony as masters of the city and territory of Chartres—thus consenting to become vassals of the French king; but, notwithstanding, several parties of marauders kept continually harassing the sea-side, to the perpetual terror, and often serious injury, of the inhabitants; and certainly those sea kings had for many years been in the habit of devastating that fertile region of the Continent, before they established themselves there in 900, and changed the name of the province (which until then had preserved its ancient Roman one, Neustria) into Normandy; that is, land of the Northmen or Normans. Indeed, they had likewise turned Christians—retaining, however, much of the contempt of danger and death, and a relish for travels, and that generosity of freedom of their old faith in Odin; which sentiments, and romantic, perhaps virtuous, love, as well as religion, led them to pilgrimages to Palestine; and they nearly all went by Magna Grecia, and had astonishing adventures.

Forty of them landing at Salerno or Amalfi, on their return from a pilgrimage to Jerusalem, repulsed the Saracen freebooters, to the delight of the natives, who invited their allies to stay, or return with others of their countrymen; and that they might be sure of grateful hospitality;

and so they did, and formed a sort of military republic. Some years later the hardy veterans, religious but inaccessible to scruples, overthrew a large Papal army—or rather multitudinous rabble with the Pope at its head; but victors, they unhelmed and knelt down to the Pope himself on the same field, and craved his forgiveness and blessing; which, with or against his will, he gave, and erected whatever they had conquered, or should conquer in those parts, into a feudal patrimony under the protection of St. Peter. Thus constituting himself feudal lord over lands to which he had no right whatever; and gaining more by having lost, than he could have by having won a battle. Another Norman gentleman, who had twelve sons, sent them to seek their fortune in a like manner; and most of them rose to royal rank. The youngest, whose sole patrimony was one horse, worked up to be king of that rich island, which had been the granary of imperial Rome. What if he and his young bride had once travelled straddle legs on the same horse? He had no other. But the day was at hand when he was to be a potent and wealthy monarch; where he and queen might (so they liked) sit on their throne, as quietly as Sir John taking his ease in his inn. And when he wore a crown, he gave his historian special directions to insert the circumstance of one horse in his annals.

The lapse of ages was to find what were styled the Gallican liberties concentrated in the King of France; but now in the tenth century, where were they to be concentred? There was no King of France, but only nominally; rather an exceedingly loose federalism. It was only mere justice to the Popes to avow that it was oftener by assent than assumption that their undue power grew. If they occasionally arrogated, they more frequently did not refuse the wide jurisdiction offered them. That Christian mercy had possibly been their motive, may be believed; and if some wily Pontiffs took advantage of it, what is there implied of peculiar badness? A foreign mediator in those times of ruthless tyranny, might have been a necessary evil. The union of temporal and spiritual in the state can hardly co-exist, except at the very highest point of civilisation—where no country tarries long. But before and after? Alas! She that is conversant with what is divine, and whose aspirations are after a far better world than this, must then assume naturally the influence which stronger minds exercise over feebler; and, when implored, lends her limping sister a helping hand along their weary way through this vale of tears. With France that unhappy infancy is supposed to comprehend the entire space from Charlemagne's death to that of Philip Augustus—or a still immenser stretch.

But the worst of that whole shocking period is precisely what we have now reached, the eleventh century. The list of the woes and grievances of the French is much too long to recite. The oppression of the people by the barons, that of these by the unworthy portion of the clergy, and of all three by the kings when they had an opportunity—all classes were deeply dissatisfied, and ripe for any extravagance. Gothic or feudal, both systems were unjust and odious. Miles justitiæ (miles meaning then, not so much soldier as knight), *Knight of Justice* was more illustrious than any rank or birth. But none but nobles could be knighted.

By an ancient law in France, no one could be imprisoned for debt, and it was lawful to rescue the debtor from any officer who had arrested him. So, how was it possible for a common person to get paid by a nobleman? Only the nobles could fish or fowl. Hunting and hawking were Norman pursuits during peace; in fact, through all France they were the chief occupations of gentlemen, and a knight rarely left his house, either on horseback or afoot without a falcon on his fist, and a greyhound following him. But such diversions were exclusively for the nobles. There was little or no trade, nor could the people, even the few who had scraped together a little cash through some chance, increase it by lending, though interest on money was at forty or sixty per cent., for usury was adjudged exclusively to the Jews, or Lombards. No glazed windows, no books, no paintings in even the houses of gentlemen; for although the abbey of St. Denis had windows, both glazed and painted, much earlier, yet glass is said not to have been employed in the best French mansions before the fourteenth century. So it may well be imagined that the cottages were wretched, and undoubtedly no domestic architecture in France was better than in England, where it was execrably bad. And I lay stress upon it the rather, that I am quite of their opinion who hold, that architecture, more than any other of the fine arts, characterises its age.

A grievous misfortune to the French was the feudal army. Better, when soldiers were hired; but these mercenary *solidarj* were later; at least the first instance I find in Hallam is in 1030, and then it was a small corps. That St. Germains had the pointed arch in 1014, only shows that pilgrims were frequent from France to Palestine even then;

by one of whom it was probably brought by a rare exception. When that style became general an age or two later, whether it came through Spain or Italy, or round by the German woods, resembling the intersection of the top branches of trees in a Druidic avenue, or if it originated in the East at all, or in what part of it, are questions that remain as undetermined as ever. Why further painful details? The sense of severe depression is apparent. The humane spirit of Christianity, the religion of love and kindness, had indeed struggled long with the manners and maxims of the world; and as far back as the thick night of the sixth century, St. Gregory had told them that nature had made all men free; and that the yoke of servitude, introduced by what was called the law of nations, was utterly repugnant to the law of Christ.

But what the poor peasant beheld was in awful contradiction to such consoling doctrines; that breathed of pure republican liberty, or St. Simonism of the eighteenth century, or even Socialism, without the dangerous, sanguinary, most illogical consequences drawn from it by insanity, ignorance, or wickedness. A vague tradition—if it existed—of some past legislation, only increased discontent. So what conclude, but that the sole resource was to turn to the priest, and follow his advice blindly?

Driven from his hovel, despised and ill-treated by his landlord, and exposed to numberless distresses, between slavery, anarchy, and famine, what was left for the cultivator of the soil, but to indulge in the expectation of some great change at hand—ready at the crisis to take any direction his clergy prescribed. Classes which had any intimacy with those handsome domineering Normans, could not but have imbibed something of their gay independent spirit, and enthusiasm both in religion and love, and their uncontrollable desire of roving— they being the greatest pilgrims of their time; one of whom was the Count de Verdun, of the illustrious family that was soon to produce Godfrey de Bouillon. To consort with them was to get restless, particularly in private hardships—and what family then but had its private hardships? Uncertainty brooding everywhere, and gradually falling into permanent forlornness and the loss of any attachment to their homes; as eager to shift them as the Nomade Arabs, who carry their pots and pans about with them, and children and tents, and whatever they possess, and a furious contempt for stone walls. Thus all the French lay on their oars.

Doubtful as may be the origin of those enterprising parties that got together in Scandinavia, yet coming thence to Germany, ancient or modern

—before or since Tacitus — they deserve to be called Northmen; just as much on the Elbe or Rhine, as on the Seine or Thames. They were a fated and dangerous race; yet carried a sort of compensation with them—the seeds of freedom. And leaping over several centuries, the landwehr, or insurrection, brings us to the times of Charlemagne; for not only in deed, but name, too, that Militia dates so far back. Yet, if it be true that the Irish missionary sent to convert those of Wurzburgh, was murdered there in the eighth century, is it not surprising that the capital of Franconia, whence so many emperors derived, should be so late of conversion? learned antiquaries informing us that also the French were from Franconia; as its very name implies, land of the French!

But neither Militia nor Christianity seem to have remedied the reigning evils much; for open robbery was more in vogue in Germany than anywhere else, since the strongholds of those they called nobles spread terror over the whole country; they making it a practice not only to plunder the travellers they seized, but likewise to sell them into slavery, when promised no sufficient ransom. Bondage within their own castles, or to somewhere in the vicinity, was their sale at first; but when there came to be Saracens, they were sold to the

Saracens — traffic of which Venice set the example. Even at a much later period the German nobles were mostly robbers; the burghers of the town no better, for they used to give the liberties of them to every stranger that offered, without the least discrimination, vagabonds for the greater part, who terrified the honest, by committing every kind of crime with perfect impunity; so that between pillage and piracy, both by sea and land, it is a wonder that in Germany any had the courage to become merchants at all. The sacred appetite for gold must have been very cogent. In Saxony, Poland, and Lithuania, the remains of Paganism were trod out with a savage eagerness to compensate for lingering rather late.

As to the Jews, they were fair game throughout the entire of Christendom; the unfortunates had to endure sackage, gross insults, and murder in every land. It was a question of more or less atrocity and injustice the vilest; but of justice or mercy never. Shame on the nefarious abusers of the religion of peace and charity! After the fowler, and the Saxon Othos, and Franconian Henries, although the surnames of Guelph and Ghibelline had not been as yet invented; nevertheless the wicked enormity itself was—the sanguinary rivalry between the dynasties of southern and northern Germany—feud that degenerated to that degree that it embraced nearly every individual, and added new distractions to the whole region from Swabia to beyond the Vistula and Alps, and down the Adriatic. Still these amazing outrages bore with them the promise of healing, and seemed too violent to last long. And in proportion as nations became fervent Christians, they looked eastwards.

Hope was in the East, and the world desirous of hope. Many devout or repentant Germans, tired of such turbulent scenes, set out to make what they perhaps did not know St. Jerome and St. Austin had made several centuries earlier—a pilgrimage to the tomb of the Founder of their Divine creed; and though some of those scolloped travellers had died on the road to or at Jerusalem, and some of them on their way back, yet some of them also returned home, and lived to enliven it with spirit-stirring stories of adventure or holy unction. One of those pilgrims, who never reached Palestine, but died in Asia Minor, had been the very first sovereign in Europe who made a law against fiefs being given to the clergy without their lay superior's permission; so that it is not quite just to suppose all the religious palmers were foolishly servile to the monks or priests. Knights were then called *brothers*, fratres, and their guests *Christ's poor*, or the *poor*, without any consideration of their poverty or wealth; for it was the name given to the most opulent and even royal or imperial personages. And I observe it, lest any one hunting out my authorities, should be misled by finding the emperor I allude to amongst *Christ's poor*, and with *fra* before his name, not as the first syllable of *frate*, friar, but knight. All liberty came from the north (according to Sismondi) in its oral descent from their most remote ancestors, and was carried by who bore the misnomer of barbarians, over the whole of Europe, where that beneficent principle was gradually extinguished, with one single exception; but if not soonest, most fiercely in Germany, through reiterated persecutions. Conversion to Christianity only heightened the warmth of that ancestral dogma by giving it a celestial foundation.

The doctrine of Christ was sympathetic with the free. The currents of liberty flowed into it readily, rejoicing towards the immortal ocean. So love was added to liberty, and the rude converts proclaimed both divine; comprehensive, indefinite, intuitive, undying, incalculable, superhuman. Love is liberty and liberty is love, may appear a lax redundancy, and even ridiculous jargon to many minds; but to others it will associate with something dear, as a struggle to express what cannot be expressed by mortal, or scarcely; that sacred, forbidden and undiscovered word, which may possibly be felt, but if it could be pronounced would enamour, or peradventure instantly destroy, the whole creation.

This German-like anticipation of future grandeur (within the limits of our present world) is curiously exemplified by an individual of the Imperial race, who, though himself generally a vagrant, and never safe even in his bed, yet was so persuaded of the high destinies of his family, that he always wrote in his books the famous Austrian device, A E I O U, initials of *Austriæ est imperare Orbi Universo*. This somewhat wild state of the imagination, productive of a voluntary death for freedom or religion, is not without an analogy to that ascetic exaltation which has spirited away myriads to the wilderness; for whom fanatics were too harsh a name. Heavens preserve us! Any how such were not idly standing with their arms a-kimbo; but in deep thought, preparatory to something out of the common run.

But the land of the free—or of humbug, pretension, and clatter, as some have presumed to call her—land of amazing contrasts and contradictions, fair and noble England, neither was she an exception. Also she had her freedom from the north. Anglo-Saxons, Danes, Normans, all such new-comers were clearly varieties of one stock. The Anglo-Saxons appear to have had very mild laws, if mildness be few or no capital punishments. The native aboriginal Britons, who had become Christians long before in the night of ages, had been all extinguished, or driven away, or reduced to slavery; but those who replaced them followed the European stream, and assumed the profession of Christianity as soon as they fixed their residence in Southern Europe. Though Alfred had saved the Anglo-Saxons, he never rooted out the Danes, a name peculiar to England for those earlier Normans; but in France and every other country they are all called Normans. So both members of the Heptarchy thought it best to recur to their common origin, and quietly unite, which was an easy fusion, and a Dane shortly became king, and had a regular standing army, as preferable for discipline and separation from the people. The pay was in all such cases enormous, incredibly beyond what is paid at present. What we should call Colonels got ninety-six shillings a-day, and common troopers fourteen shillings, and a foot soldier one shilling and fourpence. To be sure they had to furnish themselves with arms, equipments, and horses; the cavalry at which instance of Canute is, I believe, the earliest known of hired soldiery in England. Sometimes a lance signified six men, sometimes three; so it is hard to specify their numbers. Lances were long and heavy; horses big, and of a cart-like breed. Banner, coat of arms, and war-cry were common to all knights; in some of which particulars, if it be rather too soon to ascribe them to Canute, this is above controversy, that it is an error to imagine that coats of arms were not in use before the first crusade.

Inside the towns, though civilisation might have existed in some degree, yet we owe agriculture entirely to the monks; with the exception of their secluded spots, which they had received a wilderness, and reclaimed, all the rest of the land lay, from the fifth to the eleventh century, in barbarous disorder. Small or no encouragement, whole domains waste, until some monastery got a grant of them, the only chance after the ravage of a marauder; for thus they got under the protection of the Church, not always, but generally valid. Doomsday Book is more than a proof of what had preceded it, and in what lamentable plight it found the shires.

Still, how easily the lower classes are contented, is conspicuous from their often calling for the laws of Edward the Confessor in subsequent times. When discontent alarms the husbandman, we must look to some awful catastrophe. Reach that sturdy order, and some violent change is infallibly at hand! Individuals of any wealth put off the evil day in their case by frequent pilgrimages; and even one to Jerusalem was no considerable undertaking, as long as the Abassides reigned. Pilgrimages are said to have been what may be termed a fashionable recreation then, and even up to the ninth or tenth century, pilgrims were received well everywhere; for they without fail brought each a letter from his prince or bishop, pilgrims being then to the Christians, what Haggies are this day to the Mahometans, privileged persons. Some danger or distress made them only the more revered. It is well known that the Mahometans respect pilgrims still more than the Christians do, and the natural consequence was tolerance in all things, even towards those of a different creed; pious makers of a hazardous pilgrimage from the distant West. The gates of the city of God were often opened to let in two parties nearly equal; one, disciples of the Koran, directed to Omar's mosque, the other, Christians for the Holy Sepulchre. Hitherto the Mussulmen had committed no atrocities, in what was a seat of holiness to them also; as the site of the Temple, the dwellings of David and Solomon, the Almighty's chosen place, illustrious for prophets, saints, and miracles. Therefore it was that Omar left them a sort of religious liberty, though the Christians had to hide their crosses, ring no more bells, nor retain any exterior sign of being dominant; but allow of building that extensive mosque, that in some sort stands still where the Temple once stood. The Christians could not be pleased; but Omar's moderation mitigated the fanaticism of his co-religionists.

After his death, his children imitated him; nor is it improbable the caliph might have thought it politic to keep on good terms with the western emperors, and thus prevent the Franks from siding with Constantinople against him. So Bagdad became the peaceful resort of the arts and sciences, and held that the progress of reason showed the elect of God. The manners of the chiefs of Islam becoming gentler from that enlightening of their minds, and Haroun el Rascid, and caliphs of his noble stamp, were finally rendered far more tolerant than Omar himself. Jerusalem enjoyed quiet, while Rome was plundered by the Saracens, at which period it is on record that the capital of Palestine could vaunt of twelve hostelries, and as many libraries belonging to the Latin *hospitium* within it; and Venice, Genoa, Pisa, Amalphi, sent their merchandise regularly to that mart.

But such a happy state ceased with the hauling down of the black flag of the Abassides; and a failure of the Greeks to resist the Fatimites only brought persecution on the Palestine Christians. Under the triumphant Fatimite caliphs, Christian blood flowed in torrents. All Christians began to be looked on as enemies to all Moslems. Mahometan fanaticism had its swing. The Holy Sepulchre pulled down, churches, if not saved by being turned into mosques, degraded, many of them into stables; Christians of every description expelled from Jerusalem, were left to wander about wild; the story on which Tasso founded his Olinda is said to have occurred then.

By little and little the Greek Christians, as subjects, were permitted to return, not so the Latins; who were nevermore allowed to have permanent quarters there. But thirty-seven years after the demolishing of the Holy Sepulchre, it rose again under the Caliph Daher in 1044, at the expense of the Greek Emperor, by leave from the Moslems, that they might profit by a toll which they set on pilgrims. No dwelling there for the Latins, except the few days required by pilgrims; who, as such, flocked thither and paid well.

Henceforward pilgrimage was attended with some real danger and considerable cost. A service of risk and insult rather than certain death; disguise often necessary, and contumely and privations always sure. Remarkable courage or very warm devotion cannot but be predicated of a lady who under those circumstances visited Jerusalem; but what will not a new convert? She had come from Sweden, then still in idolatry, into England, where she got converted; and thence set out for the Holy Sepulchre.

It was about the date of Alfred's birth. A few years later (868) the Anglo-Saxons (who in the worst cases preferred a durable punishment, such as mutilation, death too instantaneous to be a salutary example) having condemned in their way an execrable murderer of his uncle, the convict escaped from his native place in Essex across the sea into Brittany, where he repeated the same atrocity on his own brother, and there (with notable courtesy to a foreigner) was simply doomed to undergo his former sentence; as well he as his servants, who had been his accomplices in both crimes; to go on pilgrimage to Jerusalem, frequently kneeling, and always with a mark on his forehead, and in irons and enduring various other severities, and what must have been dreadful indignities to a Baron unarmed and defenceless master and underlings; so that their surviving to return was highly problematical. Yet return he did. Was it not a better sermon than hanging, or solitary confinement, or transportation when he came back a changed man, on the best evidence, those who knew him intimately afterwards during a prolonged old age, and who declare he died regretted as a holy person? Not that it would be the proper legislation now, or perhaps at any time; but only that in his instance it succeeded. Neither should I like averring that Frotmond's case is no lesson.

But what were Fatimites to their merciless successors, who it is said hesitated awhile between Christianity and Mahometanism, but decided for the Koran at last? Reckless savages by whom customs, treaties, lucre, were unregarded. It became hard for even the richest pilgrim to purchase an entry into the Holy Sepulchre. Still neither difficulties nor dangers put a stop to pilgrimages; but rather these went on increasing, as those increased. Perhaps the whole truth was not yet quite known to Europe.

Among the pilgrims of the beginning of the eleventh century, was the Count of Anjou. A bunch of broom the device of his family, *Plant the Broom* became its war-cry; just as with the Venetians *Plant the Lion*, St. Mark's winged lion. Not then noun, but verb, not *de* genet, but *le* genet. To the same epoch is affixed the pilgrimage of Robert Duke of Normandy, the Conqueror's father. Some narrate it was to this Robert the school of Salerno directed their verses; if so, he was called king as father to a king. *Francorum* meaning of the Franks suits any Latin. Indeed we have the high authority of Gibbon for the word *French* not being given to any people during the second and third crusades by either Greeks or Orientals, and the Salernitans of that time were wholly or in great part Greeks. *Frank* then meant what it does to-day, any nation of Western Europe. The chiefs being always a little less uncivilised than their soldiery, it does not surprise, that even then we read of a Mahometan governor saying to those who proposed stopping a group of pilgrims, "I have often seen such, and they only follow a vow to their idol; let them go, they are very harmless!" And when in 1064 a body of seven thousand pilgrims, after traversing safely the whole of Asia Minor and Syria, was attacked by Bedouin robbers near Jerusalem, they owe to the Turkish governor that they were not cut to pieces, but got unhurt within the gates. That sordid Bascia might have thought the toll of so great a number not to be despised; so he sent the rescue.

Let people say what they will, yet was England in a very confused condition in those good old Anglo-Saxon and Danish times. Canute was succeeded, not by his legitimate, but illegitimate son. Even the return into the Anglo-Saxon line, on the earliest opportunity that offered, was somewhat irregular; and if pestilence and famine were characteristic of even Edward the Confessor's virtuous and holy reign, what could be worse after the Conquest? Is it not said William's domination was from the first, devastating carnage; its progress, a regular system of confiscation and oppression— its close, *famine and pestilence?* Probably this climax of evils was true of both epochs, of the comparatively good and bad; for they are the necessary consequences of bad agriculture—though in other respects the government may have been more or less abominable; since the bad agriculture lasted many ages, and did not improve much before the Tudors. Had Harold any real right to the English throne, he might have called out the Anglo-Saxon militia, or trinoda necessitas—the German landwehr; but he did not dare to do so, conscious of his having no title whatever; which is a cogent argument of his not being what he pretended, the choice of the people; so can any one say that. Ferocious William said it, too, at his coronation, pleading, vain-gloriously, that he had been chosen by the people of all England, and promising Edward the Confessor's laws; though he broke that promise so flagrantly a moment after. Canute, so long before him, had said the same; and whether or not by birth a Christian, pleased his subjects by becoming a fervent one, and a tolerable monarch; for the Anglo-Saxon oath of allegiance was like that of Arragon, conditional—"if not, no!" Canute, while King of England, compiled and published in Denmark the Danish civil and military code; also, in the Court of England, towards that time, was brought up the first Norwegian legislator. The Anglo-Saxons had become Christians in the seventh, and the Danes about the eighth century; and as to the native Britons, it is not worth counting how long previously; for what remained of them were reduced to slavery in a country where it is boasted that slavery had never existed by law, nor ended by law, but naturally and silently went out of itself. As to the Normans, they were Christians when they left Normandy.

But although Harold had none at all, William had at least a show of right, not only as adopted by Edward, but from his own father's having been the legitimate child of a Queen of England ; and if he was himself illegitimate, yet we are assured by Sismondi that in (what the Normans were so intimate with) Italy, an illegitimate succeeded in the great nobility, just like a legitimate son. Much the same in all Europe. And William signing his name *Bastardus*, seems even to have taken pride in the distinction. His mother, a nobleman's daughter, had had Robert for her first love, and was true to him till his death ; so that their union was in truth what is called a left-handed marriage—*Morganatic*, an ancient German custom. Their only son was moreover legitimized by the kings and barons of France. At nineteen William was so fine a youth that the famous Duke of Flanders, Baldwin, gave him his daughter in wedlock ; and at Hastings, he was one of the bravest knights and most enterprising monarchs in Europe. He had fifty thousand horse that day; and how many infantry, I do not know. They were all paid troops; not surprising that a single battle decided. That one loss, of not a very numerous army either, and the whole cause was lost. Another proof that Harold's party knew they had not the majority of the nation with them.

The Varangian guards at Constantinople, and

those other gallant refugees in Syria testify it was not courage or fidelity the Saxons wanted at Hastings. The disastrous consequence of that field was that almost all England was reduced to slavery--every one but Normans. Feudalism on the most extensive and exclusive scale, without any one of the influences that tempered it in other countries, embraced Anglo-Saxons, Danes, and every reminiscence of the Heptarchy, levelling them all to the Britons, and branding them indiscriminately as slaves and English; for that every Norman was a gentleman, and every Englishman a slave.

Besides the Britons and their wives and families, and some of the free-born Saxons themselves, who, from debts or crimes had lost their liberty, or even from want had voluntarily sold themselves, it was calculated before the Conquest, that slaves formed two-thirds of the population of England. But now the Conquest prostrated to the same vile station those who had before been masters. Frightful retribution! The proud, war-like, and comparatively polished Norman despised and abused the conquered. William was ferocious on principle. His victims submitted to the yoke in sullen despair; one unhappy Saxon of royal descent went on a pilgrimage to Jerusalem; and coming home, died of a broken heart in 1086. His royalty secured him notice, but many of less illustrious and private rank ended similarly. Nobility, chief clergy, all foreigners— like their king. Females violated; and men sent to prison at the beck of the lowest Norman.

Nearly every inch of land in England became Norman property. Posterity could not believe it. The king had one thousand four hundred and thirty-two manors, and an income of nearly six thousand pounds a-day. Nor legally could any earldom be otherwise than Norman. Troubles were too severe to permit of considering it any compensation that a few Anglo-Saxon ladies, who had escaped into France, were admired there for their wonderful beauty, even at that early period, so full of stern calamity. With such punctual harshness was the feudal system practised at once, that in less than two years from Hastings, we hear no more of the king's hired troops, but sixty thousand feudal cavalry; and if *lances* be meant, as likely, then we must multiply by six, and have the huge body that is most probably the truth.

The Northmen, who had never known anything feudal in Scandinavia, acquired it so well in France, that William's first care in England was to establish feudalism there in all its rigour. The Anglo-Saxon ordeal was changed by the Normans into the wager of battle, which, if it led to the trial by jury, it is a curious and serpentine path; but in truth, the trial by jury came not circuitously, but directly from Scandinavia and the Goths, and was their own unwritten law, and no distinct profession, but was brought into England by the Anglo-Saxons as a whole people; and though they became Christians, they continued to content themselves with that primitive institution, and one court for both laymen and ecclesiastics. That the Goths were acquainted with writing, not only before they came to Scandinavia, but even previous to their leaving the Euxine, is no proof that they did not explain their laws orally. Their common law and its chief institutes were both written and oral. Neither canon law, nor pandects had penetrated into Scandinavia; but William, who had learned the continental fashion, introduced two courts, one for church, and one for laity; Justinian for these, and decretals for those. Was it not a carnal error? What before had been *heriot*, became Norman *relief*. If the former was a grievance, this other was ten times worse. Later even, the English gentry led a sorry existence; no foreign luxuries, few or no male servants, save a clown for the wretched farm, ugly horses, and no carriages with four wheels, springs not to be thought of, little wine, even their hospitality very limited; an income of ten or twenty pounds a competent estate for a gentleman, and, if we multiply by twenty-four, we have the present value of that sum.

But in the eleventh century, of which I speak, things were beyond comparison worse, though chivalry was then at its full, and had been growing for above three hundred years. Still, though nobly based in honour, it could effect little, as not applying to all classes and both sexes. This religion does, or may do; but neither liberty, nor honour, fine things as these be, for they admit of several distinctions and inequalities, moral and physical, but religion not one! Why leave out what, more than gallantry or chivalry, or the refinements of society, placed woman in her proper place of a companion to man, not his slave as among the Greeks and Romans, and the very best of Paganism, but his tender friend and equal? It was indeed the Christian religion that emancipated the female, and raised her destiny to the height of our own! Yet even religion might for awhile seem too feeble to control the ferocity of that age. Rather for the savage feeling it indicates, than for the value of the thing in itself, is recorded that the Conqueror meditated extirpating its language from the island.

Out of the Saxon branch of the great Teutonic stock, arose what had been spoken in England until long after the Norman, which, whatever was his impotent wish, only somewhat impeded its progress, since the nobility for the most part went on speaking French, even after Normandy had become part of France; and as for legal documents, they were invariably in law Latin, and several of the best chronicles of England likewise; nor was it till the fourteenth century that Chaucer gave England its Dante. Till then, English was an irregular jargon made up of bad French and worse Celtic, and various dialects of old German. Whether Oxford had or not thirty thousand scholars under the Plantagenets, it seems a decided fact that it existed as a university in the time of Edward the Confessor, and many affirm it was founded by Alfred.

That gunpowder ever was discovered there, may be fiction, or how much earlier, in what corner of the East, perhaps China. But happily, in mercy or not, the Saracens kept it to themselves; nor as late as Creci, do the English seem to have had firearms there, notwithstanding all that has been advanced; for France was nearer Spain and the Moors, to get their inventions first; and so curious a particular could scarcely fail of registry by the cotemporaneous writers who described that battle *ex pro-*

fesso, and one of them an eye-witness of it, and a Frenchman. Their silence is the most eloquent of denials. As for Villani, he was far off, and only wrote what he heard. Gunpowder appeared a great thing then, and a reasonable cause for that defeat, as well as a salve for much offended vanity. But now opinions have come about, and nearly all military men prefer lances for cavalry, and some of the best judges for infantry too; and that the Greek and Roman way of good swords and lances, or any description of cold iron, even this most unwieldy weapon, the bayonet—so far as it represents a lance —is better and surer than musketry, whether for attack or defence; that artillery, both heavy and light, is a splendid treasure to be coaxed and perfected to the utmost; but that regiments of the line, horse and foot, would act more wisely to throw away firelocks, pistols, and hand-grenades altogether, as quite too cumbrous and uncertain, and to learn to be capital lancers and swordsmen, whether as infantry, to scale walls or resist a charge of cavalry, not with bayonets, but long heavy lances, requiring three men to each lance, and keeping the horses far off, which is an old English fashion—such being to depend on, and quite inimitable, and easily modified to suit cuirassiers, hussars, or Polish lancers. But now whatever would liberate men for awhile from slavery to the soil, would be a great benefit, and a bold step towards regaining what they had lost—freedom. Truly (as Mr. Hallam says) the socmen are the root of a noble plant, the free peasantry of England. But what were they in the eleventh century? How fallen must they have been, when their only hope was in the Pope! Though not the Papal only, but ecclesiastical encroachments in general, are what the laity should keep a wary and perhaps suspicious eye on. Yet some of the Popes took the popular side on most questions; and even where religious ceremonies were used, as in ordeals and wagers of battle, demurring against both as unwarrantable appeals to the Almighty, did they not therein appear the advocates of liberty and reason?

It is not perhaps possible to congregate a greater accumulation of miseries than then pressed on the English. Robbers, and plunderers, and ravishers, imitated those lawless invaders and their sanguinary mercenaries. These often, instead of pay from the needy or miserly barons whom they served, got leave to plunder indiscriminately. These from tyranny, those impoverished natives from a sort of necessity, were equally the horror and scourge of whatever was left of honesty or innocence in any class. So lawless the mercenaries (who, not content with sacking it, sometimes set fire to a town—burning it down, inhabitants and all), that a later monarch had to expel them in a body, under pain of death, without further evidence than that they were known to be hired soldiers. Not but intermarriages with the Normans effected union in the end, and all their progeny, after some generations, became free, and every inhabitant in the land a freeman ; but, for an age, it did little more than evil, by generalising it. Yet the poor English were quick learners ; and mastered the French so well, that it soon was hard to distinguish by speech between the English and the Normans.

That the laws of these different species of Northmen were all from one genus—the Gothic—is proved likewise by this, that a striking affinity was between many of their institutions; and that William, treading in the very footsteps of Alfred, had every hide of land in the kingdom surveyed by commissioners, who were to impannel a jury in each hundred; and the offspring was what exists in the Exchequer to this day, Doomsday Book. William's eldest son, another Robert, appears to have inherited something of his grandfather's piety, combined with the gigantic form and sabring qualities of his father. He soon went to Palestine, not with staff and shell, but rapier and buckler.

Then, from Robert on the highest steps of the throne, down to the lowest serf in England, all ranks were uneasy, and without one sedentary wish. No English father could give his own daughter away in marriage without his Norman lord's consent; and the latter could make her marry any man he liked, the moment she was fourteen; and heiresses were constantly sold by their lords to the highest bidder. An auction of fillies. Horrors beyond the force of any tongue, tortures the most infernal and illegal were practised by every petty owner of a crow's nest, with perfect impunity; once within his foul walls, and your case was as hopeless as in hell.

Durham Cathedral might be in the best Norman style; and several other cathedrals might afterwards display pointed arches, and rich decorations, and fantastic tracery and arabesques—built perhaps by companies of incipient freemasons; yet not only the castles of the most potent noblemen were dark, cold, unsightly erections, but also the gentry were miserably lodged; and as for the people's dwellings, they did not merit the name of houses at all, but styes or dog kennels—or something fouler and meaner still. The barons, in their keeps, were wild beasts in horrid dens. Every baron was a pitiless despot. But what results from all these observations, if not that England was no exception, but as ready as any other state in Europe for an explosion, or any radical change? and that, burning with impatience for the signal, if given from any part of Christendom, the white cliffs would be just as determined as whatsoever country to echo it and march?

In Spain the people are better bred than any in Europe, says a well-informed writer even of late; and another has ably affirmed that the fierce Spaniard never forgets he has Gothic blood in him. Now both observations are not only true at present, but also from the middle ages down; and the first from the ancient Romans. The lower classes in Spain still spoke the same Latin dialect that they had spoken in the time of Augustus probably; when the Visigoths, before the fifth century, invaded and fixed in it. The Visigoths were to Spain, what the Anglo-Saxons were to England. Their capital, Toledo; until the Moors in 712. From that disastrous downfall, Pelayo retreating with his few, planted the cross in the mountains of Asturias, where it remained for a couple of centuries. But in 914 it removed to Leon; and the Moor driven back step by step, the Christians became masters of their former metropolis, Toledo, in the eleventh century; and to know what sort of government they established there, it is necessary to have known what was that of the Visigoths ; for what was then re-set, was in substance what had been plucked out. Meagre as are the chronicles regarding each, yet by joining those of both periods, we learn indubitably at least that it was a system of rational constitutional monarchy.

It is not without feelings of deep reverence that a lover of freedom turns to Spain. Not Latins or Moors, but on its Gothic kingdom and Pelayo are his thoughts—and on the early Spanish liberties. The Cid is only a splendid instance of the heroism that has scarcely ever ceased to distinguish Spain. The Visigoths being, like all the other Northmen, a branch of the Goths, did not treat the Romans with that haughty contempt which the rest of the barbarians showed, but gave a legal sanction to intermarriages between Goths and Spaniards, much more early than in Italy or elsewhere. So Goths and Spaniards soon amalgamated, and the law declared them equal *in dignity and lineage.* Nevertheless, we know little of the manners of the Visigoths before the Moors—perhaps less than of the primitive Hungarians; for except battles, miracles, and murders, there is little in the chronicles, who seem to love throwing a dark and barbarous stain on all they relate most concisely and jejunely.

Cruel and vindictive acts brought their own ruin, and the Moorish invasion. Goth and Spaniard had already so intimately coalesced, that the barrier of language disappeared, and the *Romance* tongue spoken and written universally ; so that scarcely a Visigoth word remained. And for one of Gothic origin in Spanish, there are ten in Italian, and a hundred in French.

The law Latin is far purer in Spain than in France or Italy; for in these countries the barbarians would by no means give up their old Gothic words, when they thought they expressed the thing in question as well or better than the Latin, but laughed at Roman lawyers, and scorned them ; but the Spanish Goths, with no such harsh pride, were pleased with translating the law of the Goths into good Latin.

Money, or slavery, or mutilation, for murder, and nearly all crimes, was preferred to the punishment of death—in the Anglo-Saxon fashion. But the trial by jury had a far greater latitude of application in Spain than in England. When the throne became vacant in Scandinavia, the provinces used to choose each a jury of twelve men, and these chose a new king; which example, indeed, it is not quite clear that the earliest Spaniards rigorously followed; but their crown was elective, and the jury was used in the army and navy as well as nearly all civil and criminal cases. The ordeal was still more reprehended in Spain by the Papacy than in the Heptarchy. Not only Pope Honorius forbade it, but also the Council of Leon. No clergyman could officiate at ordeals. Still the tribunals and popular charters continued them; "although these ordeals are prohibited by Rome" (says the law book), "yet they may go on; and if no priest, nor even clerk, be allowed to give the blessing, the magistrates may give it—which will be nearly as well."

That the jury is common to all the Northmen is a proof that it was the invention of none of them, but had been inherited from their common parent, the Goth. If the juries in Spain were not so equal as in England (for a Spanish peasant had all his jury superior, while eleven of the Anglo-Saxon jurymen were of the rank of the accused, and only one a king's thane), yet this has a compensation in the fact that in Spain a woman had a jury of women.

In some Spanish towns, when there was a quarrel between man and wife, the cause was tried by a female jury, and no appeal; and as this is a great exception from Gothic rules (by which oaths of men alone were taken in cases of accused females), we may attribute it to the usual Spanish gallantry, which chivalrous respect for females, whether mediately or immediately, is the only question; and who deny that the heroic Goth had any participation, or the soul-stirring warmth of Moorish imagination either, they must refer it wholly to Christianity; and indeed, any medium of Goths or Moors were superfluous; nor could any splendour of poetry speak half as forcibly to the tender enthusiastic heart of the Spanish mother, as the simple, unclassical lines which, when fresh in the seventh century, were as popular in Spain, as lately with us when set by Rossini to his sweet music; and it is to be doubted if so complete a picture was ever drawn in a few plain words:—

> "Stabat mater dolorosa,
> Juxta crucem lacrimosa,
> Dunc pendebat filius."

No! that spiritualised creation, that brightest, most blessed sovereign Lady, she that never sinned, nor ever was otherwise than immaculate, she whose robe was the sun; whose footstool, the moon; whose crown, the stars; she far more than goddess; that dear, mysterious, ineffable union of maternal and virginal celestial love, sorrow, beauty; she may well be an object of reverence to both men and angels; and what but an inferior representative of her was all that is sacred or beautiful in the whole female race? Spanish men knew what their women personified, and Spanish women, too, were conscious of their dignity, as became them. From Molina (chief town of the Laras), the completest municipal record in Spain in 1152, we learn that unanimity in a jury was required; and in cases of extremity, a juror was withdrawn, and the accused was at liberty to name another—once practised in England likewise.

In one respect the Visigoth monarchy was happily modified in the Asturias from what it had been before the Moor. At first altogether elective—worst of governments—generally force and artifice, not the public will, elected their kings; so, they being often murdered to make room for a new king (asking the Church's assent afterwards, which was never refused); from this radical defect sprang rapacity and extortion, till lost were independence, religion, and all, to the Moorish invaders.

The Visigoth monarchs had become cruel despots, yet perhaps they have the excuse of the memory of dynasties of kings in Spain previous to their own coming, when we should refer all their liberties to their own race; and all their slavery and vice to those prior kings, who may have had much of the imperial absolutism of Constantinople, a polluted source, to whom bad doctrines are more imputable than to the Papal clergy of those times, who usually sided with what was free and honest. The odious Inquisition was long posterior, as is almost needless to remark. The Moors that overwhelmed Spain at once, would also France, had it not been for Charles Martel; but it was very gradually indeed that they lost their fine empire.

Under Ferdinand, in about the middle of the eleventh century, began the splendid course of the Cid, which, continuing under his sons, D. Sancho, who was killed at Zamora in 1072, and Alphonso VI., for whom he retook Toledo and Madrid a few years afterwards, shows delightfully with what a chivalrous spirit were carried on those wars against the Moors; inasmuch as in the very midst of them the above-named king (Alphonso VI.) married the daughter of the king of the Moors at Seville; no exception, but a fair sample of those heroic ages. The worst of elective monarchies had worn out during the day of calamity, and that long abeyance in the Asturias had reformed things so far, as that the election had become hereditary in one house, which remedied the radical defect of an elective form. The Cid's times were then worthy of him.

Whether the Spaniards learnt from the Moors—

as is pretended—or, what is more likely, that the Moors had acquired some of the generosity that characterises the Goths when not provoked, but on the contrary, met with something of the high feelings which they possessed themselves, and of that chivalry which certainly was the bud when Christianity came to blow on a northern stem; however that be, the sure incident is, that while the civil wars between Christians were less bloody and cruel than in other countries, those with the Moors were with the generous courtesy scarcely found elsewhere, except perhaps a slight tinge in England's continental expeditions of Froissart's time; and that the Cid's feats of heroism shed a wild and most romantic colouring on all Spain, until his name itself became a personification of whatever can be imagined of noblest and most brilliant, not from any other sentiment than the uncalculating valour that disdains any other reward than glory; such a magnificent, ineffable blaze, that it endures not a little from that day to this. If the Spanish sun be set, the horizon is still glowing, and flings a faint orange, as it were, of the chivalrous on everything and creature of Spanish birth, habituating us to look upon all from that region with a favouring eye, as naturally expecting more than ordinary merit. Even the sneerer who smiles to the sight, assents within; and though the Castillian grandeur be ridiculed as misplaced or vain, and may be laughable haughtiness, half admires it.

That the Cid was a chastened incarnation of Homer's Achilles, is a fact beyond controversy, and that his country merited that glorious distinction. That the poem of the Cid (of the age following his death, and said to be the finest of Spanish poems) is at least better than any in modern Europe before Dante, has been decided by unanswerable authority. The Cid, that brightest of warriors, appeared in Spain's brightest period. Ah! me! to be brief! for another Alphonso was to appear, Alphonso—called the Wise, for his astronomy, but most unwise for his policy, since his code of the Siete Partidas was to produce to him unhappiness and a turbulent reign, and to his country a civil war of fifty years, and eventually the overthrow of her ancient legislature and all her freedom.

Though the great mosque at Cordova was built in the eighth century, and is of far greater beauty and magnificence than any cathedral of that time, in France, England, or anywhere in Europe, still the architecture suitable for churches and palaces was not so for private houses—even of the prime grandees. Nor were the habitations of the Spanish nobles otherwise than very rude; and what then of the people? There is an Arabic writing in the Escurial that could make great disclosures on that head.

If the Moorish armies brought gunpowder, and measles, and small-pox into Europe, they also brought chemistry, Aristotle, and perhaps Plato; and Mahometans were to bring inoculation as well. Who but is willing to believe that when Goths and Visigoths had become an almost forgotten name— as it soon did—and merged in that of "pure Spaniard," or "old Christian"— their Gothic genealogy being locked up with their hidden treasures, to be drawn out on occasion, and displayed with pride—they did not as horribly ill treat the Jews as other lands? For the Spanish Jews denied most indignantly that they descended from the murderers of Christ, but from Hebrews that had emigrated into Spain centuries before his Divine birth; and on the contrary proved that when their forefathers heard of his being persecuted in Jerusalem, they sent ambassadors thither to dissuade those of Palestine from harming him; and the document asserting this was kept with considerable reverence at Toledo.

When it is conjectured that the Visigoths came into Spain before they had written laws, is not this an evident mistake, and in contradiction with the general belief, that the Goths had letters previous to leaving the Euxine? How could then their sons the Visigoths not? Is it not falling into the error of thinking oral opposed to written? But may not the common law be written as to the text, and oral as to the custumal, or comment of the recorder? or modified by the judge or jury? St. Isidore may only have meant the change of characters, no longer Runic, but Roman. This was the *new writing*. Traditional, or what is oral, has not only as much permanence as written, but much more. It is to inscribe not on parchment, but on men's minds; on no evanescent matter, but on what is immortal. Are not national songs and ballads older than any writing? This may get lost, or destroyed, or forgotten, like the Egyptian hieroglyphics, but the oral will be transmitted from generation to generation; but once reduced to writing, and it is liable to slip from memory, which recoils away as from a burden, and feels again vacant and free.

The Druids confided their laws to memory alone, says Cæsar. A short jingle suffices for a heap of desultory deductions. A rhyming or alliterative law is hard to obliterate from memory, nor likely to be innovated. What scroll of secretary is to be depended on like that of the memory of an illiterate warrior or wild huntsman?

When the Visigoth code was written in 466, the immediate consequence was that no former law was remembered, and so we are ignorant of the custumal of the Goths, as far as Spanish information. But from that code we see that the Visigoth kings were then obliged to have the popular consent, without which no laws could be made. The Theodosian, or some other Roman authority, may have been admitted into that Gothic collection; but the Visigoths, with a pardonable pride, corrected those foreign interpolations first. And in the fourth Council of Toledo, the whole was joined in one body, and called the *Fuero jusqo*, and was amended in another council there, in 653. Various MSS. of the *Fuero jusqo* (some clandestine) went before printing; so it is hard to discover the exact truth, save that Spain anciently had a free or constitutional monarchy, as free as that of England ever was; although, since Ferdinand and Isabella, or Charles V., the Kings of Spain have been absolute.

From the dawn of the eleventh century, town after town became Christian; the cross bore all before it—Saragossa, Valencia, and the Balearic Islands, and Murcia and Cordova and entire Andalusia, were annexed to Christianity and Castille; yet even so, and allowing that the arts and sciences of Cordova, and the sedentary habits they produce, might have rendered the Moors less hardy, these were nevertheless, to reign for two and a half centuries longer in part of Spain.

As high as twenty-five per cent, or twenty, was still to be the interest of money; and if it was only at ten at Barcelona in 1433, that was when there were insurance laws, which do not exist before regular commerce; and Spain was not of the commercial log at that period. Also in Spain Charlemagne's *caballary* were landowners and knights. There, as elsewhere, the *milites* of the middle ages were knights. " Sive *miles,* sive alius," that is, *knight* or not. " Statuimus (says one of those ancient Spanish kings) ut nullus faciat *militem,* nisi filium *militis*"—" none but who is qualified by being a gentleman," as it has very properly been translated.

Although Visigoths, Danes, Lombards, Vandales, may have differed as to pride, do not various examples prove that all the Gothic tribes were no way niggard of verbal changes, but offhanded as to taking or giving of language? Was it not characteristic of the entire stock? When they found it difficult for the Southern to acquire Gothic, they left their own and took his tongue. If this occurred in most countries, it is above all remarkable in Spain.

Willingly they gave their language and freedom,

and had in return religion and wealth. However sounding their titles, the Visigoth kings, no more than the Anglo-Saxon, were absolute; but popular will and responsible agents were mixed up with every act of the monarch. His laws were no laws until they had the national assent in a full meeting, or council, or Cortes, *universali consensu;* nor could any individual be punished without a fair trial. Alphonso I. was chosen "by the whole Gothic nation." Alphonso II., " by the whole kingdom."

In 930 Alphonso VI. abdicated " with consent of the Cortes ;" but, though the monarchy continued elective, it was in one particular family; " and in 966, notions of hereditary right had made such progress" that a child of only five years old, son of the late king, was elected to the throne by the people. When in 1064 Ferdinand divided his states between his children, he first called a meeting of his subjects and obtained their consent. Alphonso in 832 gives a charter to his clergy, both by the consent of his nobility and of his people—scriptura quam in *concilio* edimus. Ramiro in 930 calls a general council to advise whether he shall attack the Saracens. In 985, Vermuda pronounces with the consent of the *council.*

The earliest Cortes of which the acts have been preserved, in 1020, was to *assist* Alphonso V. In

1046 under another monarch, we have a Cortes consulting about the operations of a war against the Moors. In the Cortes of 1089, Alphonso VI., with its consent, appoints an Archbishop of Santiago. The same Cortes oblige that king's daughter to marry the King of Arragon, and as soon as she has a son, elect him to be their king and to succeed her father, instead of her. In 1135 a Cortes held at Leon under Alphonso VII., is convened " to deliberate on all the affairs of the Spanish monarchy." Ferdinand convenes a Cortes at Salamanca in 1178, with a similar mandate. There were no distinctions on such occasions between civil and ecclesiastical. The Cortes were the virtual representatives of the whole kingdom in 1188, and not the deputies of any particular class or community. The Cortes, like the ancient Parliaments in England, drove away the minions of one debauched monarch, and interposed to baffle the bigotry of another, who, in league with an unworthy part of the clergy, wished to oppress and expel his Moorish subjects. *Procuradores* were later, and, as from the different cities, formed a distinct part of Cortes. Matters went on thus even until the author of the Siete Partidas died in 1285, which began the funeral of Spanish liberty.

Spaniards, then, in the eleventh century, were

certainly far from as unhappy as other Europeans; yet was Spain unsettled. It had lately had great changes, and was in expectation of greater. Nor had Spaniards to look far off; their foe was in their own homes. Nor did they dream of quitting their beloved Spain; but of rendering themselves masters of it—their cherished native land! They had more patriotism a great deal, than any other people in Europe. This splendid virtue, sometimes mistaken for hatred to foreigners, has often led to benefit; as when the "erudite party" proposed classical plays, which was put down by the people, always characteristically hostile to foreign interference. So, instead of imitation, Spain has got the most national, original, independent, perhaps finest theatre in the world. Not to emigrate, but most ripe were the Spaniards to applaud loudly any project that fell in with their own heated feelings, and dislike—not to say contempt— of every description of foreigners; and glowed as always, with an ultra-devotion, an inexpressible fervour, both in religion and war; in the former a metaphysical magnificence, and in the latter not design of havoc, or to plunder the odious strangers, but love of country, sublimed to an unheard-of degree, and exceedingly lucid honour and romantic valour.

Not for having received the gospel, and to prepare mankind for that Divine gift, was the precise mission on which Socrates and Plato were sent, according to some of the Fathers, but for her having received it so badly, thinking men account by the very low ebb of morals in ancient Rome; and that, not during her decline, but the most glorious and flourishing days of her republic. In Jugurtha's times, that famous metropolis was a sink of iniquities, most enormous, most sanguinary deeds; murder being sold openly in her shops, like any other commodity; poison or dagger at your option—the highest or lowest—in reference each to his station; but every man's life had its price, none extravagantly dear. No matter what part of the civilised world he was in; though it would cost less and be more convenient to get him nearer the Romulean centre, by lure, or force, nevertheless the business could be cheapened quietly, and without the smallest embarrassment, as regularly as we now purchase cloth at a clothier's; and Tacitus avows that, when he wrote, the Germans were ignorant of even the existence of many of the crimes that were quite habitual in the Eternal City. So, though she embraced Christianity at last, yet when six centuries later the barbarians descended into Italy, they found a people they soon learned to despise.

Those first Northmen, or Ostrogoths, when they settled south of the Alps, chose a king, from some idea that it was no denial of the imperial dignity, which they had left behind them on the Danube, and which was afterwards acknowledged in the person of Charlemagne; and Italy came to be considered in all subsequent ages as a province of the great western empire established in Germany. Yet however unfavourable had been their early impression, shortly did the Ostrogoths hurry into an intimate union with the Italians, who depraved them; the balance being that, while these were in some degree regenerated, those had their native hardihood enervated; and the very name of Ostrogoth dying away, the two races merged in a single one, and were denominated Italians.

Whether the Ostrogoths had been converted previously to the Alpine barrier, admits of dispute; but they were certainly Christians when they passed the Po; and for awhile, seeing no emperor come from towards the Danube, they put up with him of Constantinople, and obeyed his delegates; so natural and necessary they found it, to be under some imperial master; nor liked to be as babes in the wood. Which craving after dependence came more from the southern than the Oltremontana moiety of their blood; for it has been remarked that the

Italians have ever loved something they could depend on, and only felt free when in numbers within walls; while Northmen felt free everywhere, but most so when in the forest or single and independent in wide space. And truly until the Ostrogoths had joined them, these others had no idea at all of the native loftiness of human nature, or patriotism, or man's inborn love of freedom.

Their emperors distant (east or west), the Popes became the only objects of great reverence that remained in Rome; particularly as there was no other chance of withstanding anarchy and baronial usurpation. And to that sacred scope, it is but justice to own, the Papacy dedicated its labours incessantly. The circumstances of that awful period, a bishop's duties, and the choice of a suffering people, form, to some apprehensions a more honourable and, as it were, superhuman title, than any the most vigorously substantiated donation of Constantine, Pepin, or Charlemagne.

Never did the Holy See cease from trying to keep the Romans faithful to the Greek Emperor, until it was forced by the popular cry to refuse equally edict and tribute, and appeal to Paris; for an old policy of the Italians is to have two masters, play off one against the other, and be false to both; and this, far more than Grecian iconoclasticism, made the mob of the Tiber roar for French protection. But scarce had the Ostrogoths vanished, without leaving even a name to state they had ever been, when, as if to vindicate their great misfortune, advanced the energetic ire of the wisest, bravest, most powerful of all the races of Northmen, the Lombards.

Nor is it certain whether they were not invited by the archtraitor Narsetes, recalled to Constantinople by as perfidious a master. It was diamond cut diamond. Slowly winding down the Alps, the Lombards ruminated sad on the woful example of the Ostrogoth; but resolved to avoid the same mishap. Even supposing them to have embraced Christianity, it nothing diminished of their severe intentions; since built upon no spirit of vengeance, but on what seemed to them the most prudential concerns. They knew that, like themselves and all the progeny of the Goth, their predecessors likewise had their Witenagemot, Cortes, or Parliament, as in Spain, France, or England; that national meeting which chose or deposed kings; that oath of allegiance qualified with the preservation of their ancient liberties; and, that those holy institutions, the same they bore with them, and planted where they settled, to think they had been already refused and made little of, filled them with fierce disdain. " We Lombards," cried one of their chiefs, " like the Visigoths, Burgundians, and others of our countrymen, so completely despise the very name of Roman, that, when in a passion with our enemies, we know of nothing more injurious than calling them Romans; for in that single term is included all that is imaginable of most ignoble, most slavish, most miserly, most corrupt, most lying—and in one word, every vice!"

So the valiant Lombard, having bought with the dearest price, his blood, the whole valley of the Po (or, as Dante calls it, " the valley between the seas"), he fixed his government within that sacred pale, and thence, as from a home, scattered about his outposts, from the Alps to Calabria, with the sternest resolution to profit by the warning, and not vitiate his own vital stream by mingling it with that of a degenerate breed; and for years did that reluctance continue; and the Lombards went on increasing, and the Romans diminishing, until nearly or quite extinct about the Milanese, or with slender exceptions, slaves; not a single native proprietor there, but, if he survived, expatriated; every acre of that whole tract of country became exclusively Lombard property. Yet, even these proudest, most intrepid of Northmen, little by little, lost some part of their attachment to those constitutional liberties which they had brought with them from Scandinavia, common heirloom from the illustrious Goth, whose legal freedom was the product of his own virtuous unbiassed will.

It might be chiefly from having had no wars but with Greeks and Italians; and still worse during peace, the effeminate habits of pampered Italy had full opportunity to eat into and corrode their souls. Thus, the coming of Charlemagne, at another plaintive invitation, from mildness that too easily deigned acceding to his people's wishes (they, not the Pontiff, being the real abject petitioners), put an end to the first (and perhaps only purely) Lombard kingdom. Scarcely more survived of it than its iron crown, and the name of Lombardy—name that in itself is a perpetual triumphal gate, proclaiming to all ages that there the Northman has a patrimonial right for ever. How, but through him, and him alone, can be proved a judicial title to any particle of that land?

Italians may consider the advent of Charlemagne to be a new barbaric irruption, if they will, but they had asked for it! and moreover they had already rejected freedom, which had been brought into their country twice (both by Ostrogoths and Lombards); so proved themselves unworthy of better than despotism. For the most part cut to pieces, but whatever remained of the Lombards, even in that extremity, had only taken one of his sons for king; but a vile populace at Rome, quite voluntarily, and without Charlemagne's requiring it, saluted him Emperor; so above all kings. What could the Lombards, but assent, and rejoice that the lot had fallen at least upon a truly great man?

The worthless electors, far from appreciating his merits, would have huzzaed for a Nero, just the same. But Charlemagne was in advance of his age. If a thicker darkness than ever, came over Europe after his death, that is no fault of his, nor of his family, that reigned for about seventy-three years after him, so that his dynasty closed in A.D. 888. The Italians have no one to accuse but themselves, if they profaned the sun of Christianity, and by their wickedness contrived to turn its good into evil; or neglected freedom, then abused, and at length suffocated. Universal influence, as both legislator and warrior, was Charlemagne's during his whole long reign; nor thus alone, but for nearly a century it decorated and kept life and sovereign power in his line after him, in spite of their inferiority of talent; and surely that is more than can be said of other noted conquerors.

Italy has always been a divided country, save a

few uncertain years when a crumb of the Roman Empire; and this is so true, that it is apparent from its geographical form, *à priori*, by a look on the mere map, without opening a page of its annals; for a long narrow slip of land, cut by mountains and rivers, cannot but comprehend various climates and national distinctions, in which neither language nor religion could be a nationality, since difference in dialect is more observable than any uniformity of written formula; and did creed suffice, then Spain, Italy, France, Portugal, and others, would be one nation.

But truth is, neither language nor religion ever formed a nationality—nor ever will; they may be characteristics of a nation; which however can change both, without for that ceasing to be a nation. And all the experience of history leads to the same conclusion. The oldest accounts of Italy (from those faint earliest glimpses where historic authenticity begins) find five distinct people there, speaking various distinct languages, which with the numerous dialects of the aborigines (none know who those aborigines were), and a large majority of words of Œolic (forefathers of Greek), winnowed by the Etruscans, formed that exquisite olla podrida, Latin.

As late as Julius Cæsar the Italian province went

no further than Rimini. All immediately north of it was called, not Italia, but Gallia. The more split into independencies, the more free in her case; of which lasting truth the Italian Republics were only dazzling instances. The exception would be while under one harsh yoke of transient servitude— which might include other nations equally well. Therefore the lower Lombards (as we say lower empire) did nothing but follow the usages of the country, when, after waiting twenty years, and no sovereign appearing with the authority of any proper election, they divided themselves into thirty independent duchies all through Italy — one at Spoleto, another at Benevento—crown and name in Lombardy might shadow forth the defunct Lombard kingdom; but in conformity with existing things, they too assumed feudalism.

Sismondi does not draw as marked a separation as desirable between the Gothic or constitutional system and the feudal. The former perished with the primitive Lombards, like the Visigothic Cortes. These limpid and fresh from the northern source, were too excellent for the vicious south. Such ask purer disciples.

The feudal system led directly to absolute monarchy in Spain and elsewhere, and in Italy to the death of freedom as well, in the end; though indirectly, after that hysteric struggle, her Republics of the middle ages. Yes, feudalism was a modification unhappily made towards brute force.

From feudalism to despotism nothing but a stepping-stone were the Republics—half of whose citizens were generally in exile for years or life. Their substance confiscated, their houses sacked or demolished. Did not Florence deprive herself of her best and most distinguished individuals? Dante and Petrarch, where did they leave their bones? Dante was condemned to be burnt to death if caught; yet he had committed nothing deserving of any punishment. I mention it, because Italian historians leave it out.

Florence since she has had the grace to be ashamed of it, tries to hide it. So even late writers doubt or forget it. Yet it is a certain fact. The original sentence exists still. It is too atrocious for silence. All mankind are interested not to permit forgetting an example of to what crimes party can climb. But that way lies digression to lose ourselves. Back to the tenth century.

After the edict of Constantinople had been formally disobeyed by Rome, also Ravenna and its entire exarchate did the same, and nothing remained to the Greek in Italy except some towns in Magna Grecia. As early as 833 had the Popes fortified

Ostia against the African buccanneers who tried to profit by Charlemagne's death. It is an assured fact that the Popes became temporal powers immediately on the fall of the Roman Empire, and during the period of many ages took every opportunity of being useful to Italy.

Nor in a Pope's lifetime—he being dependent on the Emperor only—was Rome in a bad state; but when conclaves occurred, then indeed were the Romans delivered over to the most unsparing slavery—that of their own oligarchs, which bitter irony chose to denominate freedom. Which circumstance contributed, with a variety of others, to render the Papacy popular. Whenever Popes and Emperors agreed (which was rarely), it was not at all against liberty, but against the lowest servitude, to which the barons reduced their townsmen as long as they could spin out the *sede vacante,* or some violent sedition. The Romans used thus to pass from fawning on some blaspheming patricians, hard or impossible to be pleased, to bend somewhat less to the priesthood; for religious feelings might soften the Wolsey, but nothing the domineering outlaw.

Dante in his " Monarchia" endeavoured to distinguish the temporal from spiritual; but if it was feasible in his time, it was not so in the three preceding centuries; for then it was a universal practice to jumble them together. Mahometan freebooters erected a sort of temporary colony at Naples, and besieged Gaeta in 846, but were driven off.

Amalphi declared its independence in 839 ; but unfortunately the discoveries for which it has been given immortal credit, are all three unfounded ; for the mariner's compass was certainly discovered long before; some say was known to the Etruscans previous to the founding of Rome; others in the fourth century of our era ; the Pandects, too, if in any event those laws merit the honour of having their discovery applauded or inquired into by a lover of freedom ; and as for the sea code, Oleron and Sweden are tough antagonists.

In 924, on intelligence reaching the Emperor Berenger, then on a visit in Verona, that an Italian nobleman of this name was plotting against his life, he had the generosity to send for the accused, and in private audience at supper told, and pardoned him his enormous crime ; and, taking up a golden goblet, handed it to him, and said, " Let this be an emblem between us of the sincerity both of my forgiveness and of your repentance ; accept it, and remember that your emperor is your son's god-father." And the next morning, when secure from a numerous accompaniment, this same count, meeting that emperor alone in the street, rushed at and stabbed him; and after the murder, walked off triumphing and surrounded by friends. The German, who related that to the succeeding emperor, generalised overmuch in adding, " Such were the Italians some years ago, and such are they likely to continue for a long time yet." After so shocking a lesson, it is not astonishing that Otho (deservedly called the Great) should be rather severe in his first excursion to Pavia, to be crowned with the iron crown; and on his return into Germany, before the diet, he saw a King of Italy, and son, present themselves as inferiors, to do him homage; and after doing so, they went back to reign there under his imperial protection; and Otho, again at Pavia, and recrowned, proceeded thence to Rome, where he received the imperial diadem.

Let people then talk as they please, there are ancient precedents and long-established rights for such coronations. Moreover, it is to the emperors that the Italians owe all their subsequent liberties. This union of German and Italian destinies is what has saved both. Yet the Germans might perhaps have sufficed for themselves, but the Italians, assuredly not. Ideas imported from the north, were dear to even the latest accents of liberty in

Italy. But from feudalism, easy was the stride to despotism, which, within a few years, was to reign over the whole European continent.

Rude were the manners then; man and wife ate off the same trencher; a few wooden-handled knives, with blades of rugged iron, were a luxury for the great; candles unknown. A servant girl held a torch at supper; one, or at most, two mugs of coarse brown earthenware formed all the drinking apparatus in a house. Rich gentlemen wore clothes of unlined leather. Ordinary persons scarcely ever touched flesh meat. Noble mansions drank little or no wine in summer; a little corn seemed wealth. Women had trivial marriage portions; even ladies dressed extremely plain. The chief part of a family's expense was what the males spent in arms and horses, none of which however were either very good or very showy; and grandees had to lay out money on their lofty towers. In Dante's comparatively polished times, ladies began to paint their cheeks by way of finery, going to the theatre, and to use less assiduity in spinning and plying their distaff. What is only a symptom of prosperity in large, is the sure sign of ruin in small states. So in Florence he might very well deplore, what in London or Paris would be to praise, or cause a smile. Wretchedly indeed plebeians hovelled; and if noble castles were cold, dark, and dreary everywhere, they were infinitely worse in Italy, from the horrible modes of torture; characteristic cruelty, too frightful to dwell on. Few of the infamous structures, built at the times treated of, stand at present. Yet their ruins disclose rueful corners. As to cathedrals, the age for them, though at hand, had scarcely come in the tenth or eleventh century; and when it did, it was simultaneously in Italy, England, France, and Germany.

If algebra was known in Italy in the tenth century (which might easily be, from the Moors), it was kept secret there for three hundred years; not intentionally, it is said, but simply because the Italians were not aware of what an important thing they had. The archives of all the towns of Italy, before Barbarossa, having perished, leaves many matters obscure, which probably (as is to be wished) little deserve being known. Even when the Italian cities, without being exactly independent, appeared so, was it not that the emperors were too busy at home to march across the Alps to prevent them? For though often independent *in fact*, they always acknowledged *in theory* that the emperor was their sovereign. It was only worse, before the Popes and popular party took the name of Guelph, and the Imperialists that of Ghibelline. Barbarossa's was a time of cruel civil dissensions; and the story of *non tibi sed Petro* is utterly and decidedly false, though still is shown with pride at Venice the spot on which it occurred; and not unforgiving traitors, but stout-hearted patriots are they who never pardoned Barbarossa's line, though they had sworn it; but, in spite of having made a reconciliation with the uncle, never let any opportunity escape of making war on his nephew.

The spirit of chivalry, which was called the glorious inheritance of feudalism, in other lands, was reduced by the Italians to its real philosophic value; and on their disbanding their own armies, and taking the habit of carrying on their wars by their neighbours, cunning was to succeed in esteem to courage; and if several men of talent were to signalize Guicciardini's period, yet these were to act rather from calculation, than heroism or passion; from self-interest, not sentiment. That the Venetians were Italians at all, is denied by the best authority, Dante; not in his poetry, but in his worn-out day of fullest wisdom, in plain, cogent, diplomatic prose, probably the last lines he ever wrote.

How different from the Visigoths! The Lombard Latin was found by Sismondi so barbarous as frequently to be quite illegible. And it is true of the lower Lombard, that if he conferred unlimited independence on all his citizens, he denied any whatever to those he held unworthy of being admitted into his citizenship. Regarding the Normans, why not rather sympathize with their matchless valour, than with the paltry natives, who, to clear their home from robbers and pirates, were obliged to have recourse to a handful of strangers? Not satisfied with Puglia and Calabria, and the honour of having put two emperors (both the western and eastern) to flight, Guiscard undertook to become Emperor of Constantinople himself; and, on his way, died in Cephalonia in 1085. Beginning with him, and ending with the Vespers, is it not all over? Who cares any more for Magna Grecia or Sicily? The brilliant Norman phantasmagoria has nothing in common with the lands in which it passes. But to all similar, farewell! and to philosophy, Christianity, or any religion, or anything of humanity, farewell the whole of you! Here resounds the shriek of shrieks! Here comes the king of unutterable terrors—Attila.

Illiterate, direst of savages, as yet buried in all the grossness of idolatry, reckless of every human tie or obligation, or pain or pleasure, here are the Huns who through Hungary, Bulgaria, Sclavonia,

Croatia, or whatever other devastated regions, have left one long line to track their whole road from the Scythian wilderness. Nothing of the Goth, but the very reverse (though by a casualty in some degrees contemporaries in time, but not in the least countrymen), wild, ferocious monsters who delight in creating antipathy and horror; and therefore have no objection at all to learn they are not reputed human, but vulgarly a cross between a necromancer and a she-wolf, or to pass for Gog and Magog, precursors of the day of judgment. How convey even the remotest idea of the deadly dismay and despair they caused? Every unfortified town, from Switzerland to the most southern extremity of Italy, was sacked first—then the whole of its population butchered—finally the walls and houses were all gutted and pulled down; and, the entire of its work effectually done, onward moved the hurricane! Destruction appeared their only desire! Everywhere was their passage marked by the clearest evidence, fuming ruins, property of all kinds utterly destroyed and dilapidated, and corpses all naked, and lakes of blood. But if, like the plague, nothing could stop them anywhere, they settled nowhere. And soon returned into Croatia, or beyond it, as they had come.

The first irruption of Huns was in 900; but

there were many during the two next centuries. When will there be another? And those who put that usual question shuddered, no one but shuddered. Until then, several Italian gentlemen and all the peasantry lived in the country; and the small towns were mostly unwalled. But from that hour every town was strongly walled, and every human creature slept within a town. The peasant went to work in the fields by day, but at sunset he had to seek refuge with his family within some town. Agriculture in such cases must go to ruin. Patience! Jesu Maria! from the sword of the Huns— libera nos, Domine! what a frightful litany, from Como to Otranto! And the bells never stopped ringing, as long as there were any; when the toll ceased, it was sure the Huns were there at work, and that the poor steeple would lie on the ground in a few minutes. Nor was it enough, but there were various other spoilers, all worthy of each other! Nor idolators only, but the Saracen heathens!

These last ravaging, not Naples alone, or Sicily, but likewise Piedmont, where a party of twenty of them drove all the Piedmontese before them; such terror breathed from the victors, so panic stricken the vanquished! not a captain in all Italy had the boldness to face either Huns or Saracens! And these both had the same way of making war.

Nothing but light cavalry, in small squadrons, without trying to make conquests. Not wishing to fight, but plunder and murder, they did what was consistent with those deeds of massacre to avoid their foe.

Though Huns and Saracens in their inroads often met, they never fought with each other. But seemed friends, and soon found out they were relations; for both Huns and Turks were Scythians, and once one people, they said; right proud of their mutual ugliness, and that they passed for looking more like wild beasts than the hideous negroes, or any kind of men. Now what deduce, but that Italy would rejoice for any change and think it an escape? What not preferable to such actual nudity and wretchedness—fear for the future that is close and impending—and horror at the past? If the Pope joins the cry, well; and his popularity, which is already great, will increase. He who has been always ready to assist her in her distress, will he hesitate now? Will the Papacy be but for the first time blind to such an extraordinary crisis, nor listen to the public voice? Merciful evermore, and just, and politic, will she not, at present also, side with the people—her own woe-begone people?

Who had repelled two dreadful attacks of the Arabs, and kept off all the believers in Mahomet during their three first centuries (sternness of the Damascan Omyades, munificence of the Abassides) Constantinople had now a harder task. The author of the Koran himself, when weak, had recommended patience to his disciples; when stronger, to defend themselves if assailed; when powerful, the Koran or the sword. Yet such trying periods had passed away; and even the cruelty of the Fatimites ceased to be dangerous, and had been reduced to a remote sound. The last of the Caliphs at Bagdad died in 940 A.D.

But about a hundred years later appeared a far more ferocious race than the Prophet had ever dreamt of, the Turks vomited forth from the Scythian wilderness! These who, during their idolatry, had been the worst enemies of Islamism, finished by becoming Mussulmen, and, as such, overran India, Persia, all Syria, Mesopotamia, part of Africa, and the whole of Asia Minor; and were now only stopped by the sea facing the Greek metropolis, which when it ceases to be the bulwark, must become the road to Europe. A sound of reverential was in the Roman name, even to Turkish ears, as vaguely designating something superior to Constantinople; for when their sultan settled in Iconium, he called his kingdom Roum, as well as when he removed his capital to Nice, as nearer the prey on which he gloated. A very brief though glorious struggle had been made by Eastern Christians; but in 1071 unfortunate Byzantium had its frightful assailants within sight, howling horribly along its suburban Asiatic coast—protected from them by that narrow slip of water alone.

But why not a few glimpses back into that long period? When St. Gregory, early in 600 A.D., objected to the Constantinopolitan Patriarch's being styled the universal bishop, as an antichristian title; was it not that he considered it misapplied, not as bad in itself—as applicable solely to the Pope *de jure*, though not then perhaps strong enough to wear it *de facto*; but not to the Patriarch under any circumstances? Was not this St. Gregory's tacit meaning, whether others think it an unfair pretension or not? Not to any Greek Emperor, but to Charlemagne, Haroun el Rascid sent the keys of the Holy Sepulchre, showing that, in the Moslem's opinion, the Emperor of the West, or France, is the natural protector of Palestine, and not the Greek; and however it has been since, so it was in that olden time. And thus all the nations of Christian Europe were comprised in the term *Franks;* although certainly the chief part of the population of both Constantinople and Jerusalem, were at that time Greeks, nearly as they are at present.

France, Italy, Spain, Germany, Prussia, Poland, Bohemia, Hungary, formed the vast empire of the West; and like it was the Mahometan of many nations, from the Nile to the Indus. Nor was religion an impediment; for Charlemagne crossed the Pyrenees to assist an Islamite Emir who had asked for his protection; nor Haroun el Rascid was without Christian subjects in numbers, Nestorians, Jacobites, Greeks, and Roman Catholics, and others; whence a liberal toleration was quite as necessary to him as to Charlemagne, as they no doubt both felt.

As soon as the forty-sixth year of Mahometanism, the Arabs had besieged Constantinople; and in 718 the same, without success, principally from the Greek fire, the destructive discovery of a Syrian or Egyptian, who deserted to the Greeks, bringing his secret with him; since which, these crafty Christians kept hidden the way of making it. It was a matter of conscience, a revelation from Heaven. Prince and subject, each religiously bound not to divulge the saving mystery. Grand in the extreme was the Grecian Court—its Varangian guards, famous for their splendid costume, and lofty size, and undaunted fidelity, were all Danes, Norwegians, or English. Its Emperor was the first slave of the ceremonial he so rigidly ordained; his every word and gesture regulated both in his palace and country house. This worse than monkish severity of life, and that few of his rank ever died a natural death, but that murders and conspiracies were of nightly occurrence within the imperial residence, endears the more the lot of a private citizen.

Strange, too, the destiny that forces its historian to avow that, in spite of its multitudes of law-doctors and libraries, and all its scientific and literary establishments, not one discovery was ever made at Constantinople, during a period of a thousand years, in favour of the dignity or happiness of man, " nor a single idea added to the speculations of antiquity." Even then ran the prophecy that *in the last days* barbarians should take Constantinople, which Mr. Gibbon calls " an unambiguous and unquestionable date," and which, it appears, has not been supposed executed by Mahomet (though I thought so, or might have), but stands good still with most persevering superstition.

The Magna Grecia of Pythagoras, which had been rich and full of free cities, and great artists and philosophers, had dwindled into poverty and its usual concomitants, ignorance and superstitious habits, when the Normans lifted it for a short time in the ninth century; but now in the eleventh, it had returned again into terror and obscurity.

What could oppose the torrent rushing forward? Not Arabs are they, or any of the milder and more civilized Moslem; but the Turks, Turcomans, or Seljukides, as some call them, from one of their chiefs of the name of Seljuk, the wildest of the savages of Turkestan, that region of Scythia which stretches northward from the Caspian in one frightful waste, that only terminates with the Polar Sea. Nor will they recede; but as they already had mastered India and Persia, and the Caliphs, they at present pouring destruction on Asia Minor, are to do the same with Constantinople at last, and all Greece.

In Hindostan it was a Turk that surpassed the conquests of Alexander, and the title of Sultan was invented about 1000 A.D. for him; whom a wilder tribe of his own countrymen soon vanquished. He had invited them with suspicion, but was not suspicious enough. Nor after that could the Tigris, or Euphrates, or Nile stay them; nor the Persian mountains, nor Taurus. Had they not passed the snowy Caucasus and the eternal Imäus? A Togrul from the throne of Darius sent a messenger to the Emperor of Constantinople, to require tribute and obedience. To Togrul succeeded his nephew, Alp-Arslan, who found some resistance from the unfortunate but heroic Romanus; not unworthy of the Empire of the East—nor of his French allies, and Norman and Scotch. Some brave hearts, deserving to be called Grecians, were to be found to the last, in the city of Constantine—not only its final Christian Emperor, who expired as became him—but likewise the captive, Romanus. "What treatment do you expect?" asked Alp-Arslan. "If cruel, you will torture me to death," replied the dauntless sovereign. "If proud, you will drag me at your horse's heels. If avaricious, you will put a price on my liberty!" "And what would you have done with me?" subjoined the victorious Scythian. "Ah! I would have got you scourged finely," outburst the fearless and indignant Emperor. On which the Turk smiled; and muttering about the Christian law prescribing mercy, ordained that the champion of the Cross should that instant be set free, and peace established, on the promise that an immense sum should be paid for his ransom and a large annual tribute, with an intermarriage between the Turkish and Imperial houses, and freedom for every Mahometan in the hands of the Greeks.

This agreement, hard as it was, the mournful prisoner had to sign; and disheartening it is to be obliged to add that his subjects refused to pay his ransom, but left him to pine an exile, and as such deposed, and—as far as was in them—dishonoured him. And though upon these tidings, his liberator did not withdraw the boon he had already given, but pitied him and pardoned the ransom, Romanus died almost immediately, and the generous savage was assassinated in Transoxiana some months later in the same year, 1072. After him came his son, and then his grandson, Malek-Sha; of whose three younger brothers, one had the Persian province of Kerman; another, Syria ; and the third, Asia Minor, which quickly slipped from him ; and, to avoid a civil war, he was obliged to cede it to his cousin Solyman, whose kingdom of Roum extended from the Euphrates to the Bosphorus. In this manner, Solyman and his heir apparent, Kislig-Arslan, were the tremendous lords of the inhuman hordes that, towards the close of the eleventh century, crowded all along the Asiatic edge of the cerulean tide that bathes the walls of Constantinople.

A voice of woful entreaty had been directed to the West. But conscious of their having never been friendly but in times of trouble, of their own frequent ingratitude, and former exaggerations, the Greeks asked themselves whether it would be heard now? Or even so, would it not be too late? This very evening one of the Turks could be seen putting down his foot towards the waves; but he drew it back scowling towards us, as if between dread and desire; fortunately they are without a single boat—but who knows what curious contrivance they may discover? Who at sunset can tell but long before sunrise they will have got across the straits somewhere? And then we have no resource, but are lost, utterly lost and undone! Murmuring and conspiring, the unhappy, but garrulous and dissolute Greeks, pushed to it by the extremity of their despair, supplicated whom they deeply hated.

CHAPTER II.

Now such being the universal spirit of Christendom, a consequence somewhat analogous could not but ensue. It is the only time that history presents us a simultaneous unison of so many nations; and who knows if such a sight will ever come again? With all its defects, it has certainly an air of majesty that cannot be put down by any sneer. Sneers are the trophies of what is grand. Homer and Virgil (but not their inferiors) have been travestied. What was so often in Napoleon's mouth is eminently true; "From the sublime to the ridiculous is but a step." It may be ridiculous to call ridicule a test of truth. Yet is it the sincerest homage to truth—unwilling homage.

Nor was it Christendom alone, but also the Mahometans had been long undergoing a not dissimilar preparation. Whatever be the doctrines deduced by subsequent commentators from the Koran, that book itself has much more of moral severity than sensualism, and shows so thorough a knowledge of both the Testaments that it has been reported it was from a monk called Gabriel that Mahomet had his inspirations, though he pretends it was the archangel of that name.

The *sonna* or oral law was reduced to writing two centuries after Mahomet; so the absurdities it may contain are no more to be imputed to him, than the fables of the Talmud to the Patriarchs. A collection of seventy-two thousand old popular customs and tales may easily furnish food of every kind. But is it a refined taste to select for publication whatever of most shockingly indecent can be discovered in that anonymous farrago or any of its impure appendages? Is it just to charge the Koran with that superfluous filth? Let the Koran stand on its own merits; or if to be condemned, be condemned for its own faults. Plurality of wives existed in Arabia long before Mahomet, nor could he have abolished it, if he wished; but he found adultery common, and he vigorously forbade it; and put an end to drunkenness also, and instituted prayers to the living God, instead of the idolatry of the Caaba. It is no approval of his tenets, to refuse accusing him falsely. Who grieve he went no further towards true religion, may praise him, as far as he went. That the Koran is the most classic of the language has been long ago decided, on the best possible authority and beyond all appeal —that of the whole Arab people themselves.

It is no defect of his, if, notwithstanding our cherished ideas of Oriental magnificence and an established reputation for richness, and that the Arabs have a great idea of their own superiority in everything, and contempt for all who do not speak Arabic and wear any other dress, still the Arab tongue is very poor. Will it be believed that a warlike nation has no word for *garrison?* Yet so it is, and hundreds of such deficiencies. For the Arabic in general has but one word for each thing, including all its varieties. For which I have the authority of one of the most learned Orientalists of France—Renaud, in his preface to the Arabian Chronicles. If the Ommydes were harsh and audacious, beginnings are proverbially so, and the Fatimites were weak and falling, and may have imbibed the credulous cruelty of Egypt; but the Abassides and Spain can tell whether in its best times Mahometanism was remarkable for intolerance. Nor does it not savour of tolerance, that Mahomet admits of an exception in favour of those of the *Book*, by which most understand the old Testament, which includes all Christians—and some, all who believe in God and have a written law. The superstitious corruptions of the Turks and their ferocious barbarity must go to their own account. No doubt but they were at least as superstitious as the most illiterate of the Christians could be; and the Turkish annalists recount very gravely how angels or even legions of angels joined Islam's ranks during battle; and at almost every important event the same writers accompany it with an eclipse of the sun, darkness over the whole globe, and the stars visible at broad noon day. The Turks had probably been worse when idolators in Scythia, both as to superstition and fierceness; and those of them who had become a little effeminate and luxurious, also lost something of their native coarseness.

The Arabian historians themselves avow that in the eleventh century the whole East exhibited frightful disorder; that it was indeed the most disastrous of the periods; that the empire founded by the successor of Mahomet had melted away; and a wild race from the depths of Tartary reigned over the most delicious of the countries held once by the Arab; that the Turks or Turcomans under the children of Seljuk had taken Persia, Mesopotamia, Syria and Asia Minor, and were now menacing at once Cairo and Constantinople; that nevertheless the population of nearly all the towns taken by the Turks in Anatolia, continued for the chief part Christians, Greek, Armenian, Syrian, Georgian; while the victors, habituated to the freedom of a nomade life, preferred dwelling in tents in the open fields, taking care of the cattle along with some tribes of Arab origin, and that all that remained of the famous Arabian Empire was Egypt, with a few fragments of Africa and Spain.

As early as 1010 the Turks had commenced speaking of a Christian army preparing to march against them, exercitus Francorum super Saracenos orientales commotos; and at the destruction of the Holy Sepulchre then, certain stones glittered and resisted the fire like diamonds, which, without any miracle, might really be. Signs in the skies had told the Turks repeatedly that the West was going to rise against them; and at last in 1062, a meeting was held at Omar's Mosque in Jerusalem, for the Moslem doctors to study in the Koran for an explanation of what had been seen and could still be seen in the air; and these wise men, after gazing up intently from morning until night, declared it was clear that the constellations prophesied great disorders; 'and all these expounders of the law agreed, that some dark prediction was thus foreshadowed of people, who seemed to be Christians, seizing on much of the true believers' lands, after immense victories. And every one drew the consequence, that something of great importance was at hand, since announced by such prodigies.

In truth, it is in a Mahometan mouth that I first observe the words *holy war*, calling on all Mussulmen to leave off discord among themselves, and unite in a *holy war* against the Greek; words used in about 1084, and in that very Asia Minor, and assented to by that very same Solyman, whom (or son) any army from Constantinople would have first to encounter; sanguinary Turks, lately Mahometans, and still savages, who had never seen any better Christians than Greeks, Syrians, and defenceless pilgrims, and therefore scorned and hated Christianity. These were the hyenas and lions, leopards, tigers, crowding down to the Asiatic margin of the Sea of Marmora, snuffing for blood along it, as if round where travellers have pitched their nightly camp, defended by fires in the desert.

The opinion of most Christians then was, that the end of the world was at hand; but all people were in expectance of some great event, no one knew what, yet something surpassing human vicissitudes. To popular imagination it seemed that all nature was busy announcing by prodigies of every sort and every day what was the will of Heaven, and proclaiming it too clearly and loudly for any to misunderstand. Human laws were as nothing to those who conceived themselves called on by the voice of God. Moderation was cowardice; indifference, treason; opposition, sacrilege. Subjects scarcely recognised their sovereigns, and slave and master were all one to Christians. Domestic feelings, love of country, family, and every tender affection of the heart, were to be sacrificed to the ideas and reasonings that carried away all Europe.

The whole West resounded with these holy words: "Whosoever bears not his cross, nor follows me, is unworthy of me!" So, when the hermit began riding on his mule from town to town, from province to province, a crucifix in his hand, his feet naked, his cowl thrown back, leaving his head quite bare, his lank body girt with a piece of coarse rope over his long, rugged cassock, with a pilgrim's mantle of the commonest stuff, the singularity of his attire, austerity of his manners, and his charity, had a great effect upon the people, and the morality he preached; and caused his being everywhere revered as a saint, and followed with enthusiasm by a great crowd, showing him a reverence not dissimilar to what Mahometans of our own day have shown a *Haggi* just returned from Mecca, or beyond, where their prophet sleeps in Medina.

Nor that poorly-dressed envoy of Christianity, preaching alike in churches, fields, market-places, found a scanty or unwilling auditory when he descanted on the dangers, insults, afflictions, he had undergone, and far worse, those he had been a tearful eye-witness of, where so many of their fellow-Christians were doomed to suffer all kinds of ill-treatment and bitter scoffs, and horrid tortures for their religion; and he called upon them by all they held dear, or deserving tenderness or veneration, and in the name of Him whom they feared and worshipped, and His Divine, immaculate, and far above all the rest of creation, most blessed mother, and the God-head of her uncreated Son, that thrice-sacred Redeemer, that dearest Lord Jesus; when in His sempiternal unearthly cause, he summoned every professor of this heavenly creed, to join hand in hand, without any distinction of country, sex, condition, rank, as the best preparation for that mighty day of judgment that was surely very near, in one immense crusade to expel those infidel dogs from where He left His mortal remains for our prayers and consolation, and to which no Christian but has undoubtedly a full right to go for that worthiest of purposes, and far greater right than any person can have to any earthly inheritance from any mortal parent, or any lands from a worldly father, or houses, or money, or chattels; for this is from his omnipotent, immortal Father, whose recompense is utterly superior to all earthly value, and can never die; road which was made and decreed by no creatures mortal or immortal, but the Infinite Being's self, and therefore ought most rightfully, by all laws, human and divine, to be left free for all Christians, the poorest and feeblest, as well as the richest and most powerful, and not, if they venture, be exposed to injury, whips, and death ; when he thus conjured and supplicated with most piteous exclamations, and tears and gestures of the wildest enthusiasm, he let loose a torrent that no one in his senses could even attempt to stem.

It had long been pent up; but he has now (perhaps carelessly) unsluiced it. And if it can be guided, that tremendous gush, the Lord alone knows. Yet men only heard what they were ready for; and those of any wealth or foresight began their outfit at once. Not a single syllable, I will not say of doubt, but even of delay. Thousands upon thousands were in readiness to depart forthwith. It required the hermit himself to persuade them to wait for a few months, that estates might be sold or mortgaged, and that the lowest classes that possessed anything, should convert their furniture and household goods into a little money.

Yet, where all wished to sell, and none to buy, what but hamper themselves, each with as much as ever he could, and leave the rest for any person that should pass? Heaps of articles strewed every road in Europe, and lay neglected, though they would have been all stolen at any other time; but now the meanest mendicant refused to lose a moment by looking on them. What was proposed to all, and was the duty of all, was so paramount to arms, provisions, horses, ships, in the apprehension of millions, that they smiled at such superfluous cares, and held them in supreme disdain. Yet some had the prudence to occupy themselves a little with these trifles, nor every head of a family deemed it praiseworthy to renounce his duties of providing for those whom his Creator had confided to his administration; it were a tempting of Providence! But no further deferring than was absolutely necessary.

To every class of the community the crusade

became the great business of life—the only real business—all things else were playthings for children. This was the mighty, universal law, absorbing or comprehending all other laws, civil, criminal, ecclesiastical, military, political, international. These all were mere gewgaws, or primers in comparison. Nor was there any exception even for the clergy; since they were men too! as pious and learned as you will, but still men—like ourselves in substance, mere mortal men, and bound to worship Christ and prepare for doomsday, make their souls, and get in order for salvation.

Put Satan to flight, is what is of importance. There is but one way to do this—come on the crusade. The rest is tinsel; crown or tiara, alike all tinsel. So the priests, far from inciting their parishioners, had only to follow them, and were obliged to follow them whether they wished it or not; nor when the Pope convened the councils, was either of them his own doing. His Holiness could not have acted otherwise. Certainly a large portion of the wisest and most religious of the clergy of all ranks beheld these puritanical tumults with disapprobation, and feared for the contaminating effect of such a mixture of both sexes, and of the most devout aud pure young people with the impure, repentant, and perhaps not repentant reprobates. But what could those virtuous and most prudent pastors do? No one seemed to have any time for reflection. Everywhere all was ferment and effervescence.

Even sagacious elderly men and women appeared to have lost all power over themselves or others. Nor did not some individuals act from baser motives than holiness or zeal; although the vast majority did act from these laudable motives, and no others; even owning that their zeal was often blind, and no few of the vicious really were reclaimed. But there were not wanting sprinklings of hypocrisy, and what is probably worse, a profuse assortment of iniquitous wretches, male and female, who neither changed, nor intended, nor pretended to change their lives! Swearers, cursers, pickpockets, highwaymen, robbers of every description, murderers, whole parties of the most scandalous of ruffians, and the vilest Delilahs and Jezebels, and such like, who embraced the adventure as a glorious speculation, resolved on the very reverse of any amendment of manners; but to make the most of the opportunity, in the sense of rejecting all restraint, and throwing the loosest reign to every one of their most shameless passions.

The unfortunate priest, forced to participate in the sure destruction and disgrace of such a squad, had an awful duty. Nor imagine possible that his mild voice could be heard in that outrageous confusion. Total ruin could scarcely not ensue. Undoubtedly there were persons who reprobated the crusade from the beginning, and perceived that such a reckless frenzy augured nothing good. To them it was a terrific hurricane. But, on discovering the evident impossibility of stopping it (which they soon discovered), they in every way favoured it. Some of them might even think it were self-love to suppose they saw so much better than others, and therefore joined the cry sincerely, though against their own judgment. But that this cry was in the spirit of the times, is a manifest deduction from the former pilgrims.

As often happens in great events, a strange and mighty presentiment had invaded all the nations in Europe for nearly a century; a growing disquietude that at last broke out at the same instant everywhere, north, south, east, west. Also the Turks had their presentiments, as noted. Nor was it the eloquence of the hermit, who was not eloquent, and soon was flung aside by the very crusade he had preached; for success was then considered proof of a Divine mission, and he was unsuccessful; but men were ripe for his words. It only required a word, and he said it. It was soon given. Any one else would have done as well. It was a moment too when adventurers, and idlers, and vagabonds, were unusually numerous, in consequence of the recent civil wars and discharged armies; and bands of robbers and famishing soldiery were roving everywhere at discretion. When all at once, as if at the wave of some conjurer's wand, crimes and all illegal proceedings ceased, and merged into the crusade; and Europe enjoyed, during some months, a peace she had not known for a long time. Almost everything virtuous and everything vicious took the same direction. Not one plunderer, robber, murderer was any more to be found within the precincts of all Europe. One only thought and deed pervaded every community. Nothing else was worth alluding to.

Great and little, poor and rich, literate and illiterate, folly and wisdom, males and females, parents and children, sovereign and subjects, priests and people—all had no other grave concern. Soon was there nothing but mutual encouragement, and who at first had blamed it as madness, became at last fully as mad as the rest. Impatient all to sell their property, and none to purchase but what was portable. What could not be carried was destroyed, and in like manner much provisions, which produced a famine. Kings were shelved for awhile, or if they resolved to sell or mortgage their dominions or rid themselves of them in any way—even by gift—they imitated the multitude, and joined the crusade as individuals; so they could manage to be lent money enough to buy a battle horse, it filled them with delight to enroll as a common crusader.

The heir apparent of England jumped to pledge Normandy, and left his birthright to his younger brother. Fortunately none of the great European monarchs could so easily make away with their realms, or create a national debt, to squander it; but as they were obliged to wait a little, and put their finances in some order—though resolved to take their turn, and set out as soon as the others came back—yet being of the last, they only went after men had in some degree regained their senses. But in this first crusade they could take no part, but were constrained to remain at home—sadly against their wishes—and considered themselves unhappy, and considered so by others, who sincerely bewailed their piteous lot, and the miserable elevation which condemned them to be a sacrifice for the public, and defer their felicity, and descend to the second place. Poor sovereigns, no longer in the highest, but at this most important crisis, in a quite inferior station!

The cross was the only real resource for every one, and equalled every one. If it was against the ancient discipline for the clergy to bear arms, yet that this was admitted to be an exceptional case was highly beneficial to the crusades. If a novelty, and in ordinary occurrences uncanonical, a holy war made a difference. Devoted wives followed their husbands, or induced them to permit it. Some wives asked for no permission, but their own will; and on such an excursion, no one dared to blame them. Married or unmarried pairs, set out on the adventure together, no fault could be found with them. Some priests might possibly have Asian bishopricks in their heads, even in a few instances it was so certainly; but nevertheless they stuck to their flocks, and preached the same heavenly doctrines they had always preached. Ambition also might have had much to do with several of the leaders who were laymen, and dreamed of crowns and empires in Asia, and remembered that a little nosegay of Normans had conquered Sicily and Puglia.

But notwithstanding all deductions, yet was religious enthusiasm the first and principal cause of this crusade; and put the whole Christian world in motion. Lands, castles, houses, ceasing all at once to be of any value, might well be given away *gratis* to the few who were so unhappy as to be obliged to remain at home. Domains worth little or nothing, are donations that can be accepted by even a king, so as they contribute to assuage his poignant and most reasonable grief—wretched lords—pitiable indeed their lot! The terrified Greeks, who had been sent ambassadors to the Council of Claremont, had no use for their fine harangues, but obtained a great deal more than they asked or desired. A small aid of ten thousand men or so, was all they thought of, and they beheld with perhaps some dismay, that whole nations were to flock through their country.

The first squad to whom I will not do Cromwell's wildest, the injustice to compare them (for those English fanatics were sedate prudent old gentlemen to those who under the hermit himself and his worthy associate, Sansavoir—without a penny or pennyworth—pushed off on their march in one vast irregular multitude, men and women) nearly all of the lowest classes—chiefly beggars, and knaves, and cut-throats, and virulent democrats, fanatical revellers and hypocrites, without food or money, or honesty or common sense, and imperfectly armed with long rusty knives and ancient scabbardless swords, more like saws, and greasy monks the best of them, and sturdy clowns and peasant girls, and the majority drunkards male and female, and lawless perpetrators of the grossest debauchery of every description, most of them pell mell, on foot, half-naked, with only ten horses amongst such thousands, and the most reputable in various carts and waggons drawn by their usual teams or plough cattle, and little or no provisions; for it would have been an insult to the Almighty to have done otherwise, in the estimation of the religiously mad, who furnishes the birds with food ; and the wicked having determined on ill-treating, robbing, sacking every creature, house and town they should come to, were extremely glad of that valid excuse.

Early in the spring of 1096, it was quite out of all possibility to restrain their impatience. Penitence the most austere and sincere, and piety the most fervent, were henceforth to associate with the grossest impurity, and every kind of low gaiety, worldly, and disfigured with vice. From the Tiber to the Northern Ocean, from the Danube to Portugal, all were hurrying to the crusade. These all in tears who were to remain in Europe, those marching towards Asia showed nothing but smiles of hope and joy. At every village they saw, the children kept asking, *Is that Jerusalem?* Happy in their ignorance, not a word of reason came from old or young, clerk or layman; nor did any one express astonishment at what now surprises us. All were actors; there was no audience, posterity were to be that. Immense armies, many of them, might have been formed out of that multitude; enough, and far more than enough. But the chief captains agreed among themselves to set about making the preparations absolutely necessary, and then to take different roads, and meet again at Constantinople.

But first of all was it requisite to skim off the dross, and rid themselves of that heterogeneous and most unmilitary crowd. All the various gangs of that description were to proceed in three divisions. So the Heaven-elected hermit's insane squad, that was to form the first division, departed instantly with Sansavoir leading the vanguard. The zealous Cenobite, as fit for the mad hospital as any of them, convinced that a good hot will is enough to insure success in war, and that the undisciplined mob would obey his voice, figured at the head of that oddest of columns, in his woollen gown, and with cowl and sandals, riding jovially that same she mule which had carried him over all Europe—England included. But he had outriders with his penniless lieutenant, who had been followed close by two of the horsemen; so there were only eight horses to be scattered through the main body.

Altogether this division comprised at least a hundred thousand men, followed by a long train of rude vehicles, women, children, and the old, sick, or decrepid, or valetudinarians; all relying on the miraculous promises of their more than Moses. For their holy Peter needed but to tread where he had trod already. They expected that the rivers would open to let them pass, manna fall from Heaven to feed them.

The commanders were as miserable as their soldiers. To the East asking alms! And as long as they were in France or Germany, they were not wrong in their expectations; for they were fed by the charitable. Not so in Hungary; although its king had been known to the hermit on his way home from Jerusalem, when that new convert had heard with sympathy of the poor palmer's sufferings. But his Majesty was now dead; nor did his successor, though a recent Christian also, and in correspondence with the Pope, look with a kindly eye on these lawless crusaders; nor the Bulgarians, though Christians likewise, would recognise the desperate fellows as their brethren, but treated them worse than they had ever treated former pilgrims.

Cold charity was quickly over; so the crusaders, not contented with stealing, or with the strong hand seizing, the cattle, and driving them off openly, or sacking cottages, set them on fire, insulted, beat, or even murdered the peasantry; and acted in like manner towards the outskirts of some towns, whereupon the terrified and irritated Bulgarians rushed to arms, and cut many of the others to pieces —to say nothing of sixty whom they burned in a church to which they had fled for protection, but perhaps deserved to find none; on which Sansavoir struck off into the forests and wildernesses. Nevertheless a considerable portion of the wretched forerunners got to Constantinople, and remained two months under its walls; the emperor wisely refusing to let them inside the gates, but permitting them to wait there for the hermit, where they sorrily could keep soul and body together, on the coarsest food, doled out to them with the unkindest parsimony.

At length the hermit had reached Semlin—city called by him Maleville, from the bad reception it offered them—namely sixteen, not indeed corpses, but arms and garments of so many of their own vanguard by way of a scare-crow, to deter them from following the example of those culprits; at which he in a rage gave the signal for war, and at the blast of a trumpet the desperate assailants slew forty thousand of the peaceable inhabitants. Which horrid atrocity made the King of Hungary advance with a large army. But before his arrival, hermit and congregation had all run away and contrived to cross the Save—where they found villages and towns abandoned—even Belgrade without a creature. Every one had sought refuge in the hills and woods. Thence onward did our famishing crowd labour sadly; and at last approached with expectations that were to be frustrated, the fortified town of Nyssa; but alas! they could not enter, and were only given some little food beneath its walls, on their promise of forthwith proceeding without perpetrating any misdemeanour; but a party of them, "certain children of Belial," whom a chronicler calls Germans, recklessly firing some windmills in the vicinity belonging to the citizens, these, vexed beyond all longer endurance, rushed out against the rear and put multitudes to death, and likewise took numbers of prisoners—mothers and infants, many of whom were found living there in bondage several years after. The miserable remnant crept forwards—without either food or arms, and so reduced in numbers, found themselves in a far worse condition than ever.

But this extreme misery produced pity, which answered better than force; and the Greek Emperor charitably sent what enabled them to reach the walls of Constantinople. Yet the Greeks, not liking the

Latins—and pardonably enough, if to judge by this sample—interiorly applauded the courageous Bulgarians; though the emperor himself not fearing the garrulous Peter, nor his corps, now unarmed and in the rags of indigence, advised them, with as much condescension as sincerity, to wait for the Prince of the Crusade.

But the second division had yet to come. This resembled the hermit's, but rather worse. They were, for the most part, from the north of the Rhine, and towards the Elbe, and led by a priest of the Palatinate, of the name of Gotschalk. Wholly occupied with robbing, and all kinds of pillage, rapes, quarrels, murders, these worthies soon forgot Constantinople, Jerusalem, Jesus Christ himself. If any of them had ever had any religion, they certainly soon lost the least traces of it. Not a law, human or Divine, did they consider sacred. They were quite hurried away by their passions. The slenderest temptation was irresistible to them. Their ferocity was accompanied by imbecility, and would have worn itself out probably, but that they fell victims to perfect barbarity, nor could expect to be saved by the laws of humanity, which they had broken themselves.

Yet was there a third division of such frightful eminence in iniquity, anarchy, sedition, that no one had the hardihood to be its captain. These desperadoes scorned every obedience, civil, military, ecclesiastical—all to them a grievous yoke. And they would have none, but would live and die as free as born. What property does a baby carry into the world? or a corpse out of it? What lawgivers have they? Choosing to believe that the crusade washed away all sins, they committed the most heinous crimes with the utmost indifference and a safe conscience. With a fanatical pride—or they feigned it—they despised and assaulted every one who did not join their march. Not all the riches on earth were sufficient to recompense their self-devotedness; let God and the Church know that—in whose service they are—the only service they acknowledge. They declared themselves *the Volunteers of Heaven*, and would not hear of any mixture of what is human. All that should fall into their hands was rightfully their own, and but a small part of what was due to them; an anticipated quota of the arrears of their pay, so much taken from the heathen. Of the lands they were traversing, they were themselves the true owners. The proprietors should thank them, if they left anything, and were in reality their debtors.

From such principles, you may imagine what followed. This furious troop moved disorderly;

and obeyed but the fits of their own insanity. They observed peremptorily that it was an enormous wrong to go against those who profaned the tomb of Christ, without first slaying who had crucified Him. Miraculous or pretended visions so inflamed their hate and horror and all their diabolical appetites, that they massacred all the Jews on their line of march with the most abominable and unnatural tortures. So the contents of each miserable Jewry craved for death as other men for life. But the boon without preamble of being tortured was rarely or never granted.

Since they could find no captain, they took a goose and made it march at their head, strutting pompously with a wave of its body and bobbing the pinnacle of its long windpipe, or a goat with a coquelico ribbon round its neck; and ascribed something of divine to it, and assured astonished beholders, that it was equal to any priest or bishop. For which impudent jeer they are condemned by the chroniclers more than for their deeds of tremendous guilt. This carnage of the unresisting Jews inebriated such felons, and made them as proud as if they had vanquished the Saracens. But the Hungarians exercised their implacable swords on this division to a man. At least only a very few individuals of it lived to join the hermit under the Constantinopolitan bastions.

With this offal and what remained of all three of the divisions, re-inforced by Normans, Venetians, Pisans, Genoese, and others that he had picked up, he formed a new army of a hundred thousand, quite as undisciplined, and simple, and wicked as his first, and at the head of this collection the hermit set out along with his aide-de-camp Sansavoir, to try a fresh campaign, not unlike Don Quixote and Sancho Panza making for their second excursion. Many who left home pious, their piety went out on the road. Bold men get the upper hand, and bad example gives the law. Thus their robberies roused Constantinople, and even various churches in its suburbs suffering for their neighbourhood, the emperor was engaged to give them ships to transport them into Asia, without any further delay; when advancing with the same temerity as before, a Turkish army cut them to pieces — poor Sansavoir was run through the body ten several times, and the hermit in a most cowardly manner escaped —and in one single day that whole vast gathering disappeared, and left only a great heap of bones in a valley near Nice.

So Europe was horror struck at learning that of four hundred thousand crusaders she had sent out, all were totally butchered. Yet the extermination of their less worthy parts, only increased the spirit-stirring glow of heroic and religious chivalry. The brilliant epoch of the holy war now begins. The princes of the crusade had not been yet ready. With Godfrey de Bouillon, Duke of Lower Lorraine, at their head, gathered nearly all the most illustrious captains of the time, and in a mass the nobility of France, and of both banks of the Rhine, and many of the English, and indeed of all Europe. No wonder then that the price of a war horse rose to an excessive height, the funds of a good estate hardly sufficing to arm and mount a single knight.

Germans and Hungarians were shown quite a different sight from the hermit's army, which was only a villainous mob—and re-established the honour of the crusaders in every land they went through. Hungary and Bulgaria wished Godfrey success; and he deplored the bad conduct and severe chastisement of those who had preceded him, but he did not once attempt to avenge their cause. Nor is his conduct or of any of the crusade to be ascribed to deep political views, for such matters were utterly unknown to them.

But what was purely accidental in those remote times, became to posterity, who judged of it by their own wisdom, the product of long foresight.

The brother of the King of France and the King of England's eldest son, were there mingled with their equals or superiors, many of them of the noblest birth and qualities, and as unambitious as themselves. Several of the others nourished views of earthly ambition no doubt, yet was it ambition of a very lofty kind. Monarchies, empires, diadems, and the summit of military reputation, might enter for some share, and mix with their religious feelings—even without their knowing it; still Vermandois and Robert of Normandy had no projects whatever, but heaven and glory.

Going round by Rome, the crusaders were so scandalized to see the soldiery of a Pope and of an Antipope fighting for the Lateran, the capital of Christianity serving as the theatre of a civil war, that some of them refused to go any further, and returned home. Profounder thinkers reflecting that in this life a portion of the human must ever unite with the best of the divine, and that inasmuch as it is human, it must be subject to imperfections —whence it is written, "the just man falls seven times a-day," endeavoured to shut their eyes, and after saying their prayers and visiting the curiosities, hurried away; and all the divisions of that mighty army soon met at Constantinople.

And most sumptuously were they treated in that

celebrated metropolis, and entered it with all honours, and every demonstration of joy and public welcome. Only it was expected they would do homage to the emperor, which the Count of Toulouse refused, declaring he had not come so far to look for a master. Yet by surprise or cunning something that could be explained into homage, was worked out of him, and all of them—though an idle inane show. Tancred was the single exception, and he hastened his departure as the only way to avoid taking what at present was termed nothing, but might afterwards be construed into an oath of allegiance to Alexis. The brave generous Tancred was right. He was a Norman, and would have no breath on Norman honour.

Amidst such amplitude of luxury, and a constant variety of splendid amusements, few of the crusaders but seemed to have forgotten the Turks; nearly all but Godfrey, who at last asked for boats. And the Latins crossed the Bosphorus, and had advanced but a few leagues in Asia Minor, when they accosted some slaves who had left Europe with the hermit; and further on, towards Nice, a quantity of human bones told of that slaughter. That unfortunate Christian multitude had never been buried. Wolves and vultures had well consumed their flesh. So, in sad silence, the heroes of the cross continued their march. It was a sight to end all discord, and put a curb on every worldly ambition—at least for a time; but only warmed their zeal for the holy war. So they took Nice, and won the glorious battle of Doryleum— Michaud's *chef d'œuvre* — where the valiant Duke of Normandy acquired great distinction. "O France, my delicious France, who art, indeed, superior to every other country," sang the Troubadour, "how surpassingly beautiful were the tents of thy soldiers in Romanie!" which shows that the crusaders had tents, and were not left to needlessly bivouac in the open air, and so sicken and die— whereas we never read of the hermit's tents, or Gotschalk's. It is certain they had none. But it is also certain that tents are no superfluous expense, but in every way befitting warriors. The soldier not exposed unnecessarily to the damp nights, will be the abler to endure them when it is necessary. The contrary is but a foolish, beggarly, modern pretence to what is misnamed economy. It is no economy at all, but a positive loss, not only of life but of money.

This crusade was therefore equipped as hardy warriors ought to be; and in this sense it may be doubted if the world ever possessed a fairer army than that led by Godfrey, the victors of Nice and

Doryleum. When they took the Turkish camp, at this latter place, they found camels, animals till then unknown in Europe. It was July 1st, 1097. The Franks praised the Turks highly; and vaunted of their common origin. And chroniclers avow that, were the Turks but Christians, they would be equal to the crusaders; that is, the bravest, wisest, ablest soldiers in the world. What the Turks thought is evident from their attributing the victory to a miracle. "And what wonder since St. George and St. Demetrius were with our enemy? One sees you do not know the Franks," said Kilzig-Arslan to the Arabs, who blamed his retreat, "you have never experienced their astonishing bravery; such power is not human—but comes either from God or the devil."

On the next day but one after, the crusaders renewed their march eastward, nor found any more resistance throughout all Asia Minor, so completely had it been terrified by the day of Doryleum, to which was now to be added the approach of the main body of the Frank army, to both of which was it owing that Tancred, with two or three hundred cavalry, galloping rapidly about, took town after town, the whole of Cilicia, and up to the south of Scanderoon; killing every Turk without repose or mercy. In Asia Minor had

Florine, the Duke of Burgundy's daughter, disappeared with the young Crown Prince of Denmark, and if it gave rise to much fable and rumours, yet for certain where and how they ended was never discovered; though her afflicted father went seeking her over all the then known world for several years. And if Tasso relates how they died, it is that they offered a fair field for imagination—the perhaps grandest and most difficult of a poet's attributes. What is uncertain is *common* to everybody, and open to invention; difficile est, proprie *communia* dicere; it is in some sort a creation, and makes him (what he is in no sense otherwise) a creator.

But early in Asia had the crusaders begun following the hideous example of the Turks, in cutting off the heads of the slain, and riding with them dangling from their pommels, and threw a thousand of them at the enemy within Nice, with their besieging engines; and, filling sacks with another thousand heads, sent them as a present to the Greek Emperor.

But while Tancred was so cleverly employed in Cilicia, Baldwin (Godfrey's next brother, and the English Queen's father), devoured with ambition, and thinking the East had better things than any to be expected at Jerusalem, or accomplishment of his vow at the Holy Sepulchre, set out by night to avoid the remonstrances of his friends, who all dissuaded him from that wild and shameful breach of his solemn compact, leading a small body of two thousand volunteers to assail one of the many fine cities and countries pointed out to him from the top of a lofty mountain by a fugitive Armenian adventurer.

So, passing the Euphrates at El Bir (the caravan road), at sixteen hours from Orfa, which the Talmuds affirm was founded by Nimrod, like Nineveh, he made straight for that capital of Mesopotamia, and those fragrant gardens that put one in mind of Eden, whose site they are said to be truly. A Greek governor now held it for Alexis, paying tribute to the Saracens, but, in the main, contriving to keep independent of either Bagdad or Constantinople. Both he and the people welcomed Baldwin, whom they mistook for the leader of the great Frank army. The city, fortunate enough to escape the Turks, had served as a refuge for a number of Christians; and they, rich. The bishop and twelve of the chief inhabitants met him as a deputation, telling him how wealthy Mesopotamia was, how devoted conscientiously to the cause of Jesus they were, and conjuring him to save a Christian establishment from the infidels' domination. Nor was Baldwin hard to be won. Yet having left little garrisons in all the various towns and villages he had stopped at, he had with him but a hundred horse. Curious was his triumphal entrance into that splendid, most civilised, and strongly-fortified place. The whole population walked out to receive him with olive branches and singing. But at their first interview, the prince or governor perceived he was more dangerous than a Mahometan; and, with a wish to get clear of him, offered him a considerable sum. The wily Baldwin however refused it, and threatened to go away, the towns-people, with loud cries, beseeching him to remain. But it could only be by his becoming bound to them by the binding link of duty; and by that honourable plea alone it were possible for him to be detached from the crusade, on the precise terms that the Prince of Orfa, who was old and childless, should adopt him, and proclaim him his successor; which being acceded to with eagerness, the legal ceremony of adoption was instantly gone through in the presence of Baldwin's own soldiers, and of the people, as indubitable witnesses, and according to the Oriental custom, the Greek passed the Latin between his shirt and his skin, and kissed him, in sign of his being his child. The aged wife of the prince did the same, and so Baldwin was ever after considered their son and heir, and indeed neglected nothing to defend what had now become his own inheritance. When the death of the aged prince made him sovereign, he acquired in a signal degree the respect and love of his subjects; and in their annals he is held the best monarch they ever had. Being a widower, he married the niece of another of the small Armenian despots, a marriage that brought him a vast deal of money, and enabled him by purchase to extend his principality as far west as Mount Taurus. Orfa in the end was very useful to the crusaders, as a bulwark against the Turks on the side of the Euphrates towards the north-east.

But all this while was Godfrey stopped by Antioch, hard both to take and to maintain; and for a year and a half before it or within it, besieging or besieged, equally had the Franks to endure much and to suffer immense losses. The capital of Syria, with its massive fortifications of huge blocks of stone, and the iron bridge over the Orontes, and both its banks, were in quiet possession of the Latins, and the Turkish forces driven far away eastward of the Euphrates, but consequent on—ah! what tremendous sacrifices of life! Of the five or six millions computed to have left Europe, and more than a million leaving Nice, only about sixty thousand now remained to set out for Jerusalem.

These were the ages of great things. Matters were always on a vast scale. For a few days we wander now all over a large city, or entire province, or as far as a newspaper goes; but then a father went wandering over whole continents; a great army was not of two hundred thousand men, but of five or six millions; nor of one, or of a few, but of almost all nations. A peasant now thinks it a great thing to go to a neighbouring shire, even with the aid of the railroad; but then, without any aid at all, a peasant with his entire family considered it a little undertaking to set out from the Vistula, or England, or the north of France, for Jerusalem.

Yet the sixty-thousand men that left Antioch were a far stronger body than the confused multitudes from which they were chosen; for they were every one of them excellent. After such rigid purifications—labours, diseases, battles, that along with some valuable lives, carried off almost all the useless and refuse, those that remained were veterans of rare merit. When find again a corps selected out from several millions? Nor by a fortuitous choice, but by a series of all sorts of experiments, without any danger of partiality or prejudice; for each was free to change masters, and as often as he pleased. Nevertheless they shall be still more purified, if not to so small a compass as Gideon's, yet to one third.

There are wonderful things even to this day told about the whole country round Antioch—it is all holy ground to the Arab—whose fables are all appropriated to the French by the French historian; but Franks are meant to include almost all Europe. The old iron bridge—not that it was of metal, but that it had two towers covered with plates of iron—fell in 1822, from an earthquake, I think. But nothing was more consequential in all the various battles during the siege of Antioch, than that necessity reduced the cavalry to fight on foot, having devoured all their horses during the famine; and that dismounted cavalry formed an infantry to outdo either, and far superior to all the infantry then in use; and of which the famous Spanish foot afterwards were only a faint imitation, for this infantry was quite irresistible, and broke the Turkish cavalry at once. It was a lesson, that had a great effect then, and a far greater over the whole military world in process of time. For infantry, that up to that moment had been quite neglected in the middle ages, and considered a secondary arm, began to be held in due consideration and put on a par with the cavalry, which in its turn, yielded the first place to the infantry. But it was ascertained, that to have the very best infantry, it must have been cavalry once. Particularly the English produced a celebrated corps (in their French wars, several centuries later) that used to be cavalry until they got to the field of battle, but then alighted and left their horses to the servants. "Then for the first time did Italy and France see horsemen in heavy armour that descended from their horses to fight on foot. Yet was it surely the best mode of warfare, for they thus joined the impenetrable armour of cuirassiers, to the steadiness of infantry, and it was almost impossible to break that firm phalanx. Those English too despised the most rigid winter, and never suspended their military operations at any season. And strange was the beauty of their arms and armour, all kept shining as a looking-glass; for every horseman was attended by two servants, who had nothing else to do, than clean their master's horse and accoutrements."

If the crusaders were blinded as to the holy lance, the Turks were equally so in fearing it; though some of those Mahometan writers say it was not a lance but stick. On the whole the Moslem thought it so extraordinary to lose Antioch, that some of them abandoned Mahometanism as proved untrue. Yet even then it was difficult to persuade the crusaders (or the commander-in-chief himself who had gone to Orfa to visit his brother) to quit that pleasant residence. First to avoid the heats of summer—then a fever in autumn retarded them by carrying off nearly all the women and children and beggars, at the rate of fifty thousand a month—which, though to their deep concern at the time (for the crusaders were renowned for charity), but eventually a kindness of Providence, relieved them from what would have acted as a distraction, if not temptation, and certainly an unwieldy heavy tail and impediment. And to that succeeded the cold of winter, so that it was early in March of 1099 that they at last marched; and Bohemond of the Red Flag remained there as Sovereign Prince of Antioch.

At Laodicea they were joined by several English —exiles from Hastings—noble warriors who had left their darling homes and quiet firesides to William the Conqueror, and full of pious zeal and signal valour, proceeded to deliver the Holy Sepulchre; which did not prevent the army to thin. For numbers died of distress, hunger, and sickness all along; although there was no fighting. But whatever still rested with the least tinge of indiscipline or discord kept working themselves off by death. One day a young officer saw what might well astonish him: "You alive and quite in health; you whom I saw slain in that battle?" "Know," replied the other, "that those who fight for Christ, never die." "But why are you clad in that dazzling beam?" At which his companion pointed up to the sky, where stood a palace of crystal and diamonds. "It is there I dwell, and to it owe the beauty that so surprises you. But, for you likewise, is a still more beautiful palace prepared, which you will come to enjoy very shortly. Farewell! We meet again to-morrow!" And the apparition returned to heaven. The rest was reality. For in he called the priests, received the last sacraments, and, though perfectly well, took leave of his friends. And in a sudden skirmish, early the next day, was struck in the forehead; "so went," says the chronicle, "to that fine palace."

It was certainly necessary for the counts and barons of the crusade to keep the minds of their soldiery exalted to the utmost, in order to accomplish what still awaited them; else their own authority alone would have never had weight enough. The rather that doubts began to arise regarding several of the past miracles; particularly the lance advocated by a person of dissolute manners, though well versed in letters. The Fatimite Caliph, though hating the Franks as unbelievers, hated the Turks too, as wishing to deprive him of Syria, sent an ambassador to both. But nothing could stop the crusade. These had been still further reduced, and little exceeded forty thousand men; too small a number for so great an undertaking as that to which they were hastening, picked men as they had a right to call themselves, after having been put to so many proofs, and surmounted them all; nor any longer followed by a useless disorderly crowd, fortified by their losses, they formed a body more to be feared than at the outset.

The memory of their exploits heightened their own constancy and confidence in themselves and valour; and the terror they had spread through the East made them be still held an innumerable army. If they had still somewhat of a train, all armies have camp-followers; but in their case, that idle appendage kept every day decreasing. So the Emir of Tripoli paid them a contribution for peace; and without entering his town, they continued on. It was the end of May. Admirable was the order in the army, wonder of all beholders, say the chronicles. Every movement was by sound of trumpet —the least error in discipline punished severely— a regular school for all the details of a soldier's day, on or off guard, and nightly guards and videttes; the chaplains too were active in instructing; brave, patient, sober, charitable as ever they could, were those gallant warriors. Nor did the Moslem ever dare to stop them, such respect preceded their advance; not even in those defiles of which we read, "A hundred Saracen warriors would have been sufficient to stop the entire of the human race." Beyrout's rich territory, and Sidon's and Tyre's they traversed, and reposed in the laughing gardens of those ancient cities, and beside their delightful waters; the Moslem shut up peacefully within their walls, and sending plenteous provisions to the passing pilgrims, conjuring them not to damage their flowers and orchards, decoration and wealth of their lands.

In a cool valley on the banks of *the sweet river* they encamped three days. No more dreams of ambition—no attempt at getting rich, to be able to pay their troops; the chiefs, who for the most part had become poor, took service under the Count of Toulouse, though it must have galled their fierce spirit; but the nearer they drew to Jerusalem, the more they seemed to lose something of their worldly loftiness and indomitable pride, and to have forgotten their pretensions, disputes, and piques. They passed Acre (accepting tribute from its emir), Joppa, and the plain of that St. George who had so often aided them in battle, and thence struck off to Ramla, within thirty miles of the object of all their toils and wishes. But on arriving, they had not one single loiterer or superfluous creature; but on review that morning, had barely numbered twenty thousand men.

But it was a selection of the very best warriors of all Christendom, such as it is not to be expected (perhaps scarcely desired) shall ever meet again. Most assuredly nothing similar is to be found in the history of past eras. Heroes whose likes the world never saw, and, I think, will hardly see again; and therefore is unwilling to admit they ever existed, but rather insists upon their being imaginary and inventions of story-tellers and poets. But in truth they were of the same flesh and blood as ourselves, but with sublimer minds, and more energy of purpose. I would not wrong our own period either. Perhaps, if we could concentrate the choicest of every nation in Christendom, and extract the quintessence of five or six millions, we might get together twenty thousand heroes, even now. But it is very improbable that circumstances will ever occur again to call out such multitudes of willing victims. With time and fashion, weapons and systems change.

But in substance it was the same, and will be always the same. The determined heart and bold hand and lightning mind, are of all times. Who was a capital soldier then, would be a capital soldier now—not the least doubt of it. Hardiness and exactness are the things; with them, any tactics will do; without them, no tactics can effect much. Martinets—or whatever be the name in vogue—never perform important matters. Something of what took place after the great French Revolution, took place then—I mean officers acting as privates. Not one individual of the whole twenty thousand but was an experienced able veteran warrior, both for cavalry and infantry; and several of them accomplished engineers, or for what would be now called artillery, and fully capable of conducting a siege. And to a siege they were going, and such a siege! One of the strongest fortresses in Asia, with a large valiant garrison, commanded by a noted Mahometan, chosen on purpose for that arduous station, and well furnished with every necessary ammunition, and they themselves but a handful. Who ever heard, before or since, in the usual routine of war, of the besieged army being as numerous as the besieging? Here they are three times more so. But none of the least worthy of these Franks but would have been a fit sergeant in our armies, or subaltern, or even captain—hundreds generals, and certainly several qualified to be commanders-in-chief to any army at present in Europe. Their discipline must much have struck the Arabs, for I see they continually talk of their coming on "*like one man.*"

In passing the narrow rugged defiles of the hills of Judea where the smallest resistance from an enemy would have delayed them, it is easy to believe that they interpreted their meeting none into a proof that *He* was delivering the holy city up into their hands; as, a little before too, He had informed them of their foe's designs by a dove's dropping into the midst of them, under whose wing was tied a letter from one Moslem Emir to his general; and it was perfectly clear that the sweet white bird had been sent direct from heaven, whence else could she have come? Nearer and nearer, with increase of impatience—and throbbing hearts every one of them—the venerated cupolas were now very near, though as yet unseen. So Tancred with a little vanguard was despatched round to occupy Bethlehem; and as for the centre, it halted for the night at a village within six miles of what they soon next morning came in view of—Jerusalem! Jerusalem! Jerusalem! flew from mouth to mouth and from rank to rank, and leaping from their horses, and kissing the ground, it were difficult to depict the fervour of that sublime moment.

Remounting to the highest antiquity, Jerusalem was even then the most magnificent of Asiatic cities, and it has never ceased to be a strong one. No other great metropolis was perhaps ever built from the first purposely for strength. The founders, says Tacitus, foreseeing that its difference of morals would be sure to make it the source of continual wars, had used every effort to fortify it; and under the Romans it was the mightiest fortress in Asia. And under the Moslem, who now held it, its circuit measured about three miles, in form an oblong square. The regular troops garrisoning it, were forty thousand; the militia twenty thousand; and the body of Turks and other Mahometans of every description that had come to join in the defence, were at least ten thousand, in all seventy thousand men, under the Fatimite lieutenant, an esteemed soldier, and his second in command, an Osmanli of still greater military reputation. Its garrison always numerous and brave, had been vastly increased for the occasion and in every respect excellently provided to stand a siege.

The Turks had made it an exception to their usual spirit of degradation; for finding it to be always an object of competition and by turns the ambition of every conqueror, they had not neglected its fortifications; much less the Egyptians, who supplanted the Turks. Should not all Islam united be able to beat off whom neither the ramparts of Antioch nor innumerable armies could check on their victorious march? But the crusaders, melted down as they were in numbers, were far too few to invest the entire city; so had to confine themselves to the half of it. And when, after various attempts during forty days, they took it by assault at last, without any of the aids of modern warfare and little of the engineership then practised, not from want of talent and information but want of timber, without even ladders, but only a few machines made on the spot—far from the sea —and with scarcity of wood and iron—there is something very like a miracle in their ever having taken it at all. Bloody was the struggle—indeed *a giant fight*—and too bloody necessarily the first unsparing blast of victory.

Glad am I to be able to dispense myself from speaking of atrocities committed during many days. Butchered it is said were seven thousand souls in Omar's Mosque alone; nor is it easy to flatter one's self it is a grievous exaggeration, since vaunted of by the Christians themselves, and rather admitted by the Moslem chronicles, that proclaimed it with indignation; and indeed one of them goes so far as to labour to extenuate it, by affirming that from a rumour that every Mahometan who left the town within three days, his life should be spared, a terrible disaster occurred ; for that, to be in time, numbers pressed out together, and choked up the doorway, and were many of them suffocated. But that could account for few deaths in seventy thousand; and the long space of three days. It rather makes the matter worse—and but adds an atrocious and more striking circumstance.

But it is very remarkable, that neither here nor on any occasion, do either Christians or Moslems condemn or lament their own crimes or barbarities, or those of their enemies, but quietly recite the enormity without a single word of surprise, sorrow, or blame. What a profound hatred must have been on both sides, since not one Mahometan ever came from the besieged, asking either capitulation or quarter; nor had the Christians once deigned—as was almost invariably practised everywhere else, in Palestine particularly—to summon them to surrender. Their encounter could not be otherwise than tremendous and merciless, whoever won.

With perfect justice has it been observed that Tasso introduces too much witchcraft; which is not to be in character. Witchcraft is in the spirit of the age in which the poet lived, and which was full of that superstition, but not of that of which he wrote. The crusaders were very superstitious, to be sure, but their superstition was not conversant with little things, but with the phenomena of the heavens, and the apparition of saints and angels, and revelations made by the Creator himself; but not regarding necromancy and magicians. Fairies might have come through Normandy from the Scalds; and the mythology of Odin may have had some affinity with the alchymy of the Spanish Moors. But the crusaders of the first crusade believed little or not at all in magic and witches.

The Jerusalem of that time was the Jerusalem of Titus; or like it in some degree, and displayed desperate valour and rapacity, and the very utmost pitch of unsparing cruelty. Consolatory to have the operation quickly over, the Arab historians despatch the whole doleful matter in two lines: "It was the will of God that the city should be taken; and so the Christians, rushing on *like one man*, took it—God curse them!"

But Godfrey de Bouillon did not share in any of the barbarities; but if he could not give an order in a place taken by assault, gave his example, and the crusaders saw that he who had been the first and most ardently courageous and able of warriors on the walls, appeared to change his nature the moment he entered the streets, and went straight and most meekly to pray at the Holy Sepulchre, helmless and barefooted. And after some time, the other chiefs of the crusade followed him; but grieved and ashamed am I to avow, that after that splendid act of piety, they returned to the vomit, with refreshed acrimony, and all the most un-christian passions. Yet some few tarried with their heroic lord; chiefly his own immediate servants, and one devoted youth who had long chosen him for *his man*, and been beside him during the whole crusade, and had saved his life in Natolia; and reminds us of the person who desired his own name should be forgotten, and this epitaph, and nothing else, inscribed on his tomb, *Here lies Sir Philip Sydney's friend* ; — for chroniclers rarely designate him otherwise than *Duke Godfrey's young friend*, so that it required singular chance, and much antiquarian perseverance, to discover securely whom they meant. But now all doubt has unanswerably vanished. From deserters met at Ramla, not one Latin, male or female, had remained in Jerusalem. The contrary is but a fable. Had there been one, priest or layman, one single one of any age or either sex, any such would have been eagerly caught at; if even for no other purpose, yet for this, to identify the relics intended for Europe.

But the crusaders not finding one of their own persuasion, had to put up with the authority of schismatics, and others, or those they called heretics; and, at all events, not Latin Roman Catholics, but Orientalists, Jews, Pagans, Greeks, Nestorians, Armenians, Jacobites. There was no remedy. On the faith of these, blind reliance was to be placed by Europeans. Fact is, no Latin inhabitant had been tolerated in Jerusalem for the last half century, and that as to pilgrims, or passing traders, the Latin archbishop had seen the last of them off, before he left it himself, and fled to Cyprus, soon as the crusaders had reached Antioch.

The news of the fall of Jerusalem flying fast, a deputation from the Mahometans of the neighbouring town of Assur, came the very next day to Godfrey, the Christian Malek-Nasser, or Commander-in-Chief, to capitulate on terms of lives and property, for which they sent several hostages; and in return would be satisfied with one Christian chief; and the duke, who had but his young friend then on whom he could thoroughly count, and knowing that he had determined not to return home like the rest, but sacrifice himself to their sacred cause for life, appointed him at once; whereupon he immediately delivered himself up to the deputies, and departed.

But in the next night's tumult, the Moslem hostages escaped; and when they got to Assur, tidings had come of the approach of the Egyptian army to expel the Christians; so those of that town, taking courage, refused to send back the refugees. Godfrey hastened to chastise them with what troops he could gather from the murderous sack still going on. The irritated Assurians then betaking themselves to an enormously lofty mast of a ship which had been erected as a trophy or ornament in the market-place, and shaping it into the form of a colossal cross, planted it on the walls near the Jerusalem Gate, and raising the youth to it with ropes, using a jerk, as in some of the by-gone modes of torture, must have cruelly dislocated all his limbs, and lacerated his muscles. Nailing at first had been perhaps less horrible. But they seem at the beginning to have meant only a jest; when the rescue from Jerusalem came in sight, within some paces, a voice bade them not advance, for that at their first step they would instantly kill him; or shoot, and you must shoot him. At which the poor crucified, with what strength he could, exclaimed most wofully: "Now do not forget, O most illustrious Duke, that it was under your command I was sent hither an exile and hostage amongst impious men and a barbarous nation; and therefore I beseech you to show mercy towards me, and not permit me to perish so cruelly by so dreadful a martyrdom." But Godfrey, well aware that the tribute naturally torn from his sufferings, was nowise a criterion of his resolute heart, replied, "Not at all, O most gallant of warriors, my dearly beloved young friend! Nor is it in my power to turn off the vengeance of these of mine come to pour it on this devoted town. Not were you even my own brother Eustatius of the same womb with myself, could I this day purchase your release at such a price. Believe me, it is better to die than make these soldiers falsify their oaths, and me mine, and allow this town to remain a lasting scourge to all pilgrims. Your departure is only to fly up to where you'll live for ever with our Lord Jesus!" Wonderful instance of the ruling passion strong in death, he thought of his horse and arms and the Holy Sepulchre; and that its future defenders should wear his armour and wield his sword, left as an heir-loom for the occasion, as frequently was practised in those ages: "Then, O friendliest and best of dukes, give the signal, without any longer attending to me. Only I ardently do beseech you to have my horse and arms presented as a gift and legacy to the Holy Sepulchre, for the benefit of my own soul, and to be used by those who serve God there!" And at the instant ten arrows struck him.

It could not be avoided. But Assur was not to be taken by a *coup-de-main* thus; after many ineffectual attempts, it was clear that no small force like this, but only a large army and regular siege would do. So duke and Normans returned sadly to Jerusalem, reflecting that it would require two months to prepare the necessary machines. And all mourned for the death of their leader's "young friend." Yet dead he was not totally. But on their return, they beheld other duties, and what none of the crusade had expected. The uproar of the sack had (thank Heaven) ceased. Jerusalem, utterly altered, in a few days had changed inhabitants, laws, and religion; yet louder than ever was the martial bustle. The rumour that had emboldened the Assurians was not untrue. The visier had passed the frontier, and might reach the metropolis in three days. Not be besieged, as at Antioch; meet our foes, not wait for them within these shattered walls. There we may rely on our own courage; but here, who knows whether we might not find traitors by our side? Some such fear might be a palliation for the massacres in the Temple, whose groans frightened Jordan, and were echoed back by its sandy hills.

The message had arrived in the middle of the night, and been published by torchlight and sound of trumpet, at all the principal crossings of the streets, with a proclamation in every quarter of the city, for the warriors to meet in the church by daybreak. Such the self-confidence of the crusaders, and their assurance of victory, that this sudden announcement of peril and call to battle, rousing them from slumber about half-past midnight, did not disconcert them, nor troubled the repose of darkness otherwise than by impatience for dawn; and joy-bells rang in matins.

Several hours before Godfrey's arrival, Tancred, and the other chiefs of the crusade, had come to this resolution, and now all was ready; and he warmly approving, and hardly listening while told he had been elected king during his absence, only changes his horse, and anew the trumpet, and once more their Malek-Nasser is at their head. To Ascalon! The Egyptians will have already entered it! But some of the crusaders, holding their vow of liberating the Holy Sepulchre accomplished, had already proceeded homeward, and almost all had their thoughts in that direction. But their hesitation was soon persuaded to march.

Yet very extremely small was the army of the cross, if compared to the multitude against whom it was advancing. To the myriads of the Nile were added the ablest and bravest of the Mahometan warriors from every country. Yet their vast superiority of numbers did not prevent their resorting to every stratagem they could devise, and one very extraordinary; a quantity of buffaloes, asses, mules, mares, sent wild through the fields, to create confusion among the crusaders' horses; and men too, from the temptation to plunder. But Godfrey, under the penalty of nose and ears, forbade any soldier's leaving the ranks. Nor meant more than a prohibition; with such warriors the penalty could not but be merely for form's sake; to which the patriarch added a malediction. So the crusaders no more harmed the herds and animals wandering around them, than if their shepherds.

That night, remaining under arms, and learning the foe was in the plain of Ascalon, now only a few miles off, on sunrise, the 14th of August, the heralds blew the warning of battle. The nearer they drew, the more ardent for combat, replete with hope, and a courageous glow. We look upon our opponents as so many timid deer, or innocent lambkins. They advanced to danger as to a joyous feast. The Emir of Ramla (a spectator in the

Christian army) could not but admire the hilarity of the soldiers at the approach of their formidable adversaries, and expressing his surprise to Godfrey, swore, taking him as a witness, to embrace the religion that inspired its followers with such strength and bravery. At length they got into the plain, all decorated with the Saracen flags and tents, stretching for a league eastward. Leaning back on the sand-hills to the south, were the Egyptian forces drawn up in form of a crescent, like a young stag presenting its long, unweathered horns. Nor the crusaders came without the wild herds spoken of, who, allured by the sound of their trumpets, raised clouds of dust as they kept wheeling round them, like charges of squadrons of cavalry, with a noise of strange confusion. Until then, the Saracen troops had been taught to believe that the Latins would not even dare to wait for them within the walls of Jerusalem, but would decamp for Europe at hearing of their approach, and now, seeing the direct contrary, the more they had shown security hitherto, the more they were struck with a sudden panic terror, and were sure that millions of crusaders had come fresh from beyond sea. The battle itself was not long. The new levies first, and the rest of the Mahometans ran away soon. Little resistance, but they allowed themselves calmly to be butchered. Tancred and the Count of Flanders had done wonders, and broken through the Moslem line; and Duke Robert of Normandy, penetrating even to where the visier was giving his orders, seized on the infidels' standard, which was the signal for defeat, and the whole army took to flight. All was over, except a horrible massacre. Godfrey with about ten thousand horse, and three thousand foot, made such rapid evolutions, he seemed ubiquitous, and rendered vain every attempt to rally. Of a large body of Moslem cavalry, pursued into the sea by the Christian, three thousand were drowned in an idle endeavour to reach the Egyptian fleet, that had stood in as near as it could. Other Moslems, that had mounted into the sycamores and olive trees to hide in their leaves, were burned there, trees and all, as the Arab writers confess; adding, that some whom a lance or dart might strike, fell down from the branches, like a bird shot by the fowler. Thousands threw down their arms, and bowing, had their heads cut off. As many in consternation and trembling on the field of battle stood waiting the Christian sword, which mowed them down, as a mower mows the thick grass of a meadow, or a reaper reaps the rich wheat. A few escaped into the desert to die of hunger, but by far the greater part were miserably cut to pieces to manure that melancholy flat. A crowd tried to seek refuge in the town of Ascalon, but blocked the gate up so, that two thousand of them were suffocated, or were trampled down by the horses. The visier hardly got off, and lost his scimitar. So immense had been his army that, in the words of the old chronicler, "only God could know their numbers." Yet to the Christians it was an easy victory, nor needed their usual bravery, nor miracles. They found Egyptians much less than Turks.

The Latins are said to have had seventeen thousand on that day, and Islam three hundred thousand men. But once that disorder and panic follow an army, numbers only make things worse. Godfrey might now return in triumph to Jerusalem, and the first crusade was indeed ended. But when all these heroes go back to Europe, as will happen in a few days now, who are to uphold the new kingdom? Godfrey, is he not worthier of the title of king, than his territories of that of kingdom? Sad, dark questions from which most shrank. Also there was some little discord, usual fruit of great success. Tancred's generous intercession reconciled the parties. With tears and much weeping the crusaders separated from Godfrey, Tancred, and the others left in the Holy Land. This first crusade, the only one that succeeded, had not a monarch in it. Sacred orators expatiated for the future, not on the woes of Jerusalem, but the victories and glory of the crusaders.

CHAPTER III.

1099 THE tumults of war had ceased, for it was now in October of 1099,[1] and (the victorious crusaders being come back from Ascalon some weeks), Jerusalem resumed a share of the silence and melancholy usual to it ever since Christ's death.[2] Many detachments had gone homeward, and who will not follow?[3] But the choicest of that choice army still delayed, and both officers and soldiers seemed to dread the day they were to separate from whom they loved and revered so much. Godfrey's first care in that precarious state, was to make the most

---

[1] P. Antonio Paoli: Dell'Origine dell'Ordine di S. Gio. Geros., &c., 4to, Roma, 1781, p. 445.
[2] Michaud: Corres. d'Orient, vol. iv. p. 245.—"La cité la plus lugubre du monde," Id. 289.
[3] Pez: Chronicon Austriacum, 547.—Bib. des Croisades, iii. 195.

of it, by gaining a little elbow room all round,[1] or the pressure would have crushed his little realm at once.

All Palestine is represented in a deplorable condition at the epoch of the crusades;[2] not perhaps quite as bad as in our own days, yet very bad, and totally different from what it had been under the Jews or even Romans; as if a mighty curse lay on that whole country, cut up everywhere into small bits, belonging to various people, speaking different languages, and with multitudinous customs, laws, dresses, religions; of innumerable sects of Christianity, Islamism, Paganism, besides a large minority of Samaritans, Israelites, Canaanites, and Hebrews from remotest lands, ancient nation that had once been its real proprietors. The Latins soon gave up, as of no value, what had once seemed to them wealthy estates. The lands all appeared to belong to anybody and nobody. In a house but a year and a day, and it is your own legal property. Stay away as long, and you have lost all right over it.[3] The Jerusalem kingdom itself only comprised the city, and about twenty

---

[1] Michaud: Hist. des Croisades, sixieme ed. vol. ii. p. 2, Paris, 1841.
[2] Arab. Chron. 2.—Bib. Crois. 41.
[3] Michaud: Hist., vol. ii. 3.

towns and villages in its vicinity. And these intersected by others that had Mahometan sovereigns or lords. From one castle hung the cross, from its next, the crescent. How was Godfrey to widen his domains? Yet it was absolutely necessary. He had thought of an expedition into Galilee, to possess himself of Tiberias, and some places hard by Jordan.[1]

But it required money, and his treasury was empty. If that had caused him some sleepless nights, no wonder. Yet he had been greatly rejoiced that very morning by the unexpected return of his young friend, whom he had thought slain at Assur; and on him he knew he could build, and on Tancred he had begun, with good reason; nor arms alone his hope, but also fair means. So he is to receive a deputation of Moslem Emirs within an hour, and a treaty or alliance may succeed. So there, in the court-way of his residence: "Bid them come in!" "But, Majesty, where is your ——?" and an officer would have hurried for a seat. "This will do," said Godfrey; and if he had acted on a deep-laid plan of captivating the Moslem, he could not have done better, when he seized a bundle of straw, and sat down on it. It is

[1] Michaud: Hist., vol. ii. 3.

this mixture of grandeur and simplicity that always produces most effect on the minds of men. Yet was it done by him naturally, unconscious of the effect it had on those Easterns, particularly when he replied to their observation that he was sitting very near the earth, "One may well sit *on* the earth, since we shall so soon be *under* it."[1] So much humility and so much glory! It filled them with admiration; and they, who indeed were rather spies than deputies, going away, one said to the other, "He is indeed a great man, and must be the person assuredly destined to conquer the whole East, and govern the nations!"[2] Which things agreed with the opinions already in his favour among the Turks; so that they wrote: " For honour and uprightness, Godfrey is eminent above all the Christians—brave as they are, with all their defects, and candid. Solicit his friendship; for if you obtain it, you will have that of the whole Christian body." [3]

This contrast of grandeur and modesty has always surprised mankind, and is the most commanding spectacle in history. And had he to live long, he would have succeeded in establishing a regular

---

[1] Michaud: Hist., vol. vi. 15.
[2] Id.   Id.   ii. 5.
[3] Albert Aquenis: Chron.—Bib. Crois. i. 57.

government in that discordant multitude of Armenians, Greeks, Jews, Arabs, renegades from every religion, and adventurers from every land.[1] But an audience of still more importance; the chief princes and leaders, who came from a general assembly of all the crusaders, to announce what he and they knew, but avoided speaking of, that at the close of winter they must take leave, but that they would accompany him to receive his brother Baldwin, shortly expected from Edessa, on a visit. And Godfrey rose, and affectionately embraced every one of them, and individually thanked, and presented each with some small keepsake,[2] much more pleased at their promise to stay during winter, than shaken at their departure, which he expected. Brilliant sight! with their sashes of red or white, and surcoats, and their lofty silver helmets. But one wanting, enters singly after them; he characterised as the generous and brave, where all were of signal generosity and bravery; he who had been considered rich, when he possessed but his sword and his fame—but who now had worldly treasures in abundance, six waggon loads of gold, and silver, and jewels, which it required two days to transport

---

[1] Michaud: Hist., vol. ii. 7.
[2] P. A. Paoli: 476.—Foulcher de Chartres: Chron.

from the mosque to his quarters,[1] and of which the Arab chronicles give a list, and may well call immense riches; since they included seventy large gold lamps, and one of silver of forty hundredweight, and other magnificent articles, that had been increasing through the piety of Mahometans ever since A.D. 638.[2] A law of the crusade gave the whole to him whose banner was first raised on the building, and of this fact there never had been any question, or could be. They were all his personal undivided property; as every crusader avowed, without a moment's hesitation, or sigh of envy.[3] "Sir Tancred," said Godfrey, "I thank you," and leading him to his bundle of straw, made him sit down by his side. "You know," faltered Tancred, "I have long chosen you for more than my sovereign, by your permission, and that as long as you remain, I will; so I live. But now I wish to declare it publicly, in our Norman fashion, and am come prepared!" And on sign of assent, he called in two, and rose and knelt down before Godfrey, and between both his, placing both his own hands, said, "I call you, gentlemen, to witness that I too swear fealty to him as my man; and as my

---

[1] Michaud: Hist., vol. i. 348.—P. A. Paoli: 82.
[2] Bib. Crois., vol. vi. 12.—Ibn. Agonzi.—Mines de l'Orient.
[3] Michaud: Hist., vol. i. 248.

first tribute, make him a free gift of the half of all that by my sword has been lately won at Omar's from the Saracens." " Which I accept," said Godfrey, and lifting his right hand, described a large sign of the cross from forehead to breast, and then leant both his hands on Tancred's shoulders, and kissed him on both cheeks. " Now, my vassal, rise and retire."[1]

When Baldwin and his brother met, after so long a separation, it was to their mutual delight, and Godfrey feasted him sumptuously the whole winter. That old and most melancholy of cities must have been astounded at such entertainments. And thus to the Prince of Tarentum's cousin, his squire on service, while buckling on his master's coat of arms, and cross, and broad white sash, at his lodgings in some part of that narrow street that winds south from the square of the Holy Sepulchre down towards the Temple: "Recollect, Sir, it is summer, still, the 10th of October,[2] which these fellows desecrate with their barbarous *regeb*,[3] and his Majesty, my Lord, is early; particularly with his fine weather. And if he fixed so late an hour as eight this morning, it must be for the noble sick warrior that is with him." So Tancred

---

[1] Michaud : Hist., vol. i. 248.
[2] P. A. Paoli : 485.   [3] Arab. Chron., 209.

hastened straight to Gerard's room, and had scarcely time to say "How do you do, now, Count d'Avesne?" to him who lay on his litter, and smiling affectionately, though pale, replied "Better; but we'll never play at mall again, for I am hamstrung in both legs and arms." In the East they play it on horseback. The celebrated warrior, Noureddin, was the finest rider and best player at mall, of his time.[1] But Godfrey entering, "Sir Tancred, I sent for you not to speak or debate, but to witness what my mature reflection has resolved on, and also that of my honoured young friend, who will listen, and if ever I explain his purpose wrong, correct me. It was from my knowledge of his self-devoted intention, I sent him then as hostage, and therefore that was truly the commencement of what was made public only this day. So let the 12th of August, 1099, be a holy memorial to all ages, of the founder of all to which I here consent."[2]

"We are Normans, all three. So it is not necessary to prove those sacred oral doctrines which have come down to us from our remotest ancestors, and which have only become holier from Christianity. For me, I have already begun a compilation

[1] Arab. Chron., 161. [2] P. A. Paoli: 199.

of laws, which I hope will be a benefit to this kingdom; and mean to base them on Norman freedom, and recommend them as well as ever I can to posterity by depositing the writing in what is a general object of veneration to all Christians—the Holy Sepulchre. But much finer is the way our friend has taken, by inscribing the same great truths not on paper or parchment, or even brass or marble, but on the immortal minds of generations of men— and uniting them into one civilised body; of not a nation or race, but of all the nations and races of our human kind. Whenever that comes to be imitated, it will be but imitation; but the first idea is wholly his own, and infinitely grand. To be of utility to men (under God, whose instrument he is) has been indeed his primitive scope; but I do not know that he could ever have effected it in any other way than this he has chosen; which links so appositely with these times and will with recenter too. Could any but sovereigns and Normans have possibly executed it?

"To create a corps of volunteers of the bravest warriors for the defence of the Holy Sepulchre and this kingdom—a permanent crusade—and exercise hospitality on its widest scale towards the pilgrims of all ranks and nations—are the measures proposed, and assuredly there is sublimity in the thought.

To maintain with a few, what it has required a crusade of all Europe to conquer; and day and night, in sanguinary regions and at such a distance, lodge as they are accustomed, and feed all classes, from the emperor to the peasant; and likewise attend to them when sick, and provide them with all necessaries of physic and physicians and surgeons, and all gratis, is no small undertaking. If the duties of hospitality are three—to defend the guest going and coming—to feed and lodge him when well—to try to cure him if sick; to traverse so many disturbed lands and to receive them all so that each shall be treated as far as possible according to his rank—with no vain attempt at equality, but each pretty nearly as used to—requires armies and treasures—although the third alone, an infirmary, might perhaps cost little. The rule then that my friend has determined on, is this:—

- 1st. Hospitality for all pilgrims and crusaders including defence of the Holy Sepulchre and of this new kingdom.[1]
- 2nd. A military organisation in three classes:[2] clergy,[3] knights, servants at arms.[4]

---

[1] P. A. Paoli: 199.   [2] Id.: 202.

[3] *Pro forma*, strictly limited to their spiritual duties as not of this world, but a higher. *In ragione di dignita.* P. A. Paoli: 200.

[4] P. A. Paoli: 331.

3rd. Knights to have all the proofs required of a *miles*——nullus fit miles nisi filius *militis*.[1]

4th. The not regularly professed in the order, may yet be aggregated to it.[2][3]

5th. Females also.[4]

6th. None professed can have any property of their own; but only can expect to be clothed and fed plainly and frugally;[5] and freely dedicate their lives.

7th. Therefore three vows—celibacy, obedience, and individual poverty.

8th. Celibacy cuts off from most of those domestic ties which are impediments to self-devotedness. Obedience the most implicit; particularly in battle, where, without an express command, they on no pretext whatsoever can retire; but death must be expected with heroic fortitude. Their being individually poor, means that they renounce the rights of property,

---

[1] Hallam: Middle Ages.

[2] Almost all the Norman Princes were of this class.

[3] Ever since, as old Raimond. Cod. Dipl. Geros., Num. xxii., or a Bohemond, Num. xcviii., Appendix, xliii.

[4] P. A. Paoli: 353.—Chron. Vitzburgense. Whether by vows as in 1134 at Verona, or in the world, as the King of France's daughter and sister. Appendix, Num. xlii.

[5] P. A. Paoli: 221 and passim. Bread and water are the words to this day. Reception, Vertot, vi. 21.

so that the all of each belongs to the common treasury.

9th. Their dress is that they at present wear— the cross white, now, from the founder being a Norman.

10th. Each future head is to be selected by the order from amongst themselves; and he is to have a council to which he must submit; and on important matters convene a general assembly of the order, where he may have a double vote; and then the majority decide beyond appeal.

"Now to the whole of this I entirely subscribe, in both my Norman and royal quality, and depute you, Sir Tancred, to make it generally known; and as a mark that in this I wish to take the lead, here are two deeds of donation,[1] one in Palestine,[2] and one in Europe,[3] in respect of its European origin

[1] P. A. Paoli : 26.—Seb. Paoli : Codice Diplomatico, vol. i. Num. ii.; Appendix, Num. x.—Quick then; for London, Schwerin, Sicily are near.

[2] St. Abraham near Bethlehem. Michaud: Hist., vol. ii. 5. Michaud: Orient. vol. v. 202. Hessilia was the more proper name, as we learn from Godfrey's own brother Baldwin I. "Donum quod frater meus fecit hospitali, videlicet de quodam Casale, quod vocatur Hessilia." Seb. Paoli : i. 445.

[3] The Monale is a river in Sicily. *Monboir* is for Montboisè. *Abryele* is *a l'abri* ; in Italian, *al riparo*. Paoli : Osservazioni, lxxii.—Albert d'Aix : Chron. vii.—Bosio : par. 1, lib. i., anno 1099.

and its destination to these parts. And I hope that similar, or rather far more magnificent donations, may shortly follow from my Norman brethren, and from others also; for vast sums are necessary to so vast an undertaking—urgent and simultaneous. I will announce it to Baldwin; but a favourable omen and a merciful Providence is this delay and meeting of so many of the Norman and other princes of the crusade, which permits your speaking to them at once in person. And my desire is, that their donations, though quick, be not exactly here; for it would grieve me any should attribute them rather to love for me, than to the incontestible merits of the institution itself. Not only the antedate 1100, but also the months for a year from the taking." Yet, as this is the first gift to the order, it will be fair to give a union of the three copies; two in Italian, and one in old French—all three in the appendix, in substance the same, but each with many errors of the pen, or otherwise.

"In name of the holy and undivided Trinity, I, Godfrey de Bullion, by the grace of God Duke of Lorraine, make it known to all present and future, that for the remission of my sins, having adorned my heart and shoulders with the sign of the cross of the Saviour crucified for us, I at length reached the spot where our most high Lord, Jesus Christ, trod for the last time; and, after I had visited the Holy Sepulchre and all those holy places, with the devotion of a full heart, finally I came where once stood a church of the Holy Hospital, founded in honour of God and his blessed mother, and St. John the Baptist; and seeing so many operations suggested by the grace of the Holy Ghost that it is impossible to count them, and more charity toward the sick and indigent of the faithful than human tongue can express, I promised to offer something to God also, and so now, to acquit my promise to the Omnipotent with whole effusion of spirit, give to the said house of the Hospital, and all the brethren within it, an habitation built on the Monale called Wood Mount, in the Cold Mountain (in Sicily), and of the Castle of S. Abraham (near Bethlehem), and I make this my donation in the year 1100, less than a year from the taking of Jerusalem; and I have done this for the benefit of the souls of my father and mother, and relations, and all the Christians, living and dead. And affix my seal to the same, in presence of these trusty witnesses, Arnold of Vismala, and many others."

There are many mistakes in the deed, as come down to us, and as it could not have been written by Godfrey. The Xenodochium of the order and the Church of St. John were two distinct things. Near the church says the Papal deed, "juxta ecclesiam,"[1] and that the ruins of some former hospital or church might have been found and seen there by Godfrey, and on this was built the beautiful new one, seen there a very few years later by the Vizburgensian;[2] but what Godfrey saw could not be new. The Turks had thrown down, or converted into stables, all the hospitals of the Christians and churches, except the Holy Sepulchre for pilgrims, and the Temple turned into a mosque.[3] Circumstantiality is a dangerous thing; and he that hazards it, may lose his credit as an historian—leaving himself open to the accusation of dealing rather in fancies than realities, because he could not possibly be present. But this would put an extinguisher on all history, since

[1] Appendix, Num. v. In many ancient writings the date is in the context, the most certain date; for it is not liable to errors. Here we have two facts, of which as to the years they occurred in, all good historians agree. These in the Appendix are all very old *copies*, so not in their places in the Cod. Dipl., where none but original and legal. But if these be all with incorrections, yet do they not corroborate the substance? The date most erroneous in numbers is remedied by the context *of within a year from the taking of Jerusalem*. That Godfrey made some such donation is legally proved by Baldwin's deed in the Cod. Dipl., and if none of these three are that donation verbatim, yet their being the same in substance is a very strong probability. Appendix, Num. xix., xx., xxi.

[2] Vizburgenis: Chron.—Appendix xv.—P. A. Paoli: Osservazioni, lxix.

[3] P. A. Paoli: 82.

seldom has any historian seen much of what he relates. Nor if he did, is eyesight the first class of evidence; for how easily may the eyes be deceived! But indeed the first class of historic evidence, surer than any eyesight (for your eyes may be a law to you who see, but not to him who has to trust to your word), is that of charters and law documents, and wills, and deeds of gift, and such like. The declaration of an eye-witness is to reader or hearers only a secondary sort of evidence. It is like the former without their witnesses, and therefore needing some additional testimony of context or circumstances. A formal document has its full proof in itself. It is not one man, but several. The reader has no excuse to expect, nor the writer to give. The proof would suffice any upright judges in the world; but not so circumstantiality—this is to be taken at its worth in every instance. Yet is it not a pity to neglect any of the few circumstances that have escaped the stream of time? Rather let them be given freely, though with some personal risk to the writer, occasionally adding, from what he sees, the present condition of the places in question, when his statements aspire to no more value than those of any other traveller. As to their being beneath the dignity of history, smile at it. Whoever (by whatever means) contrives to give us a true picture of the times, suggests probable motives, and is exact as to facts—he is the historian.

The care of the sick and wounded made females necessary from the very first. Except this error as to date, the rest of the current story may be quite true; that of the Hospitalleresses, the very first was a Roman lady of the name of Agnes.[1] Godfrey was right; none but Norman sovereigns could have insured success. Who were the Normans then at Jerusalem, and who, exactly as Godfrey wished, made donations of land to the order, as soon as ever they left that city? The Norman was the great party of that day, and it became a party question. Its earliest protectors were, with few exceptions, Normans; its founder, and the King of Jerusalem, Normans; and the Baldwins Bohemond, Tancred, Roger of Antioch, Raimond of Joppa. Its first establishments in Europe were in England and Sicily, where both the sovereigns were Normans. Tancred gave it large possessions about Bethlehem, and his cousin, at Bari, Taranto, and Otranto. In Flanders, Hainaut, Pannonia, what wonder, where dwelt Gerard's own nearest relatives? It was like wild fire, and at the same time quite natural.[2] That the Mahometans should

---

[1] P. A. Paoli: 349.   [2] Id.: 456.

soon send tremendous forces to win it back, was clear from the grief with which Bagdad heard of Jerusalem's fall. Their poet had adjured them[1] by everything they held most sacred: "Blood mingles with our tears. O children of Islam, many are the battles you have to sustain, in which your heads shall roll at your feet! What blood has been spilt! How many of your women left but their hands to cover their beauty? Your Syrian brothers have but the back of their camels, or the vultures' entrails! So frightful are the strokes of the lance, and the shocks of swords, that at the very noise the head of the infant whitens with fear. Methinks he who sleeps in his grave at Medina, lifts himself to cry out, 'O sons of Hashem! What! my people not fly to save religion shaken to its foundation? To fear death now is dishonour; and is not dishonour a mortal wound? The Arabian chiefs, the warriors of Persia, submit to such degradation?'"

It is nowise but simple, then, that an immense army of Saracens assembled forthwith to march

---

[1] Alivardi. It was Ramadan. So general the grief that crowds filled the mosques imploring the Divine clemency, and were so troubled *that they forgot the fast;* which is perhaps a solitary instance in the whole history of Mahometanism of such awful trouble. Arab. Chron., 13.

against the Latins. But what is really astonishing is, that an heroic handful should overthrow such great forces. But what men were at their head! Their five thousand won the day, and saved Jerusalem, yet at the price of Bohemond,[1] carried off prisoner by the retreating Turks, *who called him the minor god of the Christians.*[2] Islam annals assure us that seven French counts tried to deliver him, but they perished.[3]

His adventures are infinitely curious; and in his old age he went through the Courts of Europe recounting them. Any one of them would be too romantic for any history but this; and even in this, its substance is all that can be given. The Prince of Tarentum and three of his followers were confined in a castle in Mesopotamia, whose malek had a beautiful, virtuous, and wealthy daughter, who, prepared by all she had heard, fell in love with the Franks, and a variety of religious discussions led to her conversion, without her father being aware of it. After a courtship of two years (says the chronicler—but it is permitted to suspect the accuracy of his chronology—perhaps it is the copier's fault who should have written months), the sultan and his power marching against the malek, besieged him,

---

[1] Michaud: Hist., ii. 10.—Arab. Chron., 15.
[2] Bib. Crois., i. 314.   [3] Arab. Chron., 16.

and she in this frightful predicament directed herself to the Franks. " Admirable Lady," answered Bohemond, " allow us but weapons, and you shall see what can be effected by the sword and courage of Franks!" She then made them swear to defend her father's possessions; and after victory to resume their irons as before:—" O my friends," said she, " if that irritate my father, you will protect her who loves you with all her heart !" And on her giving them their liberty, they armed and rushing out at once with the Norman war cry, " *God's aid!*" the besiegers, struck with a panic terror, fled. Only a single combat took place between Bohemond and the sultan's son, who at length fell. Still the malek, when he learned he owed his safety to Christians, flew into a rage and called her a *wicked minx* in the midst of all his officers; but Bohemond and his Normans rushing in with naked sword raised in the very act to strike, dropped them at a sign from her, and stood, stockstill as waiting her order. After a pause she said, " For me, beloved father, I am going to become a Christian; for their law is honourable and holy; " and retiring with the Christians she said to them, " I shall always continue your sister and tender friend!" But after various days, the old malek by degrees learned to take Bohemond into his good graces, with, as it were, parental affection; so much so that he ventured to address the new convert thus after her baptism : " Noble young lady, who did prefer our creed and us its followers to your own and kindred, even while yet a pagan, choose of yourself freely, we beseech you, from the warriors now before you! Any of us will think him honoured by your choice of him as your husband. But, in conscience before all, listen to me, my sweet friend; and let me counsel you to reflect well, before you ratify your father's selection of me. He indeed has given you to me; but I advise you to choose better. I have led a life of labour from my boyhood up ; and have suffered much, and fear I have yet much to suffer. I have to defend myself both from the emperor and the infidels. Besides which I made a vow, while in irons, to go to St. Leonard's in Aquitaine, as soon as I should be set free. So how could we promise ourselves time for the delights of Hymen, since I am obliged so soon to expose myself to the risks of the seas and direct my steps to a distant country? These considerations, my dearest mistress, cannot but engage you to choose another for indissoluble partner. Behold Roger, son of Prince Richard, my cousin; he is younger and with greater talents, more handsome than I am, and, my equal in power and riches; I wish you to marry him." And in fact (adds the chronicler) Roger espoused her; and they led a life of cloudless felicity.[1]

It is nearly certain that Tancred must have had some of Gerard's recent knights, and part, at least of his eighty Norman horse, both in his Galilean expedition, and that battle near Aleppo ; but how many of them were slain there, no record remains to tell. Nor if any of them were companions of Godfrey's last feats southward, in which he caught a fever from bad air, or, as the Moslems affirm,[2] in consequence of a wound received near Acre "the light of the world" fell sick, was lifted from his horse at Joppa, and thence was carried in a litter to Jerusalem; where he lingered in dreadful pain for five weeks, and expired on the 17th of July, A.D., 1100.[3]

1100

Whether he ever swayed the sceptre, is doubtful, nor is it any matter; he had the prerogative, and deserved it. Baldwin had gone home to his own dominions of Edessa (now Orfà); but on hearing of his brother's death, and his own election, ceded Edessa to his cousin Baldwin de

---

[1] Albericus Vitalis, Angl.—Bibl. Crois., i. 315.
[2] Arab. Chron., 17.
[3] Michaud: Hist., ii. 11.—Cod. Dipl. Geros., i. 345.—Bosio, par. 1, lib. i., anno 1100.

Bourg, and with most praiseworthy ambition, vindicated his royal inheritance—his other brother having gone to Europe—and set off for Jerusalem on a most difficult march, with an escort of seven hundred horse, and some infantry; the more requisite, that dissensions disquieted the Holy City, from the undue pretensions of the Patriarch, who seems to have been somewhat of a demagogue; yet extremely wrong—for it was not, who should reign in Jerusalem, but who would defend it with his life! Nor is it clear whether any of Gerard's order formed the deputation of knights sent to receive Baldwin. But he was one of the great Normans, and followed close on Godfrey, as a donor to the order. If to be King of Jerusalem, then, was a thing to be coveted, it was at the post of peerless honour, that is of the highest danger—and not for anything else. It was rather a duty, than acquisition. For the Kings of Jerusalem were neither powerful nor rich; and Baldwin in Orfa had been both.[1] But he was eminently a soldier, and willingly gave the preference to glory. And so well was that felt at the time, that the Duke of Normandy never got any credit for refusing the Jerusalem throne, which, upon his refusal, the

[1] Bongars: Guibert.—Bib. Crois., i. 133.—Michaud: Hist., vi. 68.—Bosio, par. 1, lib. i., anno 1101.

crusaders had voted to Godfrey. But Normandy was blamed[1] as wanting heart, and that though courageous in usual things, and even distinguished at Ascalon and Nice in several battles, he had not courage enough to accept that loftiest of all earthly positions, exposed to perils and toils as supereminent. And it was attributed to the Divine wrath, and a just judgment of God on the dastard who preferred his dukedom and the crown of England, to which he was next heir, that he was never after successful in anything; but lost his birthright, and died in a dungeon. It is an injustice to Baldwin to receive the *gaudens de hereditate* in any other sense. His heritage was indeed magnanimity alone.[2] They say that his whole reign was one continuous fight, for that he was less of a politician than Godfrey.[3] So, after a week in his metropolis, he advanced on Ascalon, and in a battle between Jaffa and Ramla, overthrew the Egyptian army under Saad-eddaulè, to whom the astrologers had predicted death from a fall of his horse; so when Emir of Beyroot, where the streets are slippery and stony, he had the stones gathered and carried away. But it was labour in vain; for, in escaping

---

[1] Michaud: Hist., i. 351. [2] Id.: Id., ii. 14.
[3] Vertot: Hist. de Malte, i. 67.—Bosio, &c.

from Ramla, he fell with his horse and was killed.[1]

The victorious Baldwin then marched south-east towards Hebron and the Dead Sea, to terrify the Saracens, who had recently annoyed Christian pilgrims, whereupon the former hid in caverns they had to be smoked out of, not dissimilar from the inroads the French have been lately constrained to in Algeria. On the south of the great asphaltic lake, they took a town, and penetrated to the Arabian mountains, where they found snow, and the whole army were obliged to bivouac in holes in the rock, the entire country abounding in such hiding-places, with no other food than dates, and such wild animals as they could kill, and the pure water from occasional excellent springs and fountains.[2] And they visited with respect a monastery called St. Aaron, on the spot where Moses and Aaron spoke with God, and tarried for three days in a beautiful valley clad with palms, and full of all kinds of fruit, and the very place where Moses had made a source bubble up from the flanks of an arid rock, and where the chronicler declares he watered his mule, and Baldwin his cavalry, after which he turned towards Jerusalem, passing by

[1] Arab. Chron., 17. [2] Michaud: Hist., ii., 17.

where were buried the ancestry of Israel, and was anointed and crowned king at Bethlehem by the Patriarch; not following Godfrey's example in this quite, yet surely in part, since he was crowned at Bethlehem, not exactly in the city, where his Saviour was crowned with thorns.[1] Even so, what Baldwin took at Bethlehem was like no mortal crown, but in some degree resembled Christ's, and a pious action, full of danger, misery, and self-sacrifice.[2] The spot where his coronation took place was in a most neglected state years ago, and worse now.[3] Baldwin the First's next act was to hold a court and council of all the grandees at Jerusalem, in Solomon's palace,[4] as well as putting into effect his brother's compilation, the assize of Jerusalem, by a solemn establishment of the bench of judicature. Any difficulties were quickly overcome by the cital of Godfrey, whose very name had a sanctified authority inappealable. Again, in 1101, upon a military advance beyond Jordan, an act of sweet and noble charity merited the oath of a Mussulman never to forget the generosity of Baldwin.

[1] Hallam: Middle Ages, i., 26. Note 1.
[2] Michaud: Hist., ii. 18.
[3] Id.: Corr. d'Orient, iv. 215.
[4] Id.: Hist., ii. 19.

Assur capitulated next, and Cesarea fell by assault with frightful carnage; in all which enormities the Genoese took a conspicuous part, as their own historian testifies, who was there present;[1] and there the great emerald was taken which in our own days turned out to be a bit of glass, as all could see, when it was broken by accident.[2] A second and greater victory was gained over the Egyptians; Baldwin the First, on his courser named Gazelle, from its swiftness, leaving no safety but to such Moslems as had horses of wondrous rapidity. In new battle, Count Harpin having volunteered some prudent counsels: "Harpin," replied the monarch, "if you are afraid, go back to Bourges." Yet the Christian army was for the most part slaughtered, and, if Baldwin was saved, he owed it to the generous gratitude of the Turk he had been kind to the year before. Old Raymond of St. Gilles had taken Tortosa and Gibel, and Acre also yielded to the Christians, but after the most cruel breach of faith in the Genoese allies; till at length, by Baldwin's personal interposition, those of the Mahometans that were yet unmurdered were permitted to retire, and Acre became inhabited by Christians.

1101

[1] Caffaro: book 1.
[2] Michaud: Hist., ii. 24.—Bosio, par. 1, lib. i., anno 1131.

In 1104, Bohemond, Tancred, Baldwin de 1104
Bourg, at that time Count of Edessa, and his
first cousin, Joscelin de Courtenai, Lord of Turbessel, laid siege to Carrhes, beyond the Euphrates, that city of Abraham's father, and of Crassus, and a rescue of Turcomans coming, the Christians fled, and Bohemond and Tancred followed them with difficulty, and Joscelin and Baldwin de Bourg were made prisoners, and remained in captivity for five years. So the Mahometans resuming courage, besieged Edessa several times, and threatened both Turbessel and Antioch, and ravaged the whole country.[1]

Bohemond, leaving his capital, stole off to Europe to seek succours; and married the daughter of the King of France, and ended his stormy days by coming to die at Tarentum; though others say at Antioch, on the last of February, 1105.[2] The indefatigable and aged Count of Tripoli, about 1106, was killed by a fall from the roof of the castle of Monte Pellegrino, to-day that of the citadel of Tripoli.[3] His son came with a fleet in 1108, and died in 1109.[4]

---

[1] Michaud: Hist., ii. 25.
[2] Oderic Vitalis.—Bib. Crois., i. 318.
[3] Michaud: Histoire, ii. 41.—Cod. Dip. Geros., i. 405, 407.—Arab. Chron., 22.
[4] Michaud: Hist., ii. 41.

In 1112, Tancred died at Antioch. "It will, by Heaven, be a very vile generation when the high name of Tancred ceases to be in honour," Godfrey used to say. To boast of one's own bravery was in the purest spirit of Paganism; but only Christianity could inspire the heroic magnanimity of Tancred, when he bade his squire swear never to relate his feats to any one. Sublimer than chiefs of Homer or Virgil is he above even the love of praise. It surpasses the heroic age. Yet is this reference to another world quite in unison with our religion.[1] Many of the gallant Normans who had been the earliest protectors of the order, were now gone; yet its high-minded founder still lived— almost young indeed in years, but a broken-down, woful cripple, and with ruined health. He had once hoped to be cured, and what he had said as a melancholy threat to Tancred, turned out to be too true.

He that morning fancied he exaggerated, but did not. So in truth a decrepit, and, as it were, aged man. But he had the consolation to see his order growing up to notice, and acquiring every day well-merited fame and power, more than realising all his warmest dreams of glory. The Norman

---

[1] Michaud: Hist., ii. 46.—Cod. Dip. Geros., i. 405; vi. 12.

feats at Jerusalem may be all fairly ascribed to Gerard and his order; and rather, indeed, that it existed as a Latin or Christian city at all. The same may be said of his imitators, the Templars and Teutonics; but as yet they did not exist, or if the individuals existed, it was but as French or German Hospitallers, or their followers. It was in the spirit of those times that the local spiritual authority assented, till recourse to Rome. But, however Norman influence abbreviated that process, and hastened the Papal answers, it required a longer life than was allowed to poor Godfrey. One basis to both the assize, order, and the conduct of several of the crusade, who, returning to Europe, as the Duke of Brittany, the Count[1] of Flanders (more particularly, perhaps, in France, but also in England[2], whence Henry the First's charter, and in Germany Lothaire's[3]), these lords coming home from the first crusade, affranchised, chartered, or otherwise softened the institutions of feudalism.

All those three currents of benevolence derived from the same pure source, the principles of northern freedom, which, wherever it originated, was brought south by the Goths from Scandinavia.

[1] Michaud: Hist., i., 398.
[2] Hallam: Middle Ages, ii. 36. Note (2).
[3] Id.   Id.   i. 323. Note (1).

Assize, order, and charters had the same holy basis. The assize was a modification to Oriental ways of thinking, and the Greek; the order to its peculiar circumstances. But in both were preserved a representative body, the trial by jury, and many other seeds of true liberty, that with astonishment men now see their own glorious constitutional government was certainly in the meditation of both Godfrey and Gerard, who selected the perhaps only secure manner by which such a country, and at such a period, could preserve the treasure—not made indeed for that wild discordant multitude whom liberty could only set mad, nor for a state of permanent civil war, or hostility of any sort, but for happier ages, permitted to expect.[1] A writer not to be suspected of partiality to the crusades, regards the code as from the well-springs of freedom.

Yet Gibbon could only judge by the heavy tome compiled two hundred and sixty-six years later, and which affords food for blame and derision, and no doubt much trash and iniquitous customs were then foisted into what pretended to be a copy of the original deposited by Godfrey, which could scarcely but be brief; to be compiled, legalised,

---

[1] Ibelin, Count of Jaffa copied (as he says) the Assizes of Godfrey. But this was not " the Code so precious and so portable." Dec. and Fall, xi. p. 94, and Notes.

and consigned within a few months, since Godfrey's whole reign was limited to a year. But that the laws of Godfrey were in the general estimation of the Norman is proved by that other Baldwin, who becoming Emperor of Constantinople in 1204, "adopted the *Assizes de Jerusalem* as best adapted to a French colony in the East."[1] In the course of these first twelve years of the order, how much was effected! A chronicler, who visited Jerusalem within a few years after the first crusade, found it had its church newly built, and a splendid mansion for above two thousand men.[2] Godfrey himself had founded an hospital in Jerusalem for the poor;[3] so that in that respect there would have been no need of the order's (*and that must be specified*), for by a casualty Godfrey's was dedicated to St. John, which led to mistakes; but it stood in quite another part of the city, and had nothing to do with the order's, which was exclusively for crusaders, who then went by the name of *poor* or *Christ's poor*, without any reference to wealth. In comparison of *Him* are we not all poor? This large mansion, or *Xenodochia*, lay exactly opposite the Holy Sepulchre, alongside of its own church; both of which buildings, church and man-

---

[1] Dec. and Fall, xi. 246.
[2] P. A. Paoli : 62.   [3] Id. : 117.

sion, were so majestic and fine, that it was represented by some critics as a most indecent rivalry with that in honour of Christ.[1]

But that sneer was of posterior times. The chronicler, who came soon after the first crusade, extols the grandeur and beauty and noble hospitality. Where there were two thousand guests, and at such a time, there must often have been sick or wounded, and these were of course removed into the infirmary belonging to the house, and for none but pilgrims or crusaders. That the knights had to sustain the principal military duties in Jerusalem, and all through Palestine, from the very beginning, is quite certain; nor had they then any other of the military orders to assist them; nor in those first twelve years were there any other knights mentioned than the Hospitallers of St. John, that is, St. John the Baptist; for as to the almsgiver, it is all a humbug, nor the least worth discussion; indeed, only for the respectable publication that recently repeated the nonsense, it should not be mentioned here in the least.

That such could be accomplished only by a union of enterprising sovereigns, requires no debate. But not only sovereigns, but that these were

---

[1] P. A. Paoli: 373.

almost immediately reinforced by a group of private individuals, is likewise true; so that a multitude signalized themselves in the same way. Of the few deeds extant still, and gathered together by an Italian gentleman, that by Godfrey is followed close by Brisset and Roberts in London; and others in Sicily, the south of France, and the north of Prussia, and Hungary, and Germany. This rapidity would be altogether incredible, had Gerard not been a Norman prince.[1] Flanders and Hainaut were then included in Normandy, as they had been in the old Roman Neustria; although soon to be otherwise. In later crusades, as many colours as nations; every nation had its own. But in the first crusade, the French wore the red cross, and all other Latins the white or Norman, even the Flemings; and these, who took the green cross in every succeeding crusade, and no few Germans, then, as well as many others, were erected into a division which was called the Norman party, who, by that means, could balance France itself, and formed a full half of the crusading warriors. Geographical distinctions being then little attended to as transitory, but the ties of blood and alliances were stabler. Not merely Neustria, but all in every royal house in Europe

[1] P. A. Paoli : 456-7.

who could boast of a single drop of Norman blood, were Normans. The Counts of Flanders, Hainaut, and Bouillon, are styled Normans, and were bound by a direct treaty to keep William the Norman on the English throne. Hainaut, turned by the Germans into Egenau, and by the Latins and Italians into Anonia, or Eno, makes the sovereigns of Anonia be Anauci, and by corruption Amauci; and the same person is indiscriminately named Count of Anonia, or Hainaut, or Avesne, or Amauci, or Dell Monte.[1] So Gerard's proposal was like a circular (with Godfrey's consent as his near relative and sovereign), not only to all the Normans, but to all Europe; and indeed, more, all Christians, for that they should all benefit by what he had projected. All crusaders and pilgrims, each according to his station, and earthly circumstances; a king or emperor, like a king or emperor; a knight, a nobleman, like such; an inferior, like an inferior, each as he had been accustomed to, or a little better, all fed and lodged in the houses and halls of the order, and when sick, in its infirmaries; all protected and escorted both in coming and going. To treat all alike, would be to maltreat all.

[1] P. A. Paoli: 460, 472.

According to the best habits of each, and education and manners, and place in society, and charitable feeling on the whole; such is the cheer to be expected in the order's houses, and no vain attempt at what is impossible—equality. Their corps must therefore include many nations and languages, and different degrees of gentle birth; with a rule binding the members in the sight of God and man—honour and religion, obedience the promptest, and superhuman valour. No minor considerations, but the universally received rites of Christianity; not theologians, but soldiers; qualified, so they take the rule's oath, though rule and oath may be modified with time. Gothic freedom generalized far beyond the most exalted sentiments of patriotism. Feelings of home suffocated, nor wife nor child must weaken or distract those who are to be always exposed to such frightful dangers, and bound to escort feeble wanderers through so many hostile countries, beset with infidels, robbers, and murderers. Brave man is he, who endured for moments what must be habitual with them; permanent to death. Their hearts must so frequently be harder than iron. "I know," said Gerard to his aspirants, "that there are many valiant people now, who act as honour and their creed prescribe. Yet nothing will satisfy me, or come up to the scope of this project, except a greater generosity and valour than the world has ever yet seen, even in our own marvellous Normans. That sublime daring and existing out of ourselves, which has visited other heroes for a brief space; must in you have a perpetual residence. Reflect profoundly well then before you enter what demands such singular self-devotedness. You may be very brave, without being brave enough for us. Such supernatural excitement of mind and body must soon wear out life. That wear and tear will suffice, without any other wound. It is living ages in a minute. Yet even Pagans have thought it a fine thing to die young. And Turks, and Turcomans, and clouds of most ferocious Saracens at hand, you must be prepared to die. If you wish any chance of life, join other crusades and armies, with whom you may gain great honour, and eventually return to Europe and enjoy it there for life." And to Godfrey he had said, "Of extreme hardihood, and well mounted and armed, and of fanatical audacity are these Turks; as reckless of life as Saracens ever were, and proud of being worthy to be slaughtered in the service of Mahomet, and for the glory of Islam; and these you are to face with a minority of numbers as perfectly miraculous as ten to a hundred thousand. Divided, impoverished, helpless, as this kingdom is, none can protect it; but only possibly a corps of the transcending spirit proposed, a selection of the most valiant of all Christendom. And it must begin with those who, it is allowed, are pre-eminent above all others at present in existence, our own Normans." Was it not natural that Tancred, to whom knighthood seemed far superior to any monarchy, should have enthusiastically undertaken what he was ordered? And that the Norman chiefs heard him with applause? And other Normans all over Christendom hurried with donations, as soon as they received the circular?

Lands and tenements in Europe had been so cheapened and reduced nearly to worthlessness by the emigration of the first crusade, and in Palestine by the fluctuation of all property during so many wars, and principally the Saracenic, that so mighty a foundation was practicable and timely. It required all that patronage. It was as natural an effect of the first crusade, as the crusade of the disorderly state of Europe. Urgency brought that necessary simultaneousness, quite characteristic of the institution in all its parts, from the founder's mind, into complete action. A chronicler, while Godfrey was alive, saw their church building, and the knights mounting their horses for battle, and crowds of pilgrims in their Xenodochia, and sick in their temporary infirmary.[1] It is enough to know what they did, to know they had the means of doing it. Now, French historians tell us it required one of the richest estates in France to purchase a battle horse and equip one single knight.[2] What but a league of Norman sovereigns could have compassed it? A mind like Gerard's always finds a propitious time and fitting instrument. But had he not been a Norman prince, himself, could he have persuaded them to league? He knew how to use them, and was worthy of them. That is all—and everything. "My order must not be mere men," he said, "but superior to men, and proper companions for that S. George and S. Demetrius against whom those green demons — or angels, as the Saracens pretend— come down on green horses to join Islam in fight.[3] He must be guilty of an anachronism who thinks there was a Latin human being, or hospital or monastery, in Jerusalem, when taken at the first crusade. A little earlier or later, but not then, Godfrey built the church called Latina, and gave

---

[1] The chronicler wrote in his old age 1150, what he had seen in his youth, a great many years before. P. A. Paoli : 67
[2] Michaud : Hist., i. 83.
[3] Arab. Chron., 41.

it to the Benedictines; far from finding it there;[1] just as the Wurtzburgh Chronicler says, who writes what he saw many a year previous to William of Tyre. Then not by negligence is the Latina omitted in the Benedictine texts of that period, but really because it did not then exist.

If this remark be considered superfluous, yet it may be necessary towards an error of long standing. That the ancient period of the order was never written by contemporaries, is to be deplored, perhaps; but it does not follow that we are to exult for Tyre's writing a fable. Better nothing than learn what is false. The mystery of ignorance, as to its creation, would be more dignified than what could not be true. It would have had its heroic age. No harm for that. Such an origin as the country of Socrates, or immortal Rome. Or are you of those who believe that, body and all, Romulus went up after preparing with a fratricide? Rare capacity of swallow! Its head hidden in ambiguity like the Nile or Pyramids. But that can no longer be the case now. Off with the fables, and plain truth in their place. Legal documents have only to be accurately examined and strung together. But, unfortunately, instead of avowing ignorance, and letting the world wait

[1] P. A. Paoli: 89.

until now, there was a fable ready made, in complete contradiction to any narrative that could be formed from documentary evidence. So Pantaleone, Bosio, Vertot, and all the historians following them, found it more convenient to uphold and disseminate that fable concerning a Nineveh of which it was supposed all records were irreparably lost.

And now behold they are come to light, and the whole scaffolding is wrong, and must be overturned to get at the truth. It nettles to be obliged to do any such work. Double labour, both fable and narrative; the former more wearisome to remove, than to weave the latter. Disheartening to have to set out with what may lead to cruel, perhaps flippant ridicule. It may disgust my reader, but it is necessary to overturn the common basis of a whole progeny, some of them esteemed, and deserving of esteem, though in this particular they are in error. Then the entire of what William of Tyre says respecting the origin of the order, is totally erroneous; that is, of its having changed its institution under its second chief. The documents come down to us disprove it. They all are absolutely irreconcileable with any great change; but show that the rule was from the very commencement pretty much what has come down to our own times, modified a little occasionally, according to the times, but only a little. If that be conceded now, it will become as evident to the reader, as it is to the writer, upon glancing over the documents that shall be given in the appendix. Tyre is a good authority for the third crusade, where he was present, but not for the first. In this, France's excuse for him is, that he had too high a mind to submit to the trammels of truth,[1] and that experience must confess that on some subjects he is less intelligible and trustworthy than other chroniclers.[2] Why, with your eyes open, continue your mistake?

But before perusing the documents, recollect that words vary as to their signification in different centuries, and that in that of the crusades *pilgrim* was not a transitory thing, but a real and highly honourable title, that remained during life, like that of Haggi among Mahometans even now; that the cross of the crusaders was worn suspended from the neck in the third crusade, but that at the beginning of the first crusade was as the order wears it;[3] that the poor, Christ's poor, are not what they at present signify, but meant crusaders, brethren in arms, or wives and children of

---

[1] La verité lui parait un fardeau penible. Michaud: Hist., vi. 359.
[2] Michaud: Hist., ii. 7, Note.   [3] P. A. Paoli: 99.

knights, or such like, who came with proper certificates bearing the cross; all classes of Christians, yet but few of the lower, from the length of the journey; and most of the middling and noble, and some of the very highest.[1] Nothing was more timely or simpler than the order.[2] Hospitality included the military defence of Jerusalem. Beautiful idea, and that argued a most holy and bright mind. Universal favour and gratitude. No surprise; the chronicler cited by Paoli saw with his own eyes what others only wrote of from hearsay, forty years (or more) later. Pope Innocent Second in 1130, says the Hospitallers had been used *long* to keep cavalry (paid by themselves) to defend the Christians both in going and coming, and to protect the Holy Sepulchre and Palestine itself, and therefore he calls on all people to contribute as much as they can to so useful an institution, either by entering it, or by being affiliated to it. That was written nine years from Gerard's death, but as it speaks of *long* before, it must refer to the order in its founder's lifetime. Quite the reverse then of what is pretended. But those knights were rather for action than pen, and had a great deal too much to do to write, or attend to

---

[1] P. A. Paoli: 91, 100, 101.   [2] Id. 102.

writers, and those who wrote their annals, knew nothing about them. Baron Giordan Brisset's donation in London, as early as 1100, that in Messina in 1101, and a few others, are given now at this review of the order, twelve years after its formation.[1] But most of the documents to be cited a little later refer to these years also. Only I defer gathering them, till their respective dates. The order was born under Pasqual Second, and his bull we have. Also two documents of Calixtus Second, and of Honorius Second.[2] Neither the prudence of Bosio, nor what is called the inspiration of Vertot, are requisite to account for a change in the order, since change in the order there was none.[3]

The King of Arragon calling them to defend Spain in 1131, quite agrees with their being veteran warriors for thirty-two years before,[4] but not five or six years; warriors designated as the *Santa Milizia* under Baldwin I.[5] The Templars had not been yet established in Baldwin I.'s time.[6] Other castles to churchmen; but great fortresses were only given to those who could defend them, and that taken by Baldwin I., in 1101, was to the Hos-

---

[1] P. A. Paoli: 112 and 375.—Appendix, Num. i., ii., iii.
[2] P. A. Paoli: 119.—Ap., No. v. [3] P. A. Paoli: 120.
[4] Id.   127.   [5] Id.   134.
[6] Id.   134.

pitallers.[1] Joppa had been given to Gerard himself.[2] But most of the chief places in Palestine were given to the Hospitallers, from their creation in 1099 to 1105.[3] Bow, and in honour for the fidelity of an historian, prove the truth.[4] Yes! But give time! Later, a Grand Master of the Temple protests that his order's scope was different from that of the Hospitallers; since theirs was founded for hospitality and the military profession, whereas his was for the military profession alone.[5] Edward IV. and the English tribunals held the two institutions identically the same; or rather the nearest of relatives, the first being as the father, and the Temple as the eldest son. Who could St. Bernard have thought of, since when he spoke, there was no other military than Gerard's in the world, deserving to be called heroes and martyrs? Could nine men (as the future Templars were but then) have performed such wonders, and already gained so high a reputation?[6] For military alone would be but to imitate one (indeed the first) of the three great duties of hospitality—care of the sick was but the third.[7] Brompton goes nearer to the fact.

[1] P. A. Paoli: 136.
[2] Id. 137.
[3] Id. 138.
[4] Id. 141.
[5] Id. 144 and 145.
[6] Id. 147.
[7] Id. 168.

ST. JOHN OF JERUSALEM. 185

As Godfrey did not choose to be called King, he calls himself Advocate, or Protector (Præpositus), in his letter to the Pope.[1] As Bohemond was Præpositus of Antioch, and Baldwin of Edessa; so was Gerard Præpositus of the Hospitallers. It was then confessedly a royal title, and equivalent to a recognition of sovereignty.[2] In after ages it became insignificant; but at that time it was as said. The Pope—at that time a high authority—knew what he wrote. He likewise calls Gerard's successor Præpositus at first, but afterwards changes to Grand Master. The first was undoubtedly in consideration of Gerard's royal birth, and the latter the fixed name that was to be legal for the future.

"Servant of Christ's Poor" means, then, Protector of Crusaders and of Christian Pilgrims.[3] The Papal deeds are always very exact in giving titles; not so individuals.[4] *Venerable* was then an epithet that, as to laymen, was only given to princes and lords of the greatest consideration, including the King of France, to whom it belonged exclusively, according to Mabillon.[5] Roger, son of Bohemond, Prince of Tarentum, and afterwards of Antioch, in writing a letter to Gerard, gives him precisely the

---

[1] P. A. Paoli: 183. [2] Id. 184.
[3] Id. 186. [4] Id. 185.
[5] Id. 187 and 188.

same title he gave to his own father. How full of charity those first Hospitallers were! for there is a description come down to our day of what was an *old custom* in 1185, and would not be an old custom without sixty or seventy years' standing; which brings us back to Gerard's time—what care of crusaders' children, male or female, and abandoned infants, and of alms to the imprisoned, and that they should be clad as soon as liberated, and of marriage portions to poor girls, and of food and clothing to all who asked it three times a-week, without limit as to number; that thirty-five necessitous people shall participate in the table of the knights every day, and be given clothes first; that there shall be workmen, and a tailor's room for the indigent to have their raiment mended every day, and a thousand coats to be distributed to them on certain occasions; and many similar most generous benefactions.[1] These are taken from a fragment of what is manifestly a comment on the rule, and an explanation of it.[2]

Short-sighted politicians indeed are those who see nothing in the crusade but folly. The Christian cause was that of freedom, and led not alone to the Holy Sepulchre, but likewise to the doctrines of

[1] P. A. Paoli: 202.   [2] Id. 205.

learned and polished antiquity. Not only desire of fanatical pilgrimage, but also war against dangerous and far more fanatical invaders.[1] In 1112, there was a donation from Seville; and if a Moor was there then, yet Alphonso VI., King of Castille, was in alliance with him, and married his daughter;[2] and Alphonso had been in Jerusalem in 1099, and met his stepson, Raymond, Count of St. Gilles.[3] A house was in Cesarea in 1109;[4] and in Joppa, Accaron, Rama, St. George's by King Baldwin in 1110.[5] In 1112 in Pisa. The Pisans were a great people by sea then, and their archbishop was the first Latin Patriarch of Jerusalem; but the earliest unanswerable document come down to us is in 1113, which Papal bull confirms the donation in Pisa of the year before.[6] In 1112 in St. Gilles. More is likely; but to be so, and to prove it, are very different things. All we can now affirm is, that we have certain proof it was erected before 1113; since, in the bull of that date, this too of St. Gilles is confirmed by name.[7] In the same 1112, at Asti in Piedmont.[8] In Bari, Otranto, and

[1] Michaud: Hist. Crois.—Chateaubriant: Itin.
[2] P. A. Paoli: 396. [3] P.A.Paoli:397. Cod.Dip.,Ger.i.406.
[4] Id. 399. [5] Id. 391.
[6] Id. 392.
[7] Id. 393. Vaisette's Hist. of Languedoc, ii. 16.
[8] Id. 394.

Taranto, the same.[1] In 1111, there are several donations by Antioch proprietors, during the guardianship of Tancred, and also under Bohemond II., just out of minority.[2]

In 1107, Villedieu, in Normandy, one of the greatest establishments in the order, by Henry I., King of England; for Duchesne, Martinez, and the encyclopædias are certainly wrong by eighty years. Villedieu signifies Teopoli, which was the original name given it at Antioch.[3] But Villedieu was not a single manor, but a whole magnificent tract of country, with several parishes and a large population.[4] The pilgrims had built a fortress on a hill near Tripoli, in 1103, for Raymond of St. Gilles, or Count of Toulouse, who was soon to become Lord of Tripoli; and to commemorate its being built by them all, he gave it the name of *Pilgrim Mount*, and in 1105 left it to the Hospitallers, and in 1106 he had the fall which killed him.[5] "He fell from the roof down into a fire that we, the besiegers, had lit," say the Mahometans; "and after languishing for ten days died, and the corpse of that aged count (whom God curse) was carried to Jerusalem to be

---

[1] P. A. Paolio: 394.   [2] Id. 386.
[3] Id.   387.—Bernardus Thesaurarius Chron., 188.
[4] Id.   387.—Hist. Norman, 308, Dono, &c.
[5] Cod. Dipl. Geros., vol. i., Num. xi.

buried."[1] All which is proved by the document come down to us: "Not only Pilgrim Mount itself, with its guest-house for crusaders, but all that belongs to it, and its villa, as my father gave it, and what was given it by my grandfather, Sir Raymond, with all the trees of every kind that are under it, and the waters, the pastures, mills, gardens, &c., &c."[2] This *Chateau des Pelerins* is the citadel of the present Tripoli or Tarabolos, says Poujoulat in 1831.[3] Of Godfrey's,[4] and also of Brisset's, and that of 1101 in Messina already. The size of their residence in Jerusalem was necessary, and their wealth, what a city to defend! what charity! But it was the charity of all Christendom! Baldwin confirmed what Godfrey had done; thence more clearly Gerard's wide scope. In twelve years from the creation, what vast yet requisite acquisitions! for if the rent-roll was great, how great the expenses! how copious the proofs! Yet it is only a small part of them that could come down to us. A glance at the diplomatic compilation! In 1099, the founder chose where to build in Jerusalem; and very possibly a church may once have stood on the

[1] Arab. Chron., 22.   [2] P. A. Paoli: 383.
[3] Michaud: Orient., vi. 386.
[4] P. A. Paoli: 374.—Cod. Dipl. Geros., vol. ii., Num. xii.—Appendix, Num. xix., xx., xxi.

same spot, but that is not proved. The chronicler had seen it new many years before he wrote. He wrote in 1150 what he had seen forty years earlier, then in 1110. That is all that is certain. For aught we know, he erected his from the foundations.[1] Also in 1100, in the north of Europe; and the deed is preserved in the Brandenbourgh Collection; and by Ludwig in his work on MS. and Giorgisch.[2] The lake was called Swerin, and the country, before the town was built, and erected into a county for the sovereigns general Gunzel; as was the case in 1163,[3] under Henry the Lion. Godfrey had known Gunzel on his march to Constantinople. Respecting the Messina deed, already spoken of, p. 119, the son's confirming his father's donation is given; but that father died in 1106, so that the donation at latest must have been in some day of that year;[4] and that large and early establishment in Messina was necessary, from its being the port to sail for Palestine.[5] Several receiverships and a grand priory were there even from the first; the less surprising from the sovereign's being a Norman,

---

[1] P. A. Paoli : 372.
[2] Id.   . 376.—Appendix, Num. i.
[3] Com. Geography: i. 22, fol. London, 1709.
[4] P. A. Paoli : 379.
[5] Cod. Dipl. Geros., i. 237. Num. cxii.

and the Normans were known all over the world as the order's natural protectors.[1]

Its house at Altenmunster has the testimony of Falkenstein, who attributes it to Henry first Count Stephanig in the burgravite of Ratisbon,[2] and since that prince died in the East in 1101, it is in the same way necessary to give that date at latest to his donation.[3] The facts are likewise in the Bavarian annalist,[4] and also in Gewold.[5] That the Baldwins, Guiscard, Bohemond, Tancred, and the Normans in general, had got some smattering of Greek, Syrian, and perhaps Arabic, may be likely; and it accounts for various words, as *turcopolier*.[6] Of *Turcopili* we read in old chronicles they were light cavalry, but on other occasions they had *cuirasses*. There were a corps of them kept by the Emperor of Constantinople. Right or not, it is said they were so called from being born of a Greek female by a Turk. *Milites* meant knights or heavy horse; and *turcopili* light, whether foot or horse. But Vertot, like Paoli, seems to think that all that is not cavalry must be infantry; yet cavalry on foot had been tried with success at

---

[1] P. A. Paoli: 380. [2] Antiq. Nondg. ii., 368.
[3] Id.: 381.
[4] John Aventine: Ad. Ann. fol. 654.
[5] De Septemviratu: 89. [6] P. A. Paoli: 346.

Antioch, and had taken Jerusalem; and Hawkwood showed later that his dismounted cuirassiers were an impenetrable phalanx.[1] No reason then but we may think *turcopili* to be both cavalry and infantry, light and heavy, so mercenaries and not knights.[2] In truth if servants-at-arms and *milites* mean heavy, and *milizia a cavallo* light cavalry, and *milizia soldata* infantry; then must *turcopili* mean something else—why not both?[3] As ancient as the order were the servants-at-arms. Whoever knows anything of these times, knows that a knight could not do without them. They were the squires who rode by their master always. Each knight of the Hospitallers had *two*, and the grand master *three*. They formed an intrinsic part of the order; squires expected to become knights; but these rarely or never left their class. Nor were they like lay-brothers, who share not at all in the principal scope of a monastic fraternity, nor vote. But the servants-at-arms were not like menial servants, for the knights had menial servants too; but rather like under officers; for they principally served in the first scope of the order—its military duties— and in battle they were dressed precisely like the knights. On all occasions these admitted them to

---

[1] Sismondi: Hist. des Rep. Ital.
[2] P. A. Paoli: 348.   [3] P. A. Paoli: 345.

their table conversation and familiarity. They were in society on a kind of footing with them. They also voted for the election of the grand master.[1] Yet did they form an inferior class, and hardly rose higher, and were satisfied with it. They had sworn to it. It was with their eyes open. This also was an invention of Gerard's, and built on a profound knowledge of mankind, and a far finer matter than people think. To make a class strictly embodied and tied down to the rule by vows, as much as the knights themselves (so just as much obliged by honour, conscience and probity), yet of acknowledged inferiority; and taking an active part in the legislature and loftiest duties of the profession, and even in the voting for the chief of their superiors, was a grand idea; and in Gerard was original; but has been imitated. No base service but military service, the very leading aim of the whole. Therefore the class of the servants-at-arms were always just as much to be depended on as the knights, and they were never discontented.[2] The aggregated (devotional, or honorary, or females) without exactly forming a part of the order, were closely linked to it from the beginning by Gerard himself.[3]

[1] P. A. Paoli: 331. [2] Id.: 330. [3] Id.: 333, 336, 340.

The first crusade, that changed the whole face of society, operated first on tactics; and began the great military revolution that led to gunpowder.[1]

There were churches and established houses of the order in England, Sicily,[2] and Palestine before 1112, and at Arles in France in 1105, and many other places. *Fra* has often changed meaning. There was a time when it meant *Knight*, and that time was Gerard's; so he applied it to his companions.[3] And in English it must not be translated Sir. Baldwin is *Fra*, Robert Duke of Normandy is *Fra*. "We are all brethren and equals by the rights of brotherhood," says Bohemond, and calls Godfrey, "Prince and regulator of all his brethren." Another Robert who was an Hospitaller in England in 1100, and was mere Sir, is called in Italian *Fra*; which shows how soon that word was, as it were, appropriated by the order.[4] The Templars followed the same use, though they had no clerical class, but reformed it away, as well the two other great duties of hospitality, and only kept the first, or military.[5] As to the form of Gerard's cross, there is much idle learning, and the common, is probably the true; that like many other things, it has a

[1] P. A. Paoli: 337.   [2] Id.: 398.
[3] Id.:   247.   [4] Id.: 260.
[5] Id.: , 262.

secondary as well as its principal meaning; and besides being a general Christian sign, the crusaders' cross was made a little different to denote that particular body of Christians; and that for the same purpose Gerard modified still more that of the crusaders, to apply it as a distinctive mark for those of the permanent crusade—his own order.[1] The tunic, birro, and mantle had, all three, the sign. Under them, what you pleased, shirt, flannel, or even cuirass, but those three were the crusader's dress. The tunic might be either over or under the cuirass, and was girt round tight, and reached to just below the knee.[2] The birro was a short narrow stripe of cloth, with a hole to receive the head, and then falling on the breast and half way down the back, having the cross both behind and before; nor worn under, but over everything; and at all times this was the most essential article and never laid by; leaving the elbows quite free and answering for a coat of arms.[3] The mantle might be worn on the shoulder, or drawn round or not at all, according to the weather. This mantle is represented still by that worn by the knights at their profession, and is black with the white cross.[4] As to the purse and broad girdle, they were worn

---

[1] P. A. Paoli: 228. [2] Id.: 223.
[3] Id.: 225. [4] Id.: 229.

but by the chief of the order. So of the first grand master that abdicated (in 1170) we read "he laid down his girdle and the seals and the purse."[1]

The birro was at one time the most distinguishing part of the crusader's dress: "dressed in a birro, that is the dress of a traveller to Jerusalem," says a chronicle of the first crusade.[2] Many lament the loss of the early papers; but have never taken the pains to consult what exist, with the intention of giving the names of whatever of the ancient knights were yet discoverable; but here are a few, thanks to the two Paolis. The learned Bosio spends not a word about the founder's companions, and was led into this mistake by the person he sent to inspect the Vatican MS., as often happens to those who judge by others', not their own eyes.[3] Vertot would perhaps have tried. But where was he to obtain the information? He did what was in his power for France by publishing the list in Provence. Neither are the three, instanced by him as the founder's companions, to be held so; for it would be to make Sir Raymond de Puys one hundred and twenty-six years old—so great an age that it requires to be proved, not supposed, being extraordinary; still worse Gaston. Conon was a

[1] P. A. Paoli: 230. [2] Id.: 226.
[3] Id.: 208.

married man; nor is there any document proving that either he or Dudon were of the first brethren of the order. Out of the earlier of Paoli's two rolls " both of them from authentic deeds," let those be culled that extend not beyond these twelve years. Sir Lambert, who was with Gerard when he was tortured in 1099; Sir Robert Brisset, in 1100; Sir Roger Pagano, in 1112; Sir Bertrand, Prior at Pilgrim's Mount, in 1105; Sir Gubald, through whom the house in Messina was founded in 1101; Sir Peter Mallet, at the first crusade, and of one of the most conspicuous Norman families. His elder brother Robert was one of the magnates of the Conqueror, and fought against Harold, and saw him buried, and had two fiefs in England. Sir Gerard *Sub-deacon*, Sir William Almerico, Sir Rodolph, all three in a donation dated Beyrout 1133.[1]

Now, amongst all his troubles and labours, had not Gerard a great compensation in this review? His ails increasing every day, and carried about in a kind of chair, his spirit as clear as ever, he could not but exult internally at the wonderful progress of his wise and splendid project. All of military or knightly that he could now do was to inspect the

---

[1] Cod. Dipl. Gerosolimitano: vol. i. Num. xiv. 15.

departure of his troops and receive the victorious survivors. This was his daily duty, and it rejoiced him.

Togdekin, the Atabec or Moslem Governor of Damascus, having in those violent dissensions in Syria, partaken in various cruel treasons, murders, and robberies, so that the Assassins (or Battenians, as some call them) slew the noted robber Kalaf, a Mahometan, and the Damascan menacing Kalaf's enemies, became himself exposed to the Old Man's emissaries;[1] wherefore it is said that the unworthy Togdekin began to do everything he could, to insinuate himself into the Mountaineer's good graces. So violent and most unnatural struggles ensued, in one of which King Baldwin, with the late old Raymond's son Bertrand, took Tripoli and Beyrout, and attacked Sidon;[2] which last town paid a sum of money to Baldwin, and he raised the siege and returned to Jerusalem. Joscelin, Lord of Tel-bacher on the Euphrates, had declared war against Aleppo about 1110 (according to Kemaleddin) with a variety of success; but upon the whole, the Franks were evidently the gainers, and even forced the Moslems to retire from the siege of Edessa; besides, thoes of Sidon resolved to remove to Damascus,

[1] Ibn Mayassar: 21.—Cod. Arab.
[2] Arab. Chron., 24.

and left their native place to Baldwin.[1] Another Mahometan prince had to purchase peace with twenty thousand pieces of gold and ten horses. The Mahometan Prince of Aleppo engaged to become tributary to the Frank Prince of Antioch, at ten thousand pieces of gold a-year; and after Tancred's death,[2] the money continued to be paid to a child. Baldwin in 1112, besieged Tyre; and without taking it, advanced against Damascus, and into the Haraoun, and wrapping all in fire and blood, retreated towards Jerusalem, upon Togdekin's application for succour to Moussul. 1113 And on its arrival, a great battle ensued, in which Ibngiouzi says the Franks lost two thousand men, and that King Baldwin escaped with difficulty, and without his sword. The fact appears to be, that the Franks only removed to a good position; and that the Mahometans, by disease, the heats, famine, and severe fighting, were kept off for twenty-six days, and on a reinforcement coming from Antioch, were completely routed near Tiberias.[3] Passing through Damascus, the Moussul leader was murdered in the mosque there by the Assassins, "but I say," writes Abulfeda, "that it was the traitor of an Atabec sent the murderer. And I was

[1] Arab. Chron.: 27. [2] Id.: 31.
[3] Id.: 32.

told by my father that King Baldwin wrote to Togdekin the moment he heard of the bloody deed: "*They who deprive themselves of their protector, and even upon a festival day, and in the very temple of their God, merit well that God should exterminate them from the face of the earth.*"[1] The Mahometan also who ruled at Aleppo was a great supporter of the Assassins or Battenians at that time. And after his death in 1115, his odious son drove the emirs into a conspiracy that smothered him in his bed. Add to all which horrors an earthquake that injured Aleppo, Antioch, Haraoun, and several cities in Syria.[2] The sultan then sent Borsaki from Moussul, to attack the Franks in Palestine, which was not pleasing to all the Syrian Mahometans, who feared that under this pretext the sultan wanted to seize the whole country.

1117

So both Moslems and Christians joined against Borsaki, who passed the Euphrates without doing much, the Moslems restraining the ardour of the Franks, lest these should become the masters of Syria, if Borsaki were defeated. The end was that he and his army ran away beyond the Euphrates. All was confusion[3] and frightful im-

[1] Arab. Chron. 33.
[2] Id.: 37. [3] Michaud: Hist., ii. 49.

morality. Baldwin the First, who had never ceased from taking a pre-eminent share in all the battles round him, and in military expeditions of every sort, now was to set out on his last. From east of Jordan and the Dead Sea, and traversing the Arabian Desert and Petrea, he advanced into what is indeed the third Arabia, or Arabia Felix, and even penetrated to the Red Sea and the Nile. What time it took up, or if it was in one continuous march, being uncertain; but in the spring of 1118, he was in Egypt, and falling suddenly sick, an old wound opened; the Christians wheeled, 1118 and bearing him on a litter made of their tent poles, undertook to cross the desert near El Arish, a small town situated close to the Mediterranean, having upon three sides those vast solitudes, a mighty wilderness, where he felt himself dying and thus addressed the companions of his victories,[1] the six hundred knights, who stood in profound grief round him: "Why are you weeping so? Recollect I am but a man, whom many others can replace; do not permit sorrow to weaken you, like women, but remember you have to return to Jerusalem with arms in your hands, and to be ready to fight for the inheritance of the Lord Jesus, as we have sworn.

[1] Albert Aquensis: Chron., 81.—B. Poujoulat: vol. ii. 497.

Fellow soldiers, I ask you but for one more proof of your affection; I conjure you not to leave my remains in the land of the infidel;" and, perceiving some demur, as if he asked a thing impossible from the natural corruption, particularly in that hot country, he added: "As soon as I have given my last sigh, rip up my body with a knife, and taking out my intestines, fill it with salt, and all the aromatic drugs you can get; and wrapping it up in carpets, and putting it into a leathern case, you can carry it to the foot of Mount Calvary, and there inter it with the rites of the Christian Church, alongside of my brother Godfrey's grave." Then calling one of his household, he addressed him in these identical words, only in Norman French—"You see, my dear serf Edon, I am going to die; if you have loved me in life, continue to do so after my death, and execute exactly what I bid you; open my body, and rub it well with salt and aromatics, both within and without, no sparing of the salt; and fill my eyes with it, my nostrils, my ears, my mouth; then join my other servants and my dear associates, in transporting me to the Holy City; it will be to fulfil my last wishes, and a proof of your fidelity to me to the end." Then he spoke of the succession of the Jerusalem throne, advising them to choose his brother Eustace of

Boulogne, or his cousin Baldwin de Bourg, Count of Edessa; and finally, the Christian hero received the last sacraments, that of confession and the eucharist, and expired. His mournful brethren-in-arms then set about accomplishing his ultimate desires, his intestines were buried, and a heap of stones raised over them to mark the spot, which grave or cenotaph is to be seen to this day not far from El Arish.[1]

Then the Frank warriors set out on their long and doleful march across the desert, marching day and night to conceal Baldwin's death, and their own affliction; and crossing in silence the mountain of Judea, and the country of Hebron, they reached Jerusalem on Palm Sunday; on which day,[2] by an ancient custom, all the Christians, with the patriarch at their head, used to go in procession to the Mountain of Olives; and they were in the act of descending from it, carrying palm branches, and singing canticles to celebrate the entry of Jesus into Jerusalem, when they met in the Valley of Jehosaphat, the train of Baldwin's companions, bearing his coffin, which stopped their hymns all at once, and struck first with a grievous silence, suc-

---

[1] That is, Abufeda's time, 1330.—Arab. Chron., 38.
[2] Easter Sunday was that year on the 2nd of April. Cod. Dipl. Geros., i. 355, Note c.

ceeded by a burst of groans, sighs and lamentations. The mortal remains of Baldwin entered by the Golden Gate, followed by the procession. Latins, Syrians, Greeks, all weeping, and even the Saracens themselves wept,[1] says Baldwin's chaplain. At the same moment Baldwin de Bourg, who, quite unconscious of what had happened, was coming in at the Damascus Gate, to pass the Easter at Jerusalem, alarmed by the plaintive cries, joined the mourners, and wailed for his lord and relative, and accompanied the funeral to Calvary, where the defunct king was laid in a tomb of white Parian marble, with the greatest pomp, alongside of Godfrey's mausoleum. Until within these late years, when it is reported that some malevolent bigotry of the Greeks induced them to wall up those two ancient monuments, every pilgrim visited with reverence the two royal brothers' tombs. Seen by Chateaubriant, Michaud found them no more. As for Mahometans (with their usual brevity), they only say: "He died before reaching El Arish, coming from Egypt. From him that part of the desert is called *the Baldwin Sands*. People think he is buried there; but it is an error; there only his entrails lie; but his body was buried at Jerusalem."[2]

---

[1] Michaud: Hist., ii. 55.
[2] Arab. Chron., 38.—Bosio: par. 1, lib. i., anno 1118.

CHAPTER IV.

EUSTACE, who, at the siege of Jerusalem had stood beside Godfrey [1] on his tower, like a lion by a lion, say the chroniclers,[2] as soon as he learned of both his brothers being dead, felt it was his own turn next, so came as far as Puglia to embark; for many held him the natural heir—nor does he seem to have been one who would have avoided that inheritance of glorious danger. But he was long returned to France, and had only left it during the short interval of the first crusade, and now he was separating from many dear old friends, and European con-

[1] Michaud: Hist., i. 335.
[2] Godfrey was the eldest. Ego Godefridus, &c., fratribus meis Balduino et Eustachio. Anno 1094. Cod. Dipl. Geros., i. 352. Quæ peperit Godefridum de Bullione postea Regem Hierosolimitanum, Balduinum et Eustachium. Cod. Dipl. Geros., i. 347, (Note e) ex. annual Belg. Ægidii di Roya.

nections and habits, which was hard; so it might not have wounded him cruelly to be spared the sacrifice. Whatever were his inward feelings, as soon as informed that his cousin had already been chosen and put into possession, and would probably make some resistance before leaving the throne, he at once exclaimed, " God forbid my ambition should cause dissensions in our family," and forthwith hurried back to the West.[1]

Baldwin de Bourg, who was fortuitously at Jerusalem, as has been related, was chosen to succeed—chiefly from the time it would cost to wait for the arrival of Eustace an argument pushed strenuously by Joscelin, Lord of Tel-bacher, who was related to the new king; who if they had formerly quarrels, all these were now forgotten, and Baldwin de Bourg giving Edessa to Joscelin, assumed the Jerusalem crown himself, under the title of Baldwin II.[2] So he followed Godfrey's example, by administering justice according to the *assizes*. It was Easter of 1118, when he was solemnly proclaimed by the barons in the Church of the Holy Sepulchre, and banquet at Solomon's Palace. Penury of money, that assailed him at the very outset of his reign, was to be his permanent scourge, as well as

[1] W. of Tyre. Bib. Crois., i. 142.
[2] Michaud: Hist., ii. 59.—Arab. Chron.: 38.

of his successors, and the cause of many of the disasters of the Latin kingdom. Terrible fights near Antioch, against an irruption of Moslems from Mesopotamia.[1] A prince of Antioch fell in the place called *field of blood*—very proper name for a battle.[2] That Baldwin's first act as a sovereign was to go there and gain a victory, was considered a good omen. And so it was, regarding what was fought immediately after his return to his capital. But if scarcely one of the many conflicts in Palestine since Godfrey's reign, had been without a corps of Hospitallers, " who were the nerve of every Christian army," says the Moslem,[3] this of 1119, in the sense of being their first pitched battle so near Jerusalem, may be called their first field; but certainly in no other. The marshal that led them that day was a noted warrior, who must have acquired his experience in those more distant, and perhaps lesser actions that were very numerous, but all after the crusade, at which he could not have been, without making him far too old; even decrepid and above 106, which is not to be easily credited. That day the Christians won a bloody victory, covering themselves with glory. But, in

[1] Arab. Chron., 39.
[2] Michaud: Hist., ii. 60.
[3] Arab. Chron., 116, Note 1.

the meantime, Gerard was dying at Jerusalem—a most placid end. It is not quite certain whether he died in the last of 1120, or in the first of 1121; but that only makes the difference of a few days.[1] His ails, that had been always increasing, now left him a blessed respite of several weeks before he expired. Of Baldwin's success, he seems never to have had a doubt. And, if several of his knights had fallen in the conflicts, and that some others might do so at present, yet he rejoiced they had gone direct to Paradise. The review was consolatory in the highest degree; why should he not make it? It was his duty to make it. Before him his faithful secretary held a long roll containing the list of the knights from almost every country under heaven, where there were Christians, and deeds of gift, and regular establishments of the order made during the life of the founder, in many remarkable places of Europe and Asia. Paoli gives a list of forty, with regard to which the legal proofs still remain; yet how few that remain, in comparison of what are lost![2] Probably of as great antiquity are those of Gozlar (in the Hartz) and in Palestine, Laodicea, Tortosa, and several others,

[1] Vaissette: Hist. de Languedoc, ii. 362.—Cod. Dipl. Geros., i. 330.—P. A. Paoli: 192.
[2] P. A. Paoli: whole three chapters xvii., xviii., xix.

but direct documentary proofs are wanting. Such extension supposes many knights.[1] A glorious answer to the Papal and Norman circulars. That roll has perished; but the Paolis, with the perspicacity of a Leibnitz, and the industry of a Muratori, have collected several ancient documents, of which this abridgment allows but culling a few, chiefly English, as well as can be made out of names that are strangely *traduced* into Italian, or Latin, or old French. A more accurate eye will discover others—to the glory of our most illustrious families—under their horrible disguises.

1120

Sir William Peter, *Chancellor in* 1126.[2]
Sir Allan, *a Castellan in* 1121.
Sir Fulk, *Constable.*[3]
Sir N. Gardiner, soon *Prior of England.*[4]
Sir —— Peters, *Treasurer.*
Sir —— Gerard, *Cupbearer.*
Sir Gilbert Malemmano.
Sir Peter Alemanno, *Prior of Constantinople.*
Sir —— Gerard, *Master in Acre.*
Sir —— Ponzio, *Guardian of the Sick.*
Sir William Williams, *Preceptor in Antioch.*

[1] P. A. Paoli: 406.
[2] Id.:   412.—Cod. Dipl. Geros., i. Num. x.
[3] Cod. Dipl. Geros., i. 42, Num. xli.
[4] P. A. Paoli: 315.—Appendix, xxx.

Sir Bernard D'Ansillan, *Prior in Toulouse*.
Sir Robert Richards, Junior, *Master in England*.
Sir N. I. Gardiner, but why *called* of Naples, yet not *Napoli* in Italy, but in Palestine the ancient *Sichem*,[1] converted by the Greeks into Neapolis, and by the Syrians into Naplouse? Perhaps he was lord of it; but that he was brother of the Prior of England demonstrates his country; long afterwards to be Grand Master.[2]

Sir Raymond du Puys, *Marshal*, and soon first of the Grand Masters.

The most material thing was to enter into the spirit of the founder. But that was not well reflected on (says Paoli) by the historians of the order; for the oldest statute found being under his successor, they held he founded the institution; but on the contrary, had there been change, it would have been said in these documents.[3] Yet that there was a regular rule before 1113, is clear from the expression, that the head of the order must be chosen by the *knights professed*, which implies a rule, and approves it, which was written and lost, but orally lived in its members, and quite enough of documents survive to permit us to add, and in

---

[1] Cod. Dipl. Geros., i. 440.—Michaud: Orient., v. 467.—B. Poujoulat: ii. 451.
[2] P. A. Paoli: 427.   [3] P. A. Paoli: 196.

the minds of all Christendom. His successor, before he began to legislate, writes what decidedly supposes a rule; and we find knights in Gerard's time refusing to fight with a Christian, because they declare it would be contrary to their vow to take arms against any but Saracens alone; full proof they had made a vow, and therefore *professed* a rule.[1] All the companions of Gerard that we know of, were persons of the highest rank; no doubt but there were clerical members in the order from the very beginning, and that they formed a separate class, among whom were an Archbishop of Arles, 1117, and a priest of a very noble family in England as early as 1100. But as to the original creation, and the first twelve years, they have been spoken of before; so whatever the poor expiring founder might think on, let us endeavour to avoid repetitions.

About 1113 (at latest), the first Roger and his son had left a deed for permitting the free export of all things for the use of the Hospitallers and the Holy Land, and that the Hospitallers might go where they liked by sea or land, and that the ships to receive them should never have to pay pilot or freight; and also in Bari, and the other cities and towns of those parts, the Hospitallers

---

[1] P. A. Paoli: 200

shall have warehouses, under lock and key, to preserve their rents, and sell them when they please, for the use and necessities of their establishments in Palestine or elsewhere; and if that deed itself perished, we have extant another which confirms it, by William, King of Sicily in 1179.[1] In 1115 the order had a house in Arles,[2] and likewise near Narbonne, as a document in the archives of Toulouse shows (or showed half a century ago), and if Vaisette[3] thought it regarded the Templars, or the Holy Sepulchre, the Hospitallers were often called of the Holy Sepulchre, and sometimes of the Temple, in those remote times, which could lead to no mistake then; for in 1115 the order of Templars did not exist,[4] and were not declared a regular incorporation till thirteen years later, and had their first creation in 1119.[5] The priory at Constantinople dates 1119, that is, a year before Gerard's death; so that the prior that writes to Louis Seventh of France, appears to have seen Gerard, and lived the whole of Raymond's reign.[6] The

[1] Cod. Dipl. Geros., i. 227, Num. clxxxiv.
[2] Id.: i. 301, Num. xxi.
[3] P. A. Paoli: 398.
[4] Michaud: Hist., ii. 490.
[5] Id.: 144.—Cod. Dipl. Geros., i. 467.—W. of Tyre.—Bosio, par. 1, lib. i., anno 1118.
[6] P. A. Paoli: 313, 314.

English priory was then one of the greatest in the order. Sir William Allan was prior after Gardiner.[1] Confusion on this point is natural in northern Europe, from knowing little, and caring nothing about the origin of either Hospitallers or Templars; but turning away with a sneering smile, that says it would be a complete loss of time for them to inform themselves of such antiquarian frivolities.[2] The Wurzburgese on the other hand, are full of disdain that little is said about Germany, although many Germans were in the first crusade.[3] Of the servants-at-arms, since lay-brothers date no further back than the twelfth century, they may rather derive from servants-at-arms, than these from those; and of the aggregated and Hospitalleresses, we have already shown they made an integral part of the order from the first, as far as aggregation goes. Many of the first crusaders had brought their wives with them, as a Count of Poitiers; but immediately after it, a number of females came to Jerusalem, of the highest rank, as a Countess of Holland, with whom the Roman lady Agnes; as certain as several historical facts; not quite proved, yet on as firm ground as many.[4]

[1] P. A. Paoli: 315.—Appendix, xxx.   [2] P. A. Paoli: 383.
[3] Id.:   382.   [4] Id.:   352, 366, and passim.

But although that other body, the Donati, were not an integral part of the order, but strangers taken into its service; still they are a very ancient corps, and reaching to the founder's time with various privileges; linked to the knights, but not their equals in any way, nor members of their confraternity.[1] We have no precise deeds earlier than Gerard's successor; but these positively show that the Donati had pre-existed.[2] There is their formula of reception, as old as the thirteenth century,[3] in the Vatican. They were accepted for a time gratis, to merit to be eventually fed and clad by the order, to wear a cross somewhat resembling that of the knights (with a quarter less, difference introduced posteriorly in 1160 at least), in hopes of being considered superior to hired servants or stipendiary soldiers.[4] In the documents are to be found two Donati, one in London, in 1104, or thereabouts, and another in 1128, who gave himself (dono) and all he possessed to the order. A Count of Barcellona was a Donato some time before 1131, since he died in that year.[5] There were *Donate* too for the sisterhood of Hospitalleresses.[6] There were *Turco-*

---

[1] P. A. Puoli: 339. [2] Id.: 340.
[3] Id.: 341. [4] Id.: 342.
[5] Id.: 343.
[6] Id.: 344.—Appendix, Num. xxxi., xxxviii., xlii

pili also under Gerard.[1] Besides the mercenaries of that name, and the commander himself was a knight called *Turcopolier* (General-in-Chief of the cavalry) a title soon for ever united, not with the Prior of England, as Vertot says,[2] but with England, as always an Englishman. The prior mostly resided in his priory, and often old, and sometimes a clergyman; but the *turcopolier* was usually with fighting men in the East. Not the *capo*, but the *second* English dignity. There were no worn-out veterans yet. Then naturally the grand masters tried to have as many knights as possible on the field of battle; and one way of effecting that, was to confide commanderies of all civil and financial employments in Europe to the clerical class. But that was only at first; after a few years, we find such places occupied by the knights themselves, to whom, in the usual course, they belonged. There was a spirit of fraternization all through the first crusade, which survived it, and Gerard shared it eminently. The Emperor Barbarossa himself, the hero of forty pitched battles, the only human being that could have rivalled with Cœur de Leon in war, and with the King of France in the cabinet, held

[1] P. A. Paoli: 345.
[2] *Titres inseparables.* Vertot : liv. xi., p. 266.—Bosio, par. 1, lib. iii. anno 1166.

that, by the right of fraternization, every knight was his brother in arms and equal. Any officer that has ever been in an action will own that equality is a feeling strongly stamped in human nature. But it in no sort interfered with the subordination required; and it comforted Gerard's mind to see that many of the superiors, which his plan implied, were already established before he died. Almoner is as early as 1117, and in 1129 another. But not everything is to be found in the few deeds left. Rather let us be thankful for having these few.

Gentlemen poor, gentlemen sick would not be used towards the indigent, either then or now, but was indeed a nobler qualification than now; and certainly meant crusaders and persons of noble birth and station. The reverse were ridiculous, or worse; a very bad and ill-timed joke. "*Signori ammalati, Signori poveri*, termine in quei tempi nobilissimo."[1] Of chaplains or rectors, the oldest known of is in England, the chaplain of the Brisset donation, which comprised a church or chapel.[2] For the places certainly created by Gerard, or so very ancient that they probably were so, let us have recourse to Paoli; and we find them to be

[1] P. A. Paoli: 324.—Appendix, Num. xiv., cap. xvi.
[2] Id : 325.

Præpositus, Provost or Guardian (Grand Master), High Constable, Castellan, Turcopolier, Marshal or Master-at-Arms, Cupbearer, Preceptor, Chancellor, Treasurer, Hospitaller of the Halls or Receiver of Guests, dating all equally from Gerard's time; though it is necessary sometimes to recur to universal long-established tradition. We have the exact paper too, only taking the pains to draw the just inference. Master at first denoted a very dependent rank (for there were many masters) though, with the addition of grand, it came to be assigned to the head of the order. At Acre, Vienna, various places in Germany, France, England, everywhere in which the order had houses, there were masters, masters of infantry, of archers, of fortifications, naval masters, masters of horse, at arms; there were numbers of masters, as in these days captains.[1] The Templars—who were founded at Jerusalem, eighteen years after the Hospitallers— took divers of his titles. Their very founder was called master-at-arms.[2] Yet the Templars assumed only one of the three duties of the Hospitaller—not hospitality, for they had no seat; but they gave their chief the title held by the other duty—the army, master-at-arms. Sir Roger Pagano was

[1] P. A. Paoli: 275. [2] Id.: 276.

Gerard's first master-at-arms.[1] If he was the brother of that Sir Hugh de Pagano who founded the Templars, it is a noble origin, and agrees with the prevailing opinion that they sprang from the Hospitallers; not from their servants, as Brompton pretends, but from their knights, their knights their own illustrious equals![2]

In the first pitched battle, the knights of the order were led by the then marshal, or master-at-arms, who was afterwards to become the famous Grand Master Raymond du Puys. But that Raymond was not a precise companion of Gerard's in the first crusade (as Paoli elsewhere proves), is no impediment to his having been master-at-arms, and fought while Gerard was president or provost.[3] It is very probable that the celebrity gained by Raymond as marshal, may truly have given rise to his election to be the head of the order.[4] Bosio has Revel; but that De Moulin was in 1181, is certain. Yet the sole difference is about *the grand*, which does not merit many words. The Gardiner mentioned in England, is not the same man who became grand master after De Moulin. They may have been near relations, and probably were, or even brothers; but were two different persons,

[1] P. A. Paoli : 276.   [2] Appendix, Num. xxxvii.
[3] Id. :   280.   [4] P. A. Paoli : 283.

one a knight, and one a priest; one celebrated for valour in Palestine, and the other for zeal and piety at home; similar only in family name, and so confused, because contemporaries and countrymen.[1] The Prior of England in 1180 and 1189 could not be the same made grand master, in 1187, in Palestine. No little error in chronology will overthrow that; but it must be avowed that the good and learned Bosio was wrong; others of course.[2] Nor was it a time to have an old priest, but a brave knight to replace him slain in battle. The *Preceptor*, Sir N. I. Gardiner, became Grand Master after De Moulin.[3] The old, little known Papal bull of 1120 (which is given in the Appendix), fortifies much that is or shall be said.[4] It has been insufficiently, or not at all, examined by former historians. The constable presided over the stables, and what regarded the tables and hospitality; possibly too, used to carry the standard of the order on the field and great occasions.[5] The standard was sometimes borne by the marshal. Tudebonde the chronicler saw Bohemond's constable carry his standard in 1101; and it is likely

---

[1] P. A. Paoli : 316.   [2] Id. : 317.
[3]   Id. :   318.
[4]   Id. :   308.—Appendix, Num. vi.
[5]   Id. :   288.

the order continued the same fashion for a time, though constable ceased soon to be in vogue, and his functions were given to another. Matthew Paris says the order's standard-bearer had its proper name of Balnicafer; but perhaps that was afterwards.[1] The keeper or castellan, is implied in castles, and though several medals and seals belonging to many such functionaries found of late are all of Rhodes, still as Godfrey gave a castle, it follows that he also gave it a keeper. Essilia was the castle's name in 1100;[2] one month after the first foundation of the order, Essilia of St. Abraham, is called simply St. Abraham in Godfrey's donation, from its being close to it, perhaps an appendage of it; and many other castles in Palestine were given to the Hospitallers before 1100; and in each was a keeper, and over all there was a lord keeper. The names of two of these earliest keepers are come down to us in two documents.[3] Of the turcopolier we have spoken already at full length. There is a fixed tradition in the order, even amongst such as have not much studied its annals, that *turcopolier* is contemporary with the founding of the order; but indeed, troops of that name were used by the Turks, and even

[1] P. A. Paoli: 289. [2] Id.: 291.
[3] Id.: 293.

Christian Greeks, long before the first crusade, and fought at Nice, and other places of Asia Minor. If the *turcopili* originated with the Turcomans, these were generally light cavalry, not much dissimilar from the Cossacks, though more richly accoutred, since some of them had lances with heads of gold. Forty thousand Tartars are said to have been so equipped.[1] The marshal was a military dignity, and chiefly directed the infantry.

The pincerna, or cup-bearer, and the chancellor, and the treasurer, date equally from Gerard's days.[2] The hospitaller of the halls, or receiver of guests, was almost always then a charge confined to one of the clergy. The preceptor was the fourth charge in the order, and was over all respecting the finances. A chronicler tells us the name was particular to the Hospitallers; for others called him procurator, or economist. But the Templars and Teutonics followed the Hospitallers in this, as in many things; and called their procurator, preceptor.[3] So in speaking of them as being (to a certain extent) all three one whole in those ancient times, is only to do what they did themselves. We hear of the preceptor's being then on

---

[1] Chron. Corn. Zanffliet, 3.—Bib. Crois. i. 336.
[2] P. A. Paoli: 302.   [3] P. A. Paoli: 295.

occasions an assistant to the second dignity in the order, the master-at-arms, or marshal, as early as 1155, and cited as of long standing.[1] In Dugdale, and an old chronicle in the Cottonian (now London Museum), is "the master or preceptor." And Clement IV. appears to have considered the preceptors vice-masters, both with Hospitallers and Templars.[2] And, when we recollect that the Pope had written to all Christendom to send them money at Jerusalem, we must conclude that the preceptor had enough to do to receive and account for such sums that were to suffice for armies, and such hospitality and charity.[3] Sir Hugo de Revel, who became grand master, passed to that from this place. Also De Moulin and Gardiner had been preceptors, before elected grand masters.[4] The marshal and *turcopolier*, though often united, existed separate under Gerard.[5] When we add to all stated the two Papal bulls,[6] we cannot but allow that few founders of any human society were ever so fortunate as this one, who lived to see his order rich, powerful, and glorious in so many places of Europe and Asia. Quite enough has been substantiated to vindicate his right to a station far

---

[1] P. A. Paoli: 296. [2] Id.: 297.
[3] Id.: 297. [4] Id.: 300.
[5] Id.: 301. [6] Appendix, Num. v., viii.

above any rival in his own fraternity; not merely a brave, holy, and high-minded nobleman, but fully entitled to rank as a princely founder and sublime legislator. And after a multitude of proofs, for which there is not room here, has not Paoli a right to say? "Mine is not merely an historical truth, but an historical demonstration."[1] And if Gerard in his corps was unique in title, he was so also, I will not say in birth (many were of as high birth in that glorious order), but worth; nor is it to affirm little, since numbers illustrious for eminent worth were there among the heroic Hospitallers. Of course there was much subsequent legislation;[2] but indeed they were only comments on a rule already formed, and most certainly reduced to writing; nor are we for a moment to suppose that the Popes would have approved of what they had not deliberately read and submitted to their council. Some soreness had existed from the first elevation of a Latin Patriarch,[3] who, having a spiritual power co-existing with that temporal one of the king's, had superiority over Antioch, that like Edessa, Tripoli, Acre, &c., was but a fief of the kingdom.

But the Antiochese archbishopric aspired to be

[1] P. A. Paoli : 457. [2] Id. 215.
[3] Appendix, Num. vi.

independent (or rather dominant), and sent a deputation to the Pope, who refused to alter what had been regulated by his predecessors. And the disappointment disposed an ambitious hierarchy to discharge their acrimony (but very unjustly), not on the Papacy, of which they were afraid, but on those it protected—the Hospitallers, who had nothing to do with the matter. Still, in reference to this accusation, the Legate Berengario was sent in 1115 to Jerusalem, and deposed its Patriarch.[1] Beside the rule that disappeared at Acre, or in some preceding mischance, the few we have, show that at least four other apostolical letters to Gerard have been lost.[2] No wonder at all; rather the wonder is that these few incontestible documents have come down to us; and if that of Lucius is in the Vatican, it is, that to have sent it then to Palestine would have been highly imprudent, seeing what a confusion that country was that time in; Jerusalem to fall in less than a year, and Acre already tottering at Saladin's approach, who was then climbing towards his ascendant.[3] But when these and all the ancient records of even Gerard's successor were thought to be lost utterly, and of his successors too, then a Pope of a later epoch (Boniface VIII.) was

[1] P. A. Paoli: 310.—Cod. Dipl. Geros., i. 549.
[2] Id.: 208.   [3] P. A. Paoli: 212.

engaged to receive some scraps of bye-laws instead, on pretence of their forming the substance of the founder's rule, and putting them together and ascribing all the merit to another than Gerard, whom they did not mention at all. Some ignorant, and perhaps not ill-intentioned persons, procured an analogous bull; which, however, the Pontiff gave rather doubtfully, so that Paoli, on inspection of the original, suspects it, from the context, to be in part falsified by a paragraph anciently foisted in, not agreeing with what precedes, though with ink of a similar colour and identity of writing, and probably in the drawing up of the document formally for his Holiness to sign;[1] by which means the imposture was got up, and superseded the truth during several ages; and now these documentary proofs overthrow the entire production; but all is of little importance at present. The very dress of the knights is not mentioned in those scraps, as having been determined long before. Nor were the females separated as nuns (which became the case afterwards), but joined the knights at table and in the church, and by the couch of sickness, and attended on strangers of their own sex.[2]

That Gerard died at the age of forty-four is no ways

[1] P. A. Paoli: 213 and 214.
[2] P. A. Paoli: 216.

surprising; but that the distinguished personage[1] lived so long, that he expired peaceably, that his body was held in great reverence, that it was transported to Rhodes,[2] and thence into France, may be easily assented to; and if it was the ancient custom of the order, when possible, to elect the new grand master in presence of the corpse of the dead one, it was very likely that the marshal, who had recently gained a celebrated victory, was immediately elected to the vacant dignity. Sir Raymond du Puys, of a most noble French family—sometimes called Florentine, from its having come originally from Tuscany, or rather Lucca,[3] and himself an illustrious knight—was then made head of the order.

1121 His own proclamation[4] and a Papal rescript, prove that was in 1121;[5] and, by the context, it was early in the January of that year.[6] The proclamation itself presupposes a rule; how else should there be chapter—knights professed—duties to which they had sworn? Sworn duties imply a rule. Nor would oral remission do, where there was

[1] P. A. Paoli: 467.
[2] Id.:   476.—Cod. Dipl. Geros., i. 330.
[3] Cod. Dipl. Gros., i. 332, 335.—Bosio, par. 1, lib. i., anno 1119.
[4] "I Raymond, on the blessed Lord Gerard's death!" Appendix, Num. x.
[5] Appendix, Num. ix.
[6] P. A. Paoli : 477, and passim.

a written document to be given: "Raymond ne devoit sa place qu' a l'eclat de ses vertus."[1] Then it was to his *eclat* he owed his election, and he merited it; albeit not probably quite in the sense intended. Though the Normans themselves, and the first crusade, had shown that eminent bravery, and all military talents, and a fervent spirit of religion (or what some call superstition), which are perfectly compatible, to an attentive reader that proclamation proves he considered his election alone made him a sovereign. How could that be, but that he had become the chief of a body already organised and made sovereign by universal consent? His *per gratiam Dei* has ever been a phrase consecrated to royalty.

But the East is a curious country. Events the most opposite occur almost in the same breath; triumphs and defeats in wondrous rapidity. So, in spite of the favourable omens and the late victory, we read of Turcomans ravaging Syria the very same year; but on their misconduct, the sultan having cut off their beards, this mark of ignominy so humbled and vexed them, that they all deserted to beyond the Euphrates.[2] Nevertheless, King Baldwin is winning battles near Aleppo in the autumn

[1] Vertot: Hist., i. 72.   [2] Arab. Chron. 43.

of 1121, and sent word that he was sure to take the town he was besieging; for that he had reduced it to the state " of a horse that had lost the use of his forefeet, and whom[1] his master pampers up with barley, in the hopes of selling him to advantage; the barley all eaten, the horse dies, and the sultan has neither barley nor horse." But Baldwin failed, and the Mussulman autocrat smiled with scorn. Yet his was a short-lived exultation; for, eating mutton, and melon and other fruit, his belly swelled and gave him an oppression of the chest that killed him.[2] But his nephew Balac, near Edessa, surprised Joscelin (to whom, as a Christian, the Mahometan deals his usual *God curse him*), and wanted him to surrender his country; but the Frank, prisoner as he was, had the courage to reply: " We and our castles are like the camel and his pack-saddle; when the camel dies—but no sooner— his pack-saddle passes to another."[3] So Balac, spreading terror over both banks, went along the river like the roaring lion of Scripture, seeking whom he may devour; while he carried Joscelin with him to his hold in the north of Mesopotamia.[4] Whereat Baldwin II. sallied forth; yet, instead of setting Joscelin free, was taken himself, and

1122

[1] Arab. Chron., 45.   [2] Id.: 46.
[3] Id.: 46.   [4] Michaud: Hist. Crois., ii. 63.

consigned to share his client's captivity. But on Balac's marching against Antioch, the Karthert captives broke their bonds, and with the assistance of some Armenian deserters, murdered the whole garrison and might have escaped. "Now that we are at liberty," said the wiser count, "let us go, carrying away as much booty as we can." "But," replied the king, "I'll remain here to keep possession; and do you depart to call my troops;" and he forced Joscelin to take an oath neither to change clothes, eat flesh-meat, or drink wine, except at mass, before he came back to deliver him.[1]

1123

But Balac, hurrying east, retook the hold, and slew all the Franks, excepting Baldwin, whom he shut up in another stronger castle. When Joscelin got to Jerusalem, it was too late. Still, after various adventures, he with ten thousand men, attacked Balac in Mesopotamia, who was beaten and obliged to fly. It is said that Balac led the charge fifty several times in that battle, without being once wounded, nor had any armour, or any other weapon than sword and lance. To-day he thanked Allah fervently for his victory; on the next, had all the Christian prisoners massacred; and, on the third, had his collar bone broken by

---

[1] Arab. Chron., 47. "Men communicated in both species," says the Christian commentator on that passage.

an arrow, and but a moment to tear away the barb and spit on it and say, "There's a shot that kills all Mahometans." That he was slain in the battle would be then a Christian fable; still some affirm his death proceeded from Joscelin's hand, though the arrow came from the ramparts.[1] Baldwin remained a long time prisoner; five years, say some. The Saracens took this opportunity of invading Palestine. That Gardiner, who afterwards became grand master, and then was Count of Sidon,[2] and constable, certainly of the order, and probably of Jerusalem itself (second charge in that kingdom), and by rights regent during the king's captivity, led the Christian army, and by rights, too, the Hospitallers, their grand master being before Aleppo. Gardiner was brother or nephew to that other Gardiner who was in England as prior, and priest, and, indeed, bishop. From the name, they are often confounded, but were two separate persons.[3] Far from old,[4] he was very young, remarkably young for that charge, scarcely any more than twenty-two, at that time, Jan., 1125, since he lived till 1191.[5] Yet what was the Christian army?[6] In numbers very in-

1125

[1] Michaud: Hist., ii. 70.—Vertot: i. 89.
[2] Cod. Dipl. Geros., 484.   [3] P. A. Paoli: as already.
[4] Vertot: i. 85.   [5] Cod. Dipl. Geros., i. 339.
[6] Michaud: Hist., ii. 70.

ferior, not seven thousand. The chief dependence was on two hundred Hospitallers. They, and a miracle, put to rout the Egyptian myriads. Those sombre heights had many terrific stories to tell, and glorious; let this be of the number.

Poor Gardiner, his own name is completely altered by a writer of authority, but in truth it was not D'Agrain,[1] but Grener or Grenier, as foreigners spell it.[2] His wife had died, but left him two sons, who grew up, and we have still the deed in which one of them confirms his father's, and that which is witnessed by his other son.[3] But the ingratitude of forgetting even his name is of a piece with what mankind has always been, and perhaps will always be. Men were first ungrateful to their good God, and others have been so to them. They who were such to their Maker, may be also to each other. The Mahometans were freely plundered, having been themselves plunderers and murderers, as they are to be. Envy of the Pisans and Genoese more than anything else, appears to have decided the Venetians. The Doge landed at Acre, and went in triumph to Jerusalem. The regent

---

[1] Michaud: Hist., ii. 65. [2] Cod. Dipl. Geros., i. 453.
[3] Id.: Id.: Num. xiii. in 1133.—Num. xxiv. in 1147. These sons write of him as dead, and he was so to them from the moment he entered the order exposed to such imminent dangers.

in Baldwin's name proposed attacking Ascalon or Tyre. But the Venetians first bargained for a church, street, and oven, in any town they assisted in taking. So a third of Tyre was promised, and it capitulated, after five months' siege, in the spring of 1125, a rich commercial place still, and defended by a range of mountains from the north-east winds, in a beautiful country, though no longer the fine Tyre of the Bible. During the siege came news of Balac's death,[1] and every one foresaw Baldwin would soon be free. However, his ransom was eighty thousand pieces of gold. Timur-tach, who liberated him, admitted him to his table, and eating and drinking together, made him a present of a royal tunic, and a cap, and buskins of gold, and the same horse on which he had been made prisoner, and when he rode away, leaving as hostages his own daughter, and Joscelin's son, and others to the number of twelve, and the first of the four portions of the money, off he went, and at once forgot his promises—" God curse him!"[2]

The Christian besiegers of Aleppo did everything they could to irritate the Moslem on the walls, as, taking a Koran from one of the many little mosques in the suburbs, and tearing out some of the sacred leaves, and fastening them under the

---

[1] Michaud: Hist., ii. 72.   [2] Arab. Chron., 50.

tail of a horse, where the animal covering them from time to time with its ordure, then the infidel began to clap his hands, and burst into loud fits of laughter in derision of Islam.[1] Also at Moussul there were many Assassins, or Battenians; for the Moslem, and famous Turcoman captain, Borsaki, on his way to mosque on a Friday, in the middle of a great crowd, was assailed by eight Battenians, disguised as dervishes, and, in spite of his coat of mail, and his guards, was pierced with many daggers, and expired. The eight Battenians were all killed, except one, who escaped; whose mother, when she heard that Borsaki was slain, and that his murderers had perished, believed that her son was of the number, and quite joyful, she decorated herself, and tinged her brows and eyelashes with collyrium, and showed her exultation publicly. All of a sudden arrived her son himself, all alive, and in perfect health, on which her rapture changed to sadness, and she tore her hair and defiled her face. Miserable woman; she adored her son, but such fanaticism is in that frightful sect, which she participated, that she had rejoiced her child had got to the eternal delight of Paradise, and then she fell into despair, as natural. The Spartan mother's was a weaker sentiment. This more to

[1] Arab. Chron., 52.

be reprobated.[1] Battenians, Ismalians, or Assassins (for they are all one, the Old Man's people—though he was called Old Man, not from age, but dignity— shieckh, or elder, having a double signification, lord, or *vecchio*). These villains were sometimes in league with the Christians, who ought to be ashamed of it. So the Moslem Governor of Damascus had all the Battenians that were in that town (six thousand it is said) put to death, with the aid of the citizens, who hated them; but the officer who commanded in Paneas, being a secret Battenian, delivered up that fortress to the Christians, among whom he went to live.[2] Nothing but troubles and anarchy through all Palestine, Syria, Mesopotamia; Moslems and Christians sometimes allied, and suddenly at war. Zengui, perhaps rather just than sanguinary, was about ten at the first crusade, when his father died. Except Aleppo, Damascus, Emessa, and Humah, there was now scarce a spot where a Mahometan could exist at peace. " But God resolved to fulminate the demons of the cross, and his searching eye saw no one so proper for this Divine purpose as the jewel of religion, the blessed martyr Zengui, of the unshaken heart and firm will."[3] So he was

1128

[1] Arab. Chron., 55. [2] Id.: 56.
[3] Id.: 60.

elected Prince of Moussul and Aleppo, and the sultan ratified the election.

"At that time the Franks (whom God curse) held Edessa, and much of Mesopotamia. If God had not given them Zengui, it was all over with Syria and the Moslems; but at his appearance, the true believers lightened up their looks, and the prophet's words were verified. 'My country shall never be without a friend of God, nor religion without a protector.' The Lord did not abandon the Mahometans, but placed at their head one whose soul is to be sanctified."[1] Yet was no way scrupulous, since he put the Prince of Damascus, a brother Mussulman, whom he got hold of by no very honourable stratagem, on a bed of straw, and scourged severely by a common executioner, to extract a ransom, and make him give up a fortress. Moslems ravaged all about Laodicea, leading away to slavery nine thousand men, women, and children, and one hundred thousand head of cattle, all which dislocated the arms of the Franks. Such were the amusements of that time.

1129

Even long before this, Sir Raymond had seen his body, with a rapid success, rivalling that under its founder, go on growing till not an illustrious

[1] Arab. Chron., 64.

family in Europe but furnished a knight to one or other of the military orders in Palestine, as early as 1128; and even sovereign princes soon learned to lay down their royal pomp, to wear either the scarlet coat-of-arms of the Hospitallers, or the white mantle of the Templars.[1] The Hospitallers wore black at home, but abroad a scarlet surcoat, field for the white cross and black ribbon, their colours in memory of Gerard, from that day to this.

The moment Baldwin was free, instead of returning to the delighted Jerusalem, he assembled an army towards Antioch, and marched against Aleppo.[2] But being repulsed, though joined by the head of the Arabs, and even some emirs, he visited the capital, and after gathering a company of Hospitallers and other distinguished knights, he made an inroad on the Damascan countries, and won such large booty, that it produced a sum that sufficed to ransom the people he had left in captivity in Mesopotamia,[3] his own daughter included. It is probably the only instance of a king's having hired out his daughter into slavery. Yet perhaps the times, and not he, were to blame.

The Turkish cavalry, in 1128, was better in

[1] Michaud: Hist., ii. 82. [2] Id.: Id., ii. 71.
[3] Id. :   Id., 72.

evolutions than the Frank; but both Egyptians and Turks left the sea to the European Franks.[1] The Turks of that period were disciplined. Nor were Curds, Arabs, Turcomans, and innumerable hordes, wanting; but on the day of battle they all joined against the Christians for love of Islam or of plunder.[2] Swimming over the Tigris or Euphrates, they united to ravage Syria. Ferocious savages they were; enough that they were Mussulmans! And indeed, from one or other of those uncultured tribes, sprang many of the most distinguished Mahometans—even Saladin himself.[3] As for the Bedouins, they were sometimes in favour of the Christians; and at worst they were easily kept in order by the castles of Montreale, built by Baldwin I. between the Dead Sea and Egypt, and by the fortress of Kerak, in Arabia Petrea. The old chronicles are full of the wonderful cruelty of the nomades, they call Parthians; but these barbarians were Turcomans swarming from the eastern shores of the Caspian, beyond the Persian frontiers. Yet on the whole, the Christians had to this been on the increase. Even after the fall of Edessa itself, Joscelin had still various flourishing towns through Mesopotamia, and along both sides of the

[1] Michaud: Hist., ii. 73. [2] Id.: Id., ii. 74.
[3] Id.: Id., 75.

Euphrates, and the declivities of Mount Taurus. Antioch, Tripoli, and the whole line of sea coast to Egypt, were Christian. After Jerusalem, Antioch was by far the greatest city in those parts. Yet it is somewhat unfair to praise the Hospitallers in 1130, without adding that, from the first crusade, without the interval of one single moment, the Latin kingdom owes its existence to them. Normans liberated the Holy Sepulchre, and founded its permanent defence up to the woful, when all was lost.[1] The Hospitallers took proper pride in the Templars and Teutonics as their children—fruit of their own loins; and a historian of the Hospitallers has a right to comprise them all in that one word. Consolidated, why should a rash hand try to separate them? At most, from their legal foundation 1128,[2] the Templars may be treated as a separate body; and the Teutonics from theirs, when we come to it. Who were the Kings of Jerusalem's great and valiant lords? The Moslems tell you Hospitallers![3] The rapidity of the Christians notwithstanding the weight of their armour,[4] is very remarkable; no comprehending it—at one time here, and at the next there, a great distance off.

1130

---

[1] Michaud: Hist., ii. 81. [2] Id. : Id., ii. 490.
[3] Arab. Chron., 128, Note, Ibn Abontai.
[4] Michaud : Hist., ii. 83.

Now in Europe or Asia Minor, now on the Orontes or Euphrates, almost at the same instant in a battle beyond the Red Sea, defending Jerusalem, or making an inroad on Damascus or Aleppo. Their scorn of ambushes or stratagems was likewise great; and prudence in their leaders was too often called weakness or timidity, and many of their princes paid with their lives or liberty the vain glory of dangers that were without any utility to the Christian cause. Yet these uncalculating exploits produced results that resembled prodigies, the only policy that could have maintained the European sovereignty so long.[1] Another advantage derived from thoughtlessness (though it had an air of the political) was, that when any Mahometan population had to leave a town, they were replaced by Franks, who, marrying women from Syria or Apulia, produced a race called Pulani,[2] like Mulattoes, despised by some, yet faithful subjects to the Latin domination.

Baldwin, now old and with only two children, and both of them daughters, married the eldest to a noble warrior and pilgrim, Foulques of Anjou, who thus became at once his sovereign's presumptive heir; and the other daughter to young

---

[1] Michaud: Hist., ii. 84.   [2] Id.: Id., ii. 88.

Bohemond, Prince of Antioch. Foulques, if not a Norman, was nearly allied to the Normans of the royal family of England, and therefore of the Norman party. On return from an unfortunate attempt against Damascus, in the arms of his Melisenda and her husband, and blessing their infant son, in 1131 died the last of Godfrey's companions—and also as such loved and revered—the illustrious warrior Baldwin II., a virtuous and sagacious king.

1131

About this same time, Sir Raymond received the two bulls of Innocent II., dated 1130, both in the first year of his pontificate. " How pleasing to God, and how venerable to man, is at least one spot on earth! How commodious, how useful a refuge is that which the Hospitallers' house of hospitality in Jerusalem affords to all poor pilgrims who face the various dangers by land and sea with the pious and devout wish to visit that sacred city, and our Lord's Sepulchre, as is well known to the whole universe. There indeed are the indigent assisted, and every sort of humane attention is shown to the weak, fatigued by their numerous labours and dangers! They are there refreshed, and resume their strength; so that they are enabled to see the sacred places which have been sanctified by our Saviour's corporal presence. Nor do the brethren of that house hesitate to expose their lives for their brothers in Jesus Christ; but with infantry and cavalry, kept for that special purpose, and paid by their own money, defend the faithful from Paynims fearlessly, both in going and returning. It is these Hospitallers that are the instruments by which the Omnipotent preserves His Church in the East from the ordures of the infidels." Thus says the Pope on the tenth of March, and thus on the twelfth:[1] "The more these excellent men, the Knights Hospitallers of Jerusalem, are assailed by malicious tongues for their religion and probity, the more are we desirous of protecting them, and showing that the Roman Church is intimately persuaded of the purity of their devotion. Therefore it is that we lay our injunctions on all parish priests, and other clergy over the whole globe, to allow no one to presume to speak against the Hospitallers, but to recur to every means in their defence, even excommunication." And so this continues, and many other Papal decrees, in the same tenor.

Fulk became King of Jerusalem. His first exercise of authority was an unpleasant one; for Alice, his wife's sister, having been left widow, conducted herself so scandalously, that it was necessary

---

[1] Appendix, Num. xii., xiii.

to import a husband for her only child, the little Constance, as soon as possible; which Fulk did, in the person of the Count of Poitiers, whom he got sent from France for that purpose, or rather from England, for he was then at the Court of Henry I.[1] The delicate commission was executed by a celebrated Hospitaller, Sir Robert Joubert, whom we shall find, a few years later, grand master of the order.[2] While that was being done, and Melisend was regent during her lord's absence in Antioch, there was a grievous storm from Egypt, *viâ* Ascalon, to repress which, it was found expedient to build a fortress in that direction, and give it in care of the Hospitallers. They and the Templars made Bersabee a secure refuge for Christians, as well as a check on the Bedouin Arabs, and attacks from Egyptian or other Saracens. All the states of Christendom then saw their defence in that of the Holy Land; and none able to defend it but those knights.[3] Indeed, the renowned warrior Alphonso the Great of Arragon, Emperor of all the Spains, as runs his title, who had conquered in twenty-nine battles against the Moors, being without children, made a will of his

---

[1] Mathew Paris: 1133.—Rob. del Monte, anno 1130.—Cod. Dipl. Geros., i. 394.

[2] Vertot: i. 105.

[3] Id.: 109.—Bosio, par 1, lib. i. anno 1131.

entire dominions to those two orders in 1131. And if his last testament never came to effect, that was owing not so much to the Spaniards, whose chief grandees had signed it, as to the knights themselves, who preferred some succour towards the wars in Palestine to the affairs of royalty, in which soldiers saw but an encumbrance. In their eyes, it was a full compensation to be allowed to defend certain castles and extensive fortresses, and the honour that no peace could ever be made with the Moor without their consent.[1]

It was on his return from Spain that Raymond assumed the title of grand master; and if that of præpositus be higher, and had been given him in the Papal bulls of Innocent II., perhaps accidentally, yet this other was destined to be forevermore the distinctive of the heads of his order.[2] Fulk had reason to feel happy that the Moslems of Moussul divided from those of Damascus, who joined the Christians in taking Paneas; and satisfied in depriving the Mesopotamians of a city, left it to a Christian garrison, which defended Jerusalem on the Lebanon side.[3]

[1] Vertot: i. 116.—Bosio: par. 1, lib. i., anno 1132.
[2] Id.: 117.—Id. Id.
[3] Michaud: Hist., ii. 99.—Or Cesarea di Filippo, or Bellina according to some. Seb. Paoli: Notizie, ii. 434.—Bosio: par. 1, lib. ii., anno 1141.

1141 Vertot, like Bosio, complains that no historians relate when the change from religious to military began. Of course they do not, for no such change ever took place. From the foundation the whole was natural, and offended none of the tastes of the age, but was in its very spirit, neither more nor less than the crusade: and all Europe had given full proof of the universal way of thinking, by the voluntary progress of all the Europeans then alive. In no way could the association of nobility and servants-at-arms agree afterwards. But then it did, and they glided in together without the least difficulty; and once the rule was established, no one ever saw anything in that honourable familiarity but justice and truth; and so it has come down to our own time without a single objection. In the presence of a loftier, all lower ideas vanished. There would have been soon a difficulty, but then there was none. Gerard knew how to take the ball at the hop. Like most other great discoveries, it seemed quite easy when effected, and in the usual course, nothing to startle. I avow that after I had learned to doubt the current opinion, I yet thought that Raymond must have written something of a body of laws, or left some fine charter, to acquire the fame of a legislator, though not the order's founder, or its prime Lycurgus. But when I saw what a few meagre trivialities they are which obtained him that estimation, I was wholly astonished. Not a single principle of any importance, or generality do they contain. The very first words prove that Raymond had no idea of forming a rule; but only of commenting on some of the minor obligations contained in a rule which had been sworn to by him and the other members of the order, and therefore well known to them all. Perhaps some of the brotherhood had been a little remiss in the particulars he notices. Like most subsequent grand masters and chapters, he found something to condemn or amend, not as to the established rule, but as to the mode of executing some of its articles. But as he was the first grand master, posterity thought they could go no higher. The founder was gone, and when his rule was lost, it was not hard to pass off this as a substitute; so as not read, but received with blind or dishonest credulity; not even the shadow of a rule, but only a parcel of bye-laws, chiefly regarding the sick, or punishment for some diminutive misconduct in trifles scarce deserving notice: no few of them utterly childish and ridiculous, clownish, and but practical jests. The impression it cannot but leave in any one that has the patience to examine the rubbish, is highly to Raymond's disadvantage. Yet was he a very eminent personage. Undoubtedly this trash given in his name, was never meant by him to be the apology for a rule. Impossible to suppose it ever came from him at all, but was evidently only a collection of many little stray notes, thrown together by chance, and referring to some observations he may have made on miserable negligences in the daily service. No doubt the wording was by some of his lowest subalterns, who may have thought they were writing something very becoming; and that it was his, is not to be dreamed of, nor merits a serious objection. Forsooth it is a nasty custom to walk about naked. Kindness is due to the sick. It is wrong to speak loud and disrespectfully in the church. All indecency is to be eschewed, particularly in the company of women. Nor should females be allowed either to wash heads of knights, or feet. It is forbidden to wear foreign furs;[1] which reminds us of the sumptuary laws of the Italian Republics, in none of which, however, are found so many littlenesses as in this. So to have this exhibited as the rule of an order that never occupied itself but with things of the greatest moment, and had something of the *qu'il mourut* in all its transactions, is not unlike an insult to com-

[1] Appendix, xiv.

mon sense. One of the greatest captains of his age, "*par sa rare valeur, des plus grands capitaines de son siecle*,[1] as Raymond is represented, we have no right to impute to him anything of puerility; and to this veteran's instructions, young Baldwin owes his beginning very early to distinguish himself as a warrior. For the princely boy's father had been killed by a fall from his horse, when coursing on the thirteenth November, 1142 (which agrees ill with what is elsewhere said of his having got blind, and probably meaning only a little short-sighted),[2] and left two sons, Baldwin of thirteen, and Almeric of seven. Their mother at first assumed the regency, but in less than two years the grand master and some other of the great lords had the elder boy crowned by the title of Baldwin III., who instantly led out 1144 a body of Hospitallers and Templars on an excursion against the Saracens in the land of Moab, and came back with the fame of bravery.[3]

The Christian cause had just entered its decline by the fall of Edessa;[4] Joscelin 1145

---

[1] Vertot: i. 170.—Bosio: par. 1, lib. ii., anno 1159.
[2] Cod. Dipl. Geros., i. 362.—Appendix, Num. xxvi. It reconciles both passages to reckon from the coronation of Baldwin III. on Christmas day, 1144, and not from his father's death.—Bosio: par. 1, lib. ii., anno 1142.
[3] Michaud: Hist., ii. 99, 100.—Bosio: par. 1, lib. ii. anno 1142.
[4] Vertot: i. 118, 119, 120.—Bosio: par. 1, lib. ii. anno 1143.

being dead, and his son totally incapable to be his substitute. Edessa was one of the great fiefs of the kingdom of Jerusalem, and had been so ever since the time of Godfrey de Bouillon; but now Zengui took it with hideous slaughter. No need of a continual repetition. The Christian army there at this time means Hospitallers. The juvenile monarch's next act was a war unjust in its motive, and unfortunate in its result. An emir, who commanded at Bosra, to the south-east of Damascus in the Haouran (which has now above two hundred uninhabited towns and villages, which testify to its numerous population once), proposed giving them up his post—an offer that the Christians greedily accepted, although the prince and emirs at Damascus, astonished at the rumour, entreated them not to commence hostilities, but remain faithful to their treaty of truce, whereas an unjust war could never prosper. In vain; and when the Christian army reached Bosra, it had a fresh Damascan garrison, the treasonable officer's own wife having betrayed him. Frightful retreat; heats, and poisoned waters, and famine; and most of the gallant Hospitallers left their bones to whiten that desert, after the wild beasts had devoured their flesh; all the inhabitants having fled into caverns, and carried off every scrap of food for man or horse. There were thistles all over the plain, and the Turks set them on fire. Only for St. George on a white horse, and holding a red flag, all the Christians were lost.[1] Glorious young Baldwin might have saved himself at the beginning of these disasters, but refused to leave his army; like St. Louis in another memorable defeat.[2] Yet not calamity, but repose was the true gangrene of the Franks. So Zengui thought, and he was right. It was Joscelin the Second's enervating dissoluteness that lost Edessa, and so it shall be soon with Antioch, the two strong outworks of Jerusalem however distant; and thence the same foul disease shall go on eating its way, till it ruins Palestine and the holy city itself. Therefore it was, that Zengui (according to the Mahometans, a blessed servant) used fraud to the utmost against Edessa, before he had recourse to force. So weakened, he overcame; and by the sword condemned the people of Edessa to eternal silence; and diminished into Orfa, it is now a poor place, of little strength. Well might the Imaums sing: "O Mahomet, Prophet of Heaven, in your name have we destroyed these idolatrous sinners, and torrents of blood have run for the triumph of your law!" Edessa, that had acquired much power under the Franks (observes

[1] Michaud: Hist., ii. 102. [2] Id.: Id., ii. 102.

Ibn Alahir himself),[1] one of the stoutest fortified places in Asia, the queen of beauty, and limpid waters, the city over sixty towns, was no more. Its altars upset, its riches and songs gone, its unrivalled magnificence, as if an edifice carried from heaven to be built on earth.[2] Whatever of the atrocious massacres were subsequently perpetrated by Noureddin, his father Zengui had showed the example; so that, if the scimitar devoured its people as fire devours straw, yet on Zengui's head, the man of blood, be the whole! Some weeks later, the man of blood was himself murdered by his own Mamelouckes, while asleep in his camp.[3] The Emperor of Greece had a few years earlier come into Syria at the invitation of a cadi near Aleppo, who became Christian with four hundred of his village, and many of the natives having taken refuge in caves in the hills, the Greeks making large fires at the mouth smoked out some, and suffocated others of the unfortunates within. But it having been contrived to cause dissensions between the Greeks and Latins, the emperor had to retire.[4]

1146

On the whole, Zengui deserved his death, and the earth was liberated from a monster. News of

---

[1] Arab. Chron., 66.
[2] Michaud: Hist., ii. 177, 187.   [3] Arab. Chron., 78.
[4] Arab. Chron., 67.

the fall of Edessa, and that Islam began to advance her horns in Mesopotamia, roused Europe to the second crusade, under Lewis VII. and Conrad, which ended so unfortunately; for most of the Germans died in Asia Minor, and if a remnant of French got to Antioch, Queen Eleanor learned the vices of it, so that Louis VII. was obliged to get divorced from her, as soon as he got back to Paris. Some pretended she saw the famous Saladin there, then a very young officer, and, if it depended on her, would have run away with him. Too young, perhaps, but it seems the queen was of a different taste. Certainly he was rather twenty or twenty-four, than ten; since, within a year later, he was the second in command, under his father, at Damascus.[1]

Conrad and king met to weep at Jerusalem, and made an attempt on Damascus, that ended ineffectually, and the European sovereigns returned home with slender retinue, and no armies, though the imperial had left Europe with ninety-thousand horse, and the royal with fifty thousand of the same arm; for, as to the infantry of both, they were beyond counting.[2]

The effect of the second crusade in beautiful France, was mournful, "Our castles and villages deserted, widows and orphans are everywhere,

[1] Michaud: Hist., ii. 177, 187.   [2] Arab. Chron., 93.

whose husbands and fathers are alive.[1] Many are the historians of the first crusade, but of the second, only three; and these three all break off suddenly at Damascus. Their silence shows what people thought then of that crusade.[2]

1147

Of such wonderful strength was Raymond de Poitiers, then, by marriage, Prince of Antioch, and by birth uncle to the Queen of France, that he could bend an iron stirrup, and, one day passing on horseback under a gateway, whence hung a chain, he took the chain in both hands, and with his legs pressed the horse so prodigiously, that he stopped the animal at full gallop, and kept it there stock still, without its being able to move an inch in any direction. But he died soon, and only left a boy of the name of Bohemond, and his widow, to have some one to hold the rudder of government during the minority, and lead the troops, married Renard de Chatillon, of whom, soon again, says the Moslem;[3] but Christian chroniclers give her a less honourable motive.[4]

In Palestine, the immediate effect of the second crusade had been to show at once that there were

---

[1] Michaud: Hist., ii. 132.   [2] Id.:   Id., 191.
[3] Arab. Chron., 98.
[4] W. of Tyre: 16.—Bib. Crois., i. 144.

dissensions among the Christians; for, at a council at Acre, of the King of Jerusalem, with his knights and barons, and the King of France and the emperor, in the presence of the Queen of Jerusalem and the Christian ladies, neither among these was there the Queen of France, nor amongst those the Prince of Antioch, or the Counts of Edessa and Tripoli—sad omen, and so, as all question of besieging Aleppo was over, by Raymond of Antioch's absence, and scarce a word about Joscelin or Edessa hazarded, although the main object for calling of the council, was to decide whether to attack Aleppo or Edessa, it was resolved to besiege Damascus.

Here, for the first time, the Moslem writers distinctly mention the Knights of the Temple, and almost ever after name them with the Hospitallers. Scarcely either without the other. Indeed the historian of the crusades himself, is not much earlier; for he hardly speaks of the Templars before telling that their grand master had advanced to meet Louis VII, in Asia Minor.[1]

1148

Damascus, one of the holy cities of Islam, and famous for its fanaticism as well as its gardens of seven leagues and forest of orange trees, and almost every kind of fruit, must give up the story about

[1] Michaud: Hist., ii. 169.

Mahomet, since it cannot be possibly true; he having been never near it. Yet its wines are praised by Ezekiel.

The Christian camp was fine, and contained the chief nobility of France; small remnant of the vast army Louis VII. had led. As to the emperor and few Germans,[1] these behaved with magnificent bravery. The emperor's charge was irresistible. The French as became them. Why did the Christians then not conquer? No one knows. The Syrian lords are said to have given bad advice from corrupt motives. But treason and perfidy are always in the mouth of the vanquished.[2] On the Jordan or in Europe, treason is the cant at every failure. And it is to be generally observed that the Latin chroniclers always went with public opinion.[3] Fact is, the Christians retreated. Ayoub, father of Saladin, was the Moslem who directed the defence; and under him was the youth who was soon to be so distinguished a warrior,[4] which is perhaps the most remarkable event of the siege.[5] Dreadfully eloquent is the silence of annalists. So are the Moslems brief or mute while losing. The same spirit on both sides. No glory compensates

---

[1] Michaud: Hist., ii. 184.   [2] Id.:   Id.,   191.
[3] Id.:   Id.,   190.   [4] Arab. Chron., 97.
[5] Michaud : Hist., ii. 187.

reverses. The Christian had neglected to colonise Asia Minor and so had no retreat; which rendered a fault irreparable. Immense too the immorality. In part it was indiscretion; from St. Bernard's too easily receiving the vilest culprits. Louis VII. was a pattern of piety, and many of his leaders.[1] Too little of human prudence, too much of leaving all to Providence. In the first crusade were devotion and heroism; in the second, more of the cloister than of enthusiasm. Priests and monks had too much handling of affairs. Louis was but a martyr and common soldier; the emperor a champion utterly imprudent and presumptuous, which caused the loss of his beautiful army. Neither monarchs had extensive views, or the energy requisite for great actions. Nor heroic passions, or anything of the chivalrous, nor famous captains were in the second crusade. Also the forces of Christendom were divided. Not all were directed on Asia; but some to the north of Europe, against the Slavi; some to Spain, against the Moors; and that division contained many English knights. Normans from Sicily, were in Africa; and with them were many Hospitallers; at the very time the Christians were before Damascus. By no means did this second crusade represent the whole of Christendom

[1] Michaud: Hist., ii. 193.

like the first; and St. Bernard was blamed for sending the Christians to die in the East as if Europe could not afford them graves. Yet had he spoken with the eloquence of a mighty orator and the unction of a father of the Church of God, and he rejoiced that the public anger should rise rather against him—poor buckler of the Lord—than be guilty of disrespect to the Lord himself. Nor should those who (borrowing the words of the pious historian of the crusades)[1] speak of the "*unfortunate eloquence of St. Bernard*," do him the injustice of not avowing that it also impeded the usual enormity of that age, a massacre of the Jews.

Not long after that retreat from Damascus many Hospitallers fell in a great battle on the upper Orontes; when the Prince of Antioch was slain[2] and his head sent to Bagdad.[3] Several of the best seaports of his principality were taken by Noureddin. Young Joscelin, after various attempts to retake Edessa, was made prisoner and led captive to Aleppo and died there in misery and despair (partly it is said, from the consequence of his own vices), chained in a dungeon. It was early in 1148. What remained alive of Latin inhabitants, not of

[1] Michaud: Hist., ii. 132.   [2] Arab. Chron., 98.
[3] Michaud: Hist., ii. 202.

the town alone, but of the entire county of Edessa, decamped in a body, and sought refuge from Greeks and Turks, in Syria or Palestine, and being pursued in their flight, like the Israelites by Pharaoh, underwent a thousand dangers.

On the twenty-seventh of June, 1148, the Count of Tripoli was assassinated by an unknown hand; and all the towns of his dominions thrown into mourning.[1] In Jerusalem the queen mother was in open insurrection against her own son. Unfortunate Baldwin abandoned by France and Germany, and his whole kingdom falling to pieces, was obliged to besiege his own mother, who with her partizans had shut herself up in the tower of David![2] Which tower of David was afterwards pulled down by the Moslems, who admired the immensity of its blocks and how firmly they were fastened to each other, Cyclopean architecture.[3] To fill the chalice, two Turkish princes undertook to beleaguer the holy city, and would have succeeded, but for a few Templars and Hospitallers. Nor was Baldwin III., nor the Patriarch, nor the military orders unmoved, but sent the tidings to the Pope, who endeavoured to excite Christendom. But the recent crusade had caused discontent

1149

---

[1] Michaud: Hist., ii. 203.   [2] Id.:   Id., 203.
[3] Rothelin: MS.—Bib. Crois., i. 379.

VOL. I.   S

and even popular raillery, so that the sovereigns did not dare face new reproaches. The holy war had been ruinous to both nobility and clergy. Even St. Bernard refused his voice—holy warning! Yet on his death-bed Suger regretted he had not assisted the Eastern Christians. But how were they fallen! The Mahometan dynasties too, they had forgotten even the names of their once renowned monarchs. Their descendants were in the depths of Persia or some Indian province! Every ambitious emir set up for himself. Only each usurper offered an unmeaning homage to the Caliph of Bagdad, or Cairo, protesting he had sprung from the dust of his feet.[1] Nor did the Christians know that Aleppo and Damascus are the two keys of Syria; nor did they ever possess either.[2] But Noureddin built on his father's victories, and had much of the austere simplicity of the early caliphs, "uniting the noblest heroism with the profoundest humility," say the Arabian poets; "and when he prayed in the mosque, his subjects thought they beheld a sanctuary within a sanctuary."[3] Encouraging the sciences, cultivating letters, he likewise applied himself to making justice flourish in his states. His

1150

[1] Michaud: Hist., ii. 212. [2] Id.: Id., vide Note (1).
[3] Id.:   Id., 213.

people admired his clemency and moderation. The Christians extolled his generosity and signal heroism. He followed the example of Zengui in becoming the idol of his soldiers by his liberality to them and his zeal to combat the enemies of Islam. Noureddin then revived the fierce despotism that was nearly extinct in the East, and announced the Koran's triumph, and the destruction of the Christian colonies. Baldwin III., by trying 1153 to stop him, only afforded him an opportunity of displaying his courage. Ascalon was more than repaid by Noureddin's conquest of Damascus, always Moslem it is true, but now swayed by the most dangerous of Moslems; seduction and promises his weapons.

An interval of inaction that resembled peace, produced no event except the piratical expedition of Renaud de Chatillon (now Prince of Antioch) against tranquil Cyprus;[1] " an injustice that nearly equals what was perpetrated by Baldwin II. himself against the poor Arabs, who used to feed their flocks in the woods of Paneas by a treaty with him and his successors. His soldiers fell suddenly on the unarmed pastors, who fled in part; another part of them were killed, and their animals driven

---

[1] Michaud: Hist., ii. 219.

as booty to Jerusalem.[1] Some Flemings landing at Beyrout, formed an episode of disgrace.[2] Yet, in the midst of such scenes of calamity (what a lesson!), Baldwin married a niece of the emperor, as if all was at perfect peace[3]—nor was a stratagem wanting; the Hospitallers who had been dispensed from some formalities,[4] were entrapped into refusing what they were right in refusing, and accused of shooting at the Holy Sepulchre in scorn; which forced them to apply beyond sea—petty annoyance desired by their foes, not without a slight hope, that in the frequent succession of the Papacy, some Pope might come who was of their own and less partial to the Hospitallers, things which could scarcely be, since the Hospitallers had done no wrong, as this pitiful accusation itself proved; since their worst enemies could find but these nothings. So how unsullied indeed the Hospitallers must be, and how nobly had they merited of the Holy See[5] and all Christendom! Ecclesiastical spite! base ingratitude! Accuse them of not respecting the Holy Sepulchre; them, its best defenders![6] Had they not on all occasions risked their lives in its

[1] Michaud: Hist., ii. 220.   [2] Id.:   Id., 221.
[3] Id.:   Id., ii. 221.
[4] Vertot: i. 147.—Bosio: par. 1, lib. ii., anno 1154.
[5] Michaud: Hist., ii. 222.
[6] Vertot: i. 151.—Bosio: par. 1, lib. ii , anno 1155.

defence, with transcendent devotedness? The Patriarch was not ashamed to go with those stupid accusations; but the Pope had the honourable sagacity to turn him away, and do open justice to the injured and most meritorious Hospitallers.

Baldwin III. built another fortress against Egypt at Gaza, and gave it to the Templars.[1] But Noureddin and his Saracens set ravaging the lands around Antioch, while the sultan and Turcomans devastated the north of Mesopotamia. Baldwin the King, and two military orders, assisted the miserable Christians; but what way but this was left? So putting the entire multitude of fugitives, men, women, children, animals, baggage, and property of every sort, into the middle, he, the Hospitallers and Templars, kept up a continuous action with Noureddin during a long retreat, to keep him from the prey he was enraged to lose; but those noble warriors drove off the rabid tiger at last, and lodged the tremblers safe within Antioch. Still that absence of Baldwin nearly cost him his capital. The Egyptians going round by Damascus, attacked the Christians on that side, and advanced to the very walls of Jerusalem. In the evening, the citizens with consternation might see who hoped to take the city by escalade the next morning. Prowl-

[1] Vertot: i. 131.—Bosio: par. 1, lib. ii. [2] Id.: 133.—Id.

ing barbarians, they knew it had neither king nor garrison. Yet their very confidence made them lose the favourable moment. Had they stormed it then, they might have taken it; but waiting till morning was their ruin. The few Hospitallers and Templars that remained, took arms, and encouraged the inhabitants to resist; and, since their numbers were sufficient to man the walls, they rushed out, and finding the Moslem asleep, set fire to his tents, cut the ropes, and filled the whole camp with terror and death; so that he was struck with a panic, and ran away in remediless confusion, and flying towards Jericho, met the king and his cavalry on their way home, and these put five thousand to the sword. Of the rest, the Christians of Naplouse killed several, more still the peasantry, and a palsied residue, almost to a man, were drowned in the Jordan in a blind attempt to pass, swimming, and escape the Frank's steel.

1154 Baldwin, as reprisals for the intrusion, set off with Hospitallers and Templars and other Jerusalem forces, to assail Egypt by the coast; and after a long and sanguinary siege of seven months, took Ascalon on August 12th, 1154.[2] The Moslem garrison removing to El-Arish, was replaced by a

---

[1] Vertot: i. 135.—Bosio: par. 1, lib. ii.
[2] Id.: i. 118.—Id.: Id.

Christian one, chiefly Hospitallers. That same time, by a very inhuman and atrocious villany against his brother Mussulmen, Noureddin possessed himself of Damascus, to the vexation of the Judæa Latins, who were sorry to get so bad a neighbour.[1] And good right they had; for his first act was to gain a victory over them near Paneas; and among the spoils of their camp, was a magnificent tent for himself.[2] Damascus may balance Ascalon; so in this respect, the parties were quits.[3] The following year was terrible for earthquakes throughout the whole of Syria, principally Antioch, Tripoli, Hamah. In the last town, all the boys of a school were swallowed up the first shock, while the schoolmaster was out; and on his return, not a parent or relation came to inquire about one of them. Parents and children alike had shared the sad disaster.[4]

Noureddin had a present from the caliph, of seventy thousand pieces of gold, besides arms to the value of thirty thousand.[5] It ended by the Christians having to ask pardon of the Caliph of Cairo, to whom, at the same time, the Emperor of Constantinople sent to beg him to order his fleet to go

---

[1] Arab. Chron., 106. [2] Id., 109.
[3] Michaud: Hist., ii. 219. [4] Arab. Chron., 107.
[5] Id.:   Id.,   108.

against the King of Sicily, and that Egyptian fleet carried off the brother of the King of Cyprus, and transmitted him, as a present, to that same Greek Emperor. Fine treasons to each other amongst these Christian princes! Noureddin had tents enough, since, beside that fine one taken from the Franks, the Greek Emperor sent him a silk tent of considerable value, and several rich dresses and jewels.[1] The acquisition of Ascalon caused more joy through Christendom than any event since that of Jerusalem itself, and all knew what an active hand the Grand Master of the Hospitallers had in it; so that whether he was personally present or not—and perhaps he was not, seeing his advanced age of above eighty—matters little; for Baldwin was his docile pupil, and to Raymond's advice the fortunate resolution, whole conduct, and victorious conclusion of that gallant siege, were universally ascribed, and may very likely have been the cause of that splendid eulogium which Anastasius IV.[2] made of the order, repeating what his predecessors had said before, and even adding new marks of distinction, and rarer privileges: "Since you, my brethren, make so excellent a use of your wealth, in hospitably receiving pilgrims of every nation, and

[1] Arab Chron., 109.
[2] Vertot: i. 146.—Bosio: par. 1, lib. ii., anno 1154.

defending all Christendom, of what lowest or most exalted rank soever; therefore it is that I excuse you from paying tithes, and forbid any bishop to publish interdict on any church in your property, though the whole country round be perhaps interdicted; that no bishop can interfere with you, but any priest be in safety within your territories, if you take him under your protection; and the same too of laymen—that they cannot be touched by any ecclesiastical tribunal, while protected by you— and that you owe spiritual obedience to no one but the Holy See and your own chapters. And if the ordinary bishop refuse to ordain any one a priest whom you propose, I, the Pope, authorize you to apply for that purpose to any other bishop you choose; and we precisely prohibit the receiving any member of your order into another, under pretence of leading a life of greater sanctity. And let the Hospitallers for ever elect their grand masters in perfect and entire liberty. We confirm all that has been done, and all that shall ever be done in their favour; nor are any allowed to take them by surprise, or attempt to force them to anything under any pretext whatever." No doubt this soothing language, from such a high personage as the Pope was then, was extremely grateful to the dying Raymond; but it prepared much enmity to the Hospitallers.

Perhaps then, for the first time, the clergy began to look upon them with an evil eye. To lose the tithes of such great landlords over the whole world was a severe blow. But what wounded their pride still more was, that while the kings and princes of Jerusalem and Antioch, and other distinguished grandees, were subject to priests, patriarchs, and bishops, these were openly deprived of all authority over the Hospitallers. Nor were the Templars without sharing in the same odium. But that of churchmen is proverbially tenacious, and waits to ripen well before it shows itself. A malicious sneer at their riches, and with a malevolence quite characteristic of irritated ecclesiastics, they stuck up some arrows on their steeple, as if they had been shot at, or were in fear of their lives from the Hospitallers opposite; and observed with malignity that the Hospitallers had erected that magnificent edifice to attract admirers more than the Holy Sepulchre directly facing it. These little symptoms of ill-will sufficed at the beginning;[1] but soon after gave rise to the fable of William of Tyre, who had a brother a bishop, and became a bishop himself; fable that has

1158

---

[1] Vertot: i. 152.—Bosio: par. 1, lib. ii.

come down to our own day. On all occasions malignity—the worst construction put upon all their actions—an iniquitous motive always supposed. That eulogy and distinction—much more, that they merited them—were the primitive cause of the injustice suffered by the various military orders often, from that age to the present—all of them wounded in their original head. Belied were the Hospitallers; but still more relentlessly were the unfortunate Templars to be soon assailed, and at last brought living to the stake. Yet it was not the income of the Hospitallers or Templars that merited investigation, but how that income was employed![1] on which true question the Hospitallers (and probably Templars too) might have defied research. Most of those favours had been also granted by former Popes; and whatever the far by-gone generations might have been, or the future were to be, the Popes of that age had unrivalled power over almost all Christians; and for that very reason, considerable influence over the Paynim too. But it appears, the proverbial hatred of ecclesiastics had been growing with a silent growth; perhaps some unknown particulars might have kept it hidden. But not ungrateful were the Pontiffs, who would not

[1] Vertot: i. 156.—Bosio: par. 1, lib. ii.

authorize clerical avarice or haughtiness; and Raymond was revered generally as a virtuous man, and fearing God. Nor did his knights fail to set an example in Spain; which soon created its own knighthood in imitation.[1] If not his direct, the Spanish orders were his collateral descendants; and who can tell but they may yet rejoin their common parent, before falling into the ocean to which they all tend? Would it not be finer (and safer likewise) for them to unite and approach their ultimate delta in one broad stream? Perhaps, conjoint strength protracting their existence, they might erect another opulent Flanders in Lord knows what distant part of the world! Calatrava was formed in 1158; and from it the two others in some sort derived, that of Saint Jago in 1175, Alcantara in 1212,[2] all three with the Norman characteristics of singular bravery and religion. It is not of them alone, but of all human institutions it is true, that in a succeeding period they somewhat decline from the purity and fervour of the first. Nor does impartial history affirm that any of the six military orders were ever remarkable for degeneracy. Was it not rather for their riches they have been attacked?[3]

---

[1] Vertot: i. 157.—Bosio: par. 1, lib. iii., anno 1159.
[2] Id.: 163.—Hallam: Middle Ages, i. 279.—Mariana, etc.
[3] Vertot: i. 164.

Raymond is said to have been a Frenchman, and probably he was born in France, though that is not proved, but his parents were Italian, and the family Del Poggio, its original name, translated, or mistranslated into Du Puys, was from Lucca, and Lucchese antiquaries still boast of him as their countryman.[1] "In Avenione et Parisiis et aliis partibus Franciæ" (says the Juramentum Fidelitatis of 1331, still extant in the Lucca archives), "are living the Del Poggio, Lucanis civibus; who therefore, not to lose their privileges, claim to swear allegiance through their attorney." In every respect it could not but have been a flattering consolation to Raymond, in these his last days, that a Pope who, as a Tuscan, was his own countryman, wrote a bull, as highly laudatory of his order and himself as what Innocent II. had written; and if that bull of Eugenius be lost, yet the substance of it, and a copy of Raymond's bye-laws, which it contained, are come down through another of the Popes;[2] and that they passed for a rule was no fault of him, nor of the Pontiff either.

And here I have to prepare for leaving my best of guides, the mild, intelligent, and most conscien-

---

[1] Cod. Dipl. Geros., i. 335.—Bosio: par. 1, lib. ii. anno 1160.
[2] P. A. Paoli: 219.—Platina: iii. 23.—Appendix, xiv., first and fifth paragraphs.

tious P. A. Paoli, who had learned from his uncle to pluck the very heart of truth from the compilation he had left him, and to continue in his path. Muratori had the well-regulated library of Modena, but the undiscovered ocean of the Vatican, and the whole world, were to be the field of the diplomatist of the order of Malta, who for a considerable period completed his books, and died. After extracting the facts from each document, the nephew threw away the outside, and placing these essential facts so as to explain and elucidate each other, produced an impregnable whole, as far as he went, and then he too died. And now this unworthy pen is at the third operation, a little history from their mighty labours. But though the nephew's short volume be ended, the diplomatist's columns still continue, and I mean to try to keep close to them. P. Ant. Paoli only attended to those earliest of the order's annals, defaced by fables, which, with his aid, I have got through. After having been shown so far, the rest is easier, and with the diplomatic help, not difficult, and for that reason more adapted to me.

1159

The Del Poggio had fiefs and lordships in Tuscany, as early as the Countess Matilda. The Del Poggio were marquises and dukes, and always sign themselves with such titles in several papers still existing, as far back as the tenth century. A

Poggio was Bishop of S. Miniato, in 1038.[1] But wherever the grand master's birth-place was, or however illustrious his ancestors, he added new laurels to all that belonged to him. Nor the denying his having been the founder of his order, or its earliest legislator, is at all to try to deprive him of his fair fame, which needs no other support than its own. Far indeed was it from him to wish to tarnish Gerard's merits, or foresee that malicious fables were to make him and his great predecessor rivals; or rather, to throw our founder completely into the shade; whereas Raymond's loftiest of desires was to be his follower in worth as station. That his Hospitallers were showing themselves deserving of the name, and his royal pupil gathering honour, soothed his respected death-bed, when, valiant and saintly octogenarian, he expired placidly at Jerusalem in the first month of 1160.[2]

1160

---

[1] Borghini Discorsi: ii. 421.
[2] Cod. Dipl. Geros., i. 335.—Vertot: i. 170, &c.—Bosio: par. 1, lib. ii. anno 1160.

CHAPTER V.

In Raymond's place immediately came in 1160 Sir Otteger Balben,[1] a French gentleman of Dauphinèe, celebrated in the order for having engaged Palestine to decide in favour of the orthodox Pope in the great schism, as well as to declare itself an hereditary, and not elective monarchy; so Alexander the Third's legate was invited into Jerusalem, and Baldwin III. dying, from an ignorant Syrian doctor,[2] or poisoned as some aver,[3] and leaving no children, his brother Almericus succeeded, and was anointed, and crowned on the eighteenth of February, in 1162,[4] and the ceremony scarcely over, the Grand Master, Sir

1162

---

[1] Vertot: ii. 171.—Bosio, ut supra.
[2] Cod. Dipl. Geros., i. 363.—Michaud: Hist., ii. 223.
[3] Vertot: ii. 171.
[4] Cod Dipl. Geros., i. 365.—Bosio: par. 1, lib. ii. anno 1162.

Otteger Balben[1] was followed by another as old, from the same province, Sir Arnaud de Comps, who likewise, after a few months, was replaced by Sir Gilbert d'Assaly, or De Sailly,[2] whom some call an Englishman,[3] and some from Tyre;[4] yet both may be true, if he was from English parents, and born in Tyre, or brought thither in his childhood; however all that is quite uncertain; mere conjecture might suggest Sir Gilbert d' Estley.[5] Certainly his making for England as his last refuge, like a hare to its form, seems to denote his fatherland.[6] He was too unfortunate for any nation to be very desirous of owning him. Notwithstanding what has been written, it is most certain, from the incontrovertible evidence of three documents extant, that D'Assaly was Grand Master in January, 1163.[7] Now De Comps could have but 1163 eight months at most, which however were enough to lay the seeds of a calamitous undertaking. For having accompanied Almeric in an excursion into Egypt, it was attended with good success, the Moslems not having been able to bear the shock

[1] Cod. Dip. Geros., i. 335.—Bosio : par. 1, lib. ii., anno 1163.
[2] Vertot : ii. 193.
[3] Cod. Dipl. Geros., i. 336.—Num. xxxviii., clxiv.
[4] Id. : Num. clxxxvii.
[5] Sir Harris Nicholas : Synopsis, i. 32.
[6] Cod. Dipl., 335, 336.—Bosio.—Hoveden ibi.
[7] Id : Id.—Num. xxxviii.

VOL. I. T

of the Hospitallers and Templars,[1] which led to peace, and an alliance to defend that land from a threatened invasion; and the utmost generosity on the part of that caliph, who made splendid presents to his Latin allies, and remunerated their services well, " to send them home content," was followed by a solemn treaty between them and the Egyptians, by which these were to pay one hundred thousand gold crowns to the King of Jerusalem. The barren Judea appeared to him a sorry sight, and a sway poor and narrow compared to the fat and fertile banks of the Nile; discussing the probability of Jerusalem becoming again subject to Cairo, as it had been before Godfrey's conquest; and if the aged grand master encouraged those wanderings of the royal mind, what might be pardonable to the fervent imagination of youth, should not to the cold season of judgment and duty.

Almeric pored over the dangerous thought, and that it would be better for him to seize the Pharaohs, than wait for the Pharaohs to come and seize him. So he sent ambassadors to the Greek Emperor Manuel, whose niece he had married (like his brother in 1149), and her uncle encouraged his projects against Egypt, and offered

[1] Vertot: ii. 185.—Bosio, par. i., lib. 2, anno 1163.

him a fleet,[1] and unveiling his breast to Assaly, now Grand Master, he met with an easy, perhaps immoral assent.[2] Even if the entire political plan did not succeed, of the utter conquest of Cairo, and to make it a provincial town, dependent on Jerusalem, still great riches would be acquired by the pillage of all Egypt. Yet the grand master could do nothing without a general council of his knights; and that his opinion would be theirs, would be extremely problematic; so, to gild the pill, it was accompanied by the royal offer, that if they took Heliopolis,[3] the first city the Christian army would besiege in Egypt, and finest, except the Cairos—it would be given to the Hospitallers; and of the beauty of Heliopolis and its signal advantages, which would soon render it the centre of European commerce, Assaly spoke at great length, and how fit a residence it would be for the order, if ever it was driven from Jerusalem; as we see had already become a possibility.[4] These false reasonings, and probably some not unambitious feeling in the younger knights, and the influence of the grand master and his partisans, checked every opposition from the elders of the assembly;[5] so, shut-

[1] Michaud: Hist., ii. 232.
[2] Vertot: ii. 193.
[3] Cod. Dipl. Geros., Num. xlvii. Num. xlviii.
[4] Vertot: ii. 195.   [5] Vertot: ii. 196.

ting their ears to further attempt at calm discussion, the majority with loud cries for war voted an unlimited credit of money for its expenses.[1]

At this, Almeric made sure of the Templars. But he was wrong, for they absolutely refused to consider the matter at all, as quite contrary not only to the statutes of their rule, but to every sentiment of honour and justice. The more so that a Templar had been one of the signataries to the treaty to be broken, and had been admitted to kiss the caliph's hand on it, being the first Christian who ever had that honour, or been allowed to enter that sacred, gloomy, rich, mysterious palace.[2] For that it was of direct obligation to keep faith with all men, even Pagans; whereas here it was proposed to begin with a most flagitious act, the breach of a treaty to which they had so lately sworn and affixed their formal signature. It ended by the Grand Master of the Temple and all his order declining to take part in any such enterprise, and that they would remain quietly in their own quarters. And so they did; and Almeric, with his army and the Hospitallers, marched without them.

1167

It is not to be supposed there was much of the

[1] Vertot: ii. 197.—Bosio: par. 1, lib. iii., anno 1165.
[2] Michaud: Hist., ii. 230.—Vertot: ii. 188.—Bosio: par. 1, lib. iii., anno 1166 and 1168.

spiritual in the strife between the caliphs; though he of Bagdad blessed Noureddin, and of Cairo cursed him. To the vulgar it was religion, and had the pomp and circumstance of a holy war; yet Noureddin, in the bottom of his heart, might exclusively desire to extend his temporal kingdom. Though his thoughts were principally turned towards the Nile, yet from desultory conflicts with Christians he never ceased. In a surprise in Syria, he threw himself on a horse still picketed, and might have been either taken or killed, but for a Curd,[1] who lost his own life in assisting him. And when at some distance, he was advised to retire further, or that he might be attacked by the Franks: "I swear by the living God not to lie under a roof before revenging Islam and myself for this indignity," was his reply. On another occasion,[2] to one of his own pay-masters he said, "Give my soldiers the indemnity they ask, simply, instead of swearing them, or examining their accounts at all, without heeding the sum. What right have you to curtail my generosity?" And when his ministers, seeing his immense expenses, hinted at seizing the church property, he received the advice with serious displeasure, and answered, "Why deprive them of

---

[1] Arab. Chron., 110.   [2] Id., 110.

their revenues—these who fight for me at all times, even when I am asleep in my bed—to enrich people who only know how to fight for me when I am leading them, and whose arrows sometimes hit and sometimes miss? It is from the prayers of the little that I expect my victories; for is it not writ, '*From the little you shall draw your subsistence and your strength?*' It would be a grievous injustice in me to touch what was given them by others, learned holy saints who founded, and with what belonged to them endowed, the establishments that every good Mahometan ought to revere!"

To prepare himself for a campaign, he used to sleep on the hard bare ground, and abstain from all sensual pleasures. Mesopotamia, most of Syria, Egypt, and Arabia the Happy, composed his vast dominions when he died at Damascus[1] (of a quinsey, at fifty-six), in some hole of a room, nearly without assistance, which he shunned. Moslems say he deserved a place next the four earliest of Mahomet's followers.[2] He adhered faithfully to his marriage vow. Every day he read a chapter of the Alcoran, besides his long fervent prayers. Once, on a representation to increase his frugal expenses, he replied, "Not even for my

---

[1] Arab. Chron., 152.   [2] Id., 153.

beloved wife will I incur the risk of falling into hell's fire. The money does not belong to me, but to all Mahometans. As for me, I am extremely poor, and will not, to please her, become an unfaithful treasurer. However," added he, softening, "I possess three little shops, which I let out to rent at Edessa, and she may take them if she likes."[1] A learned and pious person having observed in a letter to him that field sports were over futile for so wise a true believer, Noureddin, highly hurt at the reproach, wrote back with his own hand: "In the presence of God, it is not to amuse myself, but to keep in training myself and my horse; for, often close to the enemy, we must be ready day and night, winter and summer; and it is a holy war, a war for Islam and the Lord's self. Repose is frequently quite necessary to the soldiery, and then, likewise, they must be kept in exercise. I ought to give the example, and be always prepared to mount on horseback, continually on our guard. Our horses must be rendered docile to the rider's voice; and for this reason accustomed to it, and know him well personally; and before the Almighty, that is my only motive for sometimes playing at mall."[2]

He had much studied jurisprudence, and loved its

---

[1] Arab. Chron., 154.   [2] Id., 155.

purity, and strictly conformed himself to its injunctions. Once he was cited, and instantly went to the tribunal or cadi, and said, "I come to defend my cause, do towards me as towards any one else." And when, after a patient trial, the sentence was given in his favour, he added, turning to the cadi and court: "I knew that my accuser was wrong; but I am glad to prove it was not my desire to injure him. At present, that it is clear justice is on my side, I wish to make him a free gift of that land, therefore I call you to witness that I give it up to him."[1] The reverse of all the Moslem sovereigns of his day, he forbade the use of torture, under any pretext. Progress, that no one would have expected at that time in such a quarter.[2] He was, indeed the first Mahometan that ever erected a court of appeal, and he presided there himself, twice a-week, in presence of his cadis; on which his greatest *effendi*, who had been guilty of much extortion, called his lawyers, and bade them instantly satisfy every one of his creditors, for that anything was preferable to appearing at the bar before Noureddin and the judges. At which he shed tears of joy, and exclaimed, "Praise be to God that our subjects do

---

[1] Arab. Chron.,157.   [2] Id., 158.

right of themselves, without its being necessary for us to constrain them to it."[1] The great object of his life—in appearance at least—was to wage war on the Christians; the decree of God against which he never attempted to struggle.[2] Also on heretics; and in the Fatimites he saw not so much their Mahometanism as their heresy, and persecuted this, rather more than he loved and revered that. With regard to free thinkers, or the sect who called themselves *philosophers*, he only followed his father in punishing them severely, and with extreme opprobrium, as atheists, and had them scourged on an ass through the whole city.[3] Towards such he was inexorable, saying, "Why then should we punish robbers and highwaymen, if not those who sap the very foundations of all religion?" Having found a piece of money too much in the accounts, he gave it back to the treasurer, saying, "I know you will think it a trifle, for which very reason I beg of you to accept it, since your shoulders are less weak than mine, and I am afraid it might be an injustice that would draw on me an affair with the Omnipotent God."[4]

He was the first to render military benefices hereditary; small fiefs, or colonies, to receive

[1] Arab. Chron., 161. [2] Id., 162.
[3] Id., 164, 170. [4] Id., 159.

veterans, and furnish recruits.[1] Many hospitals, and particularly the great hospital at Damascus, were founded by him; so vast and wealthy an establishment for all Mahometans in general, rich or poor, without distinction, that, "once asking," says the historian of the Atabecs, "for a doctor, I was directed to the great hospital, where the doctor wrote me a recipe and said, 'In a moment my apprentice will bring it to you.' To which I replied, ' But, Sir, thanks be to Heaven, I can pay for my own drugs, without trespassing on the property of the poor.' On which, he looked at me steadily: 'O Sir, I have no doubt but you can do without our drugs; but here no one disdains to accept Noureddin's benefits. In the name of God, I assure you that emirs and sovereign princes send to this hospital for their medicine, and never pay.' 'I was ignorant of that.' 'It is that his desire was to be useful to all Moslems, rich or poor!'"[2] He also erected many khans, or caravan-serais,[3] as well as forts, fortresses, and mosques, and monasteries for sophis; and he it was who erected that most useful invention, pigeon posts,[4] and magnificent colleges for every sort of science, which, at that time meant more than theology, or mere

[1] Arab. Chron., 165.   [2] Id., 167.
[3] Id., 167.   [4] Id., 150.

poetry, and comments on the Alcoran, but much chemistry, mathematics, medicine, law, astronomy, mining, architecture, at least.[1] Nevertheless, few were the mourners for his death, since there was something haughty and despotic in his manners. He scarcely permitted people to sit down in his presence, before he had told them so to do, except that on perceiving a doctor of law, or sophi, or faquir, he used to rise to do them honour, and make them sit down close by his side, as one of his own family, and converse with them amicably. The Mahometan Prince of Moussul, by proclamation, told his subjects to divert themselves, and drink as much as they liked, seeing Noureddin was dead.[2] During his battle near Tripoli, when his right wing broke, he dismounted, and prostrate was heard praying fervently: "O my Sovereign Master, do not abandon thy servant, for it is thine own Divine religion I protect." Nor did he cease humbling himself, and weeping and rolling his face in the dust, all bathed as he was with tears, till God heard the voice of his supplication, and sent him victory.[3]

Such was the manner of man had sent Saladin to Egypt, under pretence of assisting the Cairo

[1] Arab. Chron., 168.   [2] Id., 171.
[3] Id.,   120.

Caliphs, but in reality to destroy them. They were but lifeless idols, or like the *Rois faineans* of France. Their viziers were their *Mairs du palais*. This state of things led to the double invitation of both Noureddin and Christians. And finally to their honourable dismissal; after Almeric's having received a thousand pieces of gold a-day, besides feeding his pack-animals, as had been stipulated before, and other advantages to "the *Hospitallers*, who formed the nerve of Christian armies."[1] And indeed Noureddin's army likewise returned to Syria, except that, as the youngest of his emirs, Saladin, with his permission, remained in the Egyptian service.[2]

1168 It was but a triumphal march to Almeric when he returned again to Egypt; and after small opposition, he took Heliopolis. Before reaching it, he had a visit from a former acquaintance, to whom, as he entered the royal tent, Almeric said: "Hail to the Emir Schems-helkelafe!" "Hail to the perfidious king!" answered the Emir. "Yes! For if your intentions are upright, why are you here?" "I was told that the vizier's son had married Saladin's sister." "That is false; but even if it were true, that is no infraction of the

[1] Arab. Chron., 116.
[2] Id., 122, 125, 126, 135, 137, 139.

treaty!" "Then truth is," replied Almeric, "that the Franks from beyond sea have forced me!" "Well, what do they want?" "Two millions of pieces of gold." "I'll take your answer to the vizier, and do you tarry here."[1] But instead of Almeric's tarrying, he proceeded to under the walls of Heliopolis, where the vizier's grandson commanded. "Where are we to encamp?" asked the Christian. "On the points of our lances," replied the young man. "Do you think Heliopolis is a cheese good to eat?" "Yes! and Cairo shall be the cream!"[2] But Heliopolis, when taken, was cruelly sacked and partly burned, before delivering it up to the Hospitallers. This drove the vizier to despair; and it was clear the Egyptian army could make no available defence.[3] So the caliph, in his consternation, had nothing for it but to apply to Noureddin as his only protection, and added to his lamentable letter of entreaty an enclosure of the tresses of all the women in his harem, cut off in the extremity of their sorrow, to testify it and stimulate his pity to the utmost haste. "They are the hair of my wives, who implore you to save them from the outrages of the Franks"—reference to the angelic song in the Koran: *Glory be to Him who*

[1] Arab. Chron.,128. [2] Id., 129.
[3] Id., 130.—Bosio: par. 1, lib. iii., anno 1168.

has given the beard to man for ornament, and her long hair to woman."[1] And Noureddin, the moment he received the letter, wrote a command to his best general to take the flower of his troops instantly, with the greatest possible despatch, round by the Dead Sea to Cairo. The difficulty was to stop the Christian till the succour could arrive; and to do so, a desperate expedient[2] was resorted to, which exceeds by far what patriotism has displayed of most terrible in our own times.

Had the Frank shown humanity at Heliopolis, he most assuredly had taken Cairo without the least resistance.[3] But, from the moment the Caireens were reduced to desperation, they changed character and feeling like those who fight with a halter round their necks, resolved to resist unto death, and manned their walls with most formidable energy. Which was represented in glowing colours by that same emir to Almeric, who, whatever their courage, would not let himself be intimidated, but moved on. The very same authority that rates both the Cairos of that age at seven millions—three for the old, and four the new— estimates Pekin at less than two.[4] Old Cairo stood on the east bank

[1] Arab. Chron., 130.
[2] Michaud: Hist., ii. 236.   [3] Id: Id., ii. 237.
[4] Comm. Geograph.

of the Nile; the new, where it yet stands; and fortified round—in a circuit twenty-two miles (say some) and others, thirty.[1] So those of the new joined their rulers in an invitation to all of the old, to remove instantly within fortifications, that at least had the river between them and the enemy. Perhaps (deducting exaggerations) old Cairo was the largest and most thickly populated city ever in the world, after New Cairo, ancient Thebes, and Babylon on the Euphrates. Old Cairo was also called Babylon,[2] and outdid and destroyed Memphis.[3] It was in Old Cairo our Saviour spent part of his earthly life.[4] Would the citizens of that unfortunate place obey such a mandate, and, abandoning all their property, quit their native dwellings, men, women and children—every human being? Had the world till then in any age produced such examples of self-devotedness? To hurry Noureddin the more, he in the same despatch had been offered the third of all Egypt,[5] and full pay and every necessary for his army, if it got in time to save the government. The army consisted of two thousand picked Turks, and six thousand Turcomans,[6] all on valuable horses. Noureddin

[1] Comm. Geograph, ii. 189.
[2] Michaud: Hist., ii. 34.   [3] Michaud: Orient, vi. 19.
[4] Id.:   Id., Orient, vi. 20.   [5] Arab. Chron., 130.
[6] Arab. Chron., 131.

had accompanied them to Rosselma, edge of the desert, and, on taking leave of them, had given each soldier twenty pieces of gold over and above his pay; and besides splendid accoutrements to the commander-in-chief for himself, handed him as credit for the public service (to face fortuitous calls) a sum of two hundred thousand gold pieces. Human wisdom and generosity could go no further. No other Mussulman since the commencement of the crusades, had been able to go to any such expense.[1] But is all soon enough? Let them have pinions! Not the third of Egypt, but will not the whole of it be his, when he has his lieutenant there? Whatever be Saladin's Egyptian title, he to Noureddin will be but his lieutenant.[2]

An advance of Almeric produced a return of the confidential emir, who dwelt anew on the resolution of those of Cairo; and thus the vizier had bid him reason: "If your Majesty even take it, much blood at least will be lost—neither you nor I can be sure of victory—on both sides numbers of brave men must infallibly be slain; then is it not better for both of us to agree in sparing such slaughter by your receiving what I offer—four hundred thousand pieces of gold?" Some assure one

---

[1] Arab. Chron., 132.   [2] Id., 139.

million. The king assented, and receiving one hundred thousand, allowed a delay for the rest.[1] But to please the Franks, he was forced to a further advance; and, though a carrier pigeon arrived to the caliph with a note that Noureddin's forces were on the road and would arrive within fifteen days, yet the assault might be sooner; and if the tidings reached the Christians, immediate.[2] Almeric had now pitched by the lake, scarce two leagues from Old Cairo. New Cairo was indeed fortified, and might stand a severe siege; but the old was defenceless, and the soldiers at all events might have every comfort there, during several weeks of rest; and even fearfully pillage it, before going to assault the new. But the fatal Emir Schems-elk-helafè entered again the royal tent. It was night-fall, and he led the king to the canvass door and lifted it: "You see those immense flames that mount up to heaven?" "I do!" "Well, it is Old Cairo on fire, I lighted it myself, by the caliph's and vizier's orders. I had twenty thousand bottles of naphtha sprinkled everywhere on the heaps of wood and other inflammable matter; and lit it at once in hundreds of places with

---

[1] Arab. Chron., 131.   Ibn-Alatir, 151.

ten thousand matches. It has been resolved that whole city shall perish for ever and ever. There is no possible remedy. So you must retire." "You are right," said the dejected monarch. And on the same moment began his retreat, lest his own camp should be burned also.[1] Slowly he moved backwards and stopped beyond Heliopolis several days,[2] while the Hospitallers[3] evacuated the city given to them with so much pomp one month before.[4] But it was idle waiting. No transitory flame was that which he had left. Not an inhabitant remained to try to extinguish it, nor by any mortal was an attempt ever made to put out that mighty fire. Had there been, it would have been in vain; the pitiless flames were at full liberty to burn themselves out; not a roof, scarce a wall was left standing, the conflagration lasted fifty-four days. In lieu of a fine city, there is now a sorry village named Forstat; where it is possible that some of those black, half-shattered columns shown in the mosque may have survived the fire, and been afterwards furnished with gables and a roof; and still more is it not quite impossible but where our

---

[1] Arab. Chron., 130. [2] Id., 132.
    Vertot: ii. 205.—Bosio: par. 1, lib. iii., anno 1169.
[4] Cod. Dipl. Geros., 448.—Num. xlvii. and xlviii.

infant Saviour and his blessed mother sojourned, may exist; for it is a cavern or grotto.[1] Old Cairo had an amazing quantity of splendid palaces as the residences of the opulent Egyptian patricians, which rank appeared to have existed then, though there has been scarce a shadow of any such in Egypt for centuries. Its being an open town, made it more convenient for horses; and besides it contained the chief charitable and religious establishments, and its streets were neither so narrow nor so crowded and suffocating as New Cairo: but above all, there was more liberty; as not exactly under the despot's eye, nor every moment subject to his caprices, so that a menaced grandee could escape into the country or desert or Upper Egypt; and the same might be said of other classes respecting the custom-house officers, or tax-gatherers and the multifarious tools of a bad administration; as well as avoiding their inevitable consequences, frequent frantic and bloody revolutions. Once that nest of aristocracy is in cinders, tyranny may reign rampant over the whole land of Egypt. Nothing to arrest the tyrant; all moral restraint at an end, and vice and brute force are everything.[2] *Beware of Egypt* was scriptural; but into whatever effeminacy or

[1] Michaud: Orient., vi. 20.   [2] Id.: Hist., ii. 240.

profligate manners Syria or Palestine had fallen, the warning was as applicable in 1168 as in the period of the Old Testament.

One other call from the emir, before Almeric can get off, who had received a hundred thousand pieces of gold in part payment of the sum promised him; and shall he return home with them?[1] " The vizier begs you to send him back half the money."

"Assuredly." " Upon my word, your majesty is extremely generous, having an army that makes you master of our lives!" "It is, I am very certain," replied the King, " that your having spoken to me in such a way is proof something extraordinary has happened." "You are right," rejoined the Emir; "for Noureddin's troops have passed our frontiers; so you are in no safety here any longer. The vizier advises you to depart. We mean to respect the treaty. The cash we have, added to this from you, may suffice to satisfy Noureddin's general; and as to our debt to you, we'll pay it when we can." " Just as you like," answered the King; " I shall at all times endeavour to be useful to you; you have only to command." And with most melancholy reflections, the Christian continued his

[1] Arab. Chron., 132.

retreat to Palestine. For was not evident irony in the vizier's words? The king himself had broken a treaty; and why expect the Egyptians to keep theirs? The whole world shall hear of the retreat of the Christians. Villany has been punished, and perjury; and the Egyptians rejoice at it.[1] One moiety of the gold pieces was given back to them, and the other being nearly expended, this military chest would hardly suffice to keep his men alive as far as Jerusalem ; and the Constantinopolitan fleet shipwrecked![2] Not only his dreams, but all his best-founded hopes had vanished.

Nor were D'Assaly's ideas brighter; for where was Heliopolis? City, commerce, maritime power, immense revenue, sovereign rights over a vast tract of most fertile country comprising fifty villages, nearly a million of inhabitants, handed over like so many beasts of burden—all had disappeared ; and what remained to the order was a debt of four hundred thousand crowns, prodigious sum for that time.[3]

Pushed hard by Noureddin's Turcomans all along that disastrous road, when Almeric reached his metropolis, it was with an army frightfully reduced

[1] Arab. Chron., 133.
[2] Vertot : ii. 204.—Bosio : par. 1, lib. iii., anno 1169.
[3] Id. ii. 205.

by desertion, sickness, famine, and with the shame of having broken a solemn treaty, and undertaken an unjust and ill-planned enterprise.[1] On the miserable grand-master most of the public blame fell; so that this, added to his self-reproaches and those of his brethren, forced him at length to abdicate against the advice of the king, patriarch, and a large majority of his own knights; and hurrying to Normandy, he did homage to Henry II. at Rouen, and embarked at Dieppe for England, and was lost, for the ship foundering at sea, he was not among the eight saved.[2] In his place, in 1170,[3] was substituted, as *locum-tenens*, Sir Castus for a few months, and then Sir Roger de Moulin for a few months, during which the knights in full chapter drew up a memorial to the Pope, asking him to decide whether they should take back D'Assaly (of whose death, so far off, they did not know), or elect a new one;[4] but that during the interregnum, both Castus and Moulin, though only *locum-tenens*, should be called grand master in the deeds, is only following the Syrian custom; as, during young

[1] Michaud: Hist., ii. 240.
[2] Vertot: ii. 207.—Hoveden.—Bosio: par. 1, lib. iii., anno 1169.
[3] Cod. Dipl. Geros., vol. i., 336.—Num. li.
[4] Id. Num. clxxxvi.

Bohemond's minority, his guardian was called in the deeds Prince of Antioch.[1] So Moulin is called grand master in a deed still extant of 1173, though in reality he did not attain that dignity till several years later. It is thus Sebastian Paoli puts history on a fair agreement with the incontestible documents; and is he not right?[2] But in 1170 1173 we come to the regular election. Nevertheless, let Sir Castus have his place among the grand masters as sixth by courtesy; and with time Du Moulin will have his too, but in reality.

The seventh Grand Master, then, is Sir Robert, or Joubert, or De Osbert; greatly celebrated, years before, for the great ability with which he executed the plan of Fulk, King of Jerusalem, in getting over Poitiers, to espouse the young Princess of Antioch—which cleverness and royal confidence had been ever since followed up, and at length led to this remuneration. Of what country he was, is uncertain, so any may be given. It is likely that the French historian would have told us if 1173 he was from France, and a Joubert; that being his surname, and Robert, as in the Italian version, his

[1] Michaud: Hist., ii. 47.
[2] Cod. Dipl. Geros., i.—Num. lii.
[3] Id.   i., 337.

Christian. By some he is called Robert, by others Roger or Richard, Josberto or Osberto, Jesberto, or Zeberto, which equally prove it a surname; and, certainly, to translate Osberto, Osbert is less change than Joubert. So, he may very well have been a Sir Robert Osbert of the family of that Norman who was Bishop of Exeter, in 1102.[1] And, indeed, it is but fair to indulge such surmises, that agree with his being at the Court of England, under Henry I;[2] for it is quite remarkable that, where there were so many English-Norman knights, there should seem to be so few grand masters of that nation. There must have been many, but their names are disguised in the translations. But whatever country he was of by birth, he was a very charitable person, and made bye-laws for the sick, as well as Raymond; one of which, still extant, is that white bread be given to the poor gentlemen, or "*Seigneurs les povres.*" And reading the deed about bread, and all those precautions, we ought to keep in mind that it was in a country often the seat of war, and a city ever threatened with a siege, where the knights, and their healthy visitors too, might be

---

[1] Sir Harris Nicolas: Synopsis, ii. 846.
[2] Vertot: i. 105.

reduced to eat inferior or black bread; but the sick got it white, and of pure wheat.[1] He signs himself *Jobert*, in that MS. from the Vatican. Could he have used so ill-chosen a phrase as *seigneurs*, almost a sneer, if applied to mendicants? But they were crusaders—his own equals or superiors.[2]

The great historian of the order says he died in 1179, from pure sorrow at seeing what ruin was impending over the Holy Land.[3] Vertot would have it he fell prisoner and was starved to death.[4] Hoveden is Vertot's authority. But, in truth, neither opinion agrees with the sure documents; for one of them shows his successor reigning in October of 1177. So, Hoveden certainly mistook, and assigned to Sir Robert, what really befel the Grand Master of the Templars.[5] During that interregnum of three years, from 1170 to 1173, under Castus, and Du Moulin, as *locum-tenentes*, different events took place; and in 1174, Almeric and Noureddin both died.[6] [7] The former, by his first wife, a Courtenay, left a boy, then about thirteen, and a

[1] Appendix, Num. xxiii.   [2] P. A. Paoli: 260.
[3] Bosio: book i.   [4] Vertot: ii. 233.
[5] Cod. Dipl. Geros, i.338.—Num. clxx.
[6] Cod. Dipl. Geros, i.—Num. cc., cci., cii. Two of these three documents show Almeric's death, and his son crowned.
[7] Michaud: Hist., ii. 242.

daughter Sybilla,[1] and, by his second wife, niece of the Emperor of Constantinople, another daughter Isabella. The boy became Baldwin IV., whose guardian or regent was to be his nearest relative, Raymond III., Count of Tripoli, descended from the Count of Thoulouse, or St. Gilles, so famous during the first crusade.[2] And that the regent bore, amongst the Turks, as nickname, *Satan of the Franks*,[3] displayed not only his talents as a politician and soldier, but their hatred of him; which, at least, should have spared him (but did not) his countrymen's suspicion; but these were falling, and of course prompt to suspect. He was a dangerous minister, from the enmity that his unpopular manners incurred, and he was so occupied with defending himself, that little time remained for government. He had cultivated his mind, and read much during his various imprisonments among the Saracens, but his natural talents served him more; for he was too impetuous to consult his wisdom. He thought everything was due to him, and that no favour was as much as he merited. With pride he demanded the recom-

---

[1] Cod. Dipl. Geros., i. 364.   [2] Michaud: Hist., ii. 246.
[3] Michaud: Hist., ii. 228.

pense of his past sufferings and services, and saw justice and public weal nowhere but in his own elevation. So he inspired his young master with terror, and found gold the most effectual poison at both Courts, Moslem or Christian. Inheriting much of his ancestor's activity and ambition, he did also of that indomitable character which irritates the passions, and provokes hatreds the most implacable.[1]

To the Grand Master of the Hospitallers the unhappy young monarch could not but be dear, from the memory of his royal grandfather, as well as from his name of Baldwin, which recalled those matchless Normans who had been the order's earliest founders and patrons. It is said the orphan child had more than ordinary talents;[2] but his tutor told him what no kind and prudent physician would have had the heart to tell him; for it must have broken the boy's spirit for ever, and effectually deprived him of whatever palliative medical art might have attempted, or love, or hope. His cruel pedagogue informed him he was curelessly infected with that terrible disease that is in-

[1] Michaud: Hist., ii. 247.
[2] William of Tyre, book xxi.—Bosio: par. 1, lib. iv., anno 1173.

finitely contagious, and separates from communication with any healthy creature; that renders one an object of ineffable disgust and terror to every human being for a long time, and is always getting worse, and, after prodigious sufferings, moral and physical, closes by a fearful agony—the leprosy— which marks you as unworthy of every earthly society from the very first, and never admits of the least glimpse of comfort in this world. The most unfeeling of fathers could never have pronounced such an atrocious sentence on his son, much less a mother. If for nothing else, for this William of Tyre merits the severest rebuke; nor that he was that tutor, could the writer have willingly believed; but he must, since it is that same Tyre himself relates it.[1] No wonder then if the hapless youth lost all courage, and teased several with vain entreaties.

Noureddin's death brought Saladin from Egypt, and was the Latin kingdom's knell. That Saladin became a beneficent sovereign to Egypt, is still remembered by the Nilometer, or Joseph's Well, so called from his name Joseph. That he had the Cairo Caliph murdered in or out of the bath[2]—per-

[1] Michaud: Bibl. Crois., i. 159.   [2] Vertot: ii. 209.

ST. JOHN OF JERUSALEM.

haps by an order from his master at Damascus[1]—is narrated freely by the Christians, but the Moslems are silent;[2] nor is it improper to hesitate as to giving a verdict of guilty, without clear proof.[3] It were murder, aggravated by deep ingratitude, for that caliph had made him vizier, which surpassing elevation Saladin is said to have at first been afraid to accept, and it certainly brought him the envy of his own sovereign. Saladin, who was very fond of pleasure in his youth, soon reformed[4] into a grave courtly politician and saintly warrior, and decided to receive the robe, and other marks of that supreme dignity, and ascended to the palace, clothed in the caliph's presents—a white turban, embroidered with gold; a robe sparkling with jewels; a tunic lined with scarlet; a mantle of a singularly fine texture; a collar worth of itself alone ten thousand pieces of gold; a scimitar enriched with precious stones, of the value of five thousand pieces of gold; a chestnut mare taken from the caliphate's own private stables, and reputed to be the fleetest in all Egypt, the animal herself valued

---

[1] Michaud: Hist., ii. 229. The Bagdad Caliph seems to have approved of all the doings of any lord of the ascendant.
[2] Michaud: Hist., ii. 239.   [3] Id.:   Id. 241.
[4] Id.:   Id.   239.—Vertot: xi., 190.

at eight thousand gold pieces; her necklace, saddle, and bridle, studded with pearls, stirrups of solid gold, her caparisons of gold, &c., &c.[1] But notwithstanding his lofty station in Egypt, Noureddin in his letters never gives Saladin any other title than his old one of emir,[2] and having recalled him frequently to Damascus, as if to do him honour, the wary adventurer always declined the invitation, excusing himself on divers pretexts, satisfied with besieging with more or less success Petra, or Montreale, or some other of the Christian fortresses south of the Dead Sea, and then hastening back to Egypt on the approach of any Syrian Mahometans.[3] Although, in his replies to Noureddin, we find him always sign himself his Mameluke or slave.[4] And this mutual distrust made Noureddin on his death-bed recommend his only son to his friends, and that they should save his poor boy;[5] and the dying father was right in his fears, for Saladin, coming from Egypt, under covert of protecting him from those emirs, removed his real friendly protectors one by one, and at length exiled young Maleksalek to Aleppo, where, under

[1] Arab. Chron., 138.   [2] Id. 139.
[3] Id. 148.   Id. 139.
[5] Id. 140.

inhuman tortures, he died, though exactly how, was never known. But volumes are in this line from one Eastern to another. "Then happened what happened: I witnessed much I'll never mention; interpret it well, and ask me no more." [1]

As in 1171, with the Fatimite Caliph, had expired the Egyptian schism (fourteen caliphs of that race, in 250 years[2]), those of Bagdad came to extend their spiritual sway to all Egypt, where the black flag of the Abassides was instantly hoisted; and before expiring, Noureddin had the satisfaction of extinguishing a family he considered heretical.

Saladin had now only one superior, and he but spiritual and orthodox; and as Sultan—1174—was prayed for in all the mosques of his vast dominions.[3] From 1174, absolute sovereign, up and down in a succession of useful victories, Saladin settled his dynasty—that of the Ajoubites, and, overrunning the Bekaa, then a rich popular valley, though now comparatively a solitude, visited the ruins of Baalbeck, the ancient Heliopolis of Asia, which Tyre confounds with Palmyra.[4]

If the Latin kingdom, Syria and Palestine, was

[1] Arab. Chron., 176.
[2] Vertot: ii. 182.—Michaud: Hist., ii. 241.
[3] Michaud: Hist., ii. 247.   [4] Id. : Id. 248.

tumbling down, perhaps it is that the heroes of the cross had disappeared, and, with the not unfair exception of the military orders, warlike virtue was gone. The descendants of an illustrious race had degenerated from their pristine morals, and contracted what may be compared to the impure stain oozing from the olive, or rust that corrodes steel.[1] Nor is this the opinion of a fanatical monk alone, but also of a cool statesman. Immediately on return from Egypt Almeric had undertaken an imploring visit to Constantinople, with confidence in his relationship to the Greek sovereigns; but it produced nothing.[2] A little later, he had to investigate that outrage perpetrated on the Old Man of the Mountain's merchant; and the criminal Templar was thrown into prison, and after trial, sentenced to death, which certainly would have been executed, if Almeric had lived; but not being so, the Assassins considered they had a full right to put any new King of Jerusalem to death, as responsible for his predecessor's neglect of justice.[3] Another Templar, in Armenia, had become Mahometan, an Englishman, Robert de St.

[1] Michaud: Hist., ii. 245.—Vitri.
[2] Id: Id. 240.
[3] Vertot: ii. 219, 223.—Bosio: par. 1, lib. iv., anno 1172.

Alban.[1] But if one Judas did not dishonour the twelve, neither should two the Templars. But the pair of culprits furnished some cloak of reason to cite, when the storm began to rise against the whole body of those unfortunate gentlemen.[2]

Whether the following events happened exactly before or after Almeric's death is not quite certain; at least Michaud and Vertot disagree on the subject.[3] The eldest of Baldwin IV.'s sisters married the Marquis of Monferrat, called Longsword, and he dying in a few months, left Sybilla, a young widow, with an infant son, heir to the throne, and she, having seen Guy Lusignan, a Frank adventurer, at Court, he debauched her, and her brother had to make them marry.[4]

Isabella, Almeric's other daughter, was given in wedlock to the famous Thoron's son, or nephew, a boy only ten, and she eight. And, after her divorce from him, she had several husbands, among whom was not, as is pretended, Renaud de Chatillon,[5] widower of the Princess of Antioch, who may have married old Thoron's widow, and young

[1] Hoveden.—Bibl. Crois., ii. 775.
[2] Vertot: ii. 214, 218.—Bosio: par. 1, lib. iv., anno 1172.
[3] Id.: 223.
[4] Michaud: Hist., ii. 253.   [5] Id.: 249.

Thoron's mother; and now in right not of his own, but of the minor Thoron's wife as their factor or lieutenant, was called Lord of Petra and Montreale. And this is so true, that Renaud does not appear in the list of her husbands, in Seb. Paoli, or any other documents.[1] But the Hospitallers appear to have had military possession of both Petra and Montreale frequently.[2] Saladin besieged them ineffectually in Almeric's time. Montreale, Mons Regalis, so designated from its having been built by a king—Baldwin I., is called by the Arabs *Shaubec*, the name of the mountain on which the town was built. Both Petra and Montreale were reputed impregnable, and built for the express purpose of keeping the road open between Syria and Egypt, round by the Dead Sea, and of dominating Arabia and the Bedouins. The soldan, when afterwards in his hands considered them the keys of the road to

---

[1] Cod. Dipl. Geros., i. 366.

[2] William of Tyre: books xv. and xx.—Krak, or Kerak, or Petra Deserti, the Petra of antiquity, the Petra now so famous among travellers. Petra and Montreale were different fortresses, more than sixty miles asunder. Mons Regalis distat ab urbe Crac (vel Petra), xx. leucas versus Egyptum. Cod. Dipl. Geros., i. 448 —Num. lxii. Crac vel Petracensis civitas est castrum ubi civitas olim Petra. Id. Id. Sanuti makes a mistake in thinking it and Montreale the same place.—Bosio: par. 1, lib. iv., anno 1172.

Mecca, and, for that reason, refused to give them back to the Franks, though he offered to return Jerusalem to them, and to pay for reconstructing its walls. But both the King of France and the Mahometan continuing to hold Petra and Montreale a *sine quâ non*, the treaty was broken off for ever.[1] That was many years later, and only mentioned now, to show how important those places were.

But now Sidon, and Paneas, and several other places fell, and by storm was taken the Christian fortress, above Jacob's ford, on the Jordan, the defence of Galilee; in which fortress many of the Templars were slain, and their grand master made prisoner, and flung into a dungeon, where the barbarians (incensed that to their demand to get himself ransomed, his reply was that *by an old custom no Templar could give more ransom than his girdle and his knife*) made him die of hunger; and they *sawed* two of his knights asunder, with a wooden saw, like Isaiah;[2] and several Hospitallers left their corpses there, and their Grand Master, Osbert may have been severely wounded; but he got back alive to Jerusalem, for we have a document of his 1177

[1] Vertot: iii. 410.—Bosio: par. 1, lib. iv., anno 1171.
[2] Roberto del Monte: Chron.—Bibl. Crois. iii. 96.—Bosio: par. 1, lib. iv., anno 1178.

dated January, 1177, between which month and the following October, he must have expired; for another document shows Du Moulin reigning in October, 1177. Vertot may have been very right in saying Osbert died of grief, at the sure signs of the approaching ruin of the Frank kingdom, only he mistook as to the date; as he was assuredly borne out in affirming that no landed acquisitions could be a compensation for the loss of a wise and able politician, and great captain, as Osbert was.[1]

Most of the Christian forces having marched towards Antioch and to the siege of Harenc—a scene of the grossest dissipation and gambling, and diversions the most dissolute—as well as the honest recreation of hawking—Saladin advanced against Jerusalem, which compelled poor Baldwin IV. with all his ailments, to march out against him, accompanied by the Count of Tripoli, the Grand Master of the Hospitallers and many Knights Templars; and "by the goodness of God" was enabled to overthrow the Mahometan chief so completely, that he had himself to take part in the flight, 1179 nor could but scramble in haste up a dromedary and escape into the desert. Yet the

[1] Cod. Dipl. Geros., i. 338.—Num. clxix. and clxx.—Bosio : par. 1, lib. v., anno 1180.

cavalry of Baldwin is said to have been only three hundred and seventy-five; who cut all the Mamelukes to pieces in their silk surcoats of saffron (Saladin's colour), and the whole road was strewed with cuirasses, helmets, little short iron boots of the Moslem runaways, who for the most part perished of thirst, hunger, and cold—for it was now November of 1179.[1]

Nevertheless dire were the presentiments of Jerusalem.[2] When Saladin was driven back with that great overthrow, so that scarce one of the Egyptian army ever got back to Egypt, yet a victory was proclaimed at Cairo, and pigeons spread the triumphant news over Egypt *to quiet the spirits of the public.*[3] How unlike modern times! Nor had it been the fault of the Moslems (say their writers), but the leper king, before he marched, alighted and in tears prayed to the Omnipotent, who thereupon sent a violent wind, that blew the dust against the eyes of the Mahometans, that they were forced to run away, and Saladin was so sore on the matter, that he swore to abstain from the nouba till he had avenged his honour. The nouba in the

---

[1] Michaud: Hist., ii. 251.—Bosio: par. 1, lib. iv., anno 1176.
[2] Id.: Id., 252. [3] Arab. Chron., 179.

East is a kind of music that only royal persons have a right to, five times a-day at their door— a privilege which he who renounces, for even a short space, is considered as abdicating so long all his other highest privileges, and confessing he lies under a stain, which must be washed out.[1]

In one of the late battles, the son of the Lord of Ramlah—a private nobleman, was obliged to pay as ransom for himself alone one hundred thousand gold pieces and the liberty of one thousand Mussulmen; and Saladin's favourite physician, a Doctor Jssa, being made prisoner on the other side, the soldan paid sixty thousand pieces of gold to ransom him. How money had increased since the first crusade, when the ransom of a sovereign would hardly have been rated at such sums.[2]

In 1179 fell in battle Humphry de Thoron, remarkable for his wisdom and valour.[3] He was uncle or father of the youth of that name who espoused the child Isabella, younger sister of Baldwin IV., a marriage that was afterwards to be broken.[4]

That there had been some small dissensions

---

[1] Arab. Chron., 180.
[2] Id. 182, Note 2.
[3] Id., 181.
[4] Michaud: Hist., ii. 366.

between Hospitallers and Templars is a natural consequence of human defects in which both parties may have erred from the strict rule of right—weaknesses scarce meriting notice, and no doubt frightfully exaggerated; but, whatever they were, Alexander III. made the two orders agree.[1] There had been disturbances at Antioch which were appeased by umpires, the Patriarch of Jerusalem and the two Grand Masters of the Hospital and Temple.[2] As well as a mutiny at Constantinople happened, in which nearly all the Hospitallers in that city were murdered, and the great establishment there sacked, including hospital and church.[3]

1181

1183

Saladin accused his rival Moslems of leaguing with the Franks and the Assassins as if they were all one; and to his eyes they were so, or he wished it so to be thought, and that he was a staunch prejudiced Mahometan.[4] Therefore when advancing against the Christians at Beyrout, he wheeled round suddenly and marched beyond the Euphrates to attack the Moslem Prince of Moussul; because he had made a treaty of truce with the Franks

[1] Rymer: i. 149.—Vertot: ii. 235.
[2] Vertot: ii. 238.   [3] Id. :   Id., 240.
[4] Arab. Chron., 184.

for twelve years, paying them a tribute of ten thousand gold pieces a-year; Saladin also declaring there was a secret article to make war on him in Syria, Egypt, everywhere. So having threatened the Tigris, and taken Damascus and Aleppo, he was master of the most of Syria, Egypt, Arabia, and Mesopotamia. All he had to do, was to conquer Palestine.[1]

Yet if the Moslems were divided a little, greatly more so were the Christians. *The sons of Belial* (in the chronicler's words), the true workers of ruin, hates, jealousies, mistrusts, embittered and tried to profit by the royal infirmities. No consolation for weak Baldwin! Little of this time is worth recounting, except an expedition made by Renaud de Chatillon from Petra against the shores of the Red Sea; for he built some ships at Petra, and had them carried on the backs of camels to Suez, where launching them, he devastated many places along the coast. As Christians had never appeared there before, the Turks were taken by surprise; and he made a large booty, advancing to the vicinity of Mecca and Medina. But here he was stopped by forces from Egypt. The Christians on the east

[1] Arab. Chron., 185.

bank were ready to ravage the holy cities, when the Saracen massacrers let few escape; and as to the prisoners, these were handed over to the haggis, who mostly cut their throats at Mecca, in place of a sacrifice of sheep as is usual every year, or lambs; and what Christians remained after the pilgrimage, were sent to Egypt to be immolated by the devout, and the doctors of the law.[1] The real Franks were not above three hundred; but there was a large proportion of apostate Arabs. The Christians' design was to disinter the Prophet's bones, and export them to Europe, to deprive the faithful of one of their chief objects as pilgrims. The intentional desecrators were within a day of Medina when arrested. Violent was Saladin's rage when he heard of such profanation: "The infidels have dared to violate the very cradle and asylum of Islamism. They have contaminated the country with their looks. It is a deep stain. Take care that the prisoners who have once seen the road do not return to be guides. We should be inexcusable in the eyes of God and men; every tongue would curse us throughout the whole East, and parts of the West also. Purge then the earth of those

Arab. Chron., 186.

monsters who dishonour it. It is our sacred duty. Let us cleanse the air of the air they breathe, and let them all be devoted to death." Such were Saladin's secret written orders[1]—preparing the murder. And he undertook himself to besiege Petra, but did not succeed; so returned to Damascus, killing, burning, and destroying everything along the road. The Prince of Moussoul being now his vassal by force, had no longer alliance with the Franks; so Saladin had nothing else to think on but war against the adorers of the cross.[2] And to any of his emirs that wished for peace, this was his ready reply: " Allah has made it our strict obligation to carry on the holy war, without the smallest intermission. Nor are we to foresee wants or difficulties. His precepts are his orders. His promises a sure gage. Let us do our duty, and Allah will do His. He who neglects Allah, Allah will neglect him."[3]

The *Leper King*, known by that abhorred distinction, and that alone in the whole history of man, suffering from leprosy, or *king's evil*, or (are they the same?) *morbo regio laborans* being the

[1] Arab. Chron., 187.   [2] Id., 188.
[3] Id., 181.

words of at least one chronicle[1]—yet was his death to be a calamity to Palestine—the Leper King, seeing it was impossible for him to marry, or even hold the reins of government, and being now entirely out of minority, began the removal of Count Tripoli, and to associate his own brother-in-law, Guy; reserving to himself only the title of king, the possession of the metropolis, and a pension of about ten thousand crowns. But it excited the envy of the grandees; nor Tripoli disrelished such divisions.[2] Renaud, from Petra and Montreale, by his lawless incursions affording too good grounds for the reprisals Saladin desired, this called out a Christian army, and Guy at its head; and however it was, whether from his own incapacity, or want of discipline in his officers, he spent more than eight days in presence of an enemy inferior to him in numbers, without coming 1184 to battle;[3] which cowardice, and the loud protests of the chiefs of the state, prepared the sure ruin of the Latins, say Mahometans.

Both they and Christians agree in pronouncing that the proximate cause was Renaud de Chatillon's

[1] Annales Acquininctem.—Bibl. Crois., iii. 320.
[2] Vertot: ii. 241. [3] Michaud: Hist., ii. 358.

breach of the truce which Saladin, in spite of all his prejudice, had contracted with the Christians.[1] Strange that the Christians, whose best defence was that sworn truce, were the first to break it, while the infidels kept it.[2] Nor was it now alone; but Renaud was continually pouncing from either Petra or Montreale, and now, like a robber, was unable to resist the temptation of rifling a caravan passing near on its quiet way to Mecca; but finally asked for peace, when the irritated Moslem was at the very gates of Petra, the Christian's den, which, to the surprise of many there, the soldan granted; for his late fever abated much of his ambition. And the truce he would probably have maintained religiously, though in the bottom of his heart he might rejoice that such a pretext came, as it were, forced upon him; but whatever he might have felt, outwardly he exhibited great anger, and swore to put the perjured traitor to death, if ever he fell into his hands.[3] This is so contrary to the noble generosity we are frequently obliged to admire in Saladin, that it leads directly to the observation of his having unfortunately been of a religion that tended to embitter all his worst

[1] Michaud: Hist , ii. 266. [2] Id. :   Id.,   266.
[3] Arab. Chron., 189.

qualities, and to suffocate his good; and that, without meaning anything of the bigotry suspected in a monkish speech, it may be very true that had he been a Christian, he would have been a greater hero, and without many of the blemishes that stain him, and which may be fairly imputed less to him[1] than to the malignant dervishes, cadis, santons, around him, and the creed in which he was brought up. To confirm such excuses, here is a literal translation of a Moslem historian regarding another whom he evidently reverenced: "Some years before, when Saladin had a violent sickness, and that his life was despaired of, Cadi Fadel told him that undoubtedly God wished to punish him for his pitiless lukewarmness towards Islamism, and that the only way to recover his health was to promise the Almighty to turn for the future all his efforts against the Christians, adding that, as a sign of his firm purpose, he ought to begin by swearing to kill with his own hand, on the very first opportunity, Renaud of Petra for his sacrilegious enterprise against Mecca and Medina, as also Count Tripoli, firmest pillar of the Christian army. In the cadi's opinion, it was necessary to put those two wretches to death.

[1] Aboulfarage: 19.

On which Saladin gave his hand to the cadi, as consenting. When, two years after, the war broke out, the cadi took care to remind the soldan of his vow, and that it was only on this condition that God had restored him his strength. And this was the reason why he showed a more than usual fervour. It was the Cadi Fadel himself who recounted this anecdote to a friend of Emadeddin." [1]

As early as 1184 poor Baldwin IV. had lost his eyes, his extremities had fallen off putrified; he had no more either hands or feet, and abdicating the administration in favour of his sister Sybilla's husband, had his little nephew crowned as Baldwin V., with great pomp; the child (then only five) being borne in a grandee's arms to the Holy Sepulchre, a splendid banquet given in Solomon's Palace, the barons and burghers of Jerusalem serving the new king; nor since then has there ever been a feast of joy in that metropolis.[2] During his minority his father-in-law Guy was to hold the regency, which dismissed Count Tripoli, whom his many enemies accused of treasonable plots, and a secret correspondence with the Moslem; but upon

---

[1] Arab. Chron., 198, Note 1.   [2] Michaud: Hist., ii. 259.

finding Guy decidedly incompetent, and deficient in courage, and unpopular among the soldiery, and, indeed, that they refused to march to battle under such a captain, the leper resumed his powers, and ratified the child's coronation. So Baldwin IV. determined to call back Tripoli to the regency, which the count was induced to accept, only with the express stipulation that the Hospitallers and Templars should promise to command the army, and the boy be under the protection of the Kings of France and England and the Pope; so that Tripoli should be without any responsibility on that head, and then he made a new truce with Saladin, at the severe, but necessary price.[1] The object of the truce was time to ask for a new crusade; and to obtain it, an embassy was composed, as before, of the patriarch and the two grand masters. But that patriarch had been already known as a vain, presumptuous man, and the state council, fearful of his impetuosity and outrageous pride, refused at first, and would have continued their refusal, to confer a place in the embassy on him to the courts of high and haughty sovereigns, were it not for calculating on the moderation, politeness,

---

[1] Vertot: ii. 247.

and knowledge of the world of his two colleagues.[1]

1185. The trio sailed from Jaffa and arrived safe at Brindisi, and there learned that the Pope was at Verona, not to pacify Italy, but driven to it in this horrid manner. The cruel by nature, time easily changes them. Thanks be to God, nothing like what I am going to relate happens now. People are to-day of a purer porcelain.[2] In a sedition those of Rome seized on some innocent clergymen and scooped out their eyes; and putting them astride on donkeys, each facing backwards and holding the animal's tail, forced them to proceed in rueful procession to Velletri, where the Pope was then in Villeggiatura. Which barbarous sight struck the poor old virtuous Pontiff with such horror that he drove off instantly for Bologna, and thence by Modena to Verona, where he sickened severely, and after lingering a few months, died in the arms of the emperor, who had come to meet and console him.

This Pope Lucius was a Lucchese, and proud of having had the first grand master for countryman; it was a consolation to him to do justice to the order; as he did in a bull still extant, with all the

[1] Vertot: ii. 249.
[2] Platina: Vite dei Pontefici, iii. 25.

fo malities that distinguish such instruments.[1] He, like his predecessors, praises the Hospitallers, and says that the Pope was always ready to ascribe fine, holy, and noble things to them, and nothing else. Mild man, he had been bishop of his native city, and loved its quiet, and, as it were, holiness; nor was it very willingly that he sat on the Papal throne—bidding farewell for ever to his dear home, and at his age ascending the tremendous stairs of the stormy Lateran. And to overturn the politics of Jerusalem, one of the three ambassadors expired at Verona—he of the Temple—on whose courteous wisdom it had relied much. The emperor then there was the famous Frederic I., who (destined to die within three years) was soon at Pavia, issuing a confirmation of privileges to the Hospitallers in the most solemn and flattering manner. It shall be given in the Appendix.[2] The patriarch and the survivor of the grand masters went by France, where they found Philip II., a pleasing young king; crossed the Channel to visit the English monarch, on whose succour they chiefly calculated, Henry II.; where, in the presence, that rampant patriarch made a

[1] Appendix, Num. xiv.
[2] Cod. Dipl. Geros., i. 311. Num. xxxii.—Appendix, Num xlv.

most insolent speech—which is an excellent proof that the royal personage, so prudent then, could never have permitted his passion to run away with him and use words that naturally led to Becket's murder. Far from obtaining a crusade, to have consigned the brutal envoy to a dungeon would have been no infringement of international law. At this the grief and confusion of the Hospitallers were great, and presenting his Majesty with the keys of the Holy Sepulchre and the Jerusalem banner, as sent to him, "because that sacred city has a right to consider you its head and hereditary chief, and descendant of that Duke of Normandy who had been the first choice of the crusaders, though he ungratefully refused the crown offered to him, on which they had to confer it on another, who, however, also was a Norman, as nearly all their kings have ever since been. So, as Duke of Normandy, they have a right to your Majesty's protection." Nor did Henry II. object to their homage.[1] That haughtiest of kings allowed them to go back to Syria with fair words and a considerable sum of money also. The words of Hoveden also are clear, "The keys of the Holy Sepulchre, the tower

---

[1] Peterborough Chron., 14.—Bibl. Crois., ii. 846.

of David, and Jerusalem, and the royal banner;" but as they are somewhat in contradiction[1] with Michaud, the original shall be in the Appendix.[2] The Jerusalem people complained of their ridiculous passionate patriarch, and that as a Heraclius found the cross, so it would be lost now through fault of a Heraclius, whose violent temper made him odious to the whole world.[3] And to these murmurings were added the fearful prognostics, a dying king, a minor his successor, and an ambitious, irreligious regent, suspected of a partiality for the infidels, and of aspiring to the crown.[4] After all which, Baldwin IV., departed on the 15th of March, 1185; and a few days later, Baldwin V., feeble and fragile hope of the Christians, his sudden death being ascribed to poison, whether from Tripoli, or Guy, or the child's own mother, desirous to become queen, and make her lover (now husband) king. Neither Sybilla nor Guy were satisfied with her brother's decision; and they resolved on a plot, that required time, to get the mass of their opponents out of the way.

1186

[1] Michaud: Hist., ii. 260.
[2] Hoveden: 2.—Bib. Crois., ii., 773.—Appendix, Num. xxiv.
[3] Vertot: ii. 256.   [4] Id.: ii. 257.

Whoever takes the pains to scrutinise this chronology minutely, will find it very different from the usual one; but it is to be hoped, he will also find it reposes on the stablest of testimony, to examine which put the writer to much trouble, perhaps more than such small matters merit; but, he flatters himself, it is once for all, and settles them for ever.

Renaud's breach of the truce coinciding (and most iniquitously was it broken by wicked Christians, avow chroniclers),[1] Saladin sent a circular throughout his dominions, summoning every Mussulman to the holy war, and in May of 1187, marched from Damascus with the caravan for Mecca, and laid siege again to Petra; and his son, marching against Acre, fought the Day of Sephoria, by Christians called the battle of Nazareth. And indeed, the spot where it was fought, is only about five miles to the north-east of Nazareth, into which the two Grand Masters of the Temple and Hospital, with their little escort, had come that very evening, on their way to Tiberias, whither they were sent on a mission by the Jerusalem Government. The little village has disappeared,

1187

[1] Sicardi: 2.—Bib. Crois., ii. 547.

but there is a circumstance mentioned by the chronicler,[1] which marks the spot out still; and it is the threshing-floor of a farm-house of El-Majed, which, however strange it seems, survives to our own days, amid changes of everything else of much more importance, particularly in that extraordinary land, where nearly universal have been the changes during so many centuries, and a rapid succession of masters. Cities, dynasties, and empires, have gone; and here is the threshing-floor, and there is the small hamlet of Cana, still known for ever by the same name.[2] "It was there," says Mr. Gillot, with most pardonable warmth, "that the France of the East had her Leonidas and Spartans, and they expired under the shade of Mount Thabor, and their Thermopylæ were the passes through those naked calcareous rocks and precipices."[3] More astonishing still, Bonaparte's victory of 11th of April, 1799, called battle of Cana, took place on nearly the same spot; and there are not wanting Frenchmen who may consider this as reprisals of that—tremendous length of interval! And the valiant actors—Templars, Hospitallers, and

---

[1] Bernard le Tresorier: Chron.—Michaud: Orient., v. 455.—Bib. Crois., ii. 574.
[2] Michaud: Orient., v. 458. [3] Id.: Id., 461.

Republicans, were unconscious of the past or future. A fellow-countryman of Maillè's cut that Templar's name on a small rock that just peeps from the centre of the threshing-floor.[1] The chronicler says, the straw on that threshing-floor was all reduced to dust by Maillè's struggles; and so it would have been now at the same season; another Chalgrove, or Hougoumont, or rather its quiet cottage. While the heroes, so soon to die, slept at Nazareth, that very same night the seven thousand Saracens had passed Jordan, and instantly began to slaughter the peaceful peasantry, who, when they opened their eyes, it was in another world; and at daybreak a voice echoed through the streets, "The Turks, the Turks! to arms, O men of Nazareth! To arms for the true Nazarene!"[2] And the grand masters and their little escort, of about five hundred, instantly marched to meet their more than ten-fold adversaries. Their meeting was on the threshing-floor in question, fronting the farmer's, at foot of a little hill that shelters the village of El-Mazed, on the road from Nazareth to Cana in Galilee.[3] Considering their great in-

[1] Bapt. Poujoulat: Asie Mineur, &c., ii. 396.
[2] Coggleshale.—Michaud: Hist., ii. 266.
[3] Bapt. Poujoulat: ii. 397.

equality of numbers—there having been one hundred and thirty cavalry, including Templars and Hospitallers, and four hundred foot, on one side, and on the Moslem, seven thousand—it is not astonishing the Franks were worsted with a cruel slaughter; and after feats the most splendid, particularly by the Marshal of the Temple, Jacques de Maillè,[1] who, by the Moslem, was believed to be St. George on his white horse. The action was on the 1st of May, 1187, and the Grand Master of the Temple and two of his knights escaped.[2] "God declared for Islam," say the Mahometans. "He is always in favour of the larger battalion," say some Christians.[3] The Grand Master of the Hospitallers, his horse being killed, fell with him, and the illustrious rider, the sworn foe of Islam,[4] not disentangling himself fast enough, perhaps partly from the confusion, and partly from his age and the weight of his armour, left time for a crowd of Moslem lancers on foot, to gather round him, and finish him with a thousand wounds. Among whom it was pretended was Count Tripoli, under a

[1] Michaud: Hist., ii. 267.
[2] Id. :   Id., 268.—Coggleshale's Chron.
[3] Arab. Chron., 190.   [4] Id., 190.

masque—rumour noticed, because others do so—but here only to accompany it with the due stigma of declaring it a wicked falsehood, utterly disproved by the melancholy events that followed. Du Moulin had the noble fine end that became him, and was found the next day beneath a mountain of corpses.[1] The words of Hoveden are very precise, "Et eodem die, videlicet Kalend Maji, sexaginta fratres Templi et summus Magister Domûs Hospitalis, cum pluribus domûs suæ fratribus, interfecti sunt."[2] Sir Roger du Moulin was probably the first with the epithet "Grand" in any document, though Bosio and Vertot give the primacy to the bull of after years.[3]

At these tidings Saladin hurried back from Petra, and at Damascus found a body of ten thousand of choice regular horse;[4] but of the irregular, so numerous that some Moslems compare them to the entire human race collected together for the day of judgment.[5] Saladin had no more to do than divide into centre, right, and left, and vanguard and rear, and in that array advanced

---

[1] Cod. Dipl. Geros, i. 339—Vertot: ii, 265.—Bosio: par. 1, lib. v., anno 1187.
[2] Hoveden: 635.   [3] Vertot: iii. 525.
[4] Arab. Chron., 190.   [5] Arab. Chron., 190.—Emad-Eddin.

towards Tiberias for a general action, though contrary to the advice of some of his council; at which time his forces, full of enthusiasm, amounted to eighty thousand men.[1] And he moreover recalled his son with his seven thousand, flushed with victory, from Nazareth, well aware that those victorious troops could not but render his own more ardent;[2] not disdaining any way of increasing his numbers or rousing them to energy. Thus in his circular he was not ashamed to call all Moslems to join him, whether they acted from religion, or love of plunder and prodigious wealth and untold hoards of money, and all kind of luxury and delights—every morsel of land from Persia to the Nile, towns and villages for his bravest emirs, the spoils of every Christian family and every farm and estate, to be divided among the descendants of those Mussulmen who had been driven from Palestine; all spiritual blessings from the Caliph of Bagdad, and his warmest orisons for those who marched to the conquest of Jerusalem. Thus was it written on his colours: "This is the banner for all who love Mahometans or hate Christians or

---

[1] Michaud: Hist., ii. 268.
[2] Coggleshale: 4.—Bib. Crois., i. 352.

desire unbounded wealth, or lands or palaces. Welcome to all who wish for gold or silver, or jewels, or fields, or fine houses, or captives hard working or beautiful, male or female. All of you join us and fall in quickly."[1] The earlier days of June, he passed in the river.[2]

As soon as Du Moulin was found by some knights of his order, they bore his corpse into Acre; and, at a chapter holden in its presence, Sir N. Gardiner was chosen. He was at that very time grand preceptor, and had been so certainly from previous to 1180,[3] and even constable in 1125, and probably turcopolier,[4] as well as brother to the Prior of England.

But under the leper, and after his and the minor's death, and during various regencies, the plot had been going on for the last two years at Jerusalem, and divisions, which Saladin kept tacitly fomenting as much as he could. And as soon as the Grand Master of the Hospitallers had been sent on that expedition to beyond Nazareth, whence it was agreed the Grand Master of the Temple

[1] Coggleshale: 3.—Bib. Crois., i. 351.
[2] Michaud: Hist., ii. 268.
[3] Cod. Dipl. Geros., i. Num. xlviii.—P. A. Paoli: 300.
[4] P. A. Paoli: 302, 427.

should return as he did (otherwise he would have stayed to share the heroic death of Maillè, no doubt), and that all the other grandees not in the secret had gone to the states general at Naplouse to consult about who should be king—then the plot broke out, and the gates of the metroplis were shut (as we learn from an eye-witness), and no one was allowed to enter or go out for two days and nights, during which there was a meeting of those called the princes; but indeed (adds the same authority) there were no princes there, but only a few priests and the Grand Master of the Temple, and Sybilla, Countess of Joppa, and Guy and their friends— that is, the conspirators. And Sybilla being crowned by the Patriarch and told by him, that as a woman she should give that crown to the person most capable of governing the kingdom, she arose and calling her husband, there present, she said, "Sire, come and receive this crown, for I know no one who can employ it so well!" On which he knelt, and she placed the crown on his head, and so they were king and queen, and proclaimed publicly; and the gates flung open again, and the tidings reached Naplouse. The consternation of those barons was great,[1] and Tripoli exclaimed, "Have

[1] Michaud: Hist., ii. 264.—Bib. Crois., i. 368.

we not Isabella's husband?[1] Let us elect him sovereign, who is of Baldwin's blood, but Guy is a total stranger!" which frightening young Thoron, who was only fifteen, he rose and rushing forth, rode off to Jerusalem, and threw himself at Sybilla's and Guy's feet, calling for pardon and doing homage.[2] And then those at Naplouse separated; and, since it was too late to resist, hurried one by one with their allegiance to the royal pair in Solomon's Palace. And also soon came Sir N. Gardiner from Acre—though melancholy must have oppressed his soul—not for himself, he was resolved to do his duty the very best he could, and die; but he knew that the battle in which he was about to head the Hospitallers, was a vain defence, and that won or lost, Jerusalem must soon be taken, and the Latin kingdom fall. Likewise the high-minded and too injured Tripoli came to a similar resolution, and that in this public extremity, no private considerations should be listened to ; though when he met his brother Franks, it was to be thus accosted!—" We suppose you have become a Mahometan!" So Guy, hearing of

---

[1] Michaud: Hist., ii. 265.—Bib. Crois., i. 369.
[2] Id. :   Id.,   265.

his approach, proceeded out on horseback ten miles to meet him, and then they both alighted on the road, and Tripoli knelt and kissed Guy's hand,[1] and, embracing, they entered Jerusalem as devoted friends. All the garrisons from the various towns had been called in, and all the crews of every Latin ship from Scanderoon to Ascalon, and together a body of fifty thousand men occupied the valley, a few miles south-west of Naplouse, which encampment Guy and his suite joined, to hold a council of war, that same evening, and march next day perhaps.[2]

Saladin had already taken Tiberias, and Tripoli's wife and infant child retreated into the citadel, which still stood, while the Saracens scoured all the country with infinite devastation, and had even burned down the town of Tiberias itself, all but its citadel. The flames were visible from the Christian camp, as well as the ruin of the whole province, that Saladin might drive the Giaours from their position, or by a decoy, which was to succeed. For, in the council of war, when Tripoli had spoken for not stirring, "It being better to lose Tiberias, and I, my town, and wife, and child—no one sacrifices

---

[1] Bernard Tresorier: Chron., 5.—Bib. Crois., ii. 574.—Michaud: Hist., ii. 268.
[2] Michaud: Hist., ii. 269, Note 2.

so much—than lose Jerusalem. Here are wells, food and shade, but there would be neither. Those arid solitudes would soon consume our army and horses, and hunger and thirst and the burning heats of this season. The Saracens must soon remove, either to attack us at grievous disadvantage, or to retreat from sickness and want of food and water; on which we could pursue them, we and our chargers fresh and vigorous, and with that blessed Cross; for at present the Saracen numbers are in their favour, but then not. Then I swear to you, they'll all perish in Jordan, or the lake, or by thirst, or our swords, or fall into our hands prisoners." Renaud to this, "It is to intimidate us, that he has exaggerated their numbers; but at all events, the more the wood, the better the blaze!" Nevertheless, that soldierly advice of Tripoli's engaged the majority to vote for biding, and Guy adopted that salutary intention.[1] But when he was in his tent, the wily Grand Master of the Temple shook his resolution by protesting that it would destroy the spirit of the army to be lookers on at such barbarous deeds; and that he, for one, and his Templars were resolved

---

[1] Michaud: Hist., ii. 271.

not to endure the dishonour, but would lay down their white mantles; so, the unhappy monarch weakly issued orders for an advance to battle, at day-break. Some may suspect the Templar of treason; yet it probably was not, but rash impetuosity. Tiberias, that lay on the western bank of the lake, is no longer to be found; its walls had been rebuilt, but the earthquake of 1837 threw it down; so that a subsequent traveller could not find any shelter to sleep in there, and was obliged to go and bivouac on the opposite bank. For the first time, Guy was obeyed, and it was to ruin the Christian cause.[1] "We suppose you are afraid," said the unblushing Renaud, "since you advised the reverse." "As you go, I will, also," replied Tripoli, "though against my opinion. If it end disastrously, that will be no fault of mine." When Saladin perceived the Christians advance, he saw his stratagem had succeeded, and exclaimed, "We have conquered, and all Palestine is ours!"[2]

The Count Tripoli led the vanguard, as was his feudal place, on that morning of Friday, the 3rd of July, says the eye-witness.[3] The left and right

[1] Michaud: Hist., ii. 272.
[2] Arab. Chron., 192.
[3] Coggleshale.—Michaud: Hist., ii. 273.—Bib. Crois.

were composed of troops belonging to various barons of Palestine. The centre held the cross, surrounded by a picked corps, and Guy with his bravest knights; the rear was confided to the Templars and Hospitallers. These both were called a swinish race that he was resolved to exterminate, by Saladin. They rarely gave, and had never any reason to expect quarter. At about three miles from Tiberias, the Christians began to suffer from thirst and heat, and met the Saracen. There were high rocks between them and the lake. So Tripoli sent back to the king to bid him hasten his march to gain the lake before night; and the count pushed on, Guy's answer being that he would follow him close. But instead of this the king, hearing that the Turks were pressing on the rear severely, felt irresolute, and gave the command to halt and pitch the tents. So the army was separated, and had to pass a dreadful night; and indeed all was lost. Impossible to depict the sufferings and horrors of that, to them, long night. Still the Franks did not quite lose their courage: "To-morrow we'll find water with our swords." There was much of the pale blue of the country round Rome in that lowland, between the rocky lines that keep it from the most sacred of lakes—a mile off to its right, and

Mount Thabor to its left, at the distance of about three miles. All along that plain grew a quantity of tall dry grass, weeds, and brushwood, to which the Turks set fire; so that, to augment the torment of the Christians already dying of thirst and heat, they were enveloped on every side by smoke and flames, till they became black as devils and half roasted; while the shrill cries of the savages who never one moment ceased from assaulting them, caused the air to ring with the groans and clamours of the murderers and murdered, making a terrific accompaniment to the rustling and roaring of the conflagration. So passed that whole horrid night. And between them and the wavy fresh-water lake, day-break only showed the entire Saracen army in an extensive dense mass. Many were the charges to break through it; and Frank bravery did whatever could be done by valiant and desperate men, speaking of the cavalry; for as to the infantry— but in vain. And now all was confusion, death or flight; yet this was death too, for they were surrounded. Only Tripoli, after prodigies of valour, with his incomparable vanguard united like one man, broke back again through the Saracens and joined his countrymen, who were in the horrors of an irremediable, indisciplinable defeat; on which the stoutest of his peerless corps charged the Saracens once again with such determined valour, that it succeeded as before, and they were the sole large body of soldiery that escaped from that bloody field. Nor was it duplicity in Tripoli, as pretended, nor from any leniency in the Saracens, but as their own Moslem commander confessed afterwards, he saw resolute despair in the Christian looks and whole demeanour, and to avoid it, made his men divide and leave them a free passage. Some other individuals cut their road to liberation; but they were very few. Tripoli's were the only party forming anything like a regular body, and with them the count retreated to Tripoli, his capital, and in a few days died of grief. The army of Franks scarce any longer existed. The picked guards, who retreated with the cross to the right horn of the Hill of Hattim,[1] being for the most part killed, their sacred deposit was taken. It is not in a spirit of hate that Mahometans neglect the cross; but they think the real Jesus returned to heaven, and that an angel was sent down to suffer and be crucified in his place.[2] After fearful struggles, the king

[1] Rex (Guy), victus cum majoribus Tyronem. Hatti ascendit, ubi comprehensus est cum principus suis et aliis, et in captivitatem ductus.—Oliveri Scho. Chron.—Bib. Crois., iii. 137.
[2] Arab. Chron., 195. Note.

and immediate suite, and the bravest of the survivors, rode up its left horn. "I was then with my father below it," related Afdal, later, "and they charging down from the hillock upon our troops, who were beginning to mount, drove them back; and looking at my father, I saw a cloud of grief on his face. 'Make the devil a liar,' he cried to his Mamelukes, catching hold of his beard. At this they threw themselves on the enemy, and forced him to regain the top of the hill, at which I shouted joyfully, '*They fly! they fly!*' But the Franks returned to the charge, and came down to the very foot of the hillock, yet were again obliged to return up, on which I shouted again, '*They fly! they fly!*' Then my father looked at me, and said, '*Hold your tongue! They will not be truly defeated until the king's standard falls.*' And scarce had he finished speaking, when the standard fell. On the instant my father alighted from his horse, and prostrate, thanked God with many tears of joy."

"This was the way the king's standard fell," says Ibn-Alatir; and, since Mahometans and Christians come to the same conclusion, it cannot but be true. "When the Franks charged down, it was an effort like that of a dying man, for they were ready to expire from thirst; not an endeavour to rally, for the day was lost, they knew, but to gain the water. So at our repulse, they dismounted from their horses, and sat down on the grass. The Mahometans ascended the hillock, and going round threw down the king's standard. No Christian hand would have dared to do it; and there they sat mute and stupified, making no resistance." But there must have been something in their eyes that protected them; yet they were only a few. It was the whole royal party made prisoners. The king, his brother, Renaud of Petra, the Lord of Gebail, were among them; and young Thoron, the Grand Master of the Templars, and several Hospitallers and Templars. But Gardiner, and his choicest of knights, had cut their way to liberty, or perished in the attempt. Yet though the slaughter had been great, the number of prisoners was great too, including nearly all the infantry, that had refused to fight from the very first. Not so much that they were traitors or cravens, but they declared it impossible for them from the heat and thirst. Of the fifty thousand Christians, scarce one thousand escaped.[1] Never had the Franks, since their invasion of Palestine, suffered any such defeat. Saladin

[1] Arab. Chron., 199.

knew it was the conquest of every town in it, not excepting its metropolis, which must all drop, one by one, quietly into his lap, like ripe fruit, their fortifications having each been taken by storm on that day, and, as it should always be, far from the habitation of innocent women and children, and the pacific population, who ought never to be exposed to a siege. After the battle, Saladin had a tent pitched, and, retiring into it, called for the king and other principal prisoners, and made Guy sit by his side, and observing him to be thirsty, had iced water brought in. The king, after drinking, presented the cup to Renaud, which made Saladin exclaim, in reference, no doubt, to the Arab custom, which obliges you to defend the life of whomever you have once given meat or drink to, "It is not by me that this scoundrel was invited to drink. I am no wise bound towards him." And recollecting that he had twice sworn to slay him (and, in fine, all that was adduced in a former page), he, sending him a look that made every one present feel terror, reproached him with his crimes, and rose, drawing his scimitar—but let us hope it was only a signal to his emirs, and that he did not himself strike the defenceless unfortunate, whose head was instantly struck off; yet Emal-eddin, an ocular witness, says that in each case life was offered on turning Moslem, but Renaud preferred death, and the others too; so his head rolled at the king's feet, which set him trembling; but Saladin told him not to be afraid, for that his life should be spared. So was also that of the Grand Master of the Temple; certainly because to his advice the victory is to be ascribed. As to the rest of his knights and their likes, the soldan had them all beheaded. Nor his own prisoners alone; but knowing the avarice of his soldiers, and that they would conceal them for the ransom, he had it published by a regular order of the day, that he would purchase, at the rate of fifty pieces of gold each, whatever Templars or Hospitallers were brought to him, which produced two hundred of them; and they, in like manner, were slain. "For," said he, "since they like homicide so much when it favours their own religion, it is but justice to let them taste a little of it themselves." He looked upon them as at permanent war with Islam; and, in that same spirit, wrote to his lieutenant at Damascus to put to death all such knights there, whether belonging to private individuals or not, which command was executed. But, besides all slain, there were immense quantities of Christian prisoners, which reduced their price so much, that one of them was sold for a pair of slippers.[1] A letter says, "Were we even to pass the whole remainder of our life in thanking God, it would not be enough." And another, "Here is a victory without parallel. A little part, for to tell you even the half were impossible."[2]

Young Thoron, who remained a captive, was afterwards, at his mother's intercession in Jerusalem, sent with her to Petra and Montreale (by the Arabs called Karak and Shaubec), which were to be his ransom; but these fortresses refused to surrender; so he was led back to his prison at Damascus, and his mother fled to Tyre, then the only town in Palestine not yet taken by Saladin.[3]

The rest of that Saturday, Saladin kept the field; but on Sunday marched against the citadel of Tiberias, and took it, and sent to count Tripoli his lady and child. That count had, however, died of sorrow, too persuasive proof that he was no traitor.

And Saladin advancing against Acre, it resisted only two days; and in succession, Nazareth, Caipha, Cesarea, Jaffa, Sephoria, Sebaste, Naplouse, Sidon,

---

[1] Arab. Chron., 200. [2] Id., 200.
[3] Id., 211. Note 2.

Beyrout, Ramla, Hebron, Bethlehem, Gaza, Daroum, Ascalon, and other towns, were only preparation for Jerusalem. He however wished to leave it full time; and though he spoke severely, to try to frighten the Franks, his real object was to reduce it to a quiet capitulation; for it is the holiest of cities, to Mahometans as well as Christians. Nor did he wish to defile it with blood: the less so, that it would seem like imitating the Giaours. Besides, there was, what he counted on more, the treason of the unquiet Greek within it, and Melkite Christians.[1] He expected much glory from taking the city of God; and he would be the first since Omar, who took it from the Christians; that he and Omar would be the only two that ever took it from the Christians—if on a Friday,[2] the greater the glory through all Islam; and that such lofty repute would be a solid recompense.[3] "From Gebail to Egypt nothing along the coast, or near it, remains to the Christians, but Tyre and Jerusalem," wrote Saladin. "So I'll go and take the Holy City; and when it pleaseth the great God, we'll go to Tyre!"[4] And on the 21st of September he left the sea for the

---

[1] Michaud: Hist., ii. 286.   [2] Arab. Chron., 204.
[3] Ibn-Alatir: 59.—Michaud: Hist., ii. 283, 288.
[4] Arab. Chron., 204.

Mountains of Judea. On reaching the walls of Jerusalem, he employed five days in examining them;[1] next he harangued his emirs—" That if God should give them the grace to chase the enemy from the Holy house, what felicity, what gratitude we should owe Him! That, behold, the holy city has been in the hands of infidels for eighty years, during which the Creator receives but impious praise there; that the Moslem Princes had often desired to deliver it, but nevertheless this high honour was reserved for the Ayoubides, to gain them the hearts of all Mahometans. That their entire thoughts should then be directed to the conquest of Jerusalem; that there is Omar's Mosque, choicest fabric of Islam; that Jerusalem is the dwelling of the prophets, where the saints repose, which the angels of heaven visit in pilgrimage, where shall be the general resurrection and the last judgment; that it is there the elect of the Lord resort; that it contains the stone of untouched beauty, whence Mahomet ascended to Paradise; that it is there the lightning flashed, the night of mystery shone forth, and that truth beamed which has illuminated every part of the world; that one of its gates is that of mercy,

[1] Arab. Chron., 205.

and whoso entereth by that gate, is deserving of Paradise; that there is the throne of Solomon, the chapel of David, the fountain of Siloe comparable to the river of Paradise. The Temple of Jerusalem is one of the three mosques of which the Alcoran speaks. Surely God will give it to us back in a finer state, since he honoured it with a notice in his Divine book." [1]

And the siege began; and was severe for a short time. All the medical men there were not sufficient for the wounded [2] writes an eye witness, who had himself received a sore wound then, of which he was suffering still, when he wrote years after. But in less than four days [3] the citizens were driven to capitulate; and Saladin, with inward satisfaction, granted what he had offered from the first; [4] and precisely on the first Friday of October, 1187, the Moslem standard was raised on its walls; but Saladin made his triumphal entrance several days later.[5] Yet sixty thousand, able to bear arms, are said to have been at that time within the city.[6]

[1] Arab. Chron., 206.
[2] Coggleshale: 26.—Bib. Crois., i. 354.
[3] Michaud seems for thirteen days: Hist., ii. 288. Note 1; but the Arab. Chron. says decidedly four; 209. Note.
[4] Michaud: Hist., ii. 289.   [5] Arab. Chron., 210.
[6] Arab. Chron., 212.

More than one hundred thousand Christians, says Michaud.[1] Now then (may be well asked), could Jerusalem, in Godfrey's time, with a handful have withstood the immense forces of Islam? Most certain is, what has from the commencement been asserted, that without Gerard's knights the Latin kingdom could not have stood a week. His order was then a natural and absolutely necessary consequence of the first crusade.

END OF VOL. I.

[1] Michaud: Hist. ii. 290.

THE HISTORY

OF

THE HOLY, MILITARY, SOVEREIGN ORDER

OF

ST. JOHN OF JERUSALEM;

OR,

KNIGHTS HOSPITALLERS, KNIGHTS TEMPLARS,
KNIGHTS OF RHODES, KNIGHTS OF MALTA.

By JOHN TAAFFE

KNIGHT COMMANDER OF THE ORDER, AND AUTHOR OF
"ADELAIS."

IN FOUR VOLUMES.
VOL. II.

ERRATA, VOL. II

Page.
1, Note 2, for XXXVI, read XXXVII.
38, Line 8, after hapless, add a comma.
83, Note 1, for L, read LXXXIV.
85, Note 4, for XXXVI, read XXXV.
251, Note 3, for CIII, read XCV.
257, Note 1, for LXXX, read LXXXI.
271, Note 3, for CLIV, read CXXVII.
333, Note 3, for CXI, read XLVI.

THE HISTORY

OF THE ORDER OF

ST. JOHN OF JERUSALEM.

BOOK I.—(CONTINUED.)

ABEYANCE THE FIRST.

OUT on the pinnacle of the rock looking towards Jerusalem, about five miles from it, stood a horseman, evidently Christian, from the setting beams of a vivid October sun, A.D. 1187 (the very last day of that month,[1] for early in November Saladin was before Tyre with his army),[2] which sun flashing on

[1] Arab. Chron., 219.

[2] Arrivez sur un point elevé de la route; nous avons arreté nos chevaux, et nos regards se sont reportes sur Jerusalem. Quelle profonde detresse!—Michaud: Orient., iv. 297.—That Grand Master Gardiner was quite a different man from Gardiner, Prior of England, is certain also from this latter's having been still prior there in 1189.—Appendix, Num. xxxvi.

his scarlet surcoat, showed most distinctly its white cross; his eye accompanying each movement of another horseman that indistinctly in the deep shade was coming nearer and nearer, though rather slowly; and at probably two hundred paces away, as he got over some rising ground on the plain, keen gazers could observe he wanted the right arm, and wore a white cross of small dimensions. And they soon knew each other; and the younger, with as much speed as he could manage, rode climbing not straight over the rocky face, which was impossible, but round by the village. "Sir Almeric de Vere," said the Grand Master, as this knight of his drew up from behind, with a low bow, being without the hand to salute with his sword, or touch his helmet, "I am very glad to see you alive, even so." "Nor," said Sir Almeric, "did I hope evermore to meet your Grace in this world; for the last thing I recollect just as I felt falling, and before quite losing my senses, was to have seen your blood bursting out in torrents; so, in spite of all our exertions, you were severely wounded, and as I believed, killed, like such multitudes." "But death gave me only a distant shake again," answered the veteran, "for which, under God, I am to thank you, and indeed the whole of the valiant three score that were round me when we clove our passage at Hattim, and of whom the survivors are you and the seven patches you see in muster behind me. We stopped first a little beyond Nazareth, where we buried several, and afterwards in certain caverns, where others of our party died, and then it was too late to go to Acre or Ascalon; for from Tyre to Egypt, all along the coast, is Moslem. And now being better, we have come to take our last view of that thrice holy and most noble metropolis, and then endeavour to get round by the mountains into Antioch, or somewhere in those parts. But having told you of us, let me ask you how you got into Jerusalem, and what has happened there since Saladin is its master, which he has been this fortnight, as we are informed; and as many exact details as possible, for we are worried with contradictions!"

"Very little could be testified," replied Sir Almeric, "by one senseless from that bloody field, or lying wounded in a room. However, I know it was that angel, an English lady, who had me lifted, with Saladin's leave, and her sweet care recalled me to life, and had me conveyed on a litter to the Jerusalem Hospital, several days before the siege. But in a week after I had undergone amputation, there was a great noise; and I went to the street door, and behold there was a motley crowd, monks, priests, canons, Levites, hermits, anchorites bent with the heavy weight of years, and now, alas! obliged to carry arms, women, old or young, and even children; nor indeed could a finger be raised an instant above the parapets without being hit—and amongst the rush, I distinguished the English young lady (she was only seventeen) with a helmet on her head, and carrying drink and refreshments to the soldiers on the bastions. Nor did an hour pass before I saw her borne in wounded, and her brother, who had received an arrow in his face; but fortunately it glanced sideways, and slid along the bone, so that surgeons extracted the wooden part,[1] but the steel barb lies still buried in the flesh. As to my gentle Margaret, she had been struck on the shoulder by a large splinter of stone,[2] so that she cannot yet get up, and bled dreadfully, but is out of danger. To such a dreadful crisis had matters come, that I myself heard five thousand byzantines offered for fifty soldiers to man one tower for a single night. It was the public crier from Government.[3] But not a single person was to be had at that extremity. It would have been only worse, for traitors rendered all real defence impossible. The Greeks and Melkite Christians now openly regret it did not last for a

---

[1] Coggleshale : Chron., 27.—Bib. Crois., i. 351.
[2] Thomas of Beverley.—Bib. Crois., iii. 371.
[3] Coggleshale : 34.—Bib. Crois., i. 355.

few hours longer, for that they had resolved that very night to cut the throats of all the Franks.¹

"The capitulation, that each should pay a small sum of money, was not rigorously exacted; thousands of expedients to avoid it. Forty days were allowed for all who chose to betake themselves to Tyre or Tripoli.² After a week, came the time prefixed for leaving Jerusalem, and, certainly, it was a melancholy scene; all the gates were shut but one, and Saladin on a throne to see all pass, the clergy with the consecrated vessels and the ornaments and treasures of the churches, and chiefly of the Holy Sepulchre, which some fanatic Moslem wished to pull down, and plough up the place, to prevent all further Christian pilgrimages³ — the priests and their infinite riches were all allowed to file by unexamined.⁴—Even upon some of his emirs objecting that those treasures were valued at two hundred thousand pieces of gold, and that, by the capitulation, the clergy had only leave to carry away their own effects, and not the church ornaments, Saladin replied, 'Let them alone, otherwise they would accuse us of treachery. They do not well know the true meaning of the capitulation.

[1] Aboulfarage.—Arab. Chron., 207. Note.
[2] Michaud: Hist., ii. 289.   [3] Arab. Chron., 214.
[4] Arab. Chron., 211.

Let them rather have grounds to praise the kindness of our religion.'[1]—The Queen, and ladies, and barons, and knights.—And Saladin respected her grief, and his words were full of kindness.—A large crowd of women, some with children in their arms and all with shrill cries of distress; wives, mothers, daughters. And Saladin, stung with deep pity, promised them aid to support their calamity, and gave the wives their husbands, and the mothers their sons, as many as could be found among the prisoners.—Since every one was permitted to carry what they could, many left their most precious effects, and, instead, put their aged parents, or sick friends, on their shoulders.—And Saladin then rewarded them, and pitied their piety, virtue, and misfortunes. All misfortune, even of his foes, found an entrance to his pity. And he permitted all of our order to remain in the city with the sick, and continue to take charge of them, till quite recovered. Nor can I but confess that the Mahometans praised and were proud of their sultan's noble compassion.[2] Large sums did he bestow on the ladye captives, with wondrous courtesy; but, particularly, on those of them that had lost their husbands or fathers; to some more, to some less, according to their wants. And many

[1] Arab. Chron., 212.   [2] Id.: 219.

beautiful dames and young ladies had to praise God, internally and most sweetly, for the good and signal honour which Saladin had done them.[1] Fierce, glorious and lofty were his virtues; and he testified it by the careful respect shown by the soldiers he sent with each band of Christian captives; towards whom they acted with the utmost humanity, permitting none to insult them, and if a man or woman, or child, fell sick or tired by the way, those soldiers used to alight and walk, and put their prisoners on their horses. Kindness, and tenderness, and courtesies, were found in all Saladin's army. I declare it was so then, whatever it was before or since. And, to several Christian knights he gave fiefs, considering they had neither the strength nor riches for a journey to Europe, and were too accustomed to the climate to change. Nor proposed any altering of religion to them. So that of the one hundred thousand Christians, by far the greater part went free; ransomed by their own money or Moslem charity. The soldan's brother paid the ransom of two thousand, Saladin of as many, and also set free crowds of poor people and orphans. Numbers were furtively let down the walls by ropes; others borrowed Mahometan dresses, and escaped as such. One thousand grown-

[1] Bernard le Tresorier.—Bib. Crois., ii. 280.

up Christians, at most, fell into slavery, and about five thousand infants.

"Certainly this is very unlike the extermination of the first crusade, but here there was a capitulation, and there the city was taken by storm. Nor was it a cold delicacy in Saladin, that engaged him to defer his triumphal occupation of Jerusalem till after the Christians had gone. A few days sufficed for the mass of the population. Those who chose to linger, were present at the entry certainly, nor could the Moslem army wait longer under the walls. It would have been unjust. Indeed the pomp of the Mahometans was very splendid when they entered. Then, with the single exception of the Holy Sepulchre, all the churches were turned into mosques; that of Omar washed with rose-water from Damascus, and embellished as before. Inhabitants, law, religion, all is changed in unhappy Jerusalem. Name it as you will, it has wholly vanished. Like those other boasts of antiquity, it no longer exists. It is lost for ever and ever! And please your Grace, all is over, all is lost with it. As for me, I have experienced nothing but kindness, from that completest of defeats at Hattim (which in truth was the downfall of the holy city) to this moment; for when all that care and skill could do for me in the hospital had been done, Saladin ordered me to mount this good steed from his own royal stables; and sent me this honourable safe conduct, with which I may embark anywhere hereabouts, nor I or my suite subject to any examination, only if I should have a body of above fifty armed men. So you see I can take your Grace and all your retinue with me, and I believe all that are alive of Hospitallers and Templars in Palestine."

"Which cannot be, Sir Almeric, and I think every one of these will refuse as well. But I do not mean at all to decline your services; on the contrary, confide a mission of great importance to you, which no one can do half so well!" And here he called one of his troop; "For be it known to you, Sir Almeric, I am tied in my saddle, and my hands are bandaged, so that my surgeon, who leads my horse, bears my ring. Now take that ring and let him put it on one of the fingers of your left hand, and it will be your sure passport to all Christian countries to obtain ships, monies, advice, every aid you may want; and presenting it to whoever commands at Tyre or Tripoli, and taking all the Hospitalleresses, sail with them to Italy or France, and thence, after placing individuals of them in any of our houses they like, take the rest to England, where the prior will fix them pleasantly, in our various commanderies, or Buckland, or Normandy, or direct them to Prague, or our new establishment in Spain, as he judges best, and as the ladies themselves prefer—many of them are English. But I recommend them all to you equally, and to every one who sees that ring. Which may lead you to Germany or Spain, but everywhere I entreat of you to mention the straits of the Christians here; and at Rome, prostrate yourself before the Pope in my name, and come to me back with the ring. But if your physician prescribe your home air, or that you hear of my departure, in either case give that ring finally to the prior, and tell him to pray for his poor (however younger) brother's soul."

But the voice of the turtle had gone forth at the battle of Tiberias and Jerusalem's downfall, and mournfully had it echoed through the whole Christian world.[1] The then Pope is said to have died of the grief.[2] "On the 2nd of October, Jerusalem was retaken, and on the 19th, Urban hearing it at Ferrara, he dropped dead," says the Papal biographer. But Muratori objects to its coming such a distance in seventeen days. Still, of seven carrier pigeons, the fleetest reached Tyre in an hour, and, with a brisk, fair wind, a sailing ship is nearly as rapid as

[1] Anspert (Dubrowsky Ed.): Chron., 6.—Bib. Crois., iii. 259.—Pantaleonis Colonia Chron.—Bib. Crois., iii. 5.

[2] Vertot: ii. 291. -Michaud: Hist., ii. 296.—Platina: iii. 31. Note 6.

a steamer, and from Ravenna you can go in less than two hours; so from Syria to Ferrara in seventeen days is not incredible. What had been deferred too long, was undertaken at once. The aged hero, Frederick I. (Barbarossa), of forty pitched battles, was the earliest of that third crusade.[1] It is probable that so excellent an army never left Europe. Some of the Moslems make his army six hundred thousand, and his waggons carrying arms and provisions twenty-five thousand.[2] Much exaggeration certainly; but it shows the opinion. Christian chroniclers have eighty thousand horse, from every part of Germany, and fifty thousand foot.[3] Of his cavalry of fifty thousand, not one single man but was a complete soldier, and either a gentleman, or a healthy, well-built citizen, of good conduct, and independent. Every private had to furnish a written document, that he had conducted himself well in two campaigns, and fought at least in one great battle.—A letter of recommendation from his bishop. Recruits to be examined naked by a physician and surgeon; and each, for wealthy, to pay one whole year's revenue, for the poorest of them, three hundred francs to the imperial treasury, as

[1] Anspert: 9.—Bib. Crois., iii. 260.
[2] Arab. Chron., 281.
[3] Ricobaldus apud Muratori, Rer. Ital. Script., vol. ix.—Bib. Crois., ii. 612.

credit towards their expenses for two years, in going, staying, and returning. " Formidable indeed to the enemy in arms, but also entitled to the admiration of those who wished for peace in whose lands, and under whose roofs they lived, without oppression or harm."[1] One would think it impossible to raise an army on such terms, to pay, instead of being paid. Yet, it is said, many more offered than were accepted.[2] The infantry was similar. Frederick I. was ill-treated early. " I have made his troops so suffer, that they will not be able to give your Excellency much trouble," wrote the traitor of Constantinople, the imperial Greek, to Saladin.[3] But the celebrated Frederick I. was lost in a small rapid river of Cilicia, or Thessaly,[4] whether in bathing,[5] or at a hunt,[6] or to avoid the mountains, or to speak to his son, whose wing had encamped on the other side, as appears was most likely,[7] is little matter. Frederick I. was the greatest soldier of his day, as all agree.[8] " The only one that resem-

[1] Milton.
[2] Michaud: ii. 317.—Vinisauf: 1.—Bib. Crois., ii. 668.
[3] Michaud: ii. 323.
[4] Albi Chron., 15.—Bib. Crois., iii. 218.
[5] Canisius, 24.—Bib. Crois.. iii. 183.
[6] Robert du Mont.—Bib. Crois., iii. 104.
[7] Anspert (Dubrowsky)).—Bib. Crois., iii. 269, and ii. 670.
—Vinisauf: who also affirms it was close under a rock, on which had been cut long before, *here shall the greatest of mortals perish.*
[8] Michaud: ii. 333.

bled the great captains of antiquity."[1] Much, seeing it was the age of Cœur de Lion! Yet, how does our hero king's biographer exclaim at Frederick's death: "O sea! O earth! O heaven! the ruler of the Roman Empire, that august prince, who had revived the glory and power of ancient Rome, has perished, alas!"[2] Instead of burying his intestines at Tarsus, and embalming or salting his corpse, some say[3] it was boiled on the spot; that the bones, separated from the flesh, were collected and deposited at Antioch,[4] or Tyre,[5] or Nazareth, and (as Jerusalem, which the emperor's will had prescribed, was always in the power of the Mahometans) finally, he was brought back to Spire,[6] and interred with the other emperors. His fine army melted away, their horses eaten, the wood of their lances burned for fuel,[7] a mountain of metal formed in Asia Minor of their weapons and armour;[8] the very few of the German warriors that got to Palestine, like spectres, so worn by famine and incurable fever, could not possibly be of any assistance, but far better

---

[1] Ricobaldus.—Bib. Crois., ii. 614.
[2] Vinisauf.—Bib. Crois., ii. 670.
[3] Arab. Chron., 273.
[4] Anspert (Dubrowsky).—Bib. Crois., iii. 270.
[5] Nangis d'Achery.—Bib. Crois., iii. 236.
[6] Arab. Chron., 274, 380.
[7] Id., Id., 280. [8] Id., 278.

not show them for fear of discouraging the Christians. His poor son died soon—the second—for the first had remained at home as regent.[1] One good came of it, that deadly Asia Minor was renounced for ever. The sea for all future crusades![2]

Scarce had Acre fallen to Islam, when Conrad, son of that Marquis of Montferrat who as related, had been taken at Hattim by Saladin, coming in a ship from Europe, found out his mistake before landing, so remained on board as a merchant in the port; till hearing the Christian flag still flew at Tyre, profited by a favourable wind to sail out of the net, and got to the Tyrians, who were so encouraged and elated also on observing his engineering ability, that they acceded to his proposal to make him their prince. Had Saladin gone against Tyre immediately from the victory of Tiberias, he would have perhaps succeeded; but his delay followed by Conrad's coming, spoiled all.[3] As to Acre, it had become Mahometan, with the rest, which occurred immediately after the overthrow at Tiberias. And very soon after the fall of Jerusalem, a small Christian detachment had begun to observe, if not besiege Acre. Against whom Saladin marched; but went round by Tyre, and for the third time essayed to reduce it by

1187

[1] Arab. Chron., 279.   [2] Id., 282.
[3] Id., 219.

presenting Conrad's father in chains; but the valiant young prince, whom Saracens call the most voracious of wolves, the slicst of all Christian dogs,[1] chose rather to be a martyr's son than a traitor. So the Moslem had to remove to Tripoli, where the *green knight* rendered all in vain.[2] And the besiegers of Acre kept increasing in numbers every day. The desultory had soon to become sanguinary, and that small detachment grew up into an army.

Not only religious exasperation—a sort of despair—but likewise the spirit of every description of patriots, had been much changed by the remodelling of Palestine. Latin or Moslem despotism—the Hospitallers wished for neither. Yet they now had to choose; and which worst, was evident. Their affections, forced to become isolated, grew stronger. So they attached themselves entirely to what seemed possible; but, alas! was to baffle all their efforts. Inscrutable are the secrets of the Lord! They for the future saw no other refuge than the cross! Their only triumph was to plant the cross! The softener of the heart—the enlightener of the mind—Christianity! To them all the rest was dross! The present world was a glimpse—of nonsense; if they could not ascend

[1] Michaud: Hist., ii. 238.
[2] Id.: Id., 239. All known of the *green knight* is, that he was a *Portuguese*.

even the first step towards civilisation. Nor can any be civilised but Christians. Freedom flows in the same direction. To be free, you must first be a Christian.

His title of King of Jerusalem, which he had been forced, while prisoner, to swear to abdicate, was taken back by Guy, who had been liberated; perhaps from the bad motive that he might breed dissensions, and prevent the Giaours from having a better monarch. But even so, and though his oath of abdication, extorted by force, was therefore invalid, yet, when a conclave of bishops dispensed him from the obligation, it appeared as if Christians were always ready to break what had been sworn.[1] In spite of his oaths (cried the Mahometans), King Guy (whom God curse) violated the pact.[2] But Conrad (curse him), a devil for perfidy and daring, the cleverest of Tyrian wolves, the impurest and most artful of curs—not even the Tyrians would acknowledge him. So, after wandering awhile, he led his few followers to join the siege of Acre. And soon indeed we have nauseous images; the ribs of Saracens, well cleansed, being made into bows by his bowmen.[3] But better men than their

---

[1] Michaud: Hist., ii. 341.   [2] Arab. Chron., 220, 238.
[3] Florentini : Chron :—Bib. Crois., iii. 320.

royal leader soon joined the nucleus increasing every day.

Acre, just before that time, had been a strong and flourishing seaport, with considerable commerce, as transit between the East and Europe. On the land side it was thought to be defended by walls and the *Cursed Tower;* and the *Tower of Flies,* at its harbour's narrow entrance, made it pass for secure. From November of the year before, there had been a small Christian army of nine thousand at most, with Guy observing,[1] rather than besieging, the Moslem garrison within it.

Acre has long been in ruins, and since Ibrahim, more than ever. Yet man cannot deprive it of its southern glory, Carmel! Eastward the ground shorn of its woods, is marshy, but was a glorious plain.

Saladin was not far from Zook, collecting a great force to begin the new campaign of 1188, and at one of his military banquets had most beautiful apricots from Damascus, which shows the spring was far set in.[2] Yet little was there to conquer in Palestine. The two forts—one, Kaucab, belonging to the Hospitallers, the other Sefed to the Templars— were the principal things. But he had in his mind a far mightier foe—the third crusade, which certainly

[1] Michaud: Hist., ii. 344. . [2] Arab. Chron., 244.

menaced him with what does him vast honour. For he had to resist not only the three chief monarchs of Europe—Germany, France, and England—one led by *Barbarossa*, and one by *Cœur de Lion*, and the other, by a name very properly dear to France, *Philip Augustus*—but all Christendom; for Italians, Spaniards, Flemings, Swedes, Friezlanders, Portuguese, and others, composed it. They had Mahometans at home, but nevertheless Ebro and Mondego sent several to be Templars and Hospitallers; besides who was the Green Knight? Saladin might hold his head high; for he, risen from a private station, had to contend with all Europe, led by renowned warriors, to be conquered by any one of whom would have been a credit to any member of the military profession, alive or dead.

But seeing the crusade delayed, Saladin moved about, and in five weeks occupied Laodicea and Tortosa, and the iron bridge near Antioch, and all along the Orontes, and several places; yet avoided Marcab (say the Moslems themselves), for it appeared impregnable, and belonged to the Hospitallers, who were sure to defend it ably, which is a just tribute to those heroes, but may be fairly attributed to a wish in Saladin to preserve his army entire for the coming foe; though his prudence must have been pain to his self-love, for Marcab lay directly on his line of march, and he had to diverge from it. The Moslems who mention this, do not make any excuse.[1] "Glory be to God," said Saladin, " for permitting me to take so many towns all on Fridays in a few weeks, rendering easy what in itself is difficult!"[2] In the middle of Ramadan he attacked Sefed, and it soon capitulated. A few days afterwards, he heard his brother had taken Petra and Montreale; so, regarding the four places he had said he coveted,[3] his mind might be at ease.[4] Kaucab having foiled his emir, he went against it himself.[5] "Having taken Sefed, he will also take Kaucab," said the Christians, "and then it is all over with us. If the Hospitallers could only resist until the arrival of our brethren from Europe!"[6] Hear Emad-eddin, Saladin's private secretary: " We came to Kaucab, and found it a fortress as if hanging from the stars, or the nest of eagles, or domicile of the moon. There inhabited the *barking dogs* and *perfidious wolves*[7] who whispered to each other, ' While one of us is left, our name shall be unspotted.' Their walls began to shake, and several wide breaches were made; but the season

[1] Arab. Chron., 225.   [2] Id., 228.
[3] Id.   224.
[4] Id.   231.—Michaud: Hist., ii. 341.
[5] Id.   232.   [6] Id.   232.
[7] The Hospitallers, says the note on the original.

was bitterly rude, rain in torrents, wind, mud, at every moment the stones yielded, the cords relaxed, the tents fell, and had to be put up again. Notwithstanding such excessive rain, we were without good water to drink; the roads were so slippery, that our mules were continually tumbling on their bellies, and from the weather, the highway, which was wide, became choked up to a narrow passage. The soldan had left us with the baggage below, while he had his engines dragged up the mountain. Each morning and evening we used to clamber up to salute him; at last his miners got under the walls!"[1] So Kaucab was taken by storm; but very easily, since without any opposition; all its survivors having found a way out to join the Tyrians, it did not contain a human creature.[2] If Kaucab and Margat, or Marcab, were the same place, then Saladin must have been doubly pleased; but it was not with his army, but a picked corps of his Mamelukes and his guards, that he made this second approach, not unsuccessful like the first.[3] Thus he himself, in a letter to his brother: "Kaucab was the stronghold of the Hospitallers and infidelity, the ordinary residence of the grand master of the order and its head-quarters, since being expelled from Jerusalem. We waited long

---

[1] Arab. Chron., 234.   [2] Id. 232.
[3] Id., 232.

before we attacked it, and our efforts have been crowned with full success. All is safe now. We are masters of every one of those fortresses. We only want Tyre. If that city was not continually succoured from beyond sea, it would long since have been in our hands. But God be praised! the infidel rebels are in no ark, but rather in a prison. The Christians have nothing left but a few yelling curs, led astray by Satan. But for us, they would come on like outrageous lions; and falsehood would have triumphed over virtue. Our brethren from Egypt and the Emperor of Constantinople, send us word that the Franks in the west have already unsheathed their swords. The partisans of error coalesce against us. God confound them! Mad men, they will soon put back their sword into its scabbard. With the aid of Providence, we shall thrash them. Let us supplicate the Lord to strengthen our hearts and hands, and keep us united. Only great men are called to great things. Whatever God decrees, cannot but be effected." [1]

Then the soldan went into Acre, and passed most of the winter there, fortifying its fortifications, with great care.

In Europe, the Christians wore black in mourning

---

[1] Arab. Chron., 235.

for the loss of the Holy City, and took arms; their women, too. A Christian prisoner told the Moslems that his mother had no other child, and sent him on the crusade, and sold her house to equip him.[1]

Saladin, in a letter, tells the caliph that the crusaders are not individuals, but the whole body of Franks, able to bear arms. That they come by every way; easy and difficult, by land, by sea; from the remotest regions, as well as the nearer.

Yet one division of the third crusade had already perished. If the Germans had arrived, it might have been written: *"Here once reigned the Mussulman!"* [2] Some residue of Frederick's grand army reached Acre. It had been easy to impede them; *but when God wishes a thing, he prepares the causes.*[3] That remnant of a division of Franks got close to Acre on the 12th of August, 1189, and the soldan, who had advanced to cut them off, but missed the road, some day later. Truth is, the Duke of Suabia, Frederick I.'s son, and the rest of his army, had been engaged to remain on the Orontes, not to discourage the Christians by their haggard sight— living skeletons as they were, of no use to the crusaders; on the contrary, very dangerous. But a

---

[1] Arab. Chron., 242.   [2] Id., 243.
[3] Id., 244.

bribe of sixty thousand besants from Saladin persuaded a Frank prince to induce the poor Germans to join the crusaders, as if these acted from a spirit of envy in depriving them of the honour of sharing the besiegers' victory. Whereupon the imperial duke did come with his troops to Acre, and was the cause of most lamentable dissensions there.[1] So Saladin's march was a feint.

The Christians were not in numbers sufficient to enclose Acre, but only two thousand horse, and a larger multitude of foot; so left one of its gates free, of which Saladin profiting, introduced some troops and provision, and then pitched his tents on the little hill of Kissan, directly opposite the principal street of the town, with his left leaning on the ancient Belus or *Rivulet of Sweet Water*, and his right on the hill Aiadia, so as to form a crescent behind the Christians, who were between him and Acre, having their king's tent on the hill Massallaba, or Thuron, exactly facing the harbour.[2]

Combats every day, the Moslem wheeling like butterflies round a light. The soldan trying to moderate their zeal, and economise all for a great blow. He, also, was receiving reinforcements almost each day from Mesopotamia and the whole

[1] Vinisauf.—Bib. Crois: ii. 678.
[2] Arab. Chron., 245. Note.

East. Acre was now completely occupied by a forest of ships on the sea side, and there remained only a little spot open towards the land. Even that was closed about the end of August, and then really began the siege of Acre; one of the mightiest events of the middle ages. The Moslem had been two years working at its defences, under direction of one of the ablest engineers then in existence. At first Saladin's emirs had advised him to throw down Acre; but when he saw how fine a city it was, he sent for the famous Egyptian, who had built the Cairo citadel.[1] That celebrated Caracousch was then in Acre, and continued in it during the whole siege, as one of the two that directed the whole government and nearly every operation.[2] The Christians had to resist both the garrison and the Moslem army. There was much blood shed; yet conversation often ensued by mutual accord, when tired of fighting. Nor unfrequently, the belligerents disarmed and mixed, singing, dancing, gambling, friends for some minutes, and, at a signal resuming their arms, enemies as before. In those pacific intervals, their children not seldom played at battle, mimicking their fathers, for some trifle. When a boy was down, his parents ransomed him

[1] Arab. Chron., 246. [2] Id. 246.

for two bits of silver, and it is related that one wanted to retain the other, declaring he had made him prisoner, and did not wish to sell him, but to have him as his slave. At all events, he blushed deeply, and was unwilling to accept the ransom.— It was considered by the Turks a good omen, that a valuable horse leapt from a European ship, lately arrived, and swam, not to the Christian camp, as his owners intended, but into Acre.[1]—An emir falling sick, and wishing for death in battle, ordered out his charger, and mounting him with excessive pain, died a martyr.[2]—The Christian line stood like a perpendicular rock, on which nothing could have effect. One slain, another took his place instantly. They had fought till night, and lay on their arms, and renewed the battle at daybreak. Until noon, it was balanced. The Moslems' right at last penetrated to the city, by the latest spot the Christians closed, and where the works were fresh. Even Saladin himself then rode into Acre, but returned to his camp with his army, which there went to repose after such fatigue; Saladin's physician protesting that his master had not tasted nourishment from Friday morning to Sunday night[3] —so he had to retire. But for that retreat of his,

[1] Arab. Chron., 248. [2] Id., 249.
[3] Id. 247.

the Christians were lost. They made use of the opportunity, and built the spot up. Next day the Moslems came too late. The Frank camp was impregnable, and every passage to Acre impossible. The Grand Master of the Templars was taken,[1] the same who had been taken at Hattim, and given his freedom; but this time the soldan had him slain. Three Christian women, who had fought on horseback, like brave men, were made prisoners, and their sex discovered only when their armour was dragged off.[2] Ten thousand corpses of Christians (most of them knights) were thrown into the river by the soldan's orders. Christian infantry took small part in many actions. Some pious Moslem civilians, quiet lookers on, having made off on their mules, passed Jordan, frightening the whole country; and never stopping to eat or drink, but hastening forward, each with his hands firmly set on his beast's neck and breathing with difficulty; some of them never pulling in, till they got to Damascus; they were soon followed by the truth, that all was well, and that their party had gained a victory; "*at this their spirits grew calm, and they regretted having run away.*"[3]

But the stench of the slaughter caused sickness,

---

[1] Arab. Chron., 251.   [2] Id., 251.
[3] Id., 252.

and even the soldan felt sick.[1] So he and some Moslems retreated to another hill, the *Karoula*, a few leagues from Acre.[2] In October not many troops remained near Acre; so the Christians employed the time in cutting wide deep ditches and raising a high wall quite round their lines; with room behind it for a body of archers armed with the *zemboureck*, the *quadrellus* of Ducange, the French *carreau de la foudre*. This weapon appeared a moment at Constantinople among the modern Greeks, but fell out of use. The Popes, from humanity, had prohibited it to all Christians; and we first hear of it at the siege of Tyre by Saladin. Thence it went to Acre, and when Cœur de Lion came, he adopted it for some of his archers, which on his return to Europe scandalized the Christians, and it was considered a judgment on him that he was slain himself by a *coup de carreau*. Since the invention of gunpowder zemboureck (in some countries) means a kind of light artillery or field piece.[3]

Saladin's sickness soon passed, since that very winter we read of his being out hunting with his falcons.[4] The Moslems find it very curious that women (and dissolute ones too) were allowed in the Christian army—but particularly

1190

---

[1] Arab. Chron., 253.   [2] Id., 254.
[3] Id. 255. Note.   [4] Id., 257.

a company of three hundred courtezans, regularly shipped out together in the same ship, to amuse the warriors, who were some of them unmarried, and some separated from their wives—which impropriety soon becoming known, many emirs, Mamelukes, and other Mahometans, contrived to frequent the Christian camp on visits to those sprightly ladies. These appear to have been considered by the infidels as an essential part of our military discipline, to keep and direct the spirits of the soldiers towards furthering whatever plans their commander-in-chief might have.[1]

Excellent divers—who passed through the Christian camp by night—and carrier pigeons were the only communication with Acre now.[2] An embassy from the Caliph of Bagdad brought some Greek fire, as a sample, and five men, who knew how to compose and throw it.[3] Saladin next came back to Kissan and his vast and most beautiful camp. In July, Count Henry, who was related to both Philip and Richard, came with news of the French and English crusade, which from hour to hour might be expected.[4] "See the Pope of the Franks," said Saladin in a letter to the caliph, "how he imposes taxes for the holy war, and whatever he

---

[1] Arab. Chron., 258.
[2] Id., 260—286.
[3] Id., 261.
[4] Id., 282.

desires is as a law to all Christian people. But you who are of the blood of our Prophet, it is for you to do far more than that infidel high priest of Rome the great. What your servant here writes, he would dare say in the dust at the threshold of your palace. I am resigned to the will of God, and hope to be firm in danger. But you are Islam's physician, and we the sick."[1] Again. "Not only the Pope of his own authority restrains the Christians as to eating and drinking, but he menaces with excommunication whoever does not march with a spirit of piety to the deliverance of Jerusalem. Such is the obstinacy of Christians in their perverse cause. Then what should be we true believers?"[2]

All the Moslem army were now at Kissan. Their camp was like a splendid city. Several streets and an immense square. "I myself counted seven thousand well-stocked shops (wrote an eye-witness) and a hundred and forty sheds for shoeing horses. Of a multitude of kitchens, one had twenty-eight boilers, each boiler large enough to hold an entire sheep; a single seller of butter had paid seventy gold pieces to transport his utensils; of baths there were one thousand, a bit of silver being the

---

[1] Arab. Chron., 284.   [2] Id., 286.

price of a bath. As to the warehouses of new and second-hand dresses, they were too numerous to count!"[1]

About this time Guy's Sybilla died, as well as her two children; on which Conrad of Tyre resolved to marry Almeric's other daughter. But how? for she had for years been the wife of young Thoron. Yet Conrad got clergy who broke the marriage. As for Isabella, she seemed contented with any husband. Yet the Archbishop of Canterbury, to whom (as being on the spot, having come from England with some recent crusading party) the Jerusalem Patriarch delegated his authority, excommunicated the pair; at which both Conrad and she laughed. Thus he had two wives, one at Constantinople and one in Palestine. And two Kings of Jerusalem; Conrad in right of his living wife, and Guy of his dead one.[2] This, and other miseries, made Canterbury die of grief.[3]

On the 20th April, 1191, the King of France joined the Christians before Acre. A few days afterwards, the Count of Flanders, one of the most powerful of the Western lords;[4] and, on the 8th of the following June, the King of England.[5]

1191

---

[1] Arab. Chron., 262.
[2] Michaud: Hist., ii. 365, 366.
[3] Vinisauf.—Bib. Crois., ii. 681.
[4] Arab. Chron., 302.   [5] Id., 304.

Monies for the third crusade were in each parish to be paid, in presence of a priest, a prelate, a *Templar, and an Hospitaller*. The same of the tax called Saladin's penny. Those knights then became the treasurers of Europe.[1]

Some gentlemen of Bremen and Lubeck[2] added to the German Hospitallers, and a small remainder of Frederick I.'s army,[3] after having existed as a party, it is hard to say precisely how long, became one of the three military orders, ranking henceforth with Templars and Hospitallers, by the formal institution of a Papal bull, dated the 22nd February, 1191.[4] Not in Jerusalem, like the other two, yet in the most honourable position of that moment, under the walls of a city against which were now coming the united forces of France and England, after Germany's had been broken on the way. Glorious was the post where the Teutonics openly raised their nascent flag. And if their first steps were naturally weak, still they soon learnt from their elders to act as a worthy member of that celebrated trine.

All was joy and illuminations in the Christian camp. But an omen took place the very next

---

[1] Michaud: Hist., ii. 306.   [2] Id.:   Id.,   389.
[3] Werner, Martene.—Bib. Crois., i. 332.
[4] Michaud: Hist., ii. 494.—Appendix, Num. xlvi.

morning, which appeared highly consoling to the Mahometans. The King of France having a favorite falcon "of a terrific aspect, and rare in its kind, a very large, and really fine bird, milk-white—I seldom saw a finer—(says Boha-eddin), it flew away from his fist, and into the city, whence it was sent to the soldan; King Philip, who used to caress and fondle it, and loved it much, *as the falcon did him*, offered one thousand pieces of gold to ransom it: and was refused."[1]

But now the season was quite favourable. Small cavalry affairs had been rather for show; everything was ready on all sides; furious struggles, and the whole is to be decided.[2] The Pisan fleet had been off the mouth of the port from the first.[3] When the first fifty ships of Europeans were descried from Thoron, there had been a moment of cruel surmise; after which, came a joyful hurrah from the vessels, to which the Christians on Thoron sent a similar shout in wild response. They were twelve thousand Danes, Friezlanders, and Flemish, headed by Sir James D'Avesnes, of the founder's glorious family, and who was soon to die as became it.[4] Long ago with Henry of Champagne no few English had arrived, among whom the Archbishop of Can-

---

[1] Arab. Chron., 302. [2] Id., 306.
[3] Michaud: Hist., ii. 344. [4] Id.: Id., 346.

terbury; if not even some weeks, still earlier, as some chroniclers record.[1]

On the 12th of February that year, Guy, as King of Jerusalem, made a deed of gift to the Hospitallers, of an addition to their house in Acre, learning that the said house is small (*dinoscens*), and recollecting how great had been their establishment in the holy city. As he was then not in possession of Acre, nor in it, but only near it (*apud*), this at least shows he was sure of it; and of course, some months later, he executed his obligation. Of that document an extract shall be given in the Appendix: not because it praises the Hospitallers, for in that case the whole of their diplomatic codex might be copied, and it would be little; but because it proves that Gardiner had not died at Ascalon of his wounds the day after the battle of Tiberias, as Vertot and the others relate.[2] On the contrary, here he is alive four years later, after having participated in the battles of that siege; and as he is not said to be *in extremis*, or sick at all, for aught we know, there is every reason to suppose he shared the victory: at soonest, may have expired in the following autumn. When I differ from my predecessors in the history of the order, I do so

[1] Vinisauf, Brompton, Coggleshale, Beverly, &c.
[2] Vertot: liv. ii. 271.—Appendix, xlii.

unwillingly; and like to testify it, by assigning the paramount evidence.[1] It is not surprising that the King of France should be received as an angel, after two whole years of battles.[2]

If Richard had delayed a little, he had been forced at Cyprus to reduce a despot to order, and put him into chains, not of iron, but silver, as descending from the imperial Comneni. Nor did Richard take to himself that Latin kingdom, which was to last three hundred years; but with characteristic generosity gave it away. Richard is said to have been very handsome, and with chivalrous manners; and remarkable even at first sight, from a magnificence of dress, that distinguished him from every one else;[3] particularly on his noted fawn-coloured horse from Cyprus. Why so called is somewhat doubtful. When he too came, it might be truly said, all the most celebrated captains then in existence in any part of the world, were before Acre. On his voyage thither, off Cyprus, he had destroyed a monstrous Saracen ship, with stores of every known description, for Acre; and unknown also—two hundred deadly serpents, to be sent as ruin among

---

[1] Cod. Dipl. Geros., i.—Num. lxxix.
[2] Michaud: Hist., ii. 370.
[3] Vinisauf: 2.—Bib. Crois., ii. 684.

the Christians. Who ever heard, before, of poisonous serpents as instruments of war?[1]

Also the crusaders' camp was like a city, with streets, palaces, churches, as spacious as Saladin's, or more so; so that to the eye, there were three Acres, not merely one. And the army of Richard was more numerous than Philip's, for a very excellent reason, that the former gave higher pay. He too sided with Guy, and the other with Conrad. Philip's party was of French, Genoese, Germans, Templars. Richard's, English, Hospitallers, Pisans. So Conrad, who had visited the crusade, betook himself back to Tyre, resolved to make no *self-sacrifice* to unite the Christians. There was much of the noble generosity of chivalry in the relations between Saladin, and Richard, and Philip, and their mutual presents, contrasting strongly with the fanatical barbarism of the holy wars, particularly on the side of the Mahometans; which exposed all the leaders, Moslem and Christian, to an accusation of lukewarmness in matters of religion, and even of Deism and Atheism. After long debates it was resolved, first, that Guy should be king for life, and Conrad after him; second, on the days the English party attacked Acre, the French should defend the camp from Saladin; and *vice*

---

[1] Vinisauf: 2.—Bib. Crois., ii. 686.

versâ. The besieged kept fortifying, while the besiegers disputed. Giant battles ensued, minings, escalades; during one of which Richard, being sick, had himself carried in a chair to direct the action,[1] of which he must have been at the head, in the very hottest, since he struck several of the enemy with his lance.[2] At a surprise the man pre-eminent for intrepidity was a Bishop of Salisbury. The Moslems were in vast numbers from Asia and Africa. It was Asia and Africa against Europe.[3] "Only let God rest neuter, and victory is ours," cried the Franks.[4] " Impious cry," says their chronicler.[5] Fanatical enthusiasm on both sides. What worse could a cannon do than what one of Richard's machines did, throw a stone that killed twelve men in a single discharge? He had carried with him a dozen of those machines, that reduced everything else to dust, but could not resist the devouring Greek fire.[6] The despair of the garrison was terrible. They twice had asked for quarter, and were refused. The Christians wished to take it by storm. Death at all events.[7]

[1] Vinisauf: 3.—Bib. Crois., ii. 690.
[2] Id. :   Id.—   Id.,   Id.
[3] Bib. Crois., ii. 677.   [4] Michaud: Hist., ii. 349.
[5] Vinisauf.
[6] Vinisauf.—Bib. Crois., ii. 689.
[7] Id.   Id.   Id.

The Moslems were as certain to die; then why not rather with arms in their hands? The fishermen having caught one of their divers in their net, he was tortured, whipped, and beheaded.[1] All means had been employed to inform Saladin of their straits. Yet desperate violence wore out, and remained the weakness of terror. So all failing, they capitulated.

All had but to succumb; there was no other resource. Famine and distress of every kind had reached their zenith.

To apprise the soldan of their piteous resolution, they sent him this final missive. They were now less than six thousand.[2] It was on a Friday, July 17th, 1191.[3]

But he, having received their pigeon and letter that very dawn, had called a council of war to consider on a last effort to save the garrison. It was near the stroke of noon, and while the council deliberated, on a sudden they saw the Christian flag raised on the walls. The Mussulmen were in the utmost consternation at the sight. Dumb for awhile, as if struck dead by astonishment. Then burst forth their sighs and sobs like madmen. All

---

[1] Vinisauf: 3.—Bib. Crois., 679.
[2] Id.:   Id.   691.
[3] Arab. Chron., 316.

participated in that common sorrow. Only in proportion of each one's faith and piety, was his deep affliction; the deeper, the more religious. To restore the cross and one thousand six hundred Frank prisoners and pay two hundred thousand pieces of gold.—All to be the price of the city and their mere lives, and all the human creatures within Acre the hapless to remain as security in the victors' hands until full execution of the treaty.— Such the substance of the capitulation, sworn to already and hostages given.[1]

"As for me," says Boha-eddin, "I remained the whole time close to Saladin, and tried to console his anguish, which was like that of a mother for the death of her only son. I conjured him to turn his thoughts rather towards how to save Jerusalem and Palestine." The historian Emad-eddin, who was also present, tells us of the soldan's great sorrow. Nor did they as yet know the hard conditions. "It was God's decree! Towards evening Saladin shut himself up in his tent, full of black thoughts. Consolation was feeble, and hope had flown far off. In the morning we returned to see him, and found him dejected and unquiet as the evening before. We said, Islam has not perished,

[1] Arab. Chron., 317.

for losing a town. Let us confide in Him as much as ever." Saladin never fought a battle without having implored the Lord first, nor won a victory without, prostrate or kneeling, pouring out fervent thanks to Him on the field. Why should the hero be suspected of fear or hypocrisy? The Mahometans who relate it, did not mean to question either; but admired his courage and profound faith. The Frank also marched to battle "*with the ardour* of *a courser on his way to the pasture*," write the same Mahometans; often did his troops rally at his voice. "And we," said the Christians—"were also displeased at the capitulation; for above two whole years have we shown more bravery than would have sufficed to conquer all Asia; and now we are defrauded of justice!"[1]

On learning the conditions, and they sworn to and hostages already given, Saladin hesitated to stand by a capitulation in which he had no part, but his emirs to his interrogations answered unanimously, "Those Mahometans are our brothers and companions, we cannot do otherwise than ratify; no excuse, the Koran allows none; we must absolutely give really what they promised, whatever be our private opinion." So he sent immediately for money to

---

[1] Michaud: Hist., ii. 393.—Vinisauf: 3,—Bib. Crois., ii. 691.

Damascus, not having the sum with him. In such circumstances all Mussulmen are bound for each other as their Prophet expressly lays down. "So also the cross that he had taken at Tiberias. As soon as it came, deputies were deputed from the Christian camp to identify it, which they did, and knelt to it; and knew it to be the very same that had served for the crucifixion of the Messiah, and had been sent to the Bagdad Caliph, and could convince themselves of Saladin's good will and sincerity," says Emad-eddin.[1]

If there were afterwards a doubt, the Moslems refused to consider it. But before the cross was delivered up, or the money paid (for which there was a month allowed by the capitulation), the passions got inflamed on both sides. The King of France had already returned home, not only from sickness (it is said), but also from disliking the intimacy he perceived between Richard and Saladin. Thus Richard remained sole master of Acre and commander-in-chief not only of his English, but of all the Christians, including the French under the Duke of Burgundy. Cœur de Lion's first duty (if duty) was a cruel one. But if the Arab chroniclers have been often cited already,

---

[1] Arab. Chron., 318, 319.

they shall be still more frequently during the remainder of his stay in Palestine, because his English biographer or any Christian might pass for a partial authority.

From the first day the Christians entered Acre, they violated their word—not treating the Mussulmen well, but extremely rude, and threw them into prison under pretence of saving them from the crusaders.[1] If the garrison held up their heads like brave soldiers, they merited honour for it. Their most noble resignation ought to have inspired admiration and respect, not hatred.[2] - To Saladin's just proposal, for them to set all the Mussulmen free at once, and that he would pay all the money at once, not in quotas, as the capitulation prescribed, and give them the cross, which by their deputies they had already verified, they objected as unwilling to liberate any one before they were paid and had the cross; and, when he proposed *vice versâ*, only that since they did him the injury of distrusting him, he would them; and required that the Templars should be their guarantee on oath, for he supposed, that those religious gentlemen would think that what is sworn is to be observed; then the Templars denied to be guarantee or to

[1] Arab. Chron., 319.   [2] Michaud: Hist., ii. 392.

swear or to be responsible for any one or anything.[1] So the ratification was withheld—which drove King Richard (God curse him) furious, and meditating a terrible vengeance, he mounted his horse, and in the plain before the two armies drawn up, had his handcuffed and enchained hostages put to death, to the number of better than three thousand Mussulmen.[2] Yet it is affirmed, it was not the king, but the whole Christian army, that decided in a general court-martial. The sentence iniquitous or not, was theirs, not his.[3] Some Moslems blamed Saladin more-than Richard; and that their soldan, by not keeping the treaty, abandoned his co-religionists to death.

Saladin should not have allowed any sum, or any worldly consideration, to make him spur the Christian to a deed which he could not have well avoided in his station, where the interests of so many nations were confided to him alone, and many ready to accuse him of imprudence. Of his private generosity all Mahometans were convinced, and that his rigour was for the public.[4] But the whole was over as to that treaty, and cross and money went back to Damascus. "As to the cross, not from any value the soldan saw in it, nor any

[1] Arab. Chron., 319. [2] Id., 320.
[3] Michaud: Hist., ii. 395. [4] Michaud : Hist., ii. 396.

other motive, than that he knew it pained the Christians to think it was in Saracen hands," writes Emad-eddin.[1]

On the 30th of August, two days after the massacre of hostages, the fortifications of Acre being put to rights again, and in good state, and in free possession of the Franks, the Christian army set out on its march along the coast southward. They were then three hundred thousand strong, but of all different nations and manners, and some of them unwilling to quit Acre, where the wine was excellent, and the women renowned for beauty.[2] " It was at the end of August, two days after the massacre of our poor martyrs, the defenceless prisoners."[3] This was the order of the Christian march leaving Acre : King Richard headed the vanguard ; but, as he flew about everywhere, the Templars and Hospitallers were the head,[4] leaving Caiphas. The standard in the centre was surrounded by the Normans, and from it streamed the banner of England. The Duke of

---

[1] Arab. Chron., 322.   [2] Vinisauf.—Bib. Crois., 693.
[3] Mahometans' words.—Arab. Chron., 323.—Moslems and Christians come precisely to the same date as Vinisauf in his round-about manner, the Sunday next following St. Bartholomew's day. But Bartholomew's day is the 24th August, and in that year fell on a Tuesday, and a day for change of style.
[4] Vinisauf: 3.—Bib. Crois., ii. 694.

Burgundy and the French composed the rear-guard.[1] Their march was slow; for the Saracens, on their small, light Arabian horses, kept always flying round them.[2] Stopping at every town, and halting some days frequently, it was a continuous combat; and that the Christians lost immensely is proved by this, that a little beyond Cæsarea they were reduced to a third.

Richard himself had been wounded, by his avowal, without deigning to say exactly on what day, or by whom.[3] The sea was on their right; the hills and the Mussulmen on their left. Then it was that the Christians made great use of the zembourek, that kills horse and horseman together. They had a long line of carts, with mantles hanging like curtains, behind which lay those with that destructive weapon. But the mantles were only on the Mussulmen's side. In reprisals for the massacre, the soldan had the head of every prisoner he took during the whole march, cut off. He said his evening prayers, and then, as was his custom, mounted on horseback, and ended his day by having the Christian prisoner or prisoners beheaded.[4] In September, one of the greatest of the

---

[1] Vinisauf: 3.—Bib. Crois., ii. 695.
[2] Michaud: Hist., ii. 398.   [3] Id. :   Id., ii. 400.
[4] Arab. Chron., 327.

Islam champions, a Mameluke of Saladin's, remarkable for his strength, ability, and audacity, was killed, to the general grief. The first proposals by Richard were quite inadmissable. The battle of Arsouf was a[1] deep grief to the Moslems, and glorious to the Christians, by the confession of the Mahometan eye-witness as well as themselves.[2] It was given in an extensive plain. The Christians had now but a hundred thousand instead of thrice that number, as when leaving Acre; and two hundred thousand Moslems awaited them. As soon as Richard perceived the enemy, he drew up for battle in five divisions. The right wing the Templars, next those from the north of France, in the centre the English and Normans with the standard, next them the Hospitallers, and the left was composed of a strong body of archers. The first to enter the plain were the Templars, and then the different corps deployed in the order given. Count Henry, with a detached body of cavalry, observed the mountains; and Cœur de Lion and Burgundy were free to move about in all directions. The Christian army was drawn up so close that an apple could not drop but on a horse or man. They had commands not to stir; but, strictly only standing on the

---

[1] Michaud: Hist., ii. 401. [2] Arab. Chron., 329.

defensive, wait the enemy's charge. It was tremendous, but vain. The Moslem called the Franks a nation of iron.[1] At a signal of six trumpets, two at the right, two at the centre, and two at the left (but not before), they might advance. The Moslem did all they could to make them break their ranks. One of Saladin's bravest officers exposed his own life to sacrifice by insulting the Christians, and even striking some of them; but was allowed to return alive, and without one word of answer. The Grand Master of the Hospitallers then rode up to Richard, and expostulated with him on the slaughter of several of his knights in that trying manner; and that it would be out of his power to restrain them any longer. To which Richard replied that he could not be everywhere at once, and that the Hospitallers must remain even as they were. And at Gardiner's return, every one beheld with admiration the quiet magnanimity of that glorious confraternity under every form of threats, danger and death. At last two other knights, heroes not under as rigorous discipline as those of the Hospital, charged, at which the Hospitallers followed; and probably the trumpets had blown, for Cœur de Lion came on a gallop to join them, and

---

[1] Michaud: Hist., ii. 402.

the Christian gained that mighty victory. King Richard, though he does not say a word about his own exploits, affirms in his letter that Saladin had not suffered a similar defeat those forty years.[1]

Gardiner's being there shows that splendid veteran was not as yet dead, and it was now within a week of October.

There the illustrious Jacques d'Avesnes closed his earthly course at the enemy's third charge; he had resisted long, and slaughtered many; but in the third charge lost one leg and the foot of the other; on which he cried out, *Bon Roi Richard, vengez ma mort*, and, still struggling, slew the Saracen that rushed on him; and then by a crowd had his arm cut off, and fell dead with a multitude of wounds. That Richard and the crusaders buried him next day with all honours, after having attended with tears at his funeral service in the church, in presence of his corpse, is only as it should be.[2] He, also, was of Norman blood; so that he was not only a Frenchman, but, in one sense, had a right[3] to call Cœur de Lion his countryman. The interpreter, between Richard and Saladin's brother, was

[1] Mathew Paris: Chron.—Bib. Crois., ii. 796.
[2] Vinisauf: 3.—Bib. Crois., ii. 698.—Michaud: Hist., ii. 405.
[3] Brompton.—Bib. Crois., ii. 748.

that young Thoron, Isabella's first husband, made prisoner at Tiberiade; which shows that the growing generation of the highest class then learnt Arabic. After the day of Arsouf, Saladin kept aloof; so the crusaders entered Jaffa and Ascalon peaceably after the soldan, forced by his emirs, had destroyed its fortifications; so the whole road to Egypt lay open; and dismantling Ramlah too, he entered the holy city September 30th, 1191. But pressing[1] were the calls for Richard home, where John had already begun a civil war. "Palestine and the cross are the cause in dispute," said Richard in a note to Saladin. "Let us divide the first—you taking all beyond Jordan; we all on this side of it. The cross is in your sight a mere bit of wood. Give it to me, and let me return to England."

"But if Jerusalem is the cradle of your religion," replied the soldan, "it is still a holier city to us. Thence our Prophet ascended to heaven; and it is in Jerusalem the angels assemble. Only culpable Mussulmen could give it up. Palestine was ours formerly; you took it from Mussulmen that had waxed weak. Better if the cross had never existed; but as it is, it must be of use to Islam, and exchanged for something of immense value."[2] Richard next offered his

---

[1] Michaud: Hist., 410.   [2] Arab. Chron., 334.

sister, with Acre and great wealth for her dower, to Saladin's brother, who should be King of Jerusalem, and she Queen, and the city free to both Christians and Moslems; a proof that Richard considered Acre as his own, to be given where he liked. But she refused her consent, as Saladin foresaw; and therefore perhaps he gave his. Monks and priests persuaded her that it would be a denial of her faith.[1] Another proposal of Richard's was to divide Jerusalem into two equal parts.[2] But Saladin resolved to listen to none. "What guarantee? I dead; and all over again!" When Saladin made peace, it was that he was forced to it.[3] Richard had viewed Jerusalem's walls well, and declared them impregnable so long as Saladin lived, or any one that knew how to defend them, and that Moslems remained united. So he went back to his camp near Ramlah. There the tidings he first received was, that Conrad, Marquis of Montferrat, and whom he had just acknowledged King of Jerusalem, had been assassinated at Tyre; and although it was confessedly an act of the Old Man of the Mountain, in consequence of the murder perpetrated by that Templar who had been sentenced to death, and was in prison, in Almeric's

[1] Arab. Chron., 335. [2] Id., 336.
[3] Id., 336.

time, but at whose death was left free (as in Chapter V).; so that the Assassins' vengeance was directed against the new sovereign, as responsible for his wife's royal father; still that miserable crime added to the divisions that were already too general among the Christians. Then came the French,[1] calling to be led to Jerusalem. "As long as I command this crusade," he replied, "I will do nothing to incur shame. If you go to Jerusalem, I will accompany you, but not lead you to it. Saladin knows our strength. What if he descend into the plain of Ramlah, and intercept our road and convoys? What would then become of us before Jerusalem? Our army is too small to surround it. I am responsible for the evil that will ensue! There are people enough here—ay, and in France too—who would rejoice at inducing me to commit an imprudence, in order to reproach me with it. Neither you nor I know the country. Let us consult those who do, and proceed as they advise." So by King Richard's counsel, they named twenty faithful persons, and determined to abide by their suggestions—five Templars, five Hospitallers, five French, five Syrians. It is vexatious to have no record of their debate; but their verdict was against going to Jerusalem, and

---

[1] Michaud: Hist., ii. 411.

that they ought previously go and take Cairo. However strange this seems—though one of those cities seems to have nothing to do with the other—yet it assuredly exculpates Richard, and is in strict conformity with great military authority, both then and now. He who was the most celebrated for warlike qualifications at that time, and who had longer experience of each city, was of their opinion; and affirmed that Cairo was the only real key to Jerusalem. The first crusaders found the Egyptian in possession of the Holy City; and it seems Ibrahim thought the same in our own day; and that Egypt is the only military road to Palestine.[1]

So, full of the most perplexing meditations, King Richard and army marched back to the coast, and spent the rest of the winter in raising the walls of Ascalon and Jaffa that Saladin had pulled down.[2] Early in the spring of 1192, King Richard advanced into the mountains of Judea, near Jerusalem, and had several battles. In which of them precisely the subsequent facts occurred, is not specified. But the chronicler Ricobaldus gives a sure date when he says it was between Ramlah and Jerusalem, and on St. George's day; for only in 1192 did Richard advance thither, and St. George

1192

[1] Bib. Crois., ii. 712.—Vinisauf : 3.
[2] Arab. Chron., 340.

is on the 23rd of April—the difference of a day in the almanacs may fairly be attributed to passing from the old to the new style. Whatever be the opinions of Muratori, he, by the very act of rescuing it from the dust and publishing it, makes the chronicle so far his own—and of excellent authority—agreeing with five Arabic MSS. in the Ferrara Municipal Library. Tiraboschi tells us Ricobaldus wrote about 1297.

"Saladin and his brother Safadin were on a hillock directing the Moslems, who had repulsed the English, when from the right wing up hastens King Richard on Fauvell, and springing from the saddle, puts himself at the head of the archers, and stooping down to one of their companions who had just been slain, loosens the small tape with which the Kentish use to tie their sheaves of arrows in their quivers, and winding it round his own leg, just below the knee, bids all the chief knights (who were indeed his associates, and of all Christian countries) do the like, and fight that day in honour of St. George, for it was St. George's Feast, whose mass he had heard that morning, and received the host at it; and truly, though those gentlemen always fought well, they never performed such heroic actions as on that day. The consequence was, that Saladin seeing Richard a-foot pitied him—

thinking his horse slain—and in a few moments up rode Safadin, leading what Saladin had just alighted from, a beautiful Arabian in the richest housings, and though fawn coloured Fauvell of Cyprus and Lyard of Paris were fine steeds both, this was far finer. 'My brother bids me say, "Shall the pupil continue mounted when the master is on foot?" So sends your Majesty this present, and begs you to accept it for the love of him.' And the Moslems were ordered to retreat, whence ours believed we had won a victory; but indeed, had Safadin's advice been followed, and the Paynim charged then, we had been hardly put to it.

"Here was the first idea of the Order of the Garter, to which Richard afterwards gave its motto in his French wars, and made it exclusively an English order, from being common to all Christendom, as it till then had been."

A floating tradition of this had reached Ashmole; but too vague and imperfect, so he could not follow it. Still he rejected the fable about Lady Salisbury's garter. Edward was then not a creator, but a restorer. Clearly, if Ashmole had lived to Muratori's time, he would have assented to Ricobaldus at once.[1]

[1] Arab. Chron., 345.—Rerum Itali. Script., ix.—Tiraboschi: Litt. Ital., iv. 287.—Ashmole: 122.

Count Henry married Conrad's widow, as the people proposed and Richard consented to, and in her right, Henry became King of Jerusalem, *de jure*, no doubt; let him conquer it, and he is so *de facto*. It was a compliment to France as well as England, for he was nephew to both. But Palestine was a most disunited land. To every event opposite colourings. Falsity and treason. No repose or candour. No confiding in any one. Even the French disaffected. Not contented with the twenty, three hundred of the chiefs of the Franks met in a plain on horseback, and chose twelve commissaries; and these chose three arbiters, who had to decide whether to attack Jerusalem or not, and also came to the same resolution—No! This was in July, 1192. As to the Franks being on horseback in council, such is always the custom with them, says Boha-eddin.

Count Henry offered to reign as vassal of Saladin, who instantly was angry at the proposal.[1] King Richard then wrote to Saladin: "That as he did not think he had himself any right to sacrifice his own subjects, neither did he suppose the soldan thought he had any such over his; that therefore, for both Christians and Moslems, it was better to make peace. My nephew is at your service at the head of the Chris-

---

[1] Arab. Chron., 346.

tians, he and his troops. Do not refuse me the only thing I ask, the Church of the Holy Sepulchre. I renounce all the rest, and go home; for what you used to call my iron health is at length broken, and I feel sick. Whatever state that church be in, I accept it with gratitude." [1]

All the soldan's emirs desired him to accede to the offer. "Your nephew," replied Saladin, "shall be to me like one of my own children. I give it to you; it is the chief church in Jerusalem, and we call it of the Resurrection. The country to be divided; to you the coast, to me the mountains. But Ascalon and Daroum must be razed. I will give no fortresses." [2] King Richard immediately sent to thank Saladin, with also two falcons as a present, but insisted on Ascalon and Daroum as they stood. "The king only asks them to content the Franks. What are two such insignificant places to the potent soldan?" [3] So it was agreed on; yet some trifle extinguished the whole.

From Ascalon, Richard had frequently advanced towards Jerusalem, while Saladin was within its walls with expert engineers, adding to its fortifications, and Moslem troops devastating all the environs; and in an action near the fountain of

[1] Arab. Chron., 346. [2] Id., 347.
[3] Id., 347.

56 THE HISTORY OF THE ORDER OF [BOOK I.

Emaus, or Nicopolis, I find the Grand Master Gardiner again, in summer 1192, commanding, and indeed punishing one of his own knights for a breach of orders, though accompanied with signal heroism.[1]

Jaffa had to furnish another instance of the incomparable valour of Cœur de Lion.[2] He might have been thought gone for Europe; but it was not so, he was in Acre preparing to embark, but not yet embarked, when on tidings that the Moslems were besieging Jaffa, he threw himself into a ship, and sailed thither.[3] Thus the Mahometans: "Saladin had taken the town, except the citadel, when Richard appeared. At sight of sails, at peep of day,[4] those who were besieged within the citadel, mounted their horses, and rushed down

[1] Vinisauf.—Bib. Crois., 711. Then Gardiner was not only alive, but he distinguished himself in various battles subsequent to February, 1191. What, after all, shall I have done, except adding, on respectable authority, a few months (at most twenty), to the several years which Scb. Paoli proves by an unanswerable document? Manifest error of all past historians. I only corroborate what the diplomatist had the perspicacity to divine; and since Gardiner was commanding armies as late as summer in 1192, and that no chroniclers tell of his sudden death, which infallibly they would at that juncture, it is almost a moral certainty that he survived until nearly the end of autumn, and that it was he who had the honour of accepting Richard's gift, and installing the order in Acre.—Appendix, Num. xlii.

[2] Arab. Chron., 349.   [3] Id., 350.   [4] Id., 350.

all at once, like one man, and filled the town;[1] ours flying in such confusion and hurry, that many were nearly suffocated in the gateway;[2] others cut to pieces in the churches. Yet our flag was still flying on the walls.[3] At Richard's arrival at the mouth of the harbour, he hesitated an instant, thinking all lost, and that he was too late. The noise of the waves, and cries of the soldiers, made it impossible to hear. Moreover, the soldan was beating to arms. The Christians were in the utmost terror; one of them, *it was a priest*,[4] shouting '*I devote myself for the glory of the Messiah!*' sprang headlong from the top of the citadel, right down into the sea,[5] and swimming out to King Richard, let him know the truth, who was the first to leap ashore;[6] and every one of our people made off. The soldan had the pen in his hand, to sign the capitulation; but he had to retire.[7] The entire city had become Christian dogs—God confound them! The king had taken Jaffa.[8] Even Saladin's camp insecure; all was Richard's. Our master marched east on Saturday evening, the 19th of July, but came back, suddenly, five days after-

---

[1] Arab. Chron., 351. [2] Id., 351.
[3] Id., 351. [4] Vinisauf, 3.—Bib. Crois., 716.
[5] Id., 351. [6] Arab. Chron., 351.
[7] Id., 351. [8] Id., 351.

wards—that is, on Thursday, the 24th,[1] when that accursed King Richard had but ten horsemen and some hundred foot,[2] all lodged *in ten tents*, therefore outside the town, the walls of the town being in ruins and of no defence. But though our Moslems environed these few Christians, these stood rooted firm, *grinding the teeth of war*.[3] Astonishing! our cavalry kept cantering round them, without venturing to strike a blow,[4] and then returned into line. It was in the plain, quite close to the ruins of the walls, and the royal miscreant had marshalled forth his shadow of an army, as regularly facing ours in extensive array with the soldan at its head, as if there were a parity. But what struck me dumb altogether, was to see a whole division of ours at the sound of a trumpet charge like one man, and stop all at once, when they got close to the uncircumcised, as if these were a wall of steel, or something unearthly; their horsemen having their lances couched and vizors closed, but remaining motionless. And their infantry's first file were on one knee, with the ends of the handle of their lances fixed in the soil; so that they formed an angle, whose points were elevated a couple of feet, the other file up-standing, as usual; but not

[1] Arab Chron., 353. [2] Id., 353.
[3] Id., 353. [4] Id., 353.

a weapon was used on either side, nor a word spoken, but ours went back silently and slowly to their ground. Yet ours, I knew, were incited to the utmost by hate and desire to sack.[1]

"The indignant soldan then rode through our ranks, to excite them.[2] In vain his son set the example, by riding in a rush towards the Giaours.[3] An emir called out, I could not distinguish what, but it was clear that ours refused to obey.[4] So, our Saladin, after having, in vain, twice given the command, *Charge*, perceived he was committing himself uselessly, and, in a transport of rage, had a retreat sounded, and retired, and shut himself up in his tent without seeing any one, and so remained there invisible to us all for three days.[5] But our troops waited for a still more shameful scene. King Richard, advancing alone, rode along our whole front with his lance in the rest, and no one was bold enough to accept the challenge, and stir from the ranks to fight him.[6] On which he made a sign to his servants to come with his dinner, and, descending from his horse, sat down and ate and drank in the face of our army, drawn up as for battle; his small troop, and the handful of foot,

[1] Arab. Chron., 354. [2] Id., 354.
[3] Id., 354. [4] Id., 354.
[5] Id., 354. [6] Id., 354.

drawn up opposite likewise; so that he was banqueting half way between the two armies."[1]

All this being from Mahometan accounts, and not the least in contradiction with what other Mahometans write, and having come down through so many centuries, unquestioned by any of the Moslems, would it not be very hardy in us to consider it an hyperbole, if even a Christian be reduced to call it a greater feat than what is attributed to Achilles or any of the ancients, or Amadis de Gaul, or Roland, or the greatest heroes of romance?[2] Nothing equals the plain truth. See what it is to be terror-struck. Perhaps no veteran will deny the possibility of this, if he has been ever swept off by soldiers in a panic. Then it comes to be like other facts, merely a matter of evidence. It stands solitary in history. It may be wiser to disbelieve everything historic; but, if we believe any, it is hard to see why not this, which comes from the most opposite quarters. At a time when all disagreed, they agree as to this.

Some weeks later, King Richard sent to Saladin again: "How long am I to humble myself before the soldan? How long is he to remain deaf to my entreaties? In God's name grant me peace, I am

[1] Arab. Chron., 354.
[2] Vinisauf, 3.—Bib. Crois., ii. 688, 722.

unwell, and my kingdom is in an alarming state of sedition. Urgent business calls me home, and winter is approaching, when it will be too late to navigate the sea."[1] It was towards the end of August. Withal the king's sickness had increased,[2] which renders the recent exploits still more stupendous. The soldan sending to him ices and fruit,[3] as well as his renowned physician,[4] added a treaty for three years, says he who wrote, counting from September, 1192.[5] It was ratified, the rest swearing by King Richard's soul,[6] but the king giving only his hand, since kings never take an oath.[7] The swearers to it on the Christian side, were Count Henry, young Thoron, the Hospitallers, the Templars, and some of the principal barons.[8] These went, next day, to the soldan, who received and lodged them in a magnificent tent, and the day after, he gave them his hand; and his brother Malek-Adel swore by the soldan's soul, for the Moslem, to the treaty, and the soldan's two sons, and the Emir Marchtoub, and others.[9] Then peace was proclaimed, to the infinite joy of both

[1] Arab. Chron., 352—356. [2] Id., 354.
[3] Id., 354. [4] Michaud: Hist., vi. 323.
[5] Vinisauf, 3.—Bib. Crois., ii. 722.—Arab. Chron., 356.
[6] Hoveden.— Id., Id., 777.
[7] Arab. Chron., 354. [8] Arab. Chron., 356.
[9] Id., 357.

Mahometans and Christians, and that the road for as many as chose to go in pilgrimage to the Holy Sepulchre was open.[1] Several reasons combined for Richard's conduct: 1st.—Those decisions. 2nd.—The letters hastening him to England. 3rd.—The dissensions.[2] 4th.—His sickness, which kept on the increase. Any of the four would have done; but, in his mind, the first alone counted. And if to remain in Palestine was utterly useless, what right had he to defer his return home, where his presence was absolutely required? His lady mother's letter, as well as the trustiest of his noblemen, who brought it, declared his return to be, to the last degree, urgent. Several messengers, including both church and laymen, and the cream of his peerage, had followed by different routes, to hurry him. Indeed, he had tarried too long already; and left time for rebellion and a wicked alliance to be organized. His whole road, land and sea, blocked. The net was spread. Still little he or Saladin thought that, within little less than four short lunar months, both should be snatched away from this world's blue air; one to a dungeon, the other to his grave.[3] If that queen had only been on a par with her sex in ability, the English less

[1] Arab. Chron., 357.   [2] Id., 358.
[3] Michaud: Hist., ii. 451—454.

faithful, less stout-hearted the Pope, never had Richard re-ascended his throne.

Count Henry—whom the Christians called of Jerusalem, the Mahometans King of Acre[1] (but he himself appeared not to have used either titles)—left as the only protector of the Latin colonies, sent to ask Saladin for a pelisse and turban.[2] " You know neither are in dishonour with us. I mean to wear them both for your sake." It was evident Islam had nothing to fear.[3] Yet Saladin would not have made peace, had it depended on him. " Our soldan was forced to it by his emirs.[4] Had he not died soon, it might have been worse for Mahometans as well as Christians.[5] No better treaty in the circumstances could be, says the chronicler. Who say otherwise, they are in error, or it is malevolence; England had no reason whatever to hope for more advantageous terms.[6]

It had been one of his first and warmest requests to give back the property of the Templars and Hospitallers. But when he found it in vain, he never more mentioned it. It is said his last act was to give Acre to the Hospitallers, which is traditional

---

[1] Arab. Chron., 379.   [2] Id., 358.
[3] Id., 359.   [4] Id., 360.
[5] Id., 360. Note.
[6] Vinisauf, 3.—Bib. Crois., ii, 722.

and highly probable. Yet nothing remains that the Paolis could discover, to prove it. Still a comparatively modern has "Our valiant King Richard regained Acre, and gave it to the knights of St. John of Jerusalem;"[1] and it is to be supposed he had a legitimate authority for what he asserts frankly, though it has baffled the present writer's researches. He who gratuitously gave Cyprus to the Temple, could scarcely not have nobly remunerated the Hospitallers, to whom he was so publicly and affectionately devoted, although no such deed of gift be now extant. His scrupulous and earliest care, on regaining freedom (even before reaching Normandy or England), was to write a formal declaration of his gratitude, and to confess he owed them much, and took care to deposit that legal document so securely, that it has been lately printed, and therefore is now out of danger for ever, and shall be borrowed for the Appendix.[2]

A weeping train of the entire population of Acre accompanied him to the shore, where they bade farewell to him whom they loved and revered as no human creature. It cannot but strike every reader of those times that maritime matters must have been far less behind than we think, when such

[1] Comm. Geograph., ii. 18, Ed. London, folio, 1709.
[2] Appendix, Num. xxxix.

large armies of cavalry were conveyed in their ships, the King of France alone having had forty-five thousand cavalry at least when he sailed from Marseilles to Acre. Chroniclers never talk of any difficulty as to transport, nor of the Franks buying any horses in Syria. All seem to have brought their horses from Europe. The light Saracen horses may have been used by a few officers, but the soldiers were on powerful horses from Normandy, England, or Germany—remarkable for strength, as befits cuirassiers. With respect to sappers and miners, those from Aleppo were perhaps as good as any we have now. The invention of gunpowder has given an immense superiority to our artillery, no doubt. Yet the machines that could throw balls of six hundred pounds weight were dreadful things; as the steel barb from the zemboureck, that passed through three cuirasses and their contents—three human bodies.

Many are the stories told about King Richard and Saladin, some of which may be true, but some not possibly so; if no gravestone of the latter remains at Damascus now, that may fairly be ascribed to the lapse of ages. A similar reproach might for a long time have been made to England, and in truth both have their best of monuments in tradition, the lasting memory of nations. England was shortly to mourn for her monarch, captive she knew not where; and noble and holy Damascus for her soldan's death. It was now the end of November, 1192, and on Wednesday of the first week of the next following March, in spite of his celebrated physician—most learned Maimonides—died Saladin, "the Phœnix of his century, the firm and beautiful pillar of Islam," as his grateful countrymen call him;[1] and for the accuracy of the date, we have the authority of the Grand Master of the Hospitallers in his letter from Palestine to his lieutenant in Europe.[2]

Thus the order within its proper orbit had performed its first revolution of better than ninety-two years, under its Founder or Provost and eight Grand Masters.[3]

END OF BOOK THE FIRST.

---

[1] Arab. Chron., 376.
[2] Chron. Acquin.—Bib. Crois., iii. 322.
[3] Appendix, Num. xlvii.

BOOK THE SECOND—ACRE.

CHAPTER I.

IMMEDIATELY after Richard's departure, then at the close of November, died Sir N. Gardiner in Acre, and was succeeded by Sir Daps, who may have reigned for some days in January, but not longer, since a document shows Sir Godfrey de Duisson, Grand Master in January, 1193,[1] which completely agrees with that letter in April,[2] which contains no allusion to recent promotion. Of Daps nothing is known; nor if he did anything during his short reign. It is only reverence for former historians (a sort of prescription) which gives him a right to be placed in that post at all; for not a scrap of documentary evidence names him.[3]

[1] Cod. Dipl. Geros. Num. clxxiii.—Appendix, xlviii.—Bosio writes D'Aps, Sir Esmengard D'Aps, lib. vii.
[2] Bib. Crois., iii. 302.—Appendix, xlix.
[3] Seb. Paoli : Serie, i. 340.

Daps is said by some to have been an Englishman, but upon no sufficient authority. It may seem ridiculously minute, but there must have been many English. But as the order's historians have been nearly all foreigners, these names are translated or ill spelt; so as to have been too difficult to discover even formerly, and now impossible. Yet many old English names have in themselves proof of a Palestine origin, as D'Acre. England was much more connected with the Continent then than in Bonaparte's time.—But you so often speak to us of those documents as certain. Are they quite so? Are you very sure of it?— Why, yes, quite! as certain as anything human.— How? Might they not have been forged?—No!— Have not similar forgeries been? — No! never! For these only regard individuals and things of little importance to any except private interests, and each of them has been sifted and resifted thousands of times, and they all agree with each other, as well as with whatever is extant of like validity. They are neither historical nor political, but only the solid basis on which history may be raised. History must cover far wider ground, and embrace within itself not only much that is highly probable, and from coincidences acquires a moral certainty or nearly, and some particulars of more or less truth, or perhaps doubtful; but also a few quite incredible in themselves, but yet with this of verity, that they express the way of thinking of that time. Then these documents may be relied on blindly as far as they go, and that is not far, save dates and small contracts and concerns of no general value. But they may be used as a test with regard to others that are. What is in contradiction with them, in even so minor a point as date or place, must be apocryphal or necessarily be false. They are the cross-examinations of a lawyer.

Ibn-Alatir's observation, that the founder of an empire has scarcely in any instance been succeeded by his children, for that he probably lies under pollution of blood, which, however necessarily shed or legitimately, cannot but be displeasing to the Eternal—so that ambition is punished even in this life—is applied by many Moslems to Saladin himself, who leaving seventeen sons and one daughter, these and his turbaned emirs cut up his inheritance into a number of small states, and conducted themselves so ill, that Safadin was in a manner forced to become Sultan of Egypt and Damascus; and ended by concentrating in himself and transmitting to his own children the entire possessions of his mighty brother, with the single exception of

Aleppo, which small angle one of his sons contrived to keep. Had Saladin left a will, it might perhaps have been otherwise; but he died intestate, and the natural consequence was confusion.[1] He was but fifty-seven when he died.[2]

Far from indifference in religion and doubt, as is pretended, Saladin, after having lain senseless three days, at the imam who assisted his last moments coming to the line, which he read with solemn strength, " God is Omnipotent!" "It is true it is true," cried the Soldan, springing up; and then fell back and expired.[3] He was sincerely attached to his creed, and tenderly loving his children, brought them up in the same principles; yet he left no will to regulate the succession;[4] forgotten it perhaps, as what appeared to him so trifling a matter, in the magnitude of his dying thoughts. Singularly affectionate in his domestic relations, a trait is related of him that resembles what the French relate of Henry the Fourth. His private secretary recounts that, on the conclusion of peace a little before his death, some ambassadors presenting themselves for audience, when he was employed in playing with his youngest child, who astonished to see men with their beards cut, and short hair,

[1] Arab. Chron., 376, 382. [2] Id., 363.
[3] Id., 367. [4] Id., 377.

and in clothes different from what he was accustomed to see, began crying; on this the soldan begged the ambassadors to excuse him, and put off their business to the next day.[1]

But in addition to what was said already, it is proper to take a further review of Acre; for it must now be for a period what Malta has since been, the sovereign dominion and chief residence of the order; though a fief of Jerusalem, as that other of Sicily; and therefore called for the future not simply Acre, but St. John's Acre, *St. Jean d'Acre.* At the foot of Carmel, its shelter to the south, and Thabor within sight—seated on the sea, commanding the whole line of coast from Egypt to Asia Minor—not far from the celestial Nile, nor from the king of rivers, Euphrates; emporium not only of Palestine and Syria, but also what Alexandria had been before it, and was to be after it, chief transit between the Oriental countries and Europe, whether *viâ* Pisa, or Genoa, or Naples, or Venice, termination of the tongue of that beautiful and renowned plain that runs northward all along the shores between it and Libanus, and leaving the cedars, crosses to Mount Taurus, and returning to Caiphas stretches east to where our Saviour passed

[1] Arab. Chron., 365.

his boyhood, and where He pronounced His divinest discourse, and to the lake whose waters He trod, and Jordan and stern Judea's hills:—with so grand a situation, whether considered materially, relative to commerce and landscape, or morally from its historic and sacred recollections, Acre could not well but be one of the richest, most populous, and most agreeable cities of the whole world.[1] And though it had more than once been partially razed, it had always been rebuilt with increasing magnificence. If the Moslems had been its masters twice, yet they had not been long so either time, and treated it on both occasions with unusual respect; and the Franks being always lords of the sea, Acre was on the skirts of Europe, and enjoyed complete security in that direction. And if it was continually menaced, yet what foe approached close enough to injure its suburban districts? That could be only in a regular siege; rare misfortune, to which all cities are liable, and six years had scarcely elapsed since its taking in the third crusade, when its houses had been greatly embellished, and many of them re-erected, for which the not distant hills yielded a white stone nearly equal to the finest marble. Nor had those huge armies been unattended

---

[1] Michaud: Hist. des Crois., v. 119.—Corneri Chron.—Bib. Crois., iii. 135.

with considerable compensation, for they had imported and spent immense treasures, and, with all their doleful memorials, left also much wealth of every kind behind them, and refinements and fashions, and usages, from the best of every land over the civilised globe; and that long fallow and those tremendous slaughters had rendered its fertile plain more fertile than ever; so that with a gayer and more vivid vegetation than before, it lay in a labyrinth of villas and gardens. The roofs were flat, with terraces; so that you could go from one end of the city to the other in an uninterrupted walk on the same level, without descending into the street, as is partially the case in Aleppo even now; and the streets were wide for the Levant, which might be worse respecting sun, but gave air, and above all was better for riders, and all knights went then on horseback as universally as the Turks now. The whiteness of the cut stone houses, those marble terraces ornamented with jars of orange and lemon trees and flowers, the universal practice of glass windows, then a singularity everywhere else, without excepting London or Paris of that day (which is certain), but even of the present, which may be doubtful—paintings decorating the interior of the principal houses, the gilded cupolas, domes, minarets, steeples standing out from the brightness of the green and sparkling waters for horizon on one side, and on the other those gorgeous mountains, presented a most impressive view whether you approached Acre by land or sea. The population was usually calculated at one hundred and fifty thousand, a third more than Jerusalem. Acre was by far the gayest and most fashionable place then in existence. It had no duties, nor, it would appear, any other taxes than a very small capitation and an easy land tax. But the tithes were rather heavy, as were the feudal obligations on knights and large proprietors. Altogether these were the bright features which had, for counterpart, the want of order in the legislation. There are said to have been seventeen jurisdictions for various nations, each of which pretended to be governed by its own code—Venetians living exclusively in one street, Genoese in the next, Pisans, Templars, Syrians, and so on; most of those having acquired their rights long previous to the Hospitallers' reign there. Indeed Venetians, Pisans, and Genoese, date by treaties from the first crusade, nor could Richard have given away what did not belong to him; nor did he pretend to conquer, but only restore, and Acre had been a fief of Jerusalem, and those Franks had title deeds that derived from former Kings of Jerusalem; but the Hospitallers, having much of the republican in their own constitution, did not dislike this. Gerard, when he had to choose, did not choose a monarchy, but a sort of commonwealth, with a Moderator or President, with only one vote more than any other knight of the order. Indeed it was but conforming to the Norman fashion, for the first Normans established a military republic in Puglia; and, if they afterwards became royal, it was to follow the taste they found there; they only did not resist the temptation, but they had brought other usages. The Normans permitted, as an exception, the use of force as to what they considered their right to visit the Holy Sepulchre as often as they pleased. Their desire to go there might be religious, but to impede them was an attack on their liberty; and would be, had the Moslems been Christians. The holy war was then (at least at its best, the first crusade) not so much a war against Mahometanism as against tyranny; and rather defensive, than aggressive. So in strict neutrality between Christians, the order were only keeping to Norman principles, never to use force in matters of mere belief.

The Hospitallers perhaps gave the example for the Italian republics. It is not hard to credit that the reins of government were loose in Acre —too loose. Times of great trouble, as a siege, might unite; but even then, to have taken such habits of independence must have been injurious to soldierly discipline. The bad had its good also—mixture as in all human things. Many of the most illustrious rank chose Acre for habitual residence. So that at one time twenty crowned heads lived there, and kept up stately and splendid establishments and courts. Not ex-sovereigns, but rich and potent masters of far-off realms. There were the three military orders, and grandees of every country. And beside these residents, there were always Emperors of Germany, or Kings of France, Sicily, England, Spain, Portugal, Denmark, as well as troops from all those parts. There were a great number of stately palaces; and we have seen that even before the Christians took it, King Guy, foreseeing it would be soon theirs, had given a spot to the Hospitallers to erect a wide gate to their Xenodochia, and a square in front, as to increase their hospital to be worthy of the one they had left in Jerusalem.

The order having become sovereign, their hospital was no longer restricted to the crusaders alone, but received Moslems also, or any one whatever. The flimsiest disguise, if even that was requisite, sufficed. So, on that score, the current story is very possible ; but, on another it is scarcely so—

Saladin's death in March.[1] But he was so astonishing a person, that it is hard to say what he could not do. Who durst deny but in the short space of a few months, it is barely possible that what is told he may have executed, during some military recognisance into the immediate vicinity of that town, before his mortal sickness? At all events the rumour shows the public opinion at that time. "Master Saladin, King of Babylon, who commanded over thirty kings, having heard surprising matters of the hospital at Acre, determined on taking a stick, and piece of old carpet for cloak, fumbling it round him as well as he could, and came straight to Acre, feigning grievous sickness; and hobbling, inquired whether, for the love of God, they could lodge him. On which he was received at once, and invited to lie down at his ease, and a little after, asked what he wished to eat. He who desired to be thought sick, declared he did not care for eating, but for God's sake to allow him to repose, as being very tired, and that he had long wished to die, so they let him sleep all that day and night. The next day the infirmarians asked what he would eat, but he assured them that not only he did not wish to eat, but could not. 'Friend,' replied the in-

[1] Appendix, Num. xlix.

firmarian, 'eat; for, unless you eat, you cannot live long.' But Saladin remained two days and nights without bit or sup. Then the chief infirmarian returned to say, 'My dear friend, you must really take something to eat; for, otherwise, we should be much blamed, and my superiors would say you died here of starvation.' 'My lord,' replied Saladin, 'I believe I shall never eat again in all my life, and it is far better for me to die, since the only thing I could eat, and desire intensely, it is madness even to name.' 'Oh, as for that, sweetest brother, do not hesitate in the least, for the established law in this house is to use the very extreme of charity. A sick man, here, is given everything he fancies, if gold can buy it; so, ask for whatever your warmest fancy demands, and be assured of it you shall have it.' On which Saladin determined to ask: 'Then I wish for the right foot of Moriel, your grand master's favourite horse, and that it be cut off here in my presence, or I'll never eat a morsel more; so now you have my desire; see if it be not preferable I die; for I am but a poor man, and that beast is very valuable; the grand master would not take a thousand bezants of gold for him, they say.' Then the chief infirmarian went and told it all to the grand master, who reflected a little, and could not imagine how such a strange desire could come into the head of a sick person. 'However, since it is so, take my horse,' replied he to the infirmarian. 'Better that all my horses were dead, than a man; and, besides, we should be reproached with it for ever!' So the horse was led out, and thrown down alongside Saladin's bed, and tethered close, and a groom got ready, and having armed himself with a large hatchet and a small block of wood, 'Which foot is it,' said he, 'which the sick man wishes for?' Whereat he was told the right fore-foot; and he took the wooden block, and put it under that foot, and raised the hatchet with both his hands to strike with more force, on which Saladin cried, 'Hold! for my desire is satisfied; and I would be contented now with a good slice of mutton.' So Moriel was loosed and led back to the stable. And the grand master was vastly pleased, and all the brethren too. And the sick man ate and drank well, for he had fasted for four days, and then taking his cloak and stick, he thanked the infirmarians for all the honour and courtesy he had received, and returned to his own land; nor forgot to write a charter, which he sealed with his seal, to this purpose in substance: 'Let all know that I Saladin, Soldan of Babylon, leave and bequeath in perpetuity to the Hospital of Acre one thousand bezants of gold every year, on St. John the Baptist's day, to buy sheets, and secure said sum on my rent-roll of Babylon; and expressly desire that in all wars between Saracens and Christians, this continue to be paid the same, and sent to the grand master, whoever he be; and that it is in gratitude for the wonderful charity of his order.'"[1]

Margat[2] is a clear proof of what I have stated already, that the stories of dissensions between Templars and Hospitallers are likely to have been inventions of malignant idlers, to which neither of the parties themselves attended much. There could never have been any dispute between them concerning Margat; for the Templars knew just as well as the Hospitallers themselves, that given to these latter it had been years before by a regular deed of gift or sale, and with a whole cloud of witnesses among whom the Bishop of Valence, the Prince of Antioch, &c., &c., in date of 1186;[3] and was a fief of the Massocrians—*Castrum munitissimum Margatum quod fuit Hospitalis.*[4] Were the information of Mathew Paris perfectly correct, that the Templars had become enormously richer than the Hospitallers,

---

[1] MS. du Roi de France, Num. 454.—Bib. Crois., iii. 341.
[2] Michaud: Hist., iii. 12.
[3] Cod. Dipl. Geros., Num. lxxvii., vol. i. 77.—Seb. Paoli Notizie Geograf., i. 423.—Appendix, 1.
[4] Sanuti: lib. iii. 14.

these might perhaps have been goaded on to see with some displeasure their own children put over their heads; but indeed it was not so, and other chroniclers of that time say the direct contrary. The fact is, that neither orders had time for such squabbles; and it was those who hated both who tried to play them off against each other, and alas! had too quickly their intent regarding one. But all that is childish now.

Great warriors were lost in those holy wars, and Mahometanism survived. Frederick I. was held quite as valiant and as able a soldier as Alexander the Great; and they appeared on nearly the same scene. One conquered the Sultan, the other Darius; why then so different a result? Frederick had an established religion against him, Alexander not; but an established religion is what is hardest to vanquish.[1]

In 1193, another Bohemond becomes an aggregated member of the order by election;[2] and a new Pope confirms what his predecessors had said, particularly respecting the Hospitalleresses in Spain—his Holiness praising them as no doubt they deserved;[3]

---

[1] Suabian Chron.—Bib. Crois., iii. 184.
[2] Confrater factus sum S. Domûs Hospitalis. Cod. Dipl. Geros., Num. lxxx., i. 86.
[3] Cod. Dipl. Geros., Num. xxxiv., i. 313.—Appendix, Num. li.

but he does not mention what tradition adds, that they each had to hold a little silver sceptre in their hand during divine service, to remind them that some of their sisterhood had been queens;[1] nor avows that it was contrary to the ancient custom of the order that they should be thus shut up like nuns. Of Cœur de Lion's nephew, Harry Count Palatine of Troyes (or Champagne), we have a deed of gift, less remarkable for his not entitling himself sovereign for the property in Acre, than for his care to mention his wife, in whose right he could pretend to royalty.[2]

1194

But early in the next year is a letter from the grand master to the prior of his knights in England, in which he relates the shipwreck of several noble gentlemen of his order, the sore famine in Egypt, where that river of paradise had not overflowed, the menaces of Safadin, and worse still, the forlorn state of their house in Sicily, from its having been sacked by Germans and others; so that their knights were obliged to leave it; nor was it possible for it to assist the Holy Land; "Wherefore, my good brother, we entreat of you to send us all you can by the very earliest opportunity in March, for we are heavily in debt, and you know what loads

1195

---

[1] Vertot: ii. 301.—Bosio.
[2] Cod. Dipl. Geros., Num. lxxxi., i., 87.—Appendix, lii.

of money and provisions of every kind are necessary to maintain our garrisons and armies; and it is but with these that we can hope any respite from the Moslem. Fearfully monstrous is our expenditure. But our trust is in God."[1] How tender is the command "good brother!" But it is only a fair specimen of the order's affectionate fraternization!

Next comes a deed from the Empress Constance, confirmatory of all her ancestors had done for the order, and executed in Palermo.[2] Cœur de Lion's truce having been renewed by mutual accord of the parties, was broken by some Franks headed by Valeran de Limbourg, son of the Duke of Ardennes, without the knowledge of Henry, England's nephew,[3] to the great detriment of the Christians of the land; for the Paynim, in reprisal, marched against those of Jaffa, and slew five thousand of them.[4] And unfortunate Henry, who had gone thither, and returned to Acre, anxiously to prepare for inevitable war, whether in washing his hands, he backed and fell from the window, as the servant held a basin of water, or in rising by night, for whatever purpose, or in the

1197

1198

---

[1] Cod. Dipl. Geros., Num. xxxviii., i. 317.—Bosio.—Appendix, 1.
[2] Cod. Dipl. Geros., Num. clxxxv., i. 228.
[3] Michaud: Hist., iii. 24.
[4] Lamberti Parvi: Chron.—Bib. Crois., i. 334.

morning, while looking out from a terrace on his troops filing past, or in the portico, had a sudden apopletic stroke;[1] however it was, he was killed. Another Henry, Duke of Lorraine and Brabant, succeeded;[2] but in two or three months to be superseded by the defunct's widow taking a new husband—Almeric, who had followed his brother Guy, on the throne of Cyprus, and now married Isabella, by the Grand Master of the Hospitallers' means, and in her right became titular King of Jerusalem, which he hastened to authenticate by a deed, dated Tyre, in August, 1198.[3] Almeric is represented to be a good wise man by the Moslems themselves;[4] which, and the Pope's eulogy, is no contradiction to the same Pope's blame of the patriarch, for having connived at a woman's taking a fourth husband while her first one was still alive.[5]

And, what was of more consequence, a truce was again assented to, by the Moslems, for six years six months and six days, permitting the Christians a free passage to and from the Sepulchre, Jordan,

[1] Bib. Crois., iii. 284.—Arnold de Lubeck : Chron. 4.
[2] Lamberti Parvi : Chron.—Bib. Crois., i. 334.
[3] Cod. Dipl. Geros, Num. clxxxix.—Appendix, liii.
[4] Arab. Chron., 381.
[5] Seb. Paoli : Storiche, i. 376.—Muratori.—Bib. Crois., ii. 497.

and the other sacred places.[1] And in the very end of that same year, is a bull of Innocent III., requesting of the Hospitallers to defend Cyprus, whose king they had themselves elected to Jerusalem, and to defend him and his island as cordially as Palestine itself.[2]

Beautiful—which law papers rarely are—is the deed by which a lady of Holy Land certifies she has become a sister of the order, with her husband's consent, without calumny, without revocation, without contradiction.[3] 1201

Nor could De Duisson have died earlier than the last days of 1201 (Vertot mistakes much), as documentary proof shows, and in 1202, he was succeeded by Sir Alphonso, of the royal family of Portugal (probably son of Alphonso I.), who 1202 being very austere at the expenditure, called a chapter in cloaks[4] for some minute and ill-timed reforms, where, not considering it compatible with his own dignity, he had a proposal made by another, to whom a younger knight having replied sharply, that it would render harder what was already hard, that no officer could ever do with one horse—at least

---

[1] Reiner: Chron —Bib. Crois., i. 334.
[2] Cod. Dipl. Geros., Bolla iii., i. 270.
[3] Id., Num. lxxxvi., i. 91.—Appendix, liv.
[4] Bosio:—Appendix, Num. xxxvi.—Seb. Paoli: Serie, i. 340.

not the Hospitallers, in continual dangers and exertion of every sort, the warm debate was closed by one of their best veterans standing up, and reverently laying back his hood thus calmly: "Were the regulations from our Grand Master, and my opinion unfavourable to them, I should hesitate to interfere; but, as I am decidedly in their favour, I permit myself to express it, because this peace is propitious to grave proceedings, as our very conversation in this hall attests; for the sanguinary Marchtoub once commanded here in the name of the law of Mahomet, whereas Cœur de Lion drove off the Saracens for ever; and if three of the best horses were not then enough to enable me to fulfil my various duties, but I was often obliged to borrow a fourth, and on one pressing occasion, in the battle near Antioch, a fifth—that was a period of war, and very different from what we see at present."

And when he sat down, the turcopolier rose smiling, "and now let every one of you judge by what he has just heard, and give his vote without our losing more time in vain discourse." And the sequel was that Alphonso abdicated and returned to Lisbon, and it is said died badly, after having taken a prominent part in some revolutionary attempt. And on his tombstone in that country was inscribed, "Anno 1245, Kalend. Martii, obiit Alfonsus, Magister Hospitalis Hierusalem."[1]

Any considerable diversity of opinion in their chapters, or among themselves or with those of the Temple or others, is not so much to be considered a passing burst or exception, as indeed a radical consequence of the republican spirit kneaded up with the first principles of the Hospitallers from the very beginning; which however excellent, still share in the nature of all human things, and have some defects amalgamated with their excellencies. If, as a commonwealth, each individual took an intense and personal interest in every proposal, that exclusiveness easily during intervals of armistice degenerated into disputes in their own body and a facility to offend their neighbours. It was only in war and the execution of their decisions, that much of the dictatorial power entered. There are few or, I believe, no instances of disobedience, or even the smallest hesitation to obey on the field of battle in the fine times of the order; but very many of the fullest exertion of the power of a most rigid dictator by whoever happened to be their grand master, from whom all authority was then derived.

[1] Seb. Paoli: Serie, i. 340.

That Sir Godfrey Lo Rath did not succeed till 1205 (though Vertot like the rest has 1195) is clear from the document of December, 1204, in which Alphonso was still the reigning Grand Master.[1]

1205

But if the fourth crusade took place earlier about a year, yet as a war between Roman and Greek Christians, the order had nothing to do with it, but kept true to its neutrality between all such; except that individual Templars and Hospitallers went to Greece also, for it was the land of glory;[2] nor either then nor ever could the grand master prevent individual knights from taking what side they pleased; nor, though the order had a priory and much property at Constantinople, did its banner ever fly there, although it had scarce a member but had near relatives amongst those Franks, and they had certainly its sympathies and names that were very dear to it, and reminded it of its own Norman descent, and its earliest protectors and friends, and its founder, and all his glorious race. Nor is it surprising it exulted when a Baldwin was elected Emperor of Constantinople, and testified his singular esteem by sending it, as proof of his victory, the chain he had to break, to reach the

[1] Cod. Dipl. Geros., Num. lxxxvii., i. 92.—Appendix, lv.
[2] Michaud : Hist., iii. 210.

ST. JOHN OF JERUSALEM.

Golden Horn, and the gates of that celebrated Byzantium,[1] and likewise a deed in aid of its exchequer,[2]— the fourth part of his own private estate (the Duchy of Neocast)—and therefore the surer and more expressive of his warm friendship; no crown property, but entirely his own. Yet there was a person, who paid for so much glory with her life—his wedded spouse, his faithful and affectionate Margaret, who had preceded her husband to Acre to join him there on their way to Jerusalem, and whose gratification for his sake at his attainment of what she knew was the object of his ambition, that immensity of joy killed her. What brought out the chain and gates under orders to return with their young and lovely sovereign, expected with such ardour, as the fittest to preside at the coronation festivities she was to share—alas! that ship returned with no living empress, but her corpse—sad presage of what was brewing (in the not far clouds) for Baldwin himself.[3] About the same time there were various scourges of earthquakes and plague and famine in Egypt, Palestine, and Syria. More than two thousand Christians were buried in one day at Acre of plague.[4] The ground rolled

---

[1] Michaud: Hist., iii. 121, 210.
[2] Cod. Dipl. Geros., Num. lxxxviii., i. 93.—Appendix, lvi.
[3] Michaud: Hist., iii. 211.—Vertot: iii. 360.
[4] Id.: Id., 154.

about, like the rising and falling of a bird's wings,[1] and devastated what remained of the antique in the Holy Land, Baalbec, and many places round Lebanon (whose mountains opened and descended), and much of Damascus, Tyre, Tripoli, and other towns; and the walls of Acre, and even the very palace where the King of Jerusalem was staying; so that the monies raised in Europe for the crusade had to be laid out in rebuilding the walls of Acre.[2] The state of affairs could not be pleasing for people that loved quiet—every one making war *ad libitum*— —even the poet Saadi for awhile in prison, and condemned to work like a galley slave. Though Aleppo was at peace with Jerusalem, the Christians of Antioch were at open war with Saracen Hamah; so, as Almeric liked quiet, he thought it best to come and die at Acre.[3] Isabella is once more free. Will she take her a fifth husband? John de Brienne took heed of that, for disembarking at Acre with only three hundred horse and eighty thousand livres (half from the King of France, and the other half from the Pope) he was received with great pomp and married to her daughter, and in her right became King of Jerusalem—at least to the Latins, for the Moslems called him King of

[1] Michaud: Hist., iii. 255. [2] Id.: Id., 256.
[3] Id.: Id., 258.

Acre.[1] And these besieging Tripoli and threatening Acre, the new king marched out and made his valour be admired on the field of battle. Still he had no other than that shadow of feudal superiority, and no army to defend it.[2] That most shameful of crusades (with which, thank Heaven, the order had nothing to do), that against the Albigeois, in every sense belonged to Europe, and " from their persecution," says the French historian, " came the Inquisition, that disgrace to humanity, religion, and our country."[3] I am glad to copy that fervent Catholic's words. What has been said about the earthquakes, is by some referred to May, 1202; but such dates are uncertain, and let me observe once for all, that it is only the chronology in the margin that can pretend to documentary certainty, while that in the text is only extremely probable. But not only Godfrey Lo Rath was Grand Master in 1205, immediately on Alphonso's abdication, as has been shown, but also we have a deed of his the year next following which even Seb. Paoli seems not to have read with attention, 1206 probably from its coming too late.[4] And the same grand master was living in May of 1207 (though

---

[1] Michaud: Hist., iii. 260.—Arab. Chron., 379.
[2] Id.: Id., 266. [3] Michaud: Hist., iii. 271.
[4] Cod. Dipl. Geros., Num. clxxv., i. 217.—Appendix, lvii.

others say he died in 1206), not only because there is a deed wherein one of the witnesses is his successor, still marshal, as Paoli rightly says,[1] but likewise, as I remark, because Lo Rath is himself mentioned, though the name be ill printed Lirath in one word, instead of two; and still more, that in another contract of 1207, he signs to it in full, *Lo Ṙath*, Master of the Hospitallers, and writes the name correctly with his own hand. Amongst this document's witnesses (the *alii plures* of the Appendix), is Hugo de Burin, which no doubt means Byron); so the late lord (the poet) was not wrong in thinking he had ancestors in the crusades.[2] And in another document of that same year, I read among the witnesses Frater Galfridus Lo Rath.[3] Lo Rath,[4] after exerting his insinuating manners by being a peace-maker, as became his age, between the Armenian and Antioch, died in 1208, and his successor as grand master was one who until then had been marshal, Sir Gawen de Montacute,[5] whom Vertot unhesitatingly dubs Montaigu,[6] and that he was a French gentleman. And

[1] Cod. Dipl. Geros., Num. xci., i. 95.—Appendix, lix.
[2] Id.,   Num. xc., i. 94.—Appendix, lviii.
[3] Id.,   Num. x., *of the Giunta*, i. 289.—Appendix, lxxxv.
[4] Is not *Lo! Rath!* Anglo-Saxon? *Here! Early one!*.
[5] Seb. Paoli : Serie, i. 341.   [6] Vertot: iii. 367.

Bosio and even Seb. Paoli concur; but be it observed that, according to Lodge[1] and Sir Harris Nicolas,[2] the Montacute was an *old* English family in 1168, earlier than the period we are treating of, and that they did not take the name of Montaigu until two centuries later, when they merged in the Nevils and old Earls of Salisbury; so that, until the contrary be decided by greater authorities (and the historians of the order cite none), I must certainly vindicate the claim of England to the Grand Master Montacute, and that he was no further a Frenchman than that his ancestors had been Normans. But at that time, if the Montaigus belonged to Auvergne, the Montacutes did to Wiltshire; and Montacute is the name in all the documents. And he had to exercise his diplomatic talents much, in a similar pacific way; but also in a sterner sort, for they were unhappy times, and the military orders were an exception to the surrounding degeneracy, which induced people easily to have small regard for their oaths and break truces every moment without compunction. Nor is it quite clear whether Christians or Moslems were the first in that respect, since mutual are the accusations; and it is painful to decide (without the fullest

---

[1] Lodge: iv. 16.   [2] Synopsis, 2.

94   THE HISTORY OF THE ORDER OF   [BOOK II.

proof) against our own co-religionists. Nor had creeds much to do with the matter; for if the first crusades were more religious than political, the later ones were more political than religious.[1] And in lieu a great indifference of religion was observable over Syria and Palestine—all parties seeking but their interests, Christians against Christians, and Mahometans against Mahometans, with astonishing impartiality;[2] so that Pope Innocent III. wrote to the Sovereign of Aleppo to felicitate him on his having become a Christian—though he never thought of it, but only had been generous towards some of that belief;[3] which, if it scandalized the Pope of Rome the Great,[4] or Caliph of the Franks,[5] it did not less the Pope of the Infidels,[6] as the chroniclers call the Caliph of Bagdad; the Apostle of Rome, and the Apostle of the Saracens are also their terms.[7] We have a document by which a German count and his wife became aggregated to the order in October of 1208.[8] A King of Cyprus in 1210 gives various lands to Sir Gawen Montacute,

1210

1213

---

[1] Michaud: Hist. iii. 291. [2] Arab. Chron., 382.
[3] Arab. Chron., 383. [4] Id., 387.
[5] Id., 482. Note. [6] Vitri.
[7] Michaud: Hist., iii. 325. Note.
[8] Cod. Dipl. Geros., Num. xcii., i. 96.

Grand Master of the Sacred House of the Hospital of St. John, and the Hospitallers.[1] On the 13th of October, certain persons borrow a thousand Saracen bezants from Montacute, Grand Master of the Hospitallers, one of the witnesses being a Garnerius with the adjunct of *Alemannus*, the German, to distinguish him from others of the same name, English or of whatever country; for though *languages* were a posterior creation far, yet not so several leading offices being assigned to particular lands. Prior of England was always an Englishman by a custom dating from the very beginning of the order,[2] and on the 8th of the calends of August in 1216 the brief of Pope Honorius III.,[3] recommends the Prince of Antioch to the Hospitallers; and on the 9th of the same month and year, comes a letter from the said Pope to the Grand Master of the Hospitallers, bidding him to go to Cyprus to confer with the King of Hungary and Duke of Austria, as to the affairs of Palestine,[4] and in January, 1217, John of Brienne, King of Jerusalem, speaks of Gawen de Montacute Grand Master of the Hospitallers.[5] Therefore, in

1216

1217

---

[1] Cod. Dipl. Geros., Num. xcvii., i. 101.
[2] Id., Num. xi., i. 290.—Appendix cvi.
[3] Id., Num. xl. 320.—Giunta.
[4] Id., Num. xli. 320.—Giunta.
[5] Id., Num. ccxii. 253.—Pantaleone: Hist. book iii.

spite of the existing treaties, Brienne led a force against Jerusalem, and, upon discomfiture, determined on taking the road by where its resources came from; nor can there be any doubt of his being at Acre in the January of 1217,[1] and embarked for Egypt in the month of May, 1218, as the Islamites have it, whose authority as to dates is reputed better than that of our chroniclers. These differ a little, but those estimate the crusaders as (what is probably an exaggeration) seventy thousand horse and four hundred thousand foot,[2] and that while some of the fleet were only two days on the voyage from Jaffa to the Nile, others were an entire month; which, whatever it came from, it were wrong to attribute to nautical deficiency, since part of that same crusade leaving the Meuse in June, 1218, and in its way touching at ports on the south of England, and north of France and Spain, entered that of Lisbon towards the middle of July[3]—very tolerable sailing.[4] Four months hardly sufficed to take the first of the outworks of Damietta,[5] the tower of the chain, which seemed so violent a loss to

---

[1] Cod. Dipl. Geros., Num. ccxi., i. 253 —Appendix, lxxxvi.
[2] Arab. Chron., 388   [3] Michaud: Hist. iii., 313.
[4] Chron. Cologne.—Bib. Crois., iii. 20.
[5] Michaud: Hist., iii. 319.—Arab. Chron., 392.

CHAP. I.]   ST. JOHN OF JERUSALEM.   97

Islam that it broke Safadin's heart when he heard of it on the banks of the Lake of Galilee;[1] so his corpse was borne secretly into the citadel, at Damascus, and buried at night, in private, for fear of a sedition; so loved and venerated was he by every class.[2] That the Grand Master was away is implied by there being a *locum-tenens*, in his stead, during those years, as in one document;[3] and, by another, that Montacute was still in Egypt, in May of 1221;[4] by a third, that he was still there in June;[5] and by a fourth, that he was back in Acre, in October of that year, since his travelling companion was.[6] Brienne's expedition went 1219 on swimmingly at first, taking Damietta after a good defence, to his exultation, except that it was found to be an immense charnel house, scarcely containing a human creature alive; but the streets choked up with loads of carcasses, in various stages of putrefaction, dead of plague, or famine, or

[1] Arab. Chron., 392.—Michaud: Hist., iii. 320. Note.
[2] Arab. Chron , 393. Note 1.
[3] Cod. Dipl. Geros.—Num. xii.—Giunta: i. 290.—Appendix, lx.
[4] Cod. Dipl. Geros.—Num. cviii.—Giunta: i. 114.—Appendix, lxxxvii.
[5] Cod. Dipl. Geros.—Num. xiii.—Giunta: i. 291.—Appendix, lxi.
[6] Cod. Dipl. Geros.—Num. cvii.—Giunta: i. 113.—Appendix, lxxxviii.

wounds, and emitting such an intolerable stench, that it frightened back the storming party,[1] much more the whole Christian army, when they got in by one of the gates, but arrested by the same horrible smell, were obliged to retreat, and encamp anew under its walls, until the streets and houses were a little cleaned; yet a moment sufficed to inoculate them with the plague, dire disease, that continued lurking in their ranks, and growing every day; during which interval arrived the Papal legate. So there were two cardinals, and, if one of them was meek and pious, the other was a firebrand. But the former was soon killed, which only left the other's outrageous audacity without control.

1221 "Cardinal Peter is gone, and Cardinal Pelagius left living, the more the pity," says the chronicler.[2] Hospitallers and Templars, at the storming of Damietta, in which were then eighty thousand men,[3] were firmly believed by the Mahometans—not at all ashamed of being beaten by such—to be no human creatures, so transcendent was their valour, but white angels, and St. Bartholomew and St. George and company in red; the

---

[1] Olivier.—Bib. Crois., iii. 150.
[2] Michaud: Hist. iii., 325.
[3] Potestats di Reggio.—Bib. Crois., ii. 596.

Templars wearing their white mantles, and the Hospitallers their scarlet surcoats.[1] The Sultan, Malek-Kammel, Safadin's eldest son, had written the most woe-begone letters to his brothers, who, all fourteen, came, one by one, from various parts of the East on this side, and from beyond Jordan, their different dominions, with their troops to join him. Above all, the Prince of Damascus, who, before he left Palestine, took care to raze the walls of Jerusalem, lest the Franks should take them, was remarkably enthusiastic;[2] and, by a stratagem, forced his brother Arschaff, King of Armenia, who, having come with his army into Palestine, and after they had a conversation late one evening, retired to bed; the prince, who may have perceived some hesitation in the other, pulled on his little boots in the middle of the night, and roused and harangued the troops, "March!—To Damietta!" But Arschaff, in the morning, dressed, took a bath, and coming from it, was astonished not to see his soldiery. But learning what the prince had done, mounted; and without one word, marched towards Egypt after him.[3]

So now the sultan's army counted forty thousand

---

[1] Potestats di Reggio.—Bib. Crois., ii. 591.
[2] Arab. Chron., 398. Note, and 410.
[3] Id., 411.

horse, and an infinite multitude of foot;[1] while that of the Christians, according to the Moslem himself, was only the half; twenty thousand horse, and two hundred thousand foot.[2] How diminished since landing! Still the Latins were such celebrated soldiers, and their advance struck their foes with such terror, that, in both Cairos they forgot to open the gates for two days; and, though the Nile was on its increase, that which brought fertility, and decided whether they should have a good harvest or a famine, and which formed then, as at present, the usual topic of conversation in all Egyptian classes, was completely unattended to,[3] and it got tacitly full up to the very edge of its banks, before it was perceived. Fertile Egypt had more Christians in it than Palestine. Egypt was so holy and precious in the sight of the Lord, that He chose it to be the road by which thousands of Franks should reach Him: for they died very quietly of dysentery.[4] The Saracens came within our hearing, drawn up on the other side of the river, and summoned us to renounce our superstitious creed: "For either you must turn Mahometans, or we Christians." And the circumcised

[1] Arab. Chron., 412. [2] Id., 409.
[3] Id., 410.
[4] Vitri: Letters, iii. Bib. Crois., i. 429.

CHAP. I.] ST. JOHN OF JERUSALEM. 101

ate two fowls on it, to make good their oath, devouring the fowls as hungry dogs do bread. And the battle began, and in a twinkling—it was the day of the decollation of St. John the Baptist—who wanted companions, observes the chronicler, and here they were, fifty Templars, thirty Teutonics, thirty-two Hospitallers, the Chamberlain of the King of France, and that nobleman's son, several counts and princes, eighty knights, and five thousand men of different nations.[1] Unwillingly had Brienne set out from Damietta, disapproving totally of that unmilitary excursion, headlong, without any preparatives; and wished, at least, to wait for the succours promised by the emperor. But Pelagius treated his worldly misgivings with utter disdain, and arrogated to himself the supreme command, saying it was a Papal army, since composed in part of Italians, and under the Pope's protection.[2] And, although some Roman princes ran away at the first of the action, that was not very wonderful; and if, on another morning, a Spaniard was caught selling a piece of bread to two Saracens, the traitors—not Spaniards, but Saracens—were tied to a horse's tail, and dragged all through the Christian camp; no trifle, its extent being of ten

[1] Potestats di Reggio.—Bib. Crois., ii. 603.
[2] Oliveri : Hist. Damatiana.—Bib. Crois., iii. 155.

miles.[1] And when Brienne proposed that they should halt until the galleys cleared the river, Pelagius vociferated treason, and that his galley should not lower its masts till they reached Cairo, which he hoped would be within three days.[2] This utter blindness was deeply blamed by Brienne, but seems to have terrified the sultan; for he made frequent proposals for peace during the march, and now that the Christians had arrived at the southern extremity of the Delta, opposite to the new town of Mansourah, where the whole Moslem army was drawn up, continued for three weeks to send deputies proposing to give Jerusalem to the Christians,[3] and one hundred thousand pieces of gold to rebuild its walls, besides Ascalon and all the cities that had been won from them by Saladin in Syria and Palestine, in exchange for Damietta alone.[4] One would think such terms surrendered all that was wanted, and that the Christians would accept them with warm satisfaction. But not so Pelagius, who disdained any peace, and would be contented with nothing but the extermination of Islam, and effectually chasing every shadow of opposition from the face of the earth.

[1] Potestats di Reggio.—Bib. Crois., ii. 605.
[2] Michaud: Hist., iii. 352.—Arab. Chron., 419. Note 2.
[3] Id.: Id., 354.
[4] Arab. Chron., 413.

Brienne once more expostulated: " Let us encamp where we are, we can entrench the army well; believe me, it is better not to be in a hurry, and if we were twenty years in conquering Egypt, it would not be too much."[1] At which words the legate could no longer contain his rage. Brienne replied, " Well, if you will go on, I'll accompany you, and be resigned to the will of God. Lead me where you please; you will see what will come of it!"[2] And did come of it, that the deputies were given a flat refusal.

" Ho! ho," cried the Saracens and their horses too. " Now you may just wheel about and retire; for we have lost all patience, and our scimitars are thirsty, and burning our hands to dash down on you!"[3] So we perceiving them reinforced and so resolute, thought it best to take them at their word, and turned to withdraw in some confusion; but it was too late, for they attacked us, and a great battle ensued, which we lost; and had it not been for the Hospitallers, and also the other military orders, and Brienne himself, we should have been cut to pieces to a man.[4] Nor was this enough, but the sultan had the dykes broken, and

---

[1] Arab. Chron., 418.   [2] Id., 419.
[3]   Id.,   418.
[4] Potestats di Reggio. — Bib. Crois., ii. 603.

out burst the Nile, bellowing most awfully, and the entire country was a deluge. Then might you see the cardinal quite changed, and hang his head in shame, and fear, and sorrow.[1] The very first thing was, of course, that all our boats and provisions were lost. Some of our people sprang the wine and spirit casks, that they knew would soon be swamped, and died dead drunk. Many who lay down on some dry spot, the waters coming over their heads while they slept, drowned them. Every horse of ours had disappeared; and those of pitiless Arabs and Mamelukes drove through the waters to get at us and trample us, or that their riders might transfix us with their long lances. Howling famine also waylaid us, and the plague; but why further of that deplorable retreat? Worse than by the recent Berezina; for this was a Berezina of several nights. It would have been hard for Brienne to have imitated Saladin, who on losing a battle had his charger's tail cut off, by way of mourning; since there was not a horse amongst us.[2] Not one of the whole Christian army would have got half way to Damietta alive, were it not for compassion in direct opposition to the Prince of Damascus, who voted for no

---

[1] Michaud: Hist., iii. 358.
[2] Sicardi : Chron.—Bib. Crois., ii. 549.

quarter;[1] but Moslem charity allowed the residue to retire in peace, on the sole condition of surrendering Damietta, though much injured; and hostages were given, Brienne and legate on the one side, and on the other the sultan's eldest son, a boy of about fifteen. So the sultan had the dykes closed, and the land was quickly as before. Yet this did not suffice, for the unfortunate Christians were fast dying of hunger; whereupon Brienne walked into the sultan's tent, and sat down and began to weep; then the sultan looked at the king, who dolefully was weeping, and said to him: "Sire, why do you weep?"—"Sire, good right I have to weep," replied the King; "for do I not see the people, whom God has given me in charge, die of hunger?" The sultan took pity of the king, that he had seen him dolefully weeping, and began to weep himself also, and gave thirty thousand loaves of bread for poor and rich without distinction; and so for the four following days.[2] And further still did the compassionate Malek-Kammel go; for he forbade the Mussulmen to direct a word of obloquy to the retreaters. Far from taking an ignoble advantage of their distress, the Christian deputies were always received by him with great honour;

[1] Arab. Chron., 416. [2] Michaud: Hist., iii. 367.

and the sultan's own brothers and all his grandees used to stand upon their entering, and remain standing, in token of respect for them.[1] And he sent commissaries from his own Court to protect them, and defray all their expenses on the road, even unto their own ships; nor will gratitude permit us to inquire whether something is not to be subtracted from his generosity, and to be ascribed to his wisdom; inasmuch as it is good policy to assist the departure of a defeated foe.[2] Of the few Hospitallers who came back to Acre, all were more or less badly wounded; and most severely so, the grand master. Not only Montacute was at Damietta in June, 1221, quietly receiving a donation to the order by a German officer then there[3] (which proves how accurate the Arabs are in their dates, by which late in spring was the advance of the Christians, and the 28th of August that of their retreat from the Delta[4]), but likewise in October Montacute was back at Acre.[5] The other Hospitallers had been slain, and most of the Templars and Teutonics also. She who had rejoiced at their first successes, and flattered herself with the Holy Land's being free for ever, Acre, had now to mourn in con-

---

[1] Arab. Chron., 417. [2] Michaud: Hist., iii. 362.
[3] Appendix, lxi. [4] Arab. Chron., 416.
[5] Appendix, lxxxviii.

sternation at the plight in which they returned. But to console them, there was a grand procession; the Patriarch holding the true cross! How could he have it in 1222, whereas it had been taken by Saladin, who (and his descendants) always refused to restore it to the Christians? Very simply (replies the chronicler), because its thickness had been sawed in two previous to the battle of Tiberias, so that one half was preserved![1]

But scarcely two years[2] of sweet pacific giving and receiving had elapsed, when Cairenes and Damascenes fell out; the former accusing the latter of partiality to the Franks, in consequence of which there were skirmishes near Ascalon, in one of which the Templars took a Turkish grandee prisoner, whom rumour called Prince of Damascus; and if they did not kill him instantly, it could have been for no common purpose they conceded him a respite, since they seldom either were given or gave quarter. So there took place a meeting of deputies from all the military orders of Acre in their cloaks and hoods, presided over by the Grand Master of the Templars, when the president thus addressed the prisoner: "Sir Turk, it having been too long the custom to except us and our associates of the other two

1225

---
[1] Oliveri: Chron.—Bib. Crois., iii. 139.
[2] Cod. Dipl. Geros., i. 254.—Num. ccxiii.—Appendix, lxxxix.

military orders, from quarter, we propose a change and wish to send you with that intent to the sultan on this condition, that you promise to return with an answer, when if it be (which God forbid) in the negative, it afflicts me to have to state, that you must submit to fair reprisals; except only that we shall use no torture, which so many Hospitallers and Templars have undergone from you."—" Superfluous totally is your pity," replied the captive, " for I am as ready to go joyous to death as any of you; I can speak as pure English as any of you, or purer. So need none of your foreign gibberish. What, Sir Turk? What Damascus? My name is St. Alban.[1] Was not my cousin, Sir Thomas Montacute, your Grand Master? My other cousin of the same noble house your Hospitaller?[2] My father was a Knight Templar as you are, and wore the white mantle like you, but had the grace to be enlightened, and abjuring his false creed fled to the magnificent Saladin, who received him kindly, and gave him wealth, and a high command, and his own niece in marriage;[3] so (Allah be praised) I was brought up in the true religion. Look on me sharp, and you will recollect me. Is not my skin as milky as that of

---

[1] Hoveden.—Bib. Crois., ii. 775.
[2] Seb. Paoli: Osservazioni, i. 515.—Appendix, xc.
[3] Hoveden: 1187.—Bib. Crois., ii. 775.

any of you?" And he threw back his collar, and his lofty forehead was also of as dazzling a white; and his large blue eyes beneath his flaxen eyebrows shone terribly, and his expanded nostrils were transparent and immensely wide, as was perhaps necessary to feed the lungs of his capacious chest. Like almost all the Normans, he was of gigantic stature—nearly as tall as their lances.[1] "Think me a Bohemond!" and he stretched his muscular arm, and might seem an Apollo glorious from the Python, " I think I know that wolfish face, but it was then downcast, and you kept your tail between your legs. Look on me again! and remember Egypt! I am he who, when my gentle brother and master asked my counsel, answered, *Drive his owl of a soul out of the Christian.* Malek-Kammel gave you, too tenderly, your life and liberty. And now I see you here. But I repeat what I then advised, though in vain. Would you and I were with the faithful! my words would not again meet deaf ears. But I am far prouder of my maternal blood! Ought I not to be proud that I can call the King of kings father?[2] Yes, Malek-Adel, you were truly the sword of religion. The Christians feared you, and all your subjects loved and revered you, but

[1] Alexiad Anna Comnena.—Bib. Crois., iii. 400.
[2] Appendix, xc.

most your own kindred, of whom you were the defence and glory! Rejoice then, O my son, that two of the most illustrious of Islam, at the present day, were your near relatives! See then, Giaour, if you could have chosen a worse ambassador for your most infamous project? Not softness towards the infidel is what we want, but pitiless hate. Ay, by the verdant angels, and the Valley of Mecca,[1] hate! Like my fathers both Norman and Mahometan, my first shall be my last, my only love. The warm heart and true; not cold law! Plurality of wives proves the freedom of our doctrine; but many are the Moslems who have but one wife. This heart beats for only one, who responds as faithfully. What cares she for fidelity by statute? She has it more effectually by choice. Far better does the Norman war-cry, *God's aid*, suit us than you; for you believe in three Gods, we in one alone. You are the Paynims and idolators, not we. Was not my Mahometan brother, Malek-Kammel, knighted by Cœur de Lion? Did King Richard not come on purpose hither, and perform the proper ceremonies? Were I to accept your errand, I hope it would be useless; but at all events, I'll not submit to the opprobrium of having given such bad advice. Christians may.

[1] Arab. Chron., 425.

But who ever heard of a Moslem's being bribed? Thanking Him from whom all strength comes, I fling you back your offers, and reject and scorn them. What are your princes? Roaring lions in peace, or at board, or a-bed, but timid as deer in war. Shame to Latins! greater shame to Palestine! Are not its spotted hybrid Christians full of what is most base, and worse than brutal, prodigious, secret, disgusting vices and meanness? Bright eyes will be wet for my death; but she will have taught our son, the lotus-eyed David, to avenge it. Hearken to her all your days, O my dearest boy, and recollect I send my last blessing and kiss to you both. If there be any spark of feeling in any one of you, you will let them know these my dying words. I surely die while it is sweet living. Blasphemers, I defy, despise, spit on you. For I wish to die, being tired of enduring the same air with you; your smell corrupts it; the foul breath of your hypocrisy poisons me; it disgusts and sickens me! To me you are the filthiest of mangy curs, the most swinish of the grovelling swine. Yes, yes, yes, a blessed martyr am I! The honest, happy St. Alban's curse be on you all." And as he left the saloon, the grand master said in a placid and solemn tone, "At least, we have done our duty; so, Sir Hugh de Burin, see that the master-at-arms does his.[1] If ever Acre is lost, it will be lost by a renegade!" And hardly had the Mahometan passed the threshold, when in the corridor was heard the noise of a heavy fall, as of a corpse, and the rolling of, as it were, a head, which sank on the silence of that meeting; and silently, as if in mourning, they broke up.

Though old and severely wounded, the grand master assisted when the Pope (Honorius III.) met the Emperor, Frederick II., at Ferentino, in Italy, in 1223,[2] and thence hastening back, was certainly alive and at Acre in May of 1227, as we find by a Frenchman, who came thither to implore his protection for his father, who had fallen into Saracen hands, where the poor man died in slavery, just as the Grand Master Montacute was on the point of obtaining his liberation; so the son, seeing that as much as depended on the Hospitallers had been done, testified his gratitude by presenting them with this deed, obliging himself and his heirs to pay a certain annual rent into the hand of the prior of the order in France. But the document shall tell its own story, for the substance shall be in the Appendix.[3]

[1] See Note 48, page 15.
[2] Platina, iii. 66. Note F.
[3] Cod. Dipl. Geros. i.—Num. clxxvii.—Appendix, lxii.

A quarrel having arisen between (I will not say the brothers) but the ministries of Cairo and Damascus, in which the latter, threatening to call in the Karismians, the former were so terrified, that application was made to Frederick II., who had long promised, and at Ferentino had newly sworn, to go on that crusade; and he might well think that he could not act in a more friendly manner than engaging the parties to a reasonable peace, for there had existed an old friendship betwixt the sultan and that emperor, who, as having been brought up in Sicily, where there were many Mahometans, and one of them his master in logic and astronomy, was almost ranked by them as one of themselves, and they vaunted his learning as something their own. Moreover, to hasten his coming, was sent the famous Emir Fakr-eddin, as celebrated in diplomacy as war, who quickly won a high place in Frederick's esteem, as finding him, on many points, of his own opinion in philosophy, which rendered him the Egyptian sovereign's warm ally. As long as the Prince of Damascus lived, the Cairo government was accused of partiality to the Franks, and this was the true foundation of his anger; and it was then the emperor had been invited. But when the Prince of Damascus died, the sultan thought his nephew's minority was a fortunate opportunity to consolidate all Palestine, and even Syria, in his own hands, by uniting those countries to Egypt. Therefore came to Palestine, and changed so completely, that when young David entreated another of his uncles, Arschaff of Mesopotamia, to protect him (as indeed he marched with an army to do), the sultan wrote to him that he had come to curb the Christians, who were getting too audacious for a minor. "The land is without defence. The Franks have rebuilt the walls of Sidon and other fortresses that had been razed. You know that our uncle Saladin transmitted to us a name illustrious by taking Jerusalem. If the Christians had seized the Holy City, it would have been an eternal dishonour to us, and our memory would have been handed down blasted to our descendants. Become unworthy of the reputation gained by our uncle, how should we be estimated by God and men? Nor would the Franks have been contented with what they have already won, but would want to win more. However, since you are come, my presence is no longer necessary here. I'll return then to Egypt, and leave you to defend Syria. It shall never be said of me that I waged war against my brother. It is the idea furthest from me."[1] This

[1] Arab. Chron., 428.

letter had the desired effect; and the fear that the Franks might get so strong as to pay him a visit in his own dominions, made Arschaff turn against his nephew. And when Frederick II. arrived at Acre, the sultan, who was out of his embarrassment, would have been better contented he had never called him. But here he was, and must be satisfied. Nor did he arrive at Acre without presents, and forwarded them by a deputation in great pomp, which was received by the whole Mussulman army under arms; and the most intimate relations were immediately established between sultan and emperor.[1] And when the latter suspected some hesitation, he wrote thus, dissembling perhaps a tinge of resentment: "I am your cordial friend. You cannot but know I am the chief of all the sovereigns of Christendom. It was you yourself engaged me to come hither. The Pope and all the Western princes are informed of my voyage; and should I return without attaining anything, I should lose all consideration in their eyes. After all, was it not Jerusalem that gave birth to Christianity? Was it not you that destroyed it? It is now in a most miserable condition. I entreat of you then to restore it to me, in even the state it is; that when I go back to Europe, I may be able to hold

[1] Arab. Chron., 429.

up my head among our kings. I renounce every other advantage." For he had begun by asking not only for Jerusalem, but all the towns anciently possessed by the Franks, and favourable terms for commerce. "It is not," said he to Fakr-eddin, "that my motive in coming here was to deliver the Holy City! No such thing; but to preserve the esteem of the Franks. If I insist with such fervour on what I ask, it is simply that I am afraid of losing all credit in the West."

The sultan also felt great pain at sacrificing Jerusalem;[1] but he had a powerful foe, and besides argued he, we give the Franks but dismantled churches and ruined houses. And, indeed, Jerusalem, at that time, was without walls or fortifications, and the sultan gave only one road and its villages, that from Jerusalem to Acre, so that the Mahometans remained masters of the country. In the Holy City, too, they retained the mosque of Omar, and the free exercise of their religion. And, likewise, there was a clause that the Christians should not re-build its ramparts, but that it should remain an open town. So, on this basis, was sworn a peace that was to last ten years and five months and days, from the twenty-fourth of February, 1229.[2] Most Christians, says the chronicle, ap-

---

[1] Arab. Chron., 430.   [2] Id., 430.

proved of Frederick's peace; though Templars and Hospitallers could not, from their attachment to Rome.[1] Before embarking for home, Frederick chose to visit Jerusalem, and there is a narrative of it by a Moslem, who officially accompanied him.

" The emperor was bald and red haired, and with weak eyes. Had he been a slave, he might sell for ten drachms. His conversation showed little belief in the Christian religion; since, when speaking of it, he always turned it into jest. When noon struck, we of course said our prayers, and the Mahometans in the suite of the prince, without his ever attempting to prevent them. Amongst them was his ancient teacher, of Sicilian origin. The cadi had orders from the sultan to see that nothing ever happened that could displease Frederick, and, particularly, that there should be no sermon in Omar's mosque, nor prayers proclaimed from any of the minarets. On the first day this was forgotten, so the muezzins did as usual; even more, for one of them affected to recite at a most elevated pitch of voice various passages from the Alcoran against Christianity. The emperor lodged at that cadi's, whose house was quite close to Omar's minaret, and con-

[1] Gozlar Chron.—Alberic Chron.—Bib. Crois., iii., 126.— Bib. Crois., iii. 76.

sequently heard the muezzin in question, whom the cadi, much afflicted, called, and reproached, and to take care and let no one cry the next night. But the day after, the emperor asked for the cadi, and said: 'But the man I heard from the minaret say so and so, what has become of him?' The cadi, craving his excuse, said it was from fear of offending his Imperial Majesty. 'You were wrong,' replied Frederick. 'Why, on my account, renounce your duty, your law, your religion?' And he desired to see, with his own eyes, the chair in which the Imams sit, when they preach. And, while he was in the mosque, he saw a Christian priest entering it with a Bible in his hand, though it had been precisely stipulated that in the mosques the Mussulmen should be secured from all insult, and no trouble given in any case to them, or their religious ceremonies. This boldness irritated the emperor, and he forbade the priest to advance a step; swearing to punish any Christian severely who entered a mosque without a special permission; 'for,' he added, ' we are all the sultan's servants and slaves; it is he restored to us our churches, we ought not to misuse his favour.'"[1]

After this stay of two days in Jerusalem, Frederick went back to Acre, and sailed. He was

[1] Arab. Chron., 432.

CHAP. I.]   ST. JOHN OF JERUSALEM.   119

remarkable above all the princes of his time for fine mental qualifications, and knew all the branches of sciences well, particularly logic, astronomy, and medicine. Such was the impression he left in the East.[1] But these are Mahometan accounts, which must be cooled down by those of our own chroniclers. It is not a wonder the Hospitallers and Templars should be against him, if the Popes were so; since even if the Pope erred, yet at that time they owed the Holy See too much gratitude for continued favours, not to obey it almost blindly. As for the Teutonics, they as Germans and the emperor's subjects, of course did him honour. But the Popes, even Gregory IX., was he not against him? It were in most direct contradiction to a bull by that same Gregory IX. (which shall be in the Appendix), in which he strictly commands the Hospitallers to assist the Emperor Frederick II. as much as ever they can in his Palestine expedition.[2] But on reading it over with more attention, it entirely alters my mind, and convinces me that no exaggerations, as I thought, but direct falsities, are what are told on the faith of the chroniclers. But these were in truth the newspapers of that day; and, when they are not in contradiction with solemn

[1] Arab. Chron., 433.
[2] Cod. Dipl. Geros., Bolla v., vol. i. 271.—Appendix, lxiii.

documentary evidence, may be received as the opinions reigning; but where completely contradictory to it, they merit no kind of consideration whatever. Now here the Arab historians agree with this Papal record so far, that they are all perfectly silent as to that scene in the Holy Sepulchre, or that the Pope had ordered the Hospitallers and Templars not to fight under his command. Then no such things ever took place, but are only the inventions of malignancy or ignorance. And I observe on it the more, that historians of the highest estimation have copied those errors, even the most devout Roman Catholic Michaud. But they had never seen these decisive documents, or not examined them. The Mahometans and Papacy are two antipodes, and what they recount alike, cannot but be true; and what neither of them mentions cannot have subsisted at all. Is it not a fair conclusion? and even a necessary one for an honest writer, however eminent his predecessors, who have only fallen into a mistake? Truth is indeed what must prevail in the end, notwithstanding his weakness who wields it. This bull is so worthy of the head of a Church, and those fables so unworthy, and suppose such arrant dishonesty, that to drive them out of notice, is but mere justice, unless they be clearly proved. And the proofs are the other way. Frederick II. was a very remarkable personage. That he spoke jestingly of his religion, rather in reference to their disbelief, than to himself, may be in bad taste, and exaggerated, but was no crime, nor argues scepticism.[1]

My introduction of this piece a little before its date is knowingly, because written in 1236; it refers to all that had preceded, and shows that after his conduct in Palestine, the Hospitallers are commanded to obey him, which is a complete refutation. His Holiness would have then been in manifest contradiction with himself. If he had complained even, we should find it in these secret archives. Behold, they are turned inside out. We thought to discover great things, and what do we discover? Nothing. Without a command in clear writing, who would have dared to insult Frederick? It would be to suppose something extravagantly bold; as foolish, as enormous, quite incredible. Married to the daughter of John de Brienne, who had abdicated in his favour, it was *jure uxoris* that Frederick inherited the title of King of Jerusalem, and his appearing there, converted the titular into a kind of reality; and that, and the peace, form a not dishonourable close to the fifth crusade. Of which if I have spoken at some

[1] Appendix, xci.

length, it is that Sir Gawen Montacute had taken a great part in the whole Egyptian war, and if he only sent his Hospitallers with the emperor to Jerusalem, and did not go himself, he had a most valid excuse in his age and wounds. But he expired towards the close of 1231; for we have two deeds in each of which he is named reigning in October of that year.[1] And he was succeeded by Sir Bernard de Texis of whom there is no document extant, which agrees with his reign being only of a few months; but not with ten years and various other borrowed plumes given him by Vertot; since Sir Bernard was succeeded by Sir Girino, early in 1232, at least; to whom are to be ascribed all the fine things that regard the order and its grand masters from 1231 to May, 1236.[2] For a deed of the Queen of Cyprus in October of 1232 shows Girino was then Grand Master.[3] Nor were there hostile parties enough in that miserable land; but the Mogul Tartars were approaching, having left the bleak northern deserts to the spirits of their ancestors, and from some unlettered instinct or wild tradition, that

---

[1] Cod. Dipl. Geros.—Num. cxiii, cxiv.—Appendix, lxiv.
[2] Seb. Paoli: i. 341.
[3] Cod. Dipl. Geros. i.—Num., ccxv.—Appendix, xcii.

remains a secret, began advancing south; and selecting five hundred thousand of their bravest, sent them in five divisions against Poland, Russia, Persia, and driving all before them, forced the fiercest of the preceding Tartaric hordes, the Karismians, to pass the Tigris and Euphrates, with the horrid ferocity of savages in despair. Not religious enthusiasm, but plunder and destruction were their furious passion. And Mussulman ambassadors went through Europe, imploring its nations to withstand the irruption of those who massacred alike circumcised and uncircumcised, and were just as inimical to Mahomet as to Christ. That the treaty made by Frederick had pleased neither party of fanatics, was natural, neither Moslems nor crusaders. The hot and thoughtless will be always against any wise measures. It certainly was not wrong in Frederick to decline breaking a truce; yet was it the age of paying little regard to treaties; and those who signed and swore, were at that very moment meditating a breach of them. It is a poor excuse, if any; but let it stand, that it was too general to be much of a deception. Not only in the East, but everywhere, it was, in the troubadour's words, " an age of felony, envy, and treason." [1]

[1] Michaud: Hist., iv. 70.

Another branch of the Ayoubites had now seized on Damascus, and the boy David had been obliged to content himself with Petra, and those fortresses about the Dead Sea, whence as he grew up, he made continual sanguinary inroads on the Christians; for he was incited not only by creed and booty, but also that it was avenging his father. Peace or otherwise, what cared he? It was never peace for him; so a bloody war in that direction. The peace which bound the Hospitallers and all regulated people, did not a bit the reckless, who wishing for war created it. Yet a far more pleasing intercourse than war was that which made the Sultan of Cairo in this very 1232 send what a wondrous tent, as a present to Frederick II. The sun, stars, whole firmament, were represented in its ceiling, moving about regularly in their orbits by a most marvellous mechanism; and the moon, and the hours of night and day with infallible exactness. Beautiful clockwork; what a miracle of art at that time, if but as described! Yet since the description was made *then*, that it were in the head of the describer is an almost equal wonder! Arabia then, and Egypt, were they not in arts and sciences what France and England are to-day? But the price was royal, more than thirty thousand pounds, and well worthy was that splendid gift of a place in the imperial treasury, where it was long preserved.[1]

To Girino was directed a bull[2] in 1232, by which Gregory IX. exhorts him and his knights to assist his dearest son in Christ Jesus, Frederick the Roman Emperor, and King of Jerusalem and Cyprus; precisely of the same tenor as that four years later, and which has already been given as a talisman to meet whatever accusations, and reduce them to their just value.[3] 1236 It would not have been long now to wait for the treaty made by Frederick to have ended, but a great deal too long for perturbed spirits.

Many of these documents are *dentati*. Readers of ancient parchments will know very well what is meant; but others will not object to learning that it consists in writing counterparts in two different columns, divided by an alphabet, or some adage, generally pious, as *Gratiâ Dei*. This is cut all along through the middle of its letters; so the two parties take each a column, which contains one of the duplicates and halves of the letters of the adage, and by joining the two halves, if they fit and produce the adage whole, then each of the duplicates

---

[1] Cologne Chron.—Bib. Crois., iii. 22.—Arab. Chron., 435.
[2] Cod. Dipl. Geros., Bolla, iv., i. 271.—Appendix, lxv.
[3] Appendix, lxiii.

is true and valid. The duplicates are in substance the same, but not always in the same language or dialect. Something of the sort is still used on the Barbary coast, as to passports of ships, not unlike our indentures.

Only come in the Papal name, and you may with a safe conscience break any truce with the Paynim; indeed many thought that not even the Pope could sanction such truces, and so some crusaders openly against his will, sailed off. The war had indeed quite changed from what it had been in the first crusade, and even the third, and scarcely had any more the least pretence to be called religious, but one of chivalrous delight, and by a most blasphemous union, " for the love of God and the ladies." In this state of things[1] emanated that bull of 1236. How Girino ended is unknown; but it was to him that those two bulls of Gregory IX. were directed; and it was he who, in manifest unison with those bulls, upheld with such vigour the right of Frederick's son to be King of Jerusalem against the pretensions of Adelaide, widow of Hugh of Lusignan, King of Cyprus. Nor could be what Vertot writes, that he fell in the battle against the Karismians;[2] for this took place in 1243,[3] long after Girino was dead, who, though he reigned in May

[1] Seb. Paoli: i. 342.   [2] Vertot: iii. 480.
[3] Cod. Dipl. Geros.—Num. clxxviii.—Appendix, xciii.

1236,[1] yet his successor was reigning on the 20th of September of the same year,[2] Sir Bertrand de Comps, a gentleman of Dauphiny, Prior of St. Gilles, of the same illustrious family that had produced a former grand master. The lot of this Comps fell on most difficult times. All was in confusion. To make up for having lost a mistress, the crusading troubadour invokes the Virgin Mary as coming next,[3] and exhorts all ladies and misses to listen to no objection from husbands, parents, or any one, but set out East; for that all brave men flock thither, and none remain in Europe but cowards. No wonder therefore that such worthies scorned the advice of the Pope; and since he refused his consent, sailed without it, after insulting his nuncio. There was no longer even the name of religion, nor of soldiership either; but only of such extravagance as suits pipers, and drunkards, and lewd coxcombs, or who is, or fancies himself in love. It denotes an utter barbarism, that the same troubadour runs to see the 1237 burning of one hundred and eighty-four innocent men as heretics, just before he embarks.[4] At that

[1] Cod. Dipl. Geros. i.—Num. cxvii.—Appendix, xciv.
[2] Cod. Dipl. Geros., i. 126.—Num. cxvi., dated Marseilles, 1234, among whose witnesses is another, Montacute, Knight Hospitaller, and Draperius, a very ancient charge in the order.
[3] Michaud: Hist., iv. 41.   [4] Id.: Id., 48.

time Cyprus ratifies a not inconsiderable cession to the Hospitallers.[1] Among the gallant enthusiasts were the Counts de Montfort and De Bar, flowers of chivalry, who, upon hearing from the people of Acre that it was peace, treated that as of no consequence, since they had pontifical authority to break it; and on the Templars and the Hospitallers refusing to join them, for that they would strictly maintain the truce to which they had sworn, determined to go alone, which Sir Comps did all in his power to dissuade them from; it being dangerous to march with so small a number, for that the Saracens might surround them; the advice was spurned. Still some Hospitallers followed them at a distance, but were soon recalled by their grand master. Valiantly the French advanced over the frontier, and were not far from robbing the Saracens, who however soon got them entangled in the sands near Gaza, where most of them were killed, and the rest led away into captivity. Which of these misfortunes the generous-minded De Bar underwent is untold, for never more was he seen; but long did he exist, if not in the hearts, in the songs of France.[2] It is said that about this time[3] Richard Plantagenet,

[1] Cod. Dipl. Geros., i. 117.—Num. cx.
[2] Rothelin MS.—Bib. Crois., i. 382.
[3] Wikes: Salisbury Chron.—Bib. Crois., ii. 651.

Earl of Cornwall, with a large sum of money, not with an army, but sufficient body-guard, came to Acre, and was dear as a nephew of his famous namesake; and went to Jerusalem, rebuilt its walls in some degree, got Frederick's recent truce prolonged for a couple of years, procured the sultan's permission to bury the corpses of the recently slain at Gaza, and by his strictly pacific conduct did all in his power that was really useful to Palestine, more than can be averred of many who made more noise; and he bought the freedom of a vast number of Christian captives.[1] And this reasonable conduct perhaps ought to have spared him the gibe of representing his election to the empire (some years later), as barely a stratagem to degrade the imperial dignity; though he was very proud to display that vain title for the last fourteen years of his life.[2]

The citation to the knights of his order, which Mathew Paris speaks of in 1237, calling on them to come and replace those killed in the battles of Aleppo, was from Comps, and not Texis.[3] It was in the time of Comps that *the Pope asked the* 1240

---

[1] Sir Harris Nicolas: Synopsis, i. 153.—Vertot: iii. 474.—Michaud: Hist., iv. 61.—Wike: Chron.—Rothelin MS.—Mathew Paris, anno 1240.—Chron. Waverley.—Bib. Crois., i. 383; ii. 654, 651, 814.
[2] Sismondi: Rep. Ital., iii. 346.
[3] Seb. Paoli: Serie, i. 342.

Teutonics why they did not continue to obey the Hospitallers?[1] Where Comps died, seems unknown, but probably at Acre, from the consequences of former martial duties; yet not in 1243, as said, but in truth in 1241,[2] for we have a deed, proving that his successor was reigning in November of that year. It was Sir Peter de Villebride then, that was fated to meet the full shock of the Karismians; against whom Moslems and Christians joined in Acre. The former came first under the Prince of Emessa, who was received there as a liberator, and called by the people, "*One of the best Barons of Paganism.*"[3] The Grand Masters of the Temple, and of the Hospitallers, and the other Latin grandees, and if not the Grand Master of the Teutonics, it was because he was in Germany with most of his knights—so that only a few of those called in the various records, German Hospitallers, could have been in Palestine, but all who were there, went; nor is it easy to conceive with what ardour the combined forces of the two religions marched, and encountering the terrible horde near Gaza, a most destructive conflict ensued, indeed of the longest and most sanguinary of that age.[4] Both Christians and the Syrian Mussul-

1241

---

[1] Cod. Dipl. Geros., Bulla vi., i. 272.
[2] Id., i., 129. Num. cxviii.,—Appendix, lxvi.
[3] Michaud: Hist., iv. 97.   [4] Michaud: Hist., iv. 100.

men were under one banner, so were the Karismians and Egyptians. It was on the same spot where De Bar and Montfort had been worsted a few years before; but that did not terrify the Christians. The Prince of Emessa counselled a retreat; but here, as elsewhere, the fault is imputed to a priest, that the Franks refused Emessa's soldierly advice, and following one who knew nothing about what he dabbled in, decided for battle. It lasted from the rising to the setting sun, and the most part of the second day, but, at last the Syrian Moslems were broken, and though the left wing, where the Hospitallers fought, resisted most perseveringly for several hours, yet the end was most disastrous; a total overthrow on our side, with the loss of thirty thousand, and of the military orders, only thirty-three Templars, twenty-six Hospitallers, and three Teutonics, ever got back to any Christian town. Among the slain was Villebride.[1] None of the Hospitallers—nor, perhaps, of the Templars and Teutonics, only they are not named—seem to have been taken prisoners, but got into the citadel of Ascalon, and were rigorously besieged there by the

[1] Seb. Paoli: Serie, i. 342. It seems to have been hoped at first that he had been only senseless, and so made prisoner. But true to his rule, he had ceased to be.

Egyptians, as the bishop declared, before the Council of Lyons, and in that sense, prisoners.[1]

Of what country Villebride was, is not specified, but, probably, a Spaniard. He was instantly succeeded by the marshal of the order,[2] a French gentleman, named Sir William of Chateauneuf, in 1243, and not 1251.[3]

1243

The letter of the Patriarch, giving a full account of the disastrous battle of Gaza, is one of these documents, dated November 25th, 1244,[4] and, in that same year, the Bishop of Beyrout was sent with the doleful news to Europe, and led by the Pope, afterwards, to the council.[5] Great were the rejoicings at Cairo; and the Karismians, who had visited Jerusalem the year before,[6] and slaughtered seven thousand of its Christian population, kept closer to the sea-coast on their return. But other Christians must have replaced the sufferers, for David, from Karac, made an inroad into the Holy City, with an enormous havock of its Christian inhabitants, immediately after the great Gaza defeat; and the tower of David was quite demolished, which, until then, existed in at least

1244

---

[1] Bosio.—Vertot: iii. 490.
[2] Cod. Dipl. Geros., i. 133 Num. cxviii.
[3] Seb. Paoli: i. 342.
[4] Cod. Dipl. Geros., i. 321. Num. xliii. 1.
[5] Michaud: Hist., iv. 105, 107.   [6] Michaud: Hist., iv. 94.

some remnants.[1] In consequence of a sickness, Louis IX. took, and tricked some of his nobles into taking the Cross;[2] but, for some years, the French flattered themselves they should persuade him not to effectuate his threat, for though they were ready to attend their monarch on a crusade, or anywhere else, the spirit of religion, or fanaticism, was extinct, and few ever thought of Jerusalem.

There is a letter of the emperor and of the Grand Master of the Hospitallers relative to the Karismians and the invasion of those destructive savages, who in 1246 (and even further back) appear to have penetrated into Palestine.[3] The Pope himself (Innocent IV.) seems to have been far too much occupied with politics and Guelphs and Ghibellines to think seriously of the holy war, except as it might be converted into an instrument against the emperor;[4] and it was more with this intent than any beyond-sea projects (though he pretended to them certainly, and wrote to excite who needed no excitation),[5] that he convened the Council of Lyons that was sitting in 1248.[6] A letter

1247

---

[1] Arab. Chron., 442, 446. [2] Michaud: Hist., iv. 126.
[3] Mathew Paris: 2.—Bib. Crois., ii. 817.
[4] Michaud: Hist., iv. 135.
[5] Cod. Dipl. Geros. i. Num. xliv.—Appendix, xcv.
[6] Michaud: Hist., iv. 141.

from the sultan to the Pope in 1246 is given; the letter was very respectful, did words suffice. "To the highly great, highly venerable, thirteenth of the Apostles, mouth and guide of the adorers of Christ. God loves who desire peace and seek it. We venerate the Holy Scriptures, and love them. We have heard your messenger, who has spoken to us of the Christ whom we praise, and of whom we know more than you do, and honour him more. You say that you wish for tranquillity and repose, and that you have motives for calling the nations to peace. We are as desirous of it as you; we have always desired and wished it; but being bound by a treaty of amity to the emperor, we send to have his opinion. The same ambassador will afterwards visit you; and when we know what both think, we mean to answer and decide. We will do nothing which is not beneficial to all parties, and agreeable to Almighty Allah!"[1]

The reason the sultan wrote in that tenor, and that no Mussulmen dared to defile the Holy Sepulchre, when they mercilessly sacked the rest of Jerusalem is (according to some chroniclers), that "the Mahometans believe firmly that Jesus Christ was born of the Virgin Mary; that he lived without ever

[1] Zanfleit Chron.—Bib. Crois., i. 337.

committing sin; that he was a prophet, and more than a prophet; that he cured lepers, gave sight to the blind, restored life to the dead, and ascended into Heaven. Also the wisest of the Turks asked us to lend them our books of the Gospel, and then kissed them, and showed signs of the deepest veneration for the law that Jesus Christ had preached; particularly at the words of the Evangelist St. Luke, 'Missus est Gabriel Angelus.'"[1] But the rumours of Louis' preparations were noised abroad; nor is it necessary to suppose any imperial espial, for communications with Egypt and Syria were then continual—even Venetians alone sufficed, who cared little for anything but commerce and earthly interests and the grandeur of their republic. From which resulted the vain menaces of the Old Man of the Mountain: and that all the pepper and other drugs from the Levant were poisoned, in hopes of murdering the King of France, respecting whom, if the diabolical conspiracy failed, yet a great many innocent individuals died of it. Perhaps, however, they were inventions to increase hatred for the people they were going to war with. Such fables suited the ignorant vulgar.[2] As to the Old Man, he was soon settled and disposed of; for a single word from

[1] Tours Chron.—Bib. Crois., i. 392.
[2] Michaud: Hist., iv. 140.

the Templars and Hospitallers sufficed, not only to make him forthwith renounce all menaces or pretension to tribute from the king, but to impel him to solicit to become his tributary, sending him presents and his own privy seal, cut in a golden ring, and shirt, which last might denote their close alliance, the shirt being next the skin and heart.[1] Truth is, that some chroniclers aver it could not be, for that those infernal sectaries (neither Mahometans nor Christians, but rather a sort of fire-worshippers, or other Pagans) had been extinguished, as far back as Saladin's time.[2] Yet descendants of that abominable race are said to exist still, near the same spot in Mount Libanus. Why on earth do they pretend to be English?[3]

In the Council of Lyons the Bishop of Beyrout repeated what has been related of the Karismians, and that they were of so fearful a cruelty, that even the Paynim refused harbouring them, and none but the Egyptians could have invited them. "Those direst of savages have ravaged the whole of Syria, from Thoron of the Knights, to Gaza, breaking into Jerusalem, and disembowelling the priests in their vestments at the altars of the Holy Se-

---

[1] Michaud: Hist., iv. 140.—Bosio.—Vertot: iii. 514.
[2] Pipini: Henri de Champagne, &c. &c. &c.,
[3] Michaud: Orient.

pulchre, with the most horrid scoffs, and committing enormities in the Cathedral of Bethlehem that I durst not mention; but impieties far more atrocious than any ever perpetrated by the Saracens. All our military orders, and nobility, and proprietors, as well as our Moslem allies, met the savages and those of Egypt, on the vigil of St. Luke, in a great battle, which was lost, by fault of the Moslems, who ran away, and most of our chiefs and soldiers were slain or taken. The remainder of the Hospitallers, having got into the citadel of Ascalon, are besieged there by the Saracens, so we do not know what to do, unless you succour us. We have implored the King of Cyprus and the Prince of Antioch, but what avail they to protect us? Yours, or Palestine has no human aid. Come to us in March next, or the Holy Land is desolate, and the Hospitallers to a man, and Templars, and all of us, are cut to pieces; or what is much worse, led off into slavery."[1]

---

[1] Bosio.—Vertot, iii. 486.

CHAPTER II.

"WHERE are you, my son Louis?" To whom the king approaching: "What do you want, mother?"[1] And Queen Blanche, with deep sighs, and melting into tears; "Oh, my dear son, what is to be done in the terrible emergency, predicted by the news that has reached us? This invasion of Tartars threatens us with one universal ruin; us and Holy Church!" To which the king, in a plaintive tone, but not without something of divine inspiration, "Then, dearest mother, may the consolations of Heaven sustain us! If those barbarians assail us, either we shall drive them back to the Tartarus, whence they came, or better still, they send us to Paradise!" So leaving his mother as

[1] Mathew Paris.—Bib. Crois., ii. 815.

regent, St. Louis, accompanied by his wife (who could not be prevented), set out, having taken the cross nearly three years earlier, and embarking on the Mediterranean, the twenty-fifth August, 1248, reached Cyprus on the twenty-first September. A document, evidently composed with great care, being a contract, intended to stand for ages, and to anticipate a remedy in every possible case, is a fresh proof of how brittle are the designs of men; since, within the lifetime of some of its witnesses, a catastrophe was to occur rendering that and every other document of the sort perfectly null and invalid.[1] Its contents would imply the grand master's absence, probably in Cyprus with Louis IX.[2] There he passed the winter, and exerted his peacemaking qualities in various ways, and with more or less success between the Greek and Latin clergy concerning missions to Tartars, who at first were about becoming Christians, but when they saw Syria yield to Mahometanism, became Mahometans;[3] mediating with Cyprus, who, by accepting the Pope's offer of the title of King of Jerusalem, fomented discord with Frederick II., rightful owner of that vain distinction, and negotiating with the

1248

---
[1] Cod. Dipl. Geros., i. Num. ccxix.—Appendix, xcvi.
[2] Michaud: Hist., iv. 155.
[3] Villani.—Bib. Crois., ii. 624.

Empress of Constantinople, who came to implore him to succour her husband.[1] But Louis was relaxing the discipline of his army in that beautiful but immoral island, and lessening his provisions and finances. Yet in vain Templars and Hospitallers tried to engage him to an armistice with the sultan, who was no longer Frederick's old friend, Malek-Kammel, but his son. In which rejection the French nobility joined their monarch. Still, it required no very wary eye to see Louis, notwithstanding all his personal courage, and his sanctity, was a weak-minded man. This was most observable in his own family, where he allowed the queen mother to exert too great an ascendant over him, to the not unreasonable jealousy of her royal daughter-in-law, his true and faithful wife. The consequence was, that the gentle Margaret could not love the domineering, though virtuous and intelligent Blanche. The monarch's brothers, also, were turbulent spirits, nor obedient as they ought, to their sovereign; to say nothing of his rank of commander-in-chief. Which turbulence and which debility argued ill for the opening campaign, and rendered it still harder to quiet the haughty French grandees. Some want of provisions already brought

[1] Michaud: Hist., iv. 162.

distress upon the army, in consequence of their own carelessness, which was remedied by the emperor's sending a most timely supply. "But for this prince, Frederick II.," wrote Queen Blanche, in a letter to the Pope, "the king, my son, and all the Christian army, had undergone much jeopardy of life and honour."[1] The Moslems, themselves, in two or three most sanguinary battles, had entirely defeated the Karismians, who, like most savages, had an inordinate self-love, and despised all nations but their own—and their race extinguished totally, as an English bishop relates;[2] though others say the name, indeed, became extinct, but their blood is the obscure origin of the present potent dynasty of the Ottomans.[3]

But this was no stop to the Franks, more employed in thinking of the riches of their foe, than of his strength. That dissolute boastfulness was their ruin. It was contagious, too, and Louis was led into spending not only the whole winter, but spring, too, in Cyprus. The Grand 1249 Masters of the Templars and Hospitallers, who sent to advise him of the possibility of coming to accommodations with the sultan, were shrewder than to share the blind confidence of the crusaders, and,

[1] Mathew Paris.—Bib. Crois., ii. 826.
[2] Bib. Crois., ii. 826.   [3] Michaud: Hist., iv. 104.

besides, might have wished to free those of their orders who pined in captivity, or were besieged in Ascalon, since the day of Gaza. Besides they knew, by experience, that the Franks were subject to be feared at first, and begin war with brilliant success, but fall soon into discord and debility, and end with some huge disaster, and then thought only of getting back to Europe, and left Palestine Christians to suffer the full fury of an enemy, irritated by the loss he had to endure at the commencement. But Louis, with all his wisdom, still participating in his army's foible, not without superadding a little fanaticism of his own, scouted the proposal, and with violent indignation, forbade the grand masters ever again to address him in such a tone, for that it was as bitter an outrage to all Christian warriors, as injurious to himself.[1] So the crusade sailed, and beautiful was their departure from Limisso, in eight hundred or eighteen hundred ships;[2] at the mouth of the harbour falling in with the Duke of Burgundy's fleet, which had wintered in the Morea, and bore the then Earl of Salisbury, grandson of the beautiful Rosamond,[3] and son of one who, after his father's death, became an Hospitalleress,[4] Long-

[1] Michaud: Hist., iv. 166.
[2] Joinville.—Michaud: Hist., iv. 169.
[3] Michaud: Hist., iv. 143.
[4] Mathew Paris: 3.—Bib. Crois., ii. 826.

sword and his two hundred English; and of surpassing beauty likewise was their landing in Egypt, not unopposed—but what could withstand the gallantry of that body of Franks? Many of their vessels had been driven by the storm into various places along the coast, and chiefly Acre, where the two Grand Masters accused of being desirous of peace, and their Templars and Hospitallers, embarked. In their first impetuous outset, Louis' van of invaders, without waiting for their countrymen, or any one, had not only landed in the presence of an enemy, but also put to flight the entire Egyptian army, commanded by a renowned general, and taken Damietta. Nearly incredible, but so it was, and a joyful day it must have been for the Christian slaves there; fifty-three of whom had been in chains for twenty-two years.[1] And when the grand masters and "the nerve of the Christian armies" joined them, it was within Damietta; so that St. Louis in giving several of its best palaces to the military orders, it was not a recompense for any late succours, but in anticipation of their future utility, or as a tribute to the glorious reputation they had long earned. But for the contrary winds it is likely St. Louis would have landed at Alexandria, on the very spot where Bonaparte landed

[1] Rothelin Chron.—Bib. Crois., i. 384.

five centuries after him. But, even from Damietta he could have reached Cairo, if he had manœuvred like Napoleon; but to this Michaud has a full right to reply that it would have been quite impossible for St Louis' unwieldy army to have executed the manœuvres of the French, in 1798.[1]

The bravest of the Moslems despaired of Egypt when Damietta fell; but not so the sultan, though labouring under a mortal sickness, and totally unable to mount a horse. What could he do? A reproach to Fakr-eddin, who hardly forbore from murdering him, and a capital sentence on many of the deserters, were ineffectual; but what more could be done by a pale and dying man, who saw the emir's looks interrogating Fakr-eddin's, ready at the slightest assent to hasten his sovereign's departure, nor allow his life to spin out for a few hours longer? He had got himself carried to Mansourah, the precise field of Brienne's overthrow thirty years before. Could nothing open the eyes of the French? Yet not one appears to have felt a presentiment! Dissoluteness, disobedience, high living, continued in their camp outside Damietta, produced epidemics and famine. The Count D'Artois particularly, a young and effervescent prince, proud of his birth, and prouder of his reputation for military bravery,

[1] Michaud: Hist., iv. 173 and 189.

would obey no one. The king himself was but a cipher. So the Earl of Salisbury (whose mother, when widow, became an Hospitalleress and Abbess of Lacock) surnamed Longsword, having received some indignity from that hot-headed youth, and having complained in vain to St. Louis, said, "You are no king then, since unable to render justice," and went away to Acre, nor returned till after repeated invitations from the monarch. Why ever return?

They were waiting the king's youngest brother, the Count of Poitiers, with the heavy baggage, and a heel of the French van and some residue from England; but at length he arrived—the money in vast tuns, that took eleven waggons, with many horses each, to draw them. The queen was left to lie in at Damietta, and the ladies with a strong garrison; whilst the king and army, amounting to twenty thousand cavalry and sixty thousand foot, with every sort of stores, marched, whether for Alexandria or Cairo was debated, till Artois deciding for the capital, "to kill a snake, crush its head," he cried; so for Cairo was their march. On the 7th of December, they encamped at about twenty miles south-west of Damietta. It was the very road Brienne had taken; but what did they mind that? Instead of instantly dying, the sultan got a little better. It was only a gleam before death. But it sufficed to increase the pride and courage of the Moslems, who besides were getting large reinforcements every day. Still the beginnings of the march of the crusaders were triumphant. But then they encountered a small body of cavalry, only about five hundred at first, but it next day increased, and killed a Templar; and from that day forward they had to fight for every step. A storm was gathering all round them; they could not but see it, except that homeward was a meagre line of sombre light; but soon a retreat became as impossible as an advance. But the word impossible was to be erased from their dictionary.

About this time the sultan expired, and his son was far off in Mesopotamia. Yet the death was concealed by the heroic widow, " whom no woman ever exceeded in beauty, nor man in intellect; " and naming Fakr-eddin as Atabec or regent, she disclosed the secret to him alone. For weeks the guards were posted as usual at the sultan's door, and despatches brought in as usual; and his council received his counterfeited clamè, or signature, daily, to various ordinances, by which Fakr-eddin commanded the troops, and continued to face the invaders,[1] who now on the 19th of December got to the extreme

[1] Arab. Chron., 455.

south angle of the Delta, and there was only a canal between them and the Moslems at Mansourah. No mistake. It was the identical scene of Brienne's great disaster. The Turkish opinion being that, if the crusaders passed the canal, they would infallibly take Cairo or entire Egypt, there was to be a decisive battle; and they might expect the full resistance of the Moslems. Many days were lost in endeavours to make a mound across; tremendous exertions on both sides. The Greek fire from tubes of brass was horrible; and St. Louis, so fearless for himself, used to walk about praying and weeping at every explosion, in agonies, not knowing where it would fall: "Merciful Lord, protect this my poor host!"[1] Though often Turkish skirmishers came over to assail them, and returned before their faces, the misguided crusaders appear never to have thought it possible for their own army to have done the same. Were there not thoughts (if men of such inflamed and swollen eyes had then time to think) which went back to what once seemed unquiet Palestine? But it at that very day 1250 was quiet enough, since here is a document in 1250 concerning a church then building at Mount Thabor.[2] At last a Mahometan deserter told them

[1] Michaud: Hist., iv. 204.
[2] Cod. Dipl. Geros., Num. cxxii., i. 140.

of a ford (there were many fords) about a league off; and instead of waiting till next day, when the bridge they were making would be finished, and their entire army might pass, and all Islam irrevocably be lost (persuasion of even the best Christian authority), they separated the infantry from the cavalry, and St. Louis allowed himself to be persuaded to this instance of monstrous impatience, and lead this entire body of twenty thousand horse to the ford, in the presence of the enemy at broad day, three miles' distance; for though it was night when they set out, it was sunrise when they reached the water. After this example of his own, he could not well blame any one else; nor does he in his letter to the queen, but only bewails Artois' death, without accusing him (nor even himself) of any error. It was the 5th of April.[1] The cavalry having come to the ford, the Count D'Artois, with the vanguard, insisted on his right to pass first, and Louis, knowing his disobedient spirit, made him swear on the Evangelists to wait for orders, drawn up on the opposite bank, till all the cavalry had got over; but the moment Artois was there, he ordered his troops to advance. And on the grand master's interposing, it was in vain; for all

[1] St. Louis: Official Letter to all France, apud Michaud: Hist., iv. 415.

the Templars, and Hospitallers, and English, were in that vanguard. Artois' outrageous reply to the grand masters, was to accuse them of being in league with the Saracen, and that they wished to prolong the war from ambition, to which they replied: "So we and our knights would relinquish our home and country and all domestic comforts, to spend our lives in danger and fatigue in a foreign land, and all from treason to our faith?" The Grand Master of the Temple turning his head, commanded his knights instantly to unfurl the banner of his order for the charge. The Earl of Salisbury pleaded the unskilfulness of separating its vanguard from the main body. "Timid counsels," cried Artois, "are not made for us." "Then let us go forward," retorted Salisbury; "and, prince, I'll lead you such a race that you shall not reach even the tail of my horse."[1] Then a French knight said: "Sire, see the Turks, how they are running away! Would it not be *grant mauvaisete et grant couardise si nous ne chaçons nos ennemis?*"[2] "If you are afraid," said Artois to the Grand Master of the Hospitallers, "stay where you are!" "No," replied he of the Hospital, "neither I nor

[1] Mathew Paris.—Bib. Crois., ii. 834.
[2] French knight then present. MS. apud. Michaud: Hist., iv. 421.

my brethren are afraid. We will not stay, but will go with you. Yet you must know, that we doubt much if ever we return." But worse and worse, for during the colloquy, the king had perceived Artois' preparations, and sent ten knights to give him a distinct specific command in his royal name not to stir, but to stay on that very spot until the King of France in person should come up; to which he had the amazing insolence to answer, "that the Saracens were in full flight and that he would not stay, but on the contrary pursue them, *et que il demeroroit mie, ains les chaceroit.*" And at the word, off he flew, and indeed took the Saracens by surprise, and slaughtered a great number, sparing none, but rushing into their tents and putting them to the sword, even their women and children; and which being told to the atabec himself, then in the bath, and getting his beard dressed (as was the Moslem fashion at that time), he jumping up half naked and throwing himself on a horse, had no sooner mounted than he falls down dead, pierced with a hundred wounds. And a worthy warrior and statesman he was; and much esteemed by the Turks for his courage also (notwithstanding his conduct at Damietta), and had been knighted by Frederick II., and wore the imperial coat of arms along with those of the Sultans of Egypt and

Damascus. And so, after leaving the Moslem camp in blood and confusion, Artois galloped into Mansourah; but a few minutes sufficed for the Mahometans to observe his slender number, who immediately chose Bibars Boudochdar to take Fakr-eddin's place in commanding them; and the first act of Bibars was to have the gates of Mansourah shut, and leaving injunctions to slay or take all those mad Giaours, he straight led his army to meet the masses of Christian cavalry that were appearing then on the rising ground. The sounding of the trumpets, the waving of the oriflamme, and such a large body of cavalry with the French monarch at their head, all radiant as he was from his golden helmet and the dazzling of his armour in the sun, his sword of German steel drawn, and his martial air, was a grand and magnificent sight; "I promise you," says Joinville, "there never was a handsomer soldier seen by me." And the whole plain beneath was covered with broken bucklers and cuirasses and the dying and the dead; and there was a confusion of banners. Drums, kettle-drums, trumpets, Saracen nackers, playing the charge everywhere—here the Christians were conquerors, here beaten or in flight—here the Saracens the same, hundreds of small conflicts, single combats, no telling which the infidels, which the

Franks, and cries of " Montjoie St. Denis!"[1]—and of "Islam! Islam!" Who ever beheld more beautiful feats of arms? No bows or crossbows or other artillery; but only right good knocks of sweet battle axes, iron maces, swords and steel of lances all pell-mell![2] But overwhelmed were the Franks in Mansourah, and fell; yet after a fearful struggle. The Earl of Salisbury was killed, true to his noble exclamation, " God forbid my father's son should ever fly before the Saracens!" so perhaps when he might have escaped, he disdained to turn his horse, and preferred a glorious death to a life of self-reproach.[3] It is said his ghost visited his mother in England that same night.[4] And every one of the English who had been increased to three hundred, were slain, including De Vere, who tearing England's colours from the staff wound them closely round his body, and as he carried them, died in them. And what more glorious winding-sheet? Nor did the unfortunate Artois fail to display signal bravery. He had now fought ten hours, from daybreak to three in the

[1] "Crierent tous á haute voix. 'Montjoje S. Denis!"—Chron. Fiand. Montjoje is Mons Gaudium, the Mons Mars at Rome, but became the French war-cry. Vital: lib. xii.—Seb. Paoli: Osservazioni, i. 546.
[2] Michaud: Hist., iv. 211.
[3] Mathew Paris.   [4] Bib. Crois., ii. 835.

afternoon; horses and men were worn out. Covered with wounds, he dismounting retired from the streets heaped with corpses, into a house with a small remnant of the brave and devoted, and there entrenching himself made a further defence; but fell at last on a mound of dead, that seemed even in death to cast frowns that intimidated their enemies; yet Artois appears not to have been then quite dead, since Chateauneuf, who says he saw Salisbury killed, only says he saw Artois made prisoner. But mortally wounded, he must have died shortly after; for we find Louis mourning for his death that very evening late, when the Preceptor of the Hospital came to kiss his hand before bed time and inquired of his Majesty if he had news of Artois. "All I know," replied the King, weeping bitterly, "is that he is in Paradise."[1] Yet his body was never found, though sought for several days by his faithful servants amid the myriads of putrifying pestilential corpses; and indeed by the king too, for he paid a hundred of those bandits who gain their livelihood by that miserable trade, but they never found the prince.[2] Of many that had flown to save Artois, almost all of them perished. As to the two grand masters (who appear to have been the couple who remained by his royal highness to his end), he of the

[1] Michaud: Hist., iv. 215.   [2] Id.:   Id., iv. 227

Hospitallers saw all his die as became them, and then in a swoon from loss of blood was made prisoner; he was the only Hospitaller in that fight, who survived it.[1] He of the Temple, after the death of two hundred and eighty of his knights, escaped as if by miracle, and joined the French army late that evening, after loss of an eye, with his face all bloody, his garments quite torn, and his cuirass pierced through in several places, which notwithstanding availed him little, for the poor gentleman was killed in a skirmish a few days later.[2]

Louis' cavalry had for awhile stood, but ended by retreating, and some entire regiments were drowned in a most disorderly attempt to get back over the canal, not at the ford, but lower down, exactly opposite the infantry, who were also seized by a panic, and exclaimed, little and great, weeping loud, beating their feet and heads, and straining their fists, and pulling their hair up by the roots, and tearing their cheeks most wofully: "See! See! Jesus and Mary! The king, his brothers, and their whole company, all lost!"[3] Having got over the luckless bridge, which ought to have seen their horses turned the other way, Louis gave orders for

---

[1] MS. Rothelin, apud Michaud: Hist., iv. 424.
[2] Michaud: Hist., iv. 222.
[3] Mathew Paris.—Bib. Crois., ii. 835.

ST. JOHN OF JERUSALEM. 155

pulling it down, but they were not executed, and it enabled the Moslem to persecute them close; yet there were many most gallant actions, of which France has good reason to be proud. To so brave a nation, the heroism of Artois is almost a counterbalance for his faults, and it was certainly most magnificent in Louis not to have escaped when he might, but preferred sharing the lot of his soldiers; and valiant was his attempt to raise their spirits, notwithstanding all his own griefs, by appearing without either helmet or cuirass, but a sword in his hand, and on a fine Arabian.[1] Still all was vain; retreat to Damietta was cut off, and nothing remained but for king and army to surrender at discretion. So entire was the overthrow, that the Moslems say only two escaped; nor even two, since they threw themselves into the Nile and perished.[2] And in chains hand and foot, and his two brothers as well,[3] he was dragged back to Mansourah, and his soldiers tied with ropes, like so many cattle.[4] The new sultan had arrived; nor until then was his father's death published—not even on Fakr-eddin's; so steady and wise was the illustrious sultana. But her half son having been soon murdered by his

[1] Michaud: Hist., iv. 236.   [2] Arab. Chron., 463.
[3] Michaud: Hist., iv. 241.
[4] Michaud: Hist., iv. 245.—Arab. Chron., 464.

wicked emirs, headed by that upstart Bibars, as daring in assassination as in battle, she was for a short time proclaimed sovereign in right of her dead son, and her elevation astonished all Islam. The Caliph of Bagdad, in horror at the innovation, wrote to the Egyptian emirs, to ask them if there was not a single man of ability in entire Egypt, that they had recourse to a woman to govern them?[1] Yet the revolted emirs were not quite unmerciful to the Franks, but allowed St. Louis and army to embark, only taking back Damietta, and leaving hostages and property, which according to the treaty the Moslem promised to restore; but afterwards refused. And with Louis embarked all that remained of the military orders; three Templars, and four Hospitallers—of whom one was that preceptor for France, whose duty was to stay by the king's person, and another one dying of his wounds, and who in effect died previous to the ship's getting to Acre. Just before expiring it has been said, without citing authority, that he told the preceptor that Chateauneuf, just previous to their captivity, had visited him in a disguise, which he had received from the charity of a Saracen woman, whose medicaments had recalled him to life and staunched his wounds; and then she gave him his liberty. And, indeed, he was the only Hos-

[1] Arab. Chron., 472.

pitaller that got alive from Mansourah that day; and even the human beings were but four, he and two Templars, and one common man, who swam the river, naked, to carry the mournful news to the King of France.[1] "Indeed," said the dying man to the preceptor, "he forbade me to mention it then, for that it was his intention to profit by the confusion, and, disguised as he was, to traverse the Moslem parties, and make the sea-side. Yet I feel it to have been impossible, considering his weakness and many dangerous wounds, and that I shall find him in that other world, to which God calls me, within three or four minutes."

That the preceptor may have informed the king of all that afterwards, is more than probable, seeing how desirous his majesty was to learn whatever had any relation to his lamented brother's death; but this much, only, is recounted as certain, that Chateauneuf, however disabled, or in what way, got back to Acre, before August, in 1250; for that is the date of St. Louis' letter to his barons, spiritual and temporal, and the whole kingdom of France.[2] And, though Chateauneuf was naturally in too wretched a state of health to attend much to affairs (and, therefore, I see that several other authorities, who carefully mark

[1] Mathew Paris.—Bib. Crois., ii. 835.
[2] Michaud: Hist., iv. 420.

that they are in place of the grand master, continued to act, just as while he was in Egypt), the tradition is that by a great struggle he rose from his bed, and received St. Louis, on the beach, at Acre, who said, seeing him so thin and tottering, " Now, my good Grand Master, return to your bed, where I will presently visit you." Which when the monarch did, a few hours later, the grand master on his couch, in his bedroom, and the king standing, they remained some instants looking at each other in silence, and finally St. Louis spoke: " So you saw him?"—And the monarch turned very pale, and burst into a great flood of tears.

A few months after his return, he received an embassy from the Old Man of the Mountain, not of menace, like that in Cyprus, but friendship and tribute, as to a superior, and his ring and a shirt as symbols of close alliance, as the finger to the hand, and the other as worn next the skin.[1] To which the king replied, through a knight who spoke Arabic well, whom he sent to compliment the sheick. What expedition could St. Louis undertake, who found but a corps of seven hundred at Acre, and had not of his own one hundred? That disastrous retreat in Egypt produced many renegades, who were despised by the Mahometans.

[1] Michaud: Hist., iv. 303.

And strange it is, that not only then, but during all the crusades, more Christians became Mahometans than Mahometans Christians.[1] During his stay in Palestine, he fortified some of the Christian towns,[2] and did his best to allay the spirit of discord; but his holy discourse and virtuous example were forgotten too soon.[3]

Perhaps it is hard to call wasting his time what contributed to his chief object—bettering the lot of those Eastern Christians. A long time prevented by the sickness among that small Court, he brought with him from the Nile a hundred knights only—[4] the epidemic was so destructive, that Joinville tells us twenty funerals a-day used to pass under the window of his own lodgings—he might have been much occupied about the twelve thousand prisoners he had left in Egypt—while the three military orders and the Franks of Acre were never without conjuring him not to abandon them; and that he should not, was not merely the opinion of the monarch, but also of many of his best barons, including Joinville. Latterly the king was preparing for visiting Jerusalem, at that time (for him particularly) very difficult; and before any oppor-

[1] Michaud: Hist., iv. 305.
[2] Beaulieu: Chron.—Bib. Crois., i. 298.
[3] Michaud: Hist., v. 2. [4] Michaud: Hist., iv. 382.

tunity presented itself, tidings of the worst nature made it imperative on him to return to France immediately. Not at Acre, but the not distant Jaffa, seeing his confessor and the Papal legate enter, he mistrusted of some afflicting news; so retreated into what he called his arsenal against all the misfortunes of the world, and when he heard Queen Blanche was dead, calming his torrent of tears, he knelt down before the altar in that chapel, and with joined hands, prayed fervently: " O my God, who didst vouchsafe me such a mother, I thank thee for thy mercy. Thou knowest I loved her above every other creature; but it must be after all that thy decrees be accomplished: therefore, O Lord, be thy name blessed throughout the eternity of ages!"[1] When the excellent Joinville was called to Queen Margaret in the next room, he who had followed Louis to Egypt and Damietta, and thence to Palestine, could not but express his surprise, and that he never imagined her crying for the "woman whom she had reason to hate most in the world." "Very true," replied Margaret; "nor is it for her death I weep, but for the deep grief it will give the king." The jealous antipathy between the queen-mother and the queen was of old origin; and the former had acquired such an undue influ-

[1] Beaulieu: Chron.—Bib. Crois., i. 299.

ence over her son, that his wife could only see him in secret. Most curious anecdotes go of the haughtiness of Blanche, the weakness of St. Louis, and timidity of Margaret.[1] In the spring of 1254, he removed to Acre, and on the 25th of April sailed for Europe.

It was not till the August next after his departure, that Chateauneuf was able to resume the reins of government, and begins again to appear in the documents,[2] of which a few extracts shall be in the Appendix.[3] The last we have of his is in April of 1257.[4] Necessarily he had been at Mansourah, and seen the Earl of Salisbury killed with the three hundred English, and Robert, brother to the King of France, and this king himself, and the rest of his princes, barons, and army, made prisoners.[5] And in about fifteen months (during which he however had the comfort of the bull of Alexander IV., in favour of the order to the King of Hungary[6]), went

1254
1255
1257

1258

---

[1] Michaud: Hist., iv. 317.
[2] Cod. Dipl. Geros. i. Num. cxxiii.—Appendix, lxvii.
[3] Id. Id., cxxiv.— Id., lxviii., and Cod. Dipl. Geros. i. Num. cxxvi. and ccxx.—Appendix, lxix. and lxx.
[4] Cod. Dipl. Geros. i. Num. clxxxiii.—Appendix, lxxi.
[5] Seb. Paoli: Serie, i. 342.
[6] Cod. Dipl Geros. i. Bolla, xi. 276.

1259 the way of all flesh; since we find his successor, Sir Hugh de Revel, reigning in the Autumn of 1259.[1] So an authority most estimable[2] thinks (as he has full right) that it was in the spring of that year Chateauneuf died. Revel was of an illustrious family in that province which gave so many signal members to the order—Dauphiny; and if he had already acquired a high character, his reign as grand master was to be worthy of it. And in the last month of that same year, by that same Pope, is another bull on the same Hungarian affair —a sort of duplicate to the former, in consideration probably of the change of grand masters.[3] Yet it cannot be allowed that, as the other histories have it, he should be considered as the inventor of commanderies, since he was himself grand commander at the very time of his election to be grand master;[4] and had been grand preceptor for years before made grand commander.[5] Truth is, commander is a dignity that dates as far back as 1194, or much earlier.[6]

Already had Bibars (the same who destroyed the

[1] Cod. Dipl. Geros. i. Num. cxxxiii.—Appendix, lxxii.
[2] Seb. Paoli: i. 342.
[3] Cod. Dipl. Geros. i., Bolla xii. 277.
[4] Id.   Num. cxxvi.—Appendix, lxix.
[5] Id.   Id. cxxiv.— Id.,   lxviii.
[6] Id.   Id. lxxxi.— Id.,   lxxiii.

Christians at Mansourah and as emir murdered one sultan the sultana too being killed), ravaged many parts of the Holy Land and menaced Acre; but after remaining three days before it, riding up to its very gates with his scimitar drawn, at the head of a body of most terrible-looking Mamelukes, even mining one of its towers, and raising the takbir,[1] attempted its ditches, renewed the truce, and returned to Egypt;[2] where he murdered a second sultan and hurried to the Mameluke camp. "Who slew the sultan?"—"I," replied Bibars. "Reign then in place of him," said the Atabec.[3] And so Bibars assumed the sovereignty—doleful news for Christianity. Bibars had been originally a slave from the shores of the Black Sea, and, carried to Damascus, he was sold there for eight hundred pieces of silver. The emir, who bought him, sold him as unsound, for a white speck on one of his eyes. He took the name of Boudochdar from its being that of his former master.[4]

Alexander IV. by his bull however[5] honourable, calling the Hospitallers "Terræ Sanctæ athletæ—

[1] Mahometans have two war-cries, *Takbir* and *Tahlil*, in substance the same ; " God is great."—Arab. Chron., 489.
[2] Michaud: Hist., v. 9.
[3] Michaud: Hist., v. 10.—Arab. Chron., 480.
[4] Arab. Chron., 534.
[5] Cod. Dipl. Geros. i., Bolla xiii. 278.

incliti robusti electi," and his dear children, bidding them leave off their black whenever they were on military duty (which was always, except when precisely at home) and wear a scarlet mantle with the white cross wrought on it (which they had done of themselves long ago)—was no adequate compensation for the evil he had done, by publishing to the world in his reply to the ambassadors from Palestine, that his Holiness was more desirous of a crusade against others than the Mahometans; so that the Saracens must have discovered how impossible it was for any Christian prince to remain long in the East, and that it could never expect any real succour from such a distance; for that cruel truth came from his lips with dreadful weight—as disheartening to the disconsolate Christians as encouraging to their ruthless foe. Clement IV. in 1265 wrote a letter to the Grand Master of the Hospital, and to the Grand Master of the Temple as well, praising their past conduct and exhorting them to persevere in it; but what did such consoling words lead to?[1]

Bibars declared war against them at once. It was perhaps his first act of sultanship.[2] And he marched into Palestine with such an immense

[1] Tresor Matenc.—Bib. Crois., i. 426.
[2] Michaud: Hist., v. 11.

army that he compares their numbers to all the animals that people the face of the earth and the multitudes of fish in the ocean, and well it might be said, compared to the small number of the Christians; and we may form some opinion from the document come down to us of the vassals which according to the feudal agreements one of the Syrian towns had to give,[1] from which it appears that the whole of Assur had only five knights' fiefs, or fifty horse and various provisions, of not much amount, in kind.   1261

The Franks sent to him overtures of peace, and his only answer was to set fire to the Church of Nazareth.[2]

In 1266 a corps of five hundred English cross-bowmen were shipped for the Holy Land.[3]   1266

Stern was the discipline in Bibars' soldiery, and (to a Moslem) there was the severest morality, for there was no scandalous wine, and elderly well-conducted matrons gave the troops water to drink and even aided the men in transporting the machinery for war. The standard of the Prophet was planted by the sultan himself and prayers regularly said in the churches converted into

---

[1] Cod. Dipl. Geros. i., cxl.—Appendix, lxxiv.
[2] Michaud: Hist., v. 15.
[3] Cod. Dipl. Geros. i., Num. xlv., 325.

mosques.[1] The Mamelukes massacred the greater part of the inhabitants of that quarter of Palestine, and the rest of them were made slaves, and often forced to destroy their own houses. The conquered lands were divided among the emirs, maximum of generosity in Bibars, that deserves to be written in the book of Heaven.[2] So say the Moslems, but the Christians call him very ungenerous when he wrote in 1271 to Sir Hugh de Revel—"Brother Hugh, whom it is to be hoped the Lord will not put among the number of those who harden themselves against their destiny and are foolhardy enough to resist the master of victory, we let you know what the Creator has just done for us. You have fortified this castle, and manned it with a select body of the bravest of your order; well, it is all labour in vain, you have only hastened their death, and by theirs secured your own."[3] Which intimidated the old warrior, so he made proposals of peace, and it was generously granted; but the Christians affirm that Bibars acted from no such noble sentiment, but that it was simply because he had not the courage to besiege Margat, but turned, and it was to attack New Sephet of the Templars (for Old Sephet had been destroyed by Saladin), whose garrison capitu-

[1] Arab. Chron., 493. [2] Michaud: Hist., v. 17.
[3] Id., 525.

lated for their lives, but notwithstanding were all slaughtered, with the exception of two alone; an Hospitaller, that he might go to Acre to announce the terrible tidings; and a Templar, who became a renegade it is said, but is it true? Why assert it without proof? only the unfortunate Templars have to become callous to flippant accusations. It is a novelty to require proof in their case! Soon shall their whole innocent body be accused of all enormities without proof, and confess them too, but under torture, and to avoid the infamous stake, to which, however, they shall be condemned, and burn there to death, as guilty on their own avowal. Here by Bibars the rest, men, women, children—every human creature fell by the sword, whence the consternation and grief of the Acre Christians may be supposed. Nor is it an exaggeration, but much under the truth, by the Moslem accounts themselves.[1] Yet even the Christians allow Bibars a few of the redeeming qualities, so as not to be quite a monster.[2] Monfort in 1270 confirms the splendid donation made by his great-grandmother.[3] Yet Bibars was reluctant to attack Acre, for fear of Europe, to which the Patriarch and the two grand

1270

---

[1] Arab Chron., 526.
[2] Bib. Crois., i. 308.—W. of Tripoli.
[3] Cod. Dipl. Geros. i., Num. cl.—Appendix, xcvii.

masters were again sent; but if they had a doubt, it soon vanished, and they were taught how fruitless all such errands were. Mahomet uses all his power, and adds to Bibars' ferocity.[1] He is reported not to have rested a single day during his reign of seventeen years, in Syria, Egypt, on the banks of the Euphrates; often was he walking in the streets of Aleppo, while his officers were waiting in his ante-rooms at Cairo, thinking he was not yet risen. "To-day in Egypt, to-morrow in Arabia, the day after in Syria, and in four days at Aleppo!" said his Mihmandor. Bibars was a great conqueror, but the most suspicious, vindictive, sanguinary of men. By a mistake he poisoned himself,[2] intending to poison another, and in various ways, and under many pretexts, murdered two hundred and ninety of his own emirs. So these, added to the sultans and the princes, make a formidable list, and well merit him his terrible character.[3] One sole prince in Europe spent a thought on the Holy Land; St. Louis could not forget it was there he passed many of his younger days; the hope to avenge the French disasters in Egypt, and far above all, the thought it was where our Saviour had shed his Divine blood, and redeemed us from our fallen state

---

[1] Michaud: Hist., v. 30. [2] Arab. Chron., 538.
[3] Michaud: Hist., v. 107.

—another crusade in favour of that sacred country was what occupied his mind and heart. Yet he fancied it was more effectual to take people by surprise, and feared that otherwise some strong impediment might spring up in his own family. So it was with mystery he summoned his parliament, nobody knew decidedly for what. But soon did his crusade become the talk through Europe. The eldest son of Henry III. of England took the cross against his father's will. Whether it was reverence for St. Louis, Prince Edward's example was quickly followed by several of the most illustrious English. So acted the Kings of Castile and Portugal; and Donna Sancha, Queen of Arragon, having become an Hospitalleress, and died in the Hospital of St. John, in Syria, contributed to make the ladies of Spain highly favourable to the recovery of the Holy Land.[1] On the 4th of July, 1270, Louis embarked, as before, at the small port not far from Marseilles. But nothing did this seventh crusade effect in favor of the Christians in the Holy Land, except that it caused a diversion to distant Tunis; nor were there any Hospitallers that we read of there. They had enough to do at Acre. Twice had St. Louis led expeditions against the sultan, and was successful in neither. In Egypt he had been defeated, mal-

[1] Michaud: Hist., v. 44.

treated, and made prisoner; in Western Africa was to die of the plague. The spirit of the holy wars had become quite defunct. Whether good or bad, this was the fact. The French barons seem to have been ready to go with St. Louis anywhere. Jerusalem was only an accessory; nor did they care for Palestine. So it was not till off Sardinia that they determined on Tunis—St. Louis alone being led away by the hope of converting that dey, which Anjou fomented from policy, to root out the pirates who annoyed Sicily; if he was not the first to put Tunis into St. Louis's head, and so was the bad adviser Joinville alludes to. The crusades, chiefly the last, led to forgetfulness of Jerusalem. They discouraged the Christians upon the whole.[1] As to Carthage, neither St. Louis nor his grandees ever heard or read anything about it.[2]

While the reverses were going on near Tunis, and St. Louis' death, and the return of that crusade, matters in Acre continued towards its calamitous destiny. There is an air of preparation in even these documents, as of people getting ready for removal, and unwilling to leave their affairs in disorder. So here is a solemn documentary restitution of forty-four papers which had been kept

[1] Michaud: Hist., v. 95.
[2] Id.: Id., 57.—Sismondi: Rep. Ital. iii. 332-5.

in the archives of the order in friendly deposit for safety, and were now restored to the lawful owner, in the presence of many great personages, among whom was the Grand Master of the Temple.[1]   1271

Prince Edward, whose declaration may have been a little exaggerated, though no doubt he was well aware that obedience in a crusade could never be considered an act of homage from England, arriving at Carthage a few days after the King of France's death, did not indeed raise the French, or any other army, to two hundred thousand men, as a chronicler pretends, with prodigious exaggeration;[2] yet not without satisfaction can an Englishman relate that ours was the only prince in Europe who, on that occasion, kept his promise, and refusing to sign the Tunis treaty, went to Acre with his corps of one thousand picked men; though so small a force could not do much. Yet is his name sacred as the last prince that ever went on a crusade.[3] After staying at Acre about a month, he went with his own, together with the Christian army of seven thousand, on an expedition up the country, and took Nazareth, and returning to Acre, was assailed

[1] Cod. Dipl. Geros., i., Num. clii.—Appendix, xcviii.
[2] Zumfleit.—Bib. Crois., i. 338.
[3] Michaud: Hist., v. 95.

by an assassin, as is generally told;[1] except, first, that it was no emissary sent by the Emir of Jaffa, then a Christian town, but by the Moslem governor of Ramlah,[2] who following Bibars' orders, feigned a wish to turn Christian[3] (as Ibn-feral expressly avows, and justifies the homicide on the score of the English prince having put some Mahometans to the sword during his recent campaign), whence the murderer had an opportunity. Secondly, that by either word or sign the assassin must have triumphantly avowed the blade was poisoned; for how, otherwise, should it be known instantly on the felon's drawing it, as the chroniclers say? And Edward, after the wound, caught one of his hands, and wrenched the dagger, and ran it quite through the villain's body with such amazing strength, that he hurt his own forehead; so that when the courtiers intervened, and shattered the slain's head, the first words of the prince, who had swooned, were to blame them for ill-treating a corpse—noble sentiment,[4] even supposing it to be blended with a spice of anger at their attempt to arrogate to themselves what he was conscious belonged to his royal self alone, the

[1] Hemingford.—Bib. Crois., ii. 660.—Not of the Old Man of the Mountain's people.
[2] Arab. Chron., 530.
[3] Ex. lib. Saracen.—Bib. Crois., i. 307.
[4] Knighton of Leicester: Chron.—Bib. Crois., ii. 758.

honour of saving his own life. Thirdly, that if the sucking of the poison from Edward's wound by his wife be a romantic invention of some Spanish poet, and that there be greater truth in attributing his cure to a Knight Templar's antidote from beyond Jordan, or, as is more likely, to the skill of an English surgeon—though it may be replied that our medical men then were of far less celebrity than the Arabians, Neapolitans, or even Jews—yet the whole of these stories cede in extravagance to what is affirmed by another authority, of whose credibility the reader himself may judge; my own responsibility being no more than as regards the substantial fidelity of my translation, merely adding that Grandison is an ancient English name, being that of a baron, in 1299 and 1300 [1]—also in these documents as witness to some ordinary transaction: " I, Abbot Joannes d'Ypre, have heard from certain Savoyards worthy of belief, that there lived in their country, a person called Grandison, who had borne to him a male child, of whom the astronomers called to his birth declared that if he lived, he would become great and victorious, and one of them drew by inspiration (perhaps) a little billet of lighted wood from the fire, saying that as long as the spark in that brand lasted, the child should live, and

[1] Sir Harris Nicolas: Synopsis, i. 274; ii. 777.

thrust the brand into the wall, and had it built up therein, that the spark might last the longer. And it came to pass that the boy lived and grew to extreme old age. At length, tired of living, he had the brand drawn from the wall, and thrown into the fire. As soon as the spark went out by the brand being consumed, Grandison died. This same Grandison had formed part of Prince Edward's suite. It was he who, learning that the English prince was poisoned, dared suck the wound, relying on his destiny attached to the spark in the walled-up brand. It was by his means the prince was cured. Ever since which time, the name of Grandison is celebrated in England, and his race greatly honoured by the English kings; and even to this day the Grandisons enjoy a distinguished rank in that realm."[1] The good abbot assures us he only recounts what was the common opinion of his time, and his MS. is of the earlier half of 1300. The attempt on Prince Edward is said to have been precisely on the 15th of the Kalends of July, in 1271.[2] Yet not the wound may have caused his instant return home, but the news of his father's death and himself proclaimed king.[3]

1271

[1] Chron. St. Bertin.—Bib. Crois., i. 420.
[2] Salisbury Chron.—Bib. Crois., ii. 652.
[3] Seb. Paoli : Osservazioni, ii. 523.—Michaud : Hist., v. 94.

Edward's chaplain at Acre, who had come with him thither (but others say he came with some Friezlanders, yet both may agree, if these had joined Edward's fleet), and though not even a bishop, but only an Archdeacon of Liege, was elected Pope while at Acre, and went back to Europe as Gregory X., enthusiastically attached to the Holy Land, and with the warmest promises conducting with him to Rome the two Grand Masters of the Temple and Hospital;[1] but little did they gain there, but returned with sorrowful countenances; nor did it avail Revel that, true to what his rule prescribed, he declined interfering in the disputes of Sicily and Cyprus. Anjou nevertheless seized all the property of the Hospitallers in his dominions, for not siding with him; grievous loss to them, since Messina was the chief priory for communication with Acre.[2]

1274

Both his bulls to the Hospitallers and Templars are honourable to them, and if that of 1274 speaks of discords between them, that could only refer to some of their subalterns; for as to the grand masters, they were under Gregory's own eyes, and had shared his ship in their long voyage, and he saw clearly they were like loving brothers; and in the bull particularly directed to the Hospitallers in

1275

[1] Vertot: iii. 534.   [2] Michaud: Hist., v. 95.

1275 it contains but praise. And in addition to this, when the grand masters followed him to the Council of Lyons, they were given seats above the Peers of France and cardinals or ambassadors, and next to those intended for crowned kings.[1] Yet wherever Bibars went, whether to Egypt or against Cyprus, he had one reigning idea to which all his others were subservient, the conquest of Acre; though to execute this, he was resolved to employ every means and not to be in a hurry, but insure success.[2] His fleet shipwrecking off Cyprus, he indignantly swore to exterminate every Christian state; but death prevented the execution of his threats, nor did his sons stably succeed him, but were soon dethroned in turns; and the Emir Kelaoun became Sultan. It was in 1278, in which year Sir Hugh de Revel died, and was succeeded by Sir Nicholas de Lorgne—which Vertot spells wrong. It is Lorgne and not Lorgue.[3] Of what country, uncertain. But that he was reigning in September, 1278, we have a document that proves it, and from the context he appears to have been grand master several weeks previously.[4]

1278

---

[1] Cod. Dipl. Geros. i., Num. xiv. 279; Num. xv. 280.
[2] Michaud : Hist., v. 105.
[3] Vertot : iii. 534.
[4] Cod. Dipl. Geros. i. Num. clv.—Appendix, lxxv.

And that in the same year the brave and noble Beaujeu had already become Grand Master of the Templars, is clear from an inscription found in an excavation at Acre.[1] The Codex Diplomaticus has nothing of Lorgne's earlier, nor of Revel within the last years; so it is close upon certainty that he expired in the August immediately preceding, at latest.

Of whatever land De Lorgne was native, his election at such a time proves him highly esteemed.

To Acre's catastrophe every event hurries, the good as well as the bad. Christians might have been thankful for the destruction of the Karismians and similar hordes.[2] Yet it accelerated or clinched the loss of Jerusalem and various inland places, and the ruin of the whole Christian cause; for Syrian Mahometans, often in alliance with Franks, and in a certain manner their friends, were then destroyed, and the Mahometans of Egypt and all other Mahometans were their foes. Kelaoun's bare name made the Christians shudder. And good right they had. Nor did he delay, but girded himself up at once to put an end to them, as natural allies of the Franks. His Cimerian origin much more than his attachment

[1] Appendix, c.
[2] Michaud: Hist., iv. 104; vi. 127.

to Mahometanism might be his spur; yet something of what had the air of stern fanaticism mingled with his ferocity—as a new convert. Nevertheless the Hospitallers engaged him to a truce for three years; and he let it stand, only as a tiger goes back to spring the better. The storm was gathering all round them, blacker and blacker; Bibars had taken much, and Kelaoun will more—all to prepare for the crowning glory of Acre. It shall be a growing calamity. As Sephet, shall be Margat. Yet both are but outworks of Acre. Not the dismal doings themselves, but only the sure preparations for them, was the Grand Master Revel to see, kind Heaven so far sparing him; and better it was for him to die of grief (universal voice) at the coming tempest over those Providence had confided to his care. To him the order is indebted for many chapters holden opportunely, and wise statutes and custumals in the primitive spirit, but all in vain; at least as regarding its present establishment. Nothing can save it. So he expired of distress at what he foretold. Nor did that require any miraculous gift, but only not to be perfectly blind.[1] Bibars had finished his work with regard to all but the towns on the coast. So Kelaoun flew to level them to the dust. The truce he minded just as far as it answered him;

[1] Vertot: iii. 535.

and circumscribed to Acre itself. Not its closest allies, nor even its own property, but only to that individual city did he concede a respite, for the express purpose of separating it little by little from every one of its resources in the country and isolating it, leaving it nothing to depend on, except fickle Europe—and even this but partly; for had he a better fleet, he would have blocked it completely, by sea as well as land, and preserved it from all contact as his own peculiar prey. That it remained vilely neutral, while every one of its friends were disappearing, may be blamed; but what on earth could it do? The Hospitallers reduced to a mere handful—a group of officers without troops, or very few. The Templars no better. Indeed, one chronicler makes them already all killed, but this is an exaggeration. The Teutonics necessarily of trivial account, since their grand master and head-quarters were in Germany, so that in the treaty with Acre not the Grand Master of the Teutonics, but his Maggiordomo signs it, with the Grand Masters of the Hospital and Temple.[1]

Acre submitted to the condition of informing the sultan at least two months beforehand, whenever any Franks were coming. Ample proof of

---
[1] Arab. Chron., 545.

how terribly he abused the weakness of the Christians; it was the price of truce.[1]

And Kelaoun thought it expedient to remove the interference of even distant Armenia, so crossed the Euphrates; and to escape a war, that Christian king underwent the insult of swearing an oath of Kelaoun's own concoction: "I swear by God, by God, by God; in the name of God, of God, of God; by the verity of the Messiah, of the Messiah, of the Messiah; by the verity of the four Evangelists, and of the twelve Apostles, and of the three hundred and eighteen Fathers of the first Council of Nice; by the verity of the most Holy Virgin and St. John the Baptist; by the verity of the Lent, and every Christian dogma; and by the verity of the Cross, by the verity of the Gospel, by the verity of the Father, the Son, and of the Holy Ghost; and if I leave any of my promises unperformed, I vow to make thirty times the pilgrimage to Jerusalem, naked feet and head."[2] Yet not satisfied with such oaths from any party in that land, he also kept ambassadors in the Courts of Europe, and paid spies there to instruct him of any movement of Franks, and into every commercial, or other treaty, with them was foisted an article as into that of Arragon, by which that king and his brothers obliged them-

---

[1] Arab. Chron., 546.　　[2] Id., 556, 557.

selves to refuse co-operating with any crusade proposed by "the Pope of Rome or Kings of the Franks, or Greeks, or Tartars."[1] These treaties, not only insulting, but calculated to deprive the unfortunate inhabitants of Acre of all hope,[2] and dictated by fear, or ambition, or avarice, contributed, every one of them, to raise an insuperable barrier between the Christians of the Levant and those of Europe. There was not a maritime town in Italy, or along the Mediterranean, that did not show a disposition to prefer advantages to its own particular commerce with the East, to deliverance of the Holy Land.

A small garrison at Marcab had resisted pirates, though Saracens; and not only beat them back, but nobly discomfited them in a battle not far from Acre. It was in defence of the best, nearly the only home left to the order, after Acre; yet let it not swell you, poor Lorgne; it is like the north-east wind, for even success shall produce your ruin. Kelaoun returning into Syria, attacks that stronghold of the Hospitallers which Saladin had respected; and it had been gaining ever since in strength, strongest and best-provisioned of fortresses, *castrum munitissimum*.[3] There was a truce; it was dated

[1] Arab. Chron., 565. [2] Michaud: Hist., v. 114.
[3] Seb. Paoli: Serie, i. 423.

for ten years ten months ten days and ten hours,[1] and we are now only in the third year.[2] But what of that? Kelaoun accused the Hospitallers of having broken it, and of having thence made inroads on Mahometan lands. "It was like a city acting sentinel upon a mountain. The tops of the towers, surpassing those of Palmyra in height, were accessible but to few of the most soaring fowls of Lebanon. From the sea-side, one might take it for the sun perceived in the depths of blue, or through a mist. The constellations smile upon it with smiles of complacency, dogs bark up at it, but can do no more; only vultures can fly to its ramparts, and the eagles of heaven."[3]

However, in spite of every difficulty, the machines were placed, and the attack began towards the early days of April. The miners undermined the ramparts and towers; and a breach in the wall allowed of storming it. Yet, after many assaults, nothing would have been effected, but for the Moccarabins, or archangels and celestial troops,[4] who on proper invocation, like at Kaucab, as in Saladin's time, came again to aid Islam. The Christians finding there was no possibility of defending it any longer, undermined in every direction as it was,

[1] Arab. Chron., 549. [2] Id., 548.
[3] Id., 551. [4] Id., 549.

capitulated; and the Prophet's standard was planted on the bastions, and the inhabitants were treated as usual; while the garrison cut its way out into Tripoli,[1] where any surviving Hospitallers had soon to leave their bones.

Some fourteen months later, Kelaoun attacked another place of strength, called Marakia, whose ruins are still observable near Tortosa.[2] It belonged to a noted Frank warrior, and was a tower separated from the land, and so surrounded by the sea, that without a fleet, it was utterly impregnable. Here there is a confusion in some writers, as if there was a change of sultans;[3] but Michaud proceeds regularly according to the real facts.[4] It was the same Kelaoun who thereupon wrote this letter to the Count of Tripoli: "It was you that built, or permitted this castle to be built; woe to you, and capital, and people, if it be not instantly demolished." The count was terrified; and when the letter was written, the Mamelukes were already within his territory. So he offered the owner of the castle considerable lands in exchange; but no offers, however flattering, or prayers, would do. The old Frank slew his own son[5] when he showed

---

[1] Michaud: Hist., v. 115.
[2] Id.: Id., 116.
[3] Vertot: iii. 539.
[4] Michaud: Hist., v. 110.
[5] Arab. Chron., 552.

symptoms of disaffection; on which the garrison mutinied, the castle was demolished, and the irritated warrior becoming the bitterest enemy of the Christians, joined the Mahometans, and remained their most devoted friend and servant, and fanatical persecutor of Christianity as long as he lived. Next comes Laodicea. Kelaoun's pitiless hatred lost no opportunity. Everything seemed favourable. But Laodicea's citadel stood too far out in the sea to get at it; but there ensued an earthquake, and the famous Tower of Pigeons is thrown down, and the lighthouse to direct ships in the hours of darkness. "So Kelaoun had his terrible machines advanced, whose tongues sing triumph, and whose signals are the hands of victory."[1]

Now for Tripoli; since its avenues are all opened, neither fidelity to treaties, nor the fourth Bohemond's recent submissions, nor anything shall retard the fall of opulent Tripoli. As to pretended conspiracies of Templars, why believe them? The residue of Templars had enough to occupy them without plottings. The papers are certainly a forgery; not of recent, but remote times.[2] Treason were quite a superfluity. The accusation against the Grand Master of the Templars falls of itself, he having been then in

[1] Michaud: Hist., v. 117.
[2] Confessio Guidonis, apud Michaud: Hist., v. 416.

Europe. Why should the Templars have interceded for a culprit? Their refusal testifies their ignorance of the plot, and that they had no participation in it whatever.

But such are trifles! What cares Kelaoun, whether Bohemond be guiltless or culpable, alive or dead, or as to his sister or mother? Seventeen huge machines battered the walls for thirty-five days, while fifteen hundred miners wrought underground, and showers of Greek fire flew in all directions. On the thirty-sixth day the Mahometans penetrated into the city, steel and flames brandishing and rolling with them. Butchered were first of all what remained of the Hospitallers, who, between siege and shambles, were lost, every one to a man; not only forty tried knights profest, but one hundred other individuals of the order, and arms and horses to a great amount.[1] And, after them, seven thousand other male Christians underwent butchery; their wives and children being carried off into slavery. A crowd of unfortunates sought an asylum in an islet: but he who visited it a few days after, found nothing but corpses. Some escaped on board ships that were afterwards driven on the coast, and all were murdered by the Saracens. Not only almost the entire population of Tripoli perished, but the

[1] Cod. Dipl. Geros., i. Num. ccxxv., 268.—Appendix, lxxvi.

sultan had the town itself burned down, and utterly razed. Yet, until then, it had flourished, with an excellent port of considerable traffic, and four thousand silk manufactories,[1] many rich palaces, walls so thick that three knights could ride on them abreast,[2] and towers, and various strong fortifications. Even as late as 1278, a document shows Bohemond's tranquillity, choosing arbiters in a small disagreement.[3] Such sources of prosperity in peaceful times, and security in time of war, all were broken, destroyed, consumed by fire, the hatchet, the sledge, every sort of violence. A new town was afterwards built near the spot, and took the name of Tripoli.[4] Rapine, and murder, and destruction, even entered into Saracen policy, to exterminate the Christians totally, and leave no trace of them or their power and riches all along the Syrian coast; so as nothing should remain to induce the princes and warriors of the West to send it succours, or be tempted to unfurl their banners in that land evermore. Thus, on the fourth of April, in 1289,[5] fell Tripoli, that had belonged to the Christians for one hundred and eighty years.[6] Yet one effect, quite

---

[1] Michaud: Hist., v. 119.   [2] Arab. Chron., 562.
[3] Cod. Dipl. Geros., i. Num. clv.—Appendix, lxxv.
[4] Michaud: Hist., v. 188.
[5] Arab. Chron., 561.—Appendix, lxxvi.
[6] Id.,   563.

opposite to the sultan's desire, ensued. These, his atrocities, and others still worse, that may pass nameless, not to disgust readers so near the outset, and frighten them away from these pages, which must lead you to sup with horrors before I have done with you, but it shall not last long—his inhuman enormities depriving those of Acre of every hope, mere castles in the air, mountains in the moon, were trainings for a desperate defence, which stands as a memorial to far future generations. More than any languid ruin, the fiery overwhelming at hand, was to warn, terrify, petrify, myriads of nations all alike interested to arrest the march of such ruthless, lawless, diabolical invaders.

On the fall of Tripoli, the sultan had menaced Acre with the same, if not instantly, yet in the next month of March.[1] But finally, since the other longer truce had been broken by the Christians themselves, he, out of his inexhaustible generosity and compassion, accorded them instead a new truce for two years two months two weeks two days and two hours, at the expiration of which time they might surely expect his avenging sword for any ill conduct; and at the same time, with most horrible sincerity, handed them a copy of Bibars' letter to the refugee when within Tripoli after

[1] Michaud: Hist., v. 123.

having lost his metropolis, Antioch. " Glorious Count, magnificent, elevated in honour, magnanimous with the courage of a lion, Bohemond, glory of the nations of Messiah, champion of the cross, leader of the people of Jesus, but to whom no higher title than count can now be given, since fallen from that of prince by surrender of the principality of Antioch; may the Lord aid this count to remember and understand fully what we are going to write to him. Let this count recollect our late expedition well; our ravage of his fields into their very hearts, the desolation we have spread over his provinces, our devastation of his tillage and sown lands, our ruin to the inhabitants; how we swept the churches clean from the face of the ground; how our wheels have passed over where mansions smiled until that inauspicious day; how we have raised out into the sea a peninsula of crowds of corpses massacred by us—all the men, but the children were carried off into captivity; how the free have been made slaves—the timber cut down, except what we left for our own machines of war when we return, please God, to besiege your present asylum; how we plundered your riches, and those of your subjects, including your womankind and their cubs, and the beasts of burden; how those of our soldiers who were unmarried, found themselves all of a sudden with wives and family; how our poorest, basest beggars became opulent, our menial servants rigid masters; our foot, horsemen. As to you, you see all that with the eye of a person struck with death-like palsy; or when you are able to speak or hear our voice, you cry, *How terrible it is!* You know also how we leave Tripoli, like such as intend to return; willing to allow you a respite, but hours numbered and determined! You know that when we left your country, there did not remain a single flock behind us, nor one young girl but had been subjected to our will and pleasure; nor a column but had fallen under our pickaxes; how we destroyed all your pleasant places; not a harvest but we reaped, not a thing in existence worth having, but we deprived you of it. No obstacle could stop us; nor wizard caverns nor precipitous mountains, nor visionary valley; but we took Antioch before any rumour of our advance had reached it; we got the city while you thought us still far away from you. If we at present depart, be assured of it we will return. We now are going to tell you of a matter that is quite and naturally over; to instruct you of a disaster that has swallowed up your whole happiness beyond all remedy. We set out from before Tripoli on the

24th of Shaban, and arrived under the walls of Antioch at the commencement of the great Ramadan. At our approach, the civic troops came out to fight us, but were completely routed, and the constable who commanded them made prisoner. He offered to treat with us in the name of his Giaours; so we permitted him his entering the city, and he brought us a squad of clergy and principal citizens. Conferences were opened; but as we soon observed they had a culpable object in view (exactly following your example), which could not but turn to their own ruin, and that differing as to the good, they agreed only as to proposing what was bad, we perceived nothing could be done with them, and that their destruction was decreed by God; and therefore sent off the deputies with these words: 'We are going to attack you; this is the last and only warning you are to expect from us.' So they retired, imitating your actions and conduct, expecting you to come and succour them with your horse and infantry. As to the marshal, who commanded in place of the constable, his affair was wholly done up in less than an hour; and we hammered terror into the inmost soul of the monks. Misfortune environed the castellan; death came to the besieged on all sides; we took Antioch by the sword on the fourth hour of the morning of Saturday, the 4th of the grand Ramadan. Of all to whom you confided the guard and defence of that city, not one of them but we slew, not one of them but possessed something worth taking. At present there is not one of ours but shows something taken from them. Ah, had you seen how cruelly your knights were trampled under our horses' feet—how your beautiful Antioch was given up to pillage, victim to the violence of a rude licentious soldiery, unhappy prey of every description of ruffians, felons, outlaws, who tossed about and divided your treasures by the hundredweight—and each bought any four of your chief ladies for a single gold piece, or at whatever viler price he liked—if you had seen the churches and crosses overturned, the leaves of the sacred Gospel dispersed, or most irreverently torn and thrown away, the sepulchres of your saints and their holy bones profanely trod upon—if you had seen your enemy, the Mussulman, marching up the altar, and breaking open the tabernacle, and monk, deacon, priest, patriarch in his pontifical robes, all butchered on its consecrated steps—ah! the patriarchate itself abolished for ever and ever — and those who had been men in power, in the power of others—had you seen your palaces given to the flames, and those devoured by fire in this world before their being so in the next—your castles and their dependencies annihilated, the Cathedral of St. Paul destroyed from the very foundations — had you seen such monstrous defilements! ah! had not this been your exclamation, *Would to God I had been dust? Would to God I had never received this paper, which brings me such sad tidings!* Your soul would be exhausted with sighing; your tears would be abundant enough to seem to extinguish what burns and devours you; but it would be only in seeming, for in reality it would be quite impossible. Had you but seen the place once so rich, and now fallen into such an extreme of misery, poverty the most squalid having there its lasting residence—if you had seen the port Seleucia and its shipping— how your vessels were at war with each other— alas! then you would have known that beyond question, the same God who had given you Antioch had now taken it from you; that the Master had wholly withdrawn his gift, and effaced it from the surface of the earth. You then certainly could not but have felt that the Divine grace was now assisting Islam to regain the edifices of which your ancestors had robbed them. We have chased all of you from these countries. We have dragged the Giaours by the hair of the head, and thrown them here and there; and many to a great distance. There is no other rebel but the Orontes, whose name is rebel;[1] and no doubt it would wish to change it, if it could; and flows through Antioch, not with limpid and pure tears, as in your time, but turbid and of a dirty red to-day, from the blood with which we stained its banks.

"This letter is to rejoice with you on the favour Heaven showers on you, and to wish you a prolongation of life. The life you now have, is due to your absence from the siege; for had you not absconded from your home, you assuredly were a corpse at present, or a prisoner riddled with wounds. Your delight ought to be very great indeed; for the sensation of existence is never so dear, as when we have escaped a grievous disaster. Who knows, but the Creator indulges you with this respite, to give you time to repair your past disobedience? As not a human being has been left to acquaint you with the dreadful fact, and congratulate with you on your deliverance, we take that duty on ourselves. So you now are acquainted with the whole, and can draw up your own account, and cannot accuse us of hiding the truth from you; besides we save you the trouble of applying to another. Farewell!"

Such was the letter of Bibars, of which Kelaoun now handed a copy to those of Acre. What an

[1] That is in the Arabic.

excellent and charming epistle, cries the Mahometan! How courteous! What delicate irony! Severe blame and cutting to be sure, but in the most agreeable, placid, elegant words![1]

Their immense expenses increasing in immensity every day, while all their feudal rent-roll in various parts of Syria had been for some time diminishing, and lately extinguished altogether, so that they were absolutely reduced to what they got from their estates in Europe, or European generosity, which at the best rendered them subject to the uncertainties of a long voyage; how were the Hospitallers to get on? It was a severe weight on poor De Lorgne's shoulders. They must have been strong, not to have broken down sooner. The vineyards on the hills, fine gardens, villas and verdure, and fruit in the vicinity of Acre, had been severely injured long before by Bibars; and the gates continually kept shut, all intercourse with land was over, and the population had to live wholly on what was imported. Their port closed, and they must have died of famine. By degrees all the succours this side of the sea had been removed, and of all the towns won by Godfrey de Bouillon or his successors, Acre alone remained

[1] Arab. Chron., 507, 511. And truly the original is held remarkable for its *elegance*.

in real independence. The weather made, from late in spring to early in autumn, the season of what were called *passages;* and navigation at any other season was considered very perilous and almost always ended badly. So Acre could only count on a provision of food twice a-year, which made large warehouses necessary; and a commensurate command of ready money. Lorgne considering all these matters, and highly alarmed at the sultan's threats, and that from the different nations mixed up at Acre, this, which should be its strength, was its weakness, and that without Messina and its ports in Puglia it must cease to exist, and Palestine be totally lost, set off on a mission to Europe; but could obtain nothing but good words, and from the Papacy a few soldiers of the worst description. He who then wore the tiara was Nicholas IV. "poor both in money and soldiers," says his biographer; "and the two thousand five hundred he sent, were at his own private expense, and did more harm to the Christians than to the Saracens." [1]—" I have been assured by some Florentine merchants then at Acre, that the breach of truce was the real cause of its ruin," says Villani.[2] So without either cash or army De Lorgne

---

[1] Platina: iii. 156.—According to others, 1500
[2] Villani: Hist. Fior.—Bib. Crois., ii. 621 and 637.

returned to Acre, where within a short time those unpaid Papal ruffians [1] first insulted and finally murdered some Mahometan merchants, and in a most disorderly sally infringed the truce. According to Ebendoffer the legate had Papal orders from Rome to break it; and the Leoben Chronicle says, that when he in his pontificals ascended the pulpit, as the people thought, to bless them, it was to pour anathema on them and all those who kept truce with the Paynim, and upon that, quitted the city.[2] And if that be in contrast with the character of the then Pope, that is no sufficient answer; for how much have Roman ministers, and all ministers done, and will do without their master's knowledge or even directly contrary to his well-known intentions! Which, it was easy to see, could not but bring down sure and speedy ruin upon the Christian cause. At which new displeasures, this afflicted grand master, too, died of that most honourable of deaths, a broken heart, like his predecessor; and also like him, we have no other certain date of Lorgne's death than that it must have ensued before his successor's election. And he was reigning on the 22nd of August in 1289;[3]

[1] Muratori: Annal., 1289.
[2] Coll. Pez.—Bib. Crois., iii. 196, 290.
[3] Cod. Dipl. Geros. i., Num. ccxxv.—Appendix, lxxvi.

namely, Sir John de Villiers of France. And Tripoli having been taken at the end of April, as the Arabians in that year affirm,[1] Lorgne must have gone to Europe and back, and have died between April and August, which leaves scanty room for error—at most a month.

The indication of disorder, the death of Lorgne, the installation of his successor, the murderous breach of the truce, and the sultan's indignant departure for Egypt with the threat to be back as he had first said in March and effectually punish them, being all parts of one whole, it is fair to conclude that they took up a short time; and it is distinctly noted that the three last (*viz.*, breach, sultan and threat) occurred under Villiers.[2] But if it broke two stout hearts to have even a dim foresight of the calamities in the next chapter, should I not shudder at approaching it?

---

[1] Arab. Chron., 561.　　[2] Bosio.—Vertot: iii. 542.

CHAPTER III.

WHAT had been a fine town, and strong, in Saladin's day, had now, in a century, become finer and stronger; far stronger than when it had resisted all the forces of Europe for three years. Its villas and gardens already had been somewhat wasted, but not completely. Its fortifications added to by nearly all the Franks of eminence who visited it; amongst whom, St. Louis. The commerce of the East and Europe, during a hundred years, gradually increasing its riches, the treasures of Asia and Europe for or from the shipping that thronged its harbour, everywhere life and industry, buyers and sellers, shops, artizans, warehouses; if seaward, its walls were so thick that two chariots could go abreast, its walls and ditches were all double or treble towards the land, and every one of its gates was flanked with towers; the towers along the ramparts being never at above a stone's throw distance from each other. Within it, its squares were all spacious and airy; coloured glass in nearly all its houses was what most distinguished it from the whole globe.[1] If no people in all Syria were so effeminate as of Acre, luxurious habits and laxity of morals are they not the almost inevitable evil consequences of great wealth? Streets and houses almost all rebuilt, with a wideness and magnificence till then unrivalled in other countries—otherwise its original features kept to in this, that all the buildings were of white marble or cut stone, all equal in height, with flat roofs and terraces, by which you could walk, or even ride, from one end of the city to the other, without descending, but bridging the streets; the principal of which had silk awnings, transparent enough for light, but of soft tints, and keeping off the sun. If glass was no longer singular in Europe,[2] yet here it was in far greater abundance, and in almost every window, great or small, poor or rich. Even the ancients had glass, says a very respectable authority; for though it be true that they kept the doors open much more than we do, yet in Pompeia and Hercu-

[1] Corneri Chron.—Bib. Crois., iii. 135.
[2] Michaud : Hist., v. 120.

laneum, we find that patricians had as fine panes in their windows as the best Bohemian crystal. What M. Taylor affirms in his letter to Chateaubriand, this latter doubles its weight by making it his own. To prevent surprise at Acre's having glass windows fully equal to our own, we must only be contented to consider that city as the great mart for all the commerce of the world in the thirteenth century, and the aggregation of everything that was then splendid in existence, and not as the miserable Arab village before us. It is on the same fifty times sacked and devastated spot, that is all. But the grand commercial Acre in question was razed (and the very ground scraped clean, for having been profaned by the feet of Giaours) six centuries and a half ago; and if Venice became remarkable for large plate-glass, it is likely enough she learned the art from Acre.[1] But stained, or painted glass, with us still somewhat of a singularity and reserved once to a few European cathedrals, was then much used in Acre, and also *pointed* arches, to credit antiquarian tradition, and some recent artists. Not only merchants, and habitual residents of high, or royal rank, there was a continual influx of strangers of all classes, but chiefly the most elevated, from every

[1] Chateaubriand: Itin. de Paris à Jerusalem, ii. 418.

country under heaven, and shows of some sort or other every day in the twelvemonth.—Not to speak of processions more or less religious, there were jousts, tourneys, tournaments, balls, masquerades, assemblies, concerts, parades, and other military displays, horse and foot, from all the services in Christendom, and several of the Pagan or Mahometan too—a perpetual fair and merry-making. Crowds of municipalities; if disorder, they also indicated liberty, independence, patriotism; and that with laudable pride, those of Acre never forgot their distant homes; nor be the same not said, as to the rivalry between Genoese and Venetians, and what was general to all Italians, the separation into Guelphs and Ghibellines; and it was the period of the Republics of the middle ages in Italy.[1] Resort of diplomatists from every nation in the world—if some of these soon disappeared on the darkening of events, as the Papal Legate, yet the greater part of them remained at their post to the last; and amongst these are especially noted the ambassadors of France and England, one of whom certainly, and probably both, were afterwards killed on the ramparts, gallantly heading their compatriots at the bloodiest moment of the siege. And each one had his own law and tribunal, and national flags were

[1] Michaud: Hist., v. 122.

always hoisted, which must have made a very gay sight—commensurate with the variety of splendid dresses and uniforms, and modest, or even wanton females (many of them, no doubt, very beautiful), adorned in the pink of innumerable fashions, mutable or immutable.—Acre was assuredly during no short period the most agreeable hubbub in the whole world.[1] Must all that vanish, and be as if it never had been? Worse! Woe! woe! woe!

Villiers' first act is said to have been a circular to all the knights of the order in Europe, to hurry to join him at Acre, of which this given in the Appendix may have been a kind of specimen, though of the circular itself no copy remains; this we have only presupposing it, and being rather a particular letter to some confidential lieutenant or other high dignitary.[2] It is to be supposed the delivering him from any contention about dues to the Church, would have given a sort of satisfaction to the grand master at any other time; but he was too occupied then; particularly that bull of Nicholas IV., given in the Appendix, chiefly for 1290 the date: but also because the *quiet* and *prosperous state* spoken of in it was in curious contradiction to the sad fact.[3] A few

---

[1] Michaud: Hist., v. 121. [2] Appendix, lxxvi.
[3] Cod. Dipl. Geros., i., Bolla xvi., 280.--Appendix, lxxvii.

weeks after the breach of truce, and the murder of some Mahometans, as has been related, a meeting of citizens was held at Acre, where, after some fierce and vain debates, the majority resolved to send an embassy to Egypt with presents to excuse the city, and impute the blame to the real criminals, the strange recruits.[1] And on the deputation's design being known, yet previous to regular audience, a privy counsel at Cairo took lamentable cognisance of the business; "it having been decided already that we should take advantage of the least pretext to arm, and finish the ruin of the Christian colonies, (though our emirs began to desire repose, and to wish enjoying the riches acquired in their numerous victories), the treaty was extended on a table before us, to look out for anything to authorize what we desired;[2] and, after ripe reflection, Fakr-eddin divided with those who found no just reason for recommencing hostilities. "As for me," said Moha-eddin, "I had not spoken one word up to that moment, when turning round towards me, he asked my opinion. I replied, 'Mine? I am always of the sultan's. If he wish to annul the treaty, I declare it null; if to maintain it, valid!'—'It is not of that I speak,' retorted Fakr-eddin; 'we know the sultan is for war.' I

---

[1] Michaud: Hist., v. 125.   [2] Arab. Chron., 568.

repeated, 'I am of the sultan's opinion,' and I cited an article of the treaty, which said, 'If Christians from the West come with evil designs against the Mahometans, the magistrates of Acre are to repress them.' I added that 'in the present case the magistrates ought to have prevented the murder, or at least have punished it; which, if they were without the power of doing, they ought to have denounced it themselves to us, that we might try to remedy it.' At these words the sultan rubbed his hands, unable to contain his joy, and forthwith he began his preparations." [1]

Yet it was no fault of the government of Acre; but most of the scum sent by his Holiness as soldiers, were adventurers, ready for every crime, as our own chroniclers avow; yet if the Saracen had the appearance, he had not the substance of right, and the city was an innocent victim. The ruffianly injurers took to their galleys and absconded, and left the injured inhabitants to be cut to pieces. So it was then; and so shall often be.

Nor had Kelaoun's spies not informed him of the great war breaking out between France and our King Edward, nor of the Pontiff's pusillanimity; and that, though it was reported the French mo-

---

[1] Makrisi: Vie de Kelaoun.

narch was sending a hundred and fifty thousand crusaders under his son, it had no foundation, and was but a bomb—open the casement, and let it fly out. At all events, they would arrive a great deal too late to save Acre; so that the security, as to any intervention from Christendom, combined with the resolution of his privy council to harden his severity, when summoning the Christian deputies, though his paleness indicated a dying man (and he was indeed to die of that decay within a few weeks), yet those exhilarating news, and the heat of the recent debate in council, gave a feverish colour to his cheeks, and more force to his voice than could be expected from so emaciated a frame. Nevertheless, he heard the deputation out, and their protestations, excuses, and desire of a renewal of truce. " No such thing," replied he, " most treacherous Christians. Your words are as oily sweet as your alliance with us is false. What poisonous bitterness you hide under such honey! You mean venom, and not having the courage to say it, disguise it beneath a coat of the varnish of whining adulation. Your wicked humours begin to inflame, and you require a copious blooding, and by the blessing of Allah, you shall have it; our good swords shall be your leeches. There are poisons that taste delicious; but he who allows himself to be deceived into drinking of them, his heart is infected, and he is killed. Alas! your fawning caresses, like those of a wheedling courtesan, have too often taken us unawares, and seduced us into letting our vigilance wax drowsy, and neglect the care of our own security; but, invoking our holy law, our conduct shall be otherwise for the future! What a rage of lying has come upon you, O Giaours! What canine madness deprives you of reason, that you shamefully renounce the good faith of your ancestors? When, with an outside of simplicity, and in the gentlest terms, you gave us your solemn promise, by your trust in that Christ who you say is omnipotent, we believed you; and to the same constant peace which you swore, we also engaged ourselves by the trust we have in our invincible Mahomet; but when we see our people cheated by your falsity, and that, abandoning the truth which you affirm is in Christ, and is the foundation of your religion, you endanger our own dignity and the safety of our empire, what is to be done except not dispense ourselves from duties assumed of our own accord, but promptly take vengeance, and punish your enormous crime? Fully are we persuaded, that if Christ has the power of aiding you, through the faith you have in him, you have not any longer to count on his assistance when you refuse him your faith, and prove that you have none; but profound is our conviction that by a just judgment of God we shall be permitted to overthrow you. Stand then must our determination, that while you retain and protect traitors who compromise your safety and ours, we must not endure your seductions and lies; so at the appointed hour we shall visit your perverse city, take it by storm, and with the strong hand crumble every resistance, and you shall all perish by the edge of the scimitar. Farewell; only in regard of your ambassadorial functions, we permit and command your being allowed to return safe and sound to those who sent you."[1]

Full of sorrow, the deputies re-entered Acre, and the dolorous recital of their mission took place before a meeting, which included the Patriarch of Jerusalem, the French ambassador, Count de Gresli, and the English Sir Otho de Grandison, and the principal citizens. Nor can it be seen why Michaud adds the grand masters (the Teutonic was in Germany), whereas his authority mentions none of them;[2] and it is not discordant with sovereign right to give audience in their own house alone; as we shall see the Hospitallers do the very last day of their reign in Acre. Wherefore it is pro-

[1] Arab. Chron., 569.—Michaud. Hist., v. 125.
[2] Michaud: Hist., v. 424.

bable the city had authority from the grand master, and sent its deputation without referring to any military orders, and received the answer and reported it to their common sovereign; for, however loose the reins of government, he had them from Cœur de Lion.

On hearing the sultan's reply (though astonished at the novelty, and possibly terrified at his late cruelties at Tripoli) they all agreed it was their express duty as Christians and men to stand by each other, and not easily yield this city to the infidel, this only remaining road from Europe to dear revered Jerusalem; but that besides love of the Christian faith, they, who had been always accustomed to fight for their liberty, ought never, never submit to even the least idea of perpetual slavery; that so it was necessary to prepare for an honourable defence, even should they have to die by the barbarian sword; that any other conduct would be an eternal blot on their name; still that they ought to inform the princes of Christendom, and most of all the chief of it— the Pope; and no doubt valid succours would be sent them. And that they should exhort their immediate leaders to solicit universal piety and pity by an instant embassy to the West, since there was full time of which they had only wisely to profit; it being more than six months from this to next spring; and certainly the Mahometans would, in *this*, keep strictly to their word.

The excellent old Patriarch, at passing the resolution, rose, and casting his eyes towards heaven, his long gray hair flowed back, and crossing his hands on his breast, he rendered thanks to God with sighs: " Blessed be the Holy Trinity that the inhabitants of Acre are of one mind, and on a subject of such importance, have had their spirit enlightened, and their heart. Persevere in this noble determination, O men of Acre! Faith and liberty! This be your banner; and with them you will obtain the Lord's aid!" [1]

Villiers let not the opportunity slip of testifying his alacrity by sailing that day itself on the desired embassy. Why must I say all his efforts were ineffectual? Though he may have set out on his mission in August, he could scarcely have reached Rome until the middle of October, so, after Nicholas had written.[2] But even Rome, like the rest of Europe, was too much taken up with its own intestine squabbles, to have men or money for Palestine. And when he re-entered Acre on the first days of January he knew full well, (and, though he did not reveal it to every one, lest it might have dispirited them, yet several of the leaders knew) that theirs

1291

---

[1] Michaud: Hist., v. 126. [2] Appendix, lxxvii.

VOL. II. P

must be the very nearly hopeless struggle of a small minority against illimitable numbers. No! The moon is not entirely made of green cheese! Nor lay stress on idle will-o-the-wisps, that cannot but mislead. Hopes in Europe are no better. Calculate but on your own resources. And what are they? Alas!

There were the Templars, but of them little remaineth but glory, though their grand master and his twelve score of knights are worthy of their splendid name. The Teutonics, if you go look for them in the fine German battles; but here are only fifteen under a lieutenant. Other orders, too, there were, but altogether of slender amount. The Hospitallers—and every one of them is to be counted on —all heroes; each may be considered fifty according to the Mahometan superstition, that some Christians have many souls in them; and certainly the vulgar Saracens believed to have seen the same Christian killed several times, and beheld many living men proceed from within one Christian corpse.[1] If authority would do, there are a cloud of authorities, Christian too, to verify a fact that none can credit;[2] but even so, what of success can

---

[1] Frustra contra Christianos pugnamus, quia uno mortuo alius statim ex ore ejus nascitur, et ab hoc numerus nullatenus minuitur. Leoben Chron.—Bib. Crois., iii. 197.

[2] Appendix, ci.

be based on the Hospitallers? We have seen forty of them slain at Tripoli, and that it was held by the Grand Master to have almost extinguished his order in Asia. We do not know of any coming from Europe. But, supposing that some did come, with that self-devotion for which they are celebrated. Let them equal those they were to replace; and Acre, itself, gives sixty; yet, in all, we have only one hundred and forty, and that is the very most. Vertot tells us in one line,[1] that between Hospitallers and Templars, there were killed, at Acre, four hundred of them; and, in the next,[2] that the Templars lost three hundred there, and only ten of them escaped alive, which leaves the Hospitallers less than one hundred to be killed; and killed they were, almost all. But Vertot was not, perhaps, scrupulously exact, and did not mean to include their leaders, neither Villiers, who survived, nor Clermont or Beaujeu, who were slain. They had hired troops, but with little money they could have few, and their feudal, which used to be their chief forces, lay wholly extinguished. Knights may serve as officers, leaders, examples. But, after all, the main defence of Acre depends on its inhabitants, to whom are to be added five hundred Cypriots, brought by the king of that island, some few

[1] Vertot: iv. 72.   [2] Id.: iv. 72.

French under Count Gresli, and individuals from Picardy, with one hundred and fifty English under Grandison, as well as a sprinkling of warriors from various places, but not exceeding two score; in fine, the entire came to nine hundred horse, and eleven thousand foot,[1] or, in all, twelve thousand.[2] If a population, which, after the going away of many, amounted still to one hundred thousand, produced only twelve thousand soldiers, that was noted at the time, and shows Acre was far more mercantile than military.

Time advances rapidly.[3] Hard to reconcile divers accounts; one says the assault lasted forty days and forty nights, without a moment's intermission.[4] In this they agree, that it was one of the most fearful which history records.

Exact in his dealings, Kelaoun, at the beginning of March, finding his feebleness would not permit him to proceed, returned to Cairo himself, but sent on his seven or twelve emirs, with each of them four thousand horse and twenty thousand foot. So even now there were twenty-nine to one, in cavalry, against the Christians, and eight to one in infantry, or more.[5] Yet these were only an

---

[1] Michaud: Hist., v. 126.   [2] Bosio.—Vertot: iii. 546.
[3] Cod. Dipl. Geros., ii., Num. i., pag. 1.
[4] Ebendorfer: Col. Pez.—Bib. Crois., iii. 201.
[5] Milan Chron.—Bib. Crois., ii. 638.

earnest of what was coming, and to make due preparations, in a vast horse-shoe line, from the sea, at the foot of Mount Carmel, to that on the shore, towards where Tyre lately stood, curving east along the crests of Thabor and Lebanon; that from one extremity to the other, round by the curve line, was a day's journey.[1]

The real siege was to be on the arrival of the sultan in person.[2] Sappers and miners might have begun their burrowing, but little more, and engineers and hatchets begun to hew down the cedars of Lebanon, or in the mountains about Galilee, and the oaks of Naplouse,[3] and erect their battering machines; while men and horses refreshed after their march from the Nile, and their cuirasses got burnished, and their arms, that they should glitter well when his Highness arrived, and their chargers be fat and sleek, and restored to all their fierceness and mettle by proper repose and good grooming, food and exercise. So that the multitude of noises and human cries, and the neighing of horses, resounded the whole day through that vast enclosure; and by night the tents in the moonlight, and the challenges of sentinels, inspired a beholder or

---

[1] Ebendorfer.—Bib. Crois., iii. 200.
[2] Michaud: Hist., v. 127.   [3] Michaud: Hist., v. 128.

hearer, with, it is difficult to say, what deep melancholy.

In the interim, Kelaoun was expiring; yet before it, had an interview with his son Chalil, and in presence of many of his emirs, charged him to promise he would not celebrate his father's funeral rites until after he had taken Acre, and put its inhabitants to the sword; and Chalil swore solemnly to execute the paternal commands. He thereupon urged his emirs to serve his son as faithfully as they had him, and then breathed his last, with devout peace of mind, as they said.[1]

As soon as he was a corpse, the ulemas and imams placed him in the middle of a lighted chapel, and kept reciting prayers over his remains, reading verses from the Koran the whole night, to invoke their Prophet against the Giaours; and it may be understood that the same mode was to continue until when the regular funeral should ensue after Chalil's return from Acre, for the which he instantly set out with his entire army according to his oath.[2] Tremendous were the battering engines now ready, the several pieces of one of which were hardly contained in a hundred waggons. And, had cannons been among them, it would not have astonished

[1] Bosio.—Vertot: iii. 545.—Arab. Chron., 569.
[2] Michaud: Hist., v. 127.

me; but I am a little so, that there were not, or at least they are not mentioned, for the Mahometans had them before that time—not indeed muskets or light artillery, but heavy guns for sieges—and used them at Algesiras and other places in Spain.[1] However, these exterior batteries, though so huge, and three hundred in number, were only secondary, and rather to cover the attacks of the soldiery than to breach the defences; for which they relied on what was more deadly sure, though somewhat slower and far less noisy. And by degrees their sappers and miners had driven the Christian from all his outworks and fairly demolished them. And now, murderous moles, they had passed under the ditch and undermined a great portion of the main wall itself, and that mine had only to be sprung by firing the wood that sustained it; operation awaiting the moment the sultan should arrive to order it.

It was on the 4th of April,[2] that the new sultan arrived at Acre, and that the siege really began; though several divisions had been already there above a month; so that those who during it had been accustomed to see masses of soldiery, when they looked

---

[1] In 1249, and even earlier. Hallam: Middle Ages, i. 254.
—The Arabs had gunpowder, and fired it from cannons first of wood, next of metal, in 1230, Mines de l'Orient, Num. i. 248.

[2] Arab. Chron., 570.

from its ramparts a little after sunrise, saw no one; and, at the sudden disappearance, flattered themselves the Saracens had retreated. But not so, they had only gone to meet their sovereign, and returned with him in most magnificent triumph that same afternoon.[1]

At a really fine sight even the humblest-minded becomes poetical, and the chronicler tells us: " Now it was, that splendour was to be seen, and the earth trembled to its centre at the aspect (*rewart*, old Fr.) of such mighty forces moving as far as the eye could reach in every direction. From Arabia had come, and the Nile, Euphrates, Tigris, the different divisions composing that brilliant army and that strange variety of music. And as they passed, the sun was reflected by their golden targets, and the hills glittered to within their cores. The polished steel of their lance-points resembled the shining of heaven's stars on a serene night. And on the host's advancing, it was like a forest for the multitude of lances all held upwards; and well might it be, for they were four hundred thousand fighting men that covered the entire plain and mountains."[2]

Why talk of the coursers of Khorassan or Tur-

---

[1] Michaud: Hist., v. 128.
[2] MS. apud Michaud, Hist., v. 425.—It is said to be by a French knight there present.

comania? If surefooted and hardy, slippery is the flagging and intricate the stone work they'll have to scramble up, or down; and on broken walls and the smoking fragments of fallen towers, is where they must charge. Ah, little the Frank battalions, gazing from the ramparts, are aware that sudden death is beneath their feet, where all seems sleeping in its strength! Though discordant and sufficiently rude, yet the music when softened, as now by some distance, was martial; and the sultan riding surrounded by so splendid a staff, and the sacred banner on his right, showed extremely grand.

And when two hours before sunset, he looked upon the innumerable force occupying nearly thirty miles, from the sea on one wing to the sea on the other, and then on the small town facing him, he almost regretted so much pains as superfluous. "A pity we have not our Alma girls here," said the sultan. "For our mercenary hussies to storm it would be laughable, I protest, and more applicable to the case than breaches and Mamelukes! But some one of our black-eyed wenches might perhaps be killed, and inasmuch, as they are Mahometans, it would be a shame to risk the ugliest of them. Still, since the worthless Giaours refused their weasands to my father, I owe his shade satisfaction; so let us stun them to death!"

Whereupon out came four hundred camels with two drummers upon each, and being led down into the plain, raised a monstrous peal. " I would order them to continue all night," cried the sultan, " but that it might prevent our sleeping, and dare say the uncircumcised have already enough; and, on reflection, will surrender at discretion, to sue for which we shall find a deputation of their curs waiting at our tent door by daybreak! Depend upon it!"[1]

Yet not thus; but dawn beheld the Christian files as before. So to the miners: " By the sultan's orders, fire the mine!" And towards sunrise there was a hideous crash, and behold a large breach, practicable, if not for others, for Delhis. But when these rushed forward, they were suddenly stopped by a wide deep ditch, till then invisible for a curve in the ground. And they had to be recalled from its edge, where they left a ridge of about five thousand corpses, and many others scattered all over the plain. Then in anger the sultan ordered a general charge of the cavalry, and truly it was a gallant sight. But the same ditch arresting them at every point, they had to retire, after suffering severely from the shots of numerous zemboureks,

[1] Michaud says three hundred camels; but what difference? Hist., v. 130.

and other missiles, from behind the parapet, while they could not themselves return a single blow. And so it was during five successive days of a vast number of charges; the two first days of cavalry, and the three last of cavalry and infantry by turns, or united;[1] till the sultan lashed himself into a rage, and the whole plain a Golgotha. At last the senior emirs convinced him he must give up his idea of taking it by a *coup de main*, and have the ditch filled; for which it was necessary to drain it first, and collect the stones from the neighbouring acclivities. So the sappers and excellent engineers soon succeeded in discharging the water. It was now May.[2] And the stones had been brought in heaps near the ditch, and fascines, and carrions, and other materials, enormous quantity to the eye, yet not enough, according to the measurement of the engineers, who intended two days longer of such labour; but the impatient sultan forbade all further waiting, and the heaps were flung into the ditch, not without considerable loss from the zemboureks anew; yet, as foreseen, the ditch wanted a full yard of being full; at which the sultan, quite out of his senses, called—and here what is related so surpasses credibility, pure truth as it is, and

[1] MS.—Michaud: Hist., v. 131.
[2] Arab. Chron., 570.

must be, since from both Christians and Mahometans, that I should abstain from noticing it, were it not that it would be too dastardly in a writer to conceal what such authorities recount— Chalil, in the midst of his Mamelukes and Delhis, called upon the Chages (new sect of Moslem fanatics), and with most impetuous gesticulations thus: "You who entitle yourselves the devoted of Islam, I call upon you to testify it by at once flinging yourselves into the ditch, that my Mamelukes may ride over you!" Nor did the Chages hesitate, but instantly ran and flung themselves into the ditch, and the whole body of cavalry charged over that pontoon of living human flesh.[1] Furiously mad as the fanatics must have been, some similar madness seems to have been infused by them into the Mamelukes and their horses, since they rushed up the breach, though in doing so most of them were necessarily killed. But their riders were incited by the hope of sabring or lancing the Christians; and some few of them they may have butchered; yet it could be but a few, for they soon met again an insurmountable obstacle, even thicker

---

[1] Michaud: Hist., v. 132.—Ebendorfer 3. De Perditione Accharon Civitatis.—Muratori.—Arsenius, who declared he was an eye-witness of what he relates.—Bib. Crois., iii. 201.—Hist., Gen. Concilii Lyons.

than the old wall, a new one built during those short days, with admirable dexterity and steadiness, faced with oak beams, all hung with bales of woollen or cotton, as continued to be much used by those of Acre during the whole siege at the several breaches;[1] when out burst—but an actor in the scene shall speak for himself, who survived his wounds to write, long years after, what he then saw and participated:[2] "I had been allowed to join the Hospitallers; and, all horse, we had their Marshal Claremont, at our head. At the onset, in such a desperate precipitous spot, and against most able swordsmen, many of us were slain; but that was over in a twinkling, and what I can scarce myself believe, now that I am an old monk writing alone by this feeble lamp, is, that headlong down that breach, and over the bodies in the ditch at full gallop, I followed Claremont, who, like a wolf after a flock of sheep, flew, pursuing what remained of the Mamelukes across the entire plain, and to the very foot of the hills, cutting to shivers every creature on his way.[3] My hand trembles, and my heart bounds, and my pale, withered cheeks glow at thinking of the exaltation of that moment. But

[1] Villani.—Bib. Crois., ii. 621.
[2] Michaud: Hist., v. 133.—Relation MS.—MS. Accon.
[3] Michaud: Hist. v. 134.

we had to return; and return we did and slowly, in by that same glorious aperture. . . . . .

"From that day out, though I had not the honour to be of the Hospitallers, or even knight, I continued in their corps till I was utterly disabled.[1]

"But the losses of the Saracens were quickly remedied; those of the Christians were irreparable. After a short respite, also that second wall (according to one authority there were double walls and profound ditches, and to another, three walls and ditches, and the walls so thick that two chariots could pass each other[2])was undermined, and then we had to maintain our post by dint of hard fighting. We always killed many more of our foe than we lost of ours. Still we were at last reduced to a few. What was worse, King Hugh and his Cypriots abandoned us; it was nightfall, and he said some repose was requisite for his men, who had neither slept nor eaten for three days. I thought I might say more; and my companions, and the marshal, for I do not know how many, but a great many; but his majesty never came back, which did not surprise me, for my right-hand man in the file (a Frank like myself) and my mother were of the same vil-

---

[1] MS. Accon.
[2] Eccard: 2, Hermann.—Bib. Crois., iii. 135.—Ebendorfer, 3, Pez.—Bib. Crois., iii. 200.

lage in Normandy, he and I had become great, and I held his horse while he retired during some minutes, and on his return, pointing to a corpse that I had just seen fall, 'overheard (he said) his discourse with King Hugh, who bade him not go on, but join him, for that the Saracens were hastening in at the breach, irresistibly.' To which that black cassock replied, 'If you were going east, I'd accompany you to death; but since your face is turned west, I'll not,[1] but hasten to die with the defenders of our religion and liberties, and leave you the anathema of a martyred priest.' Nevertheless in our cruelly abandoned situation, by the exertion of the Teutonics, who came to our assistance, and Templars, we contrived to keep the post the whole night, and great part of the next day, under reiterated, or rather, never-ceasing charges, and after losing half of our small body, it was only in the afternoon that we were driven from it, but rallied in a street that began with two strong towers, and a massive chain from one to the other,[2] which we drew, and manning the towers, there was a most desperate struggle which,

[1] Which resembles what the French relate more diffusely of another. Mathew Villani.—Bib. Crois., ii. 625.
[2] Corneri Chron. Eccard.—Bib. Crois., iii. 135. The main thoroughfare in Acre, leading to St. Anthony's Gate.

with the aid of a parcel of stout citizens, was upheld for two entire days, until at length Heaven sent us victory, and we drove the infidels back through the breach; and on the right of it, lo! my poor friend, who was mighty vigorous sprang from his horse, and seizing three of the enemy, one by one in his arms, threw them clear over the rampart down into the ditch; but the third struggled so, that just as his heels disappeared in the fall, he undid Tom's helmet, whose throat was instantly pierced through and through by the shot from a zembourek; whereupon I also dismounted, but in vain, for the faithful Christian was quite dead. And I too had my share, for while in the act of rising from my knees over his corpse, I was struck on the breast-bone by something very small, so suppose it a zembourek's bullet, which must have killed me but for my cuirass, which however it broke to pieces, and glanced off. As it was, I was dreadfully wounded, nor to this day can I make the least exertion without a spitting of blood, not even ascend a horse; and Marshal Claremont, seeing me drop, got down, and with his own hands examined my wound, and pronounced it severe and dangerous, but not mortal, and added, " Were you not thus, I should tell you to become an Hospitaller, but never attempt it; for you are an invalid for life, and will require to be always very careful. I am at present your superior, and command you, by holy obedience, to swear to use every precaution not to be killed in Acre; but (as I know you use the pen) to write the truth of what you have seen; and is not this defence for faith and liberty? Both as Norman and as Christian, I wish to be useful, not only during this brief interval, but hereafter by example. So believe it no blameable vanity to tell you to transmit to distant ages how Claremont fought and died, and likewise assure our grand master that we have all done our duty. I think I shall never see you again. That way no more. I have too much to do. You, remember your oath.' "

But he said all that far more succinctly. At such moments mind and lips are quicker, both of who hears, and who speaks. Their words are winged, and their full meaning absorbed with rapidity, and deeply graven. But such was the substance of our irrevocable contract; nor I intend, but to be able to say I kept it, meeting in futurity. That success changed affairs,[1] and something similar a few hours later at St. Anthony's Gate, where the Grand Master of the Templars (who truly had been elected commander-in-

[1] Michaud: Hist., v. 134.

chief, for his celebrity as a warrior[1]) spoke thus to the Grand Master of the Hospitallers, " Unless we make a diversion, the town is lost. Let us hazard a *sortie*." And as large a body as could be gathered was formed that evening, but not above five hundred, and bravely they attacked the infidel's flank, and would have taken his camp by surprise, had his sentinels been less alert;[2] but in spite of the discomfiture, the immense disproportion of numbers told, and many of the Hospitallers and most of the Templars were slain, and though re-entering Acre as victors, those were carrying their grand master, badly wounded, and these had too much reason to fear that theirs had been struck by a poisoned arrow;[3] which somewhat uncertain as yet, he rode, but very pale. This was on a moonlight night, and the bravest began to be oppressed with a presentiment of destruction, quite imminent, yet not less determined to sell their lives dearly. And, before dawn,[4] the Grand Master of the Hospitallers convoked not only his order, but a meeting of Templars and Teutonics, as well, and of the surviving leaders of the city, including the sick commander-in-chief himself, and the magnanimous

---

[1] Bosio.—Vertot: iii. 547.   [2] Bosio.—Vertot: iii. 550.
[3] Michaud: Hist., v. 140.—Seb. Paoli: Osservazioni, i. 536.
[4] Michaud: Hist., v. 135.

Patriarch, as also the two ambassadors Gresli and Grandison. Nor is it wondrous that every one of them was pale in the first light of morning, since most were wounded, and all of them felt doomed; and that not only themselves, but every human creature in that city had but a few hours to live. Nor was there much to say; nor time for it. But the short debate was wound up worthily by the chief of their common creed, him of the long milky locks, and sweet, wan, unrugged face, their own dear, calm Patriarch: nor spoke of love of country, for he knew they were of all countries; nor reproved any creature, for all reproof should be extinct; nor praised, for fear of jealousies; nor flattered them with earthly hope, for he knew no one could reasonably have any; and this very moment a paper had been laid before them that their eighteen thousand, soon twelve thousand, dwindled into nine thousand two days ago, had now been reduced to seven thousand—too small a number even to man the ramparts, although none of those heroic bands could be accused of want of exertion certainly; since but yesterday they had left several thousands of Saracen corpses, and two thousand of their own between towers and breach, as counted by those who were charged with putting them into graves, lest a plague should ensue. And in the dead body of one single Christian knight, the iron heads of forty lances were found. Nor is this strange fact to be doubted, since it is an Arabian, not merely impartial, but unwilling witness, that writes it.[1] "Those twenty thousand are as nothing to the Saracens. But your two thousand, who replaces them? Then what remains, O my dear children, but to die valiantly, and confiding in the Creator, with arms in your hand. Calculate that one Christian is equal to five or six infidels; which will not give you victory indeed, but engage you to put your lives at their just value. Not a single one of you, but would a thousand times rather die by the sword, than be deficient in honourable fidelity to his legitimate prince, and stain his own name for ever. Why not as well in the cause of Christ? Are we not His lieges? Do we not owe salvation to Him? Let each of you think then that he has the cause of Christ to defend by the right of feudal servitude, which is merit and honour; the only difference being, that our earthly lord gives a temporal reward, and He an eternal. Nor fear that for your sins, or some other unknown motive, He will deprive you of His inheritance; and that therefore you may yield to those accursed miscreants, who have no just pretension, since not

[1] Arab. Chron., 40.

a shadow of trust can be reposed in them; but that whatever they pretend, they will infallibly massacre you, either in open war or by treachery, or some horrid torture—they, who always accomplish their threats, never their promises. Since no possible escape from them is left, why then let despair (as to earth) be your weapons, as long as you have the power to make a single struggle; and then recommend your soul to God, in the firm conviction that His tender charity can never be extinguished. His immense love will make up for our defects; and do not doubt but that without further penitence, or suffering after death, your spirit will ascend at once to a blessed eternity. So now confess your sins each to each other; be your death glorious to yourself and useful to Christianity, and be sure of pardon." [1]

Then did every man kiss his neighbour; and many who had been long enemies, died warm friends. Mass was said, and they took the sacrament. Now to your posts!—The Grand Master of the Templars had determined upon his,[2] and with heavenly resignation and self-devotedness, went straight to the sultan's tent, and had less difficulty than he expected in persuading him of the peril of reducing the Christians to despair; so the Saracen was

[1] Michaud: Hist., v. 427.   [2] Id.: Id., 129.

willing to take a not intolerable ransom and depart. But when the generous veteran perceived a repugnance in those of Acre, he perhaps was not displeased, lest the sultan should not abide by his promises—the more that renegades were busy[1] blowing and blowing like a fierce desolating wind to heat their hatred to redness against those who were their own former co-religionists; which reminds us of his predecessor's prediction at St. Alban's sentence. Still, though the poison circulating through his veins must have killed him shortly, it is said the illustrious Beaujeu was slain in the ultimate battles; an end as becoming him as the Temple. By a stratagem of one of those renegades, the unhappy breach was left, and by that very gate of St. Anthony's the Mahometans broke into the city; and the rest is one scene of confusion. ".I know versions are different, but prefer trusting my eyes corroborated by all I have heard from people likely to be well informed; nor may I shuffle from it. But the last I saw of them was on the rampart by St. Anthony's Gate, where remained at most a thousand men against the whole Mussulman army.[2] It was dark; but a gleam of Greek fire showed me them all on foot, with couched lances, and Grandison with his

[1] Chron. Estense.—Bib. Crois., ii. 638.
[2] Michaud: Hist., v. 142.—MS. Accon.

drawn sword; and Gresli stood a little further off, with his behind him in precisely the same way; and within two or three yards of them, was the head of the Moslem column, that rushed impetuously through the gate—and by the yellow they were the Mameluke horse. So I have no hesitation whatever to assert that all the English died in a corps as at Mansourah, and the French also, as well fits that valiant nation. The reverse seems to me idle stories, mere ridiculous inventions, as if English and French could have been cowards, where so many other nations were so brave. Not a true, but a pretended revelation ; it would appear to me a trick of the devil! . . . . . What if iron chains and rings had been thrown into the streets for the Moslem cavalry? They were now covered with corpses, a bitter, albeit rather unsteady footing; and after them, the savage infantry inundated the streets. Not a palace, or square, or house, but was a fort, and had to be stormed; not a lane but was the theatre of frightful carnage, battles, single combats. I cannot exactly tell what day, or if it was day or night; for the Greek fire never ceasing its infernal blaze, it made little difference whether the sun was up or not, for that lurid gleam and the noises continued the same."

But here other authorities enable me to come to

the assistance of my MS. And to say it was the 18th of May,[1] a sable day in the Almanack of Christian Acre, when in burst the Mahometans, and what of soldiery of the cross survived joined the population in a wild and rapid current that ran in the direction of the House of the Templars in the very inmost heart of the town, down towards the sea; while one hideous crape of death seemed drawn over Acre, and all was fury, dismay, and massacre!

"None thought of sleep, nor can I tell how I existed. But kept steadily to my resolve to see and remember all I could, and do my best to survive. It was bitter cold, rain and hail—strange in that climate — and towards the end of May; but nature itself seemed to have changed, and the elements to sympathise, participate, and emulate the fury of men. And wild stories circulated. Every one ready to believe anything, and I think it would have been dark, but for the Greek fire, and my tread told me there had been hard fighting in that street. And then I saw Claremont come riding slowly (not rapidly as he had passed and repassed often before), and his direction was that of returning from where the battle at that time was, a desperate defence of the Templars' residence; but the Christians were so completely losers, that

[1] Michaud: Hist., v. 140.

they must have been all killed or gone in some other direction; for except him, I did not observe any one else retreating, and I heard the Saracens approach. He seemingly as much done up as his horse, lay resting on its neck; yet holding his sword, and struck his charger with his heavy spurs and repeated hard checks of the bridle, but in vain, and I had myself known what it was to have a horse so fatigued as not to answer either aids. Claremont's refused, and stood still trembling, and in a moment fell, I thought, dead. But at that, while I was bawling to him now on foot, which either he could not hear from the screeches, or I had not the strength to raise my voice; the Saracens came rushing with a loud howl and charging furiously between him and me; and, not to be ridden over, I stepped under a vault—and they must have cloven him down instantly and galloped on; for when, the next moment, I reached his body, it was all covered with blood and quite dead. And think his spirit must have attended me and kept assiduously protecting me, the rest of that awful period; that ever I got alive out of the wilderness, blackest, direst, most murderous, most atrocious!"[1]

"Then I too made for the port, which I knew must be at hand, and walking on corpses and

[1] Michaud: Hist., v. 143.

turning from the middle of the street, to where they were in a great number of layers one over another, heaped high at the angles, like bridges, I crossed by them and beheld—would I were rather blinded than ever see the like again—long lines of something of a speckled white, piled up against the wall, and supported by others of the same dirty white, thrown transverse, as if somebody had been opening a passage, but left the sad work not half done; and on approach those spectral white things, lo! they were dead females in their gowns and coifs, dabbled thickly with blood and utterly hideous! 'O most desolate old woman, whither are you hurrying, and who are these?' And she hobbling past, 'Are what you see, but were once a goodly company. I owed them my existence, but their charity ended thus pitifully. So I may now die. What matter where I go? The wildest would scorn to touch me. These were mostly young and beautiful virgins—a whole nunnery, nuns, novices, girls in education, who all following their mother abbess' example, scarified and furrowed themselves and breasts and faces frightfully with those great scissors, that used to be kept with a long chain and padlock, fixed to the great working table for the whole community. The abbess unlocked it, and, after wounding herself, handed the steel round, and each of them took it, and inflicted it on herself unsparingly, and being without succour, every one of them bled to death; and better, since they escaped what they most dreaded from some inhuman ugly brute.' Indeed they could not be objects of anything but horror.[1] I now understood what I just had heard, a Saracen cursing most blasphemously at their not having waited to satisfy his lust before they died. And he spoke of the martyrs, as if they had done him an injury, and round from behind the corner of the house came stretched out what seemed a hairy brawny arm, and a large foul hand; and in a twinkling there was no longer that ancient hag, but I heard plunderers in an infidel tongue. And her shrieks were soon drowned by louder shrieks in the quarter towards which I was going.

"But I must get on. I am in too great a hurry to answer many questions. Quickly! What are yours? The way is frightful, but not of length. On! On!

" How describe the harbour whose shipping stood a little out, else the rush of the crowd would have foundered them at once? The boiling oil of the Greek fire, which once it catches hold of the outside of a ship's bottom, all is lost; its stink, and livid

[1] Wadin : Annales Franciscorum., vi. 96.—Michaud: Hist., v. 141. Note.

flames extending to a great distance—stones, iron, brass, every metal devoured and eaten up by it; nor can it ever be extinguished, but by a mixture of sand and vinegar in certain proportions. How horrid its hiss!![1] And though the city was all in a glare from the Greek fire, and that it whizzed terribly, with long traces of greasy blue, along the waves, showing their watery mountains rolling with a terrific violence, yet the sea itself looked dark and gloomy, nor can I be sure whether it was from the tempest, or that it was night; and the ball of Greek fire expanding to the size of a cask, with its several yards of undulatory tail shining and hissing most viciously, died away at last, after piercing more or less into that abyss of obscurity, whose dreadful bellow would have been fearful at any other time. That lasted for I do not know how long; no difference then between day and— it seemed always, night. Days were years, minutes days. Who minded sun or moon? Heaven seemed in a fury, and that it was the end of all things.

"Such a multitude, but chiefly women and children—some of them young ladies of the highest rank, endeavouring to persuade the boatmen to take them—not only offering jewels and money, but even their own persons, and that they would

[1] Vinisauf.—Bib. Crois., ii. 676.—Oliveri.—Bib. Crois., iii. 143

marry any man that would save them.[1] In the surf thousands and thousands perished."[2]

It is said sixty thousand Christians fell then, and may be no exaggeration. Of the rich, who escaped, not at that time, but weeks sooner, it is much to calculate them at twenty-five thousand, mostly women, and children, and invalids. And it can be hardly supposed that the carried into captivity came to another twenty-five thousand. And this leaves one hundred thousand, of whom nearly all must have died either during the siege, or at the final hour, and fifteen thousand, at most, can have fallen in those fair battles; leaving eighty-five thousand for ultimate butchery. All which is on the supposition of the correctness of the usual opinion that Acre contained one hundred and fifty thousand souls when Tripoli fell.

"On! On! You as you like, but I must not stop. But we are close to the shore. Stout to push through such a crowd. Yet even women can do much when desperate, and children themselves, as you now see, for most of these are such. Ah, what their frenzy and wail! And not few of the infants are killed by the press and the carelessness of their own mothers. And now the infuriated Delhis, and the likes, are cutting at them with

[1] Michaud: Hist., v. 143. [2] MS. Accon.

their scimitars, and pushing their horses after them into the very sea. Driven, pursued, ah, what will become of them? Alas! My God have compassion on them.[1]

"Unable in those floods of rain, and pelting hail and roaring wind, to get near the water for perhaps two hours (though no judging of time then, things seemed very long or very short accordingly), so beset was it by that deplorable multitude; not even at the charge of the pitiless Mamelukes, from my fear that my wounded breast would be crushed, did I stir; till there came so tremendous a crash, that one might think it an earthquake dividing the globe, and glancing towards the Templars' Tower, I saw their flag drop, and the tower itself tumble down, at which, believing all Acre was falling to pieces I, almost frantic, flew right through the crowd, and flung myself into the sea, and some paces out, was fished up into a boat. And who fished me was the pious Patriarch; but whose compassion had allowed such numbers to embark, that we shortly went down in the harbour; and better for me, for we certainly should have foundered, and been lost, every soul of us, when out in those boisterous waves; but here, though most of the unfortunates were drowned, and amongst them the

[1] Michaud: Hist., v. 144.

venerable Patriarch himself, yet a few who swam well were saved, and I found myself on board a galley belonging to the Grand Master of the Hospitallers, with a large company of fugitives, and amongst them five of his own knights, all wounded like himself.[1] Fact is, all remaining of Templars had got into that tower, where many of the townsmen's women and children had also taken refuge; and a first capitulation made of what the underground Saracens had already mined, without perhaps the sultan's knowledge; three hundred of his had been admitted, and instantly began to maltreat the females. At which the few Templars, rising like one man, attacked the brutes, and flung them down from the roof dead, and would never hear of capitulating any more. So the sultan was forced to order the tower to be scaled; and when Saracenic multitudes, scimitar in one hand and ladder in the other, were in the very act of scaling, down it toppled, by fortuitous yielding of wooden props in the mine, and Templars, scalers, males, females, it buried them all together."[2]

How many days or nights after that is not known. Various accounts, each contradictory to the other. Like Saragossa, the streets were fields of battle for

[1] French MS.—Michaud: Hist., v. 421.
[2] Michaud: Hist., v. 145.

several days, and each house a fortress, and communications cut from one to the other through the walls, and the hole closed up again as soon as the house was taken; and pass on to the next.

"Imprecations were what I could distinguish, as hastily we weighed, and weathering Carmel Cape, the last sounds borne on the storm were hellish laughter, groans of dying men, and the long, long shriek of violated women."[1]

---

[1] MS. Accon.

ABEYANCE THE SECOND.

WITH grief Europe heard of the fall of Acre, and quickly was it followed by that of Tyre, and all the towns along the Syrian coast, from which the Latin inhabitants who could, fled by sea.

Beyrout was the last Christian town to fall, according to some,[1] but others say Nicopolis lasted two years after.[2] Glory to the Hospitallers, for of these was the little garrison, whose abandoned valour rendered it inexpugnable so long under reiterated assaults; nor did it ever yield to human arms, but was thrown down by an earthquake,[3] which buried the whole—soldiers, citadel, city. Ill-printed, or inexact, Sanuti has Venetians, and truce, and Sycopolis. There were several places

[1] Chron. St. Bertin.—Bib. Crois., i. 423.
[2] Sanuti.—Bib. Crois., ii. 634.
[3] Seb. Paoli: Not. Geo., i. 443.

called Nicopolis, as Prevesa,[1] and in Hungary;[2] but this Nicopolis was the ancient *Emmaus*.[3] The present may be in the immediate vicinity of the same spot; but otherwise no vestige of its predecessor.[4]

Besides the Pilgrim Castle near Tripoli, the Templars built another of nearly that name between Caiphas and Cesarea, of which the ruins still exist. This was a very strong fortress, an outwork of Mount Thabor, and the road to Jerusalem, and was once called Detroit. It fell after Acre.[5] Its foundations were an old tower that had long belonged to the order of the Temple, and was on the sea-side;[6] and in the new erection they were assisted by various pilgrims and the German Hospitallers. Many antiquities, and ancient coins, and treasures were found in digging the mountain. The Templars built also a Castle in Acre, the chief[7] there.

Thus miserable outcasts filled Christendom with their doleful tales, and increased the poverty of

[1] Eusebii Chron.
[2] Bosio.—Vertot: vi. 322.—Michaud: Hist., v. 210. Bib. Crois., iii. 157.
[3] Seb. Paoli: Osservazioni, ii. 591.
[4] Appendix, ciii.
[5] Sanuti.—Bib. Crois., i. 195.
[6] Pantalcone: Chron.—Bib. Crois., iii. 21, and i. 427
[7] Vitri: Letters.—Cologne Chron.—Bib. Crois., iii. 136.

every country; and from the fall of Acre, Villani dates the beginning of the decline of the commercial towns in maritime Italy, since from that day out (he says), they lost half of the advantages that Eastern traffic brought. " For Acre was a universal resort, and in the middle of Syria, nay, in the middle of the civilised earth, as at equal distances between Levant and West, and almost on the European frontier, and transit for commerce from all those distant lands, and had interpreters of every language, and people of every class, and inhabitants of every climate; and therefore, in losing Acre, the world lost one of its elements.[1] " And the Holy Land, with its thickly populous districts, and its innumerable clusters of villages, quantities of strong castles, and eighty cities inhabited by Franks for the most part, and owing their defence to the Latins,[2] were all reduced to a devastated wilderness; "state in which it shall remain, please God, until the day of judgment," is the devout aspiration of a Moslem.[3]

What other circular was necessary than what Villiers had written already? And it had sufficed to

---

[1] Hist. Fior.—Bib. Crois. ii. 621.—Appendix, cii.—Hallam: Middle Ages, ii. 250.
[2] Michaud: Hist., v. 147.
[3] Arab. Chron., 575.—Michaud : Hist., v. 148.

call the knights of every age and rank, who instantly renouncing everything else, hurried down into the various ports of Christendom with most laudable ardour, young or old, in health or not, no delay, no excuse, but each one striving to be first, and embarking in any ship to be found, and all these put into Cyprus, so that not a day passed but some Hospitallers arrived from Europe. All of them might be bound for Acre, but Cyprus was on their road, and there, alas! learned they had to go no further. The nearly exterminated order reduced to half-a-dozen wounded men, without money, and in proportion, to perfect beggary; this European flow made it revive. The same of the Templars.

Nor in this island, within forty leagues from Palestine, had they not both some property already. Henry II., descended from Guy de Lusignan, was then its king, and so of Norman blood.[1] Nor did he not show it, by the cordiality with which he received the rest of the Templars and Hospitallers after their irreparable loss, and placed them in Limisso, one of his chief towns.[2] Perhaps it was from pure compassion, or that it was the advice of some evil-wisher, for Pope Nicholas IV. had the repute of loving those peerless knights; but he appears to have taken a most undue advantage of their miser-

[1] Bosio.—Vertot: iv. 4.   [2] Vertot: iv. 2.—Bosio.

able state, when he proposed uniting the Hospitallers and Templars into one order, whose common grand master, to prevent jealousy, should be elected by neither of them, but by himself, and likewise always for the future by the Holy See.[1] But that project was soon rejected.[2] The same Pope showed his liberality by applying to the schismatic Greek Church, to join him in renouncing for a time all religious differences for defence of universal Christianity against the Saracen, and also had recourse to the Pagan Tartars;[3] but of the whole powers of Christendom, not one, except the Templars and Hospitallers alone, took any real part in the attempt.[4] Yet before it there was a general chapter held at Limisso, of who so faithfully responded to the circular, that scarcely ever before, since the foundation of the order, such a number of Hospitallers of all nations as then appeared.[5] There (it is tradition) the grand master, hardly recovered from his wounds, entered with a sorrowful countenance, yet that magnanimity which usually is seen in virtue, and in a calm and slow tone said, " Of the ancient rule of our order, my

1292

---

[1] Vertot: iv. 6.—Cod. Dipl. Geros., ii., Num. i. and ii.
[2] Cod. Dipl. Geros., ii., Num. xv.
[3] Michaud: Hist., v. 158.   [4] Michaud: Hist., v. 159.
[5] Vertot: iv. 9.—Bosio.

being present may possibly appear an infraction; and therefore, not to scandalise you, cherished brethren, I have some documents to prove I had sworn to the population that, useless as I had become from my wounds, I should endeavour to survive for the purpose of leading away as many as I could from the Acre slaughter, as was likewise my duty, as sovereign of that unfortunate city. And I plead it is an exception no way derogatory to what continues our standing statute, that none shall recede without command, and that a knight of ours made prisoner is a knight dead. With regard to the few of our knights who came with me, they have no excuse to make, since they had my orders, for which the entire responsibility is mine, in consideration of their wounded condition, and that it would be an idle sacrifice of lives. Read these affidavits then; and I am ready either to be deposed, or even suffer death, or obtain your entire approval of my conduct, according to what you may determine, for which I retire."

And after some minutes the whole chapter followed Villiers, and declared him completely vindicated, and humbly besought him not to abandon them.

"Then abandon you I will not, but persevere in being your grand master and loving father; and allow me to begin by thanking you," as, re-entering the hall, he sat down, " for the promptitude with which you obeyed my orders; and far better than had Divine Providence allowed you to be in time for Acre, since there you could only have increased superfluous deaths, but here you show that Holy Land has not lost all its defenders. But, by the courage that animates you, I see we have still men worthy of the name of Hospitallers, and capable of remedying all our losses; St. John's Acre is indeed ours, as sepulchre of so many of our gallant brethren. It is for you to replace them, and liberate Jerusalem from the barbarian's iron despotism."[1]

And observing Limisso to be an open town, with only a well-fortified citadel in the centre, too small for the order's residence, some proposed removing to one of the Italian ports, which was instantly quashed with indignation by the grand master and chief knights, as contrary to the spirit of their institution, which did not permit them to go far from Palestine, but be always at hand, and ready to profit by any opportunity. And this sentiment met universal applause, and was immediately drawn up as a sort of perpetual statute.[2] And the chapter

---

[1] Bosio.—Vertot: iv. 10.   [2] Id.—Id.: 12.

ended by determining to fortify Limisso, and erect it into a regular establishment of Hospitality.

Nor is there any earlier approximation to the naval, than when it was resolved that the ship which had conveyed them from Acre, should be used in learning to clear the coasts from the continual attacks of Saracen pirates. Nor did this prevent cavalry from being the order's principal care still; as we find (even five years later) certain lands set apart for forage for their horses, whereas there is little or nothing about galleys in these documents as yet.[1]

Such was the commencement of the navy of the Order of Malta; no auspicious one certainly, to commence in a period of abeyance (which some called decline or extinction), after having lived the trifle of above two hundred years; far from promising future maritime glory.

Fortunately their young efforts were not crushed by the sultan, enraged that the two bodies (Templars and Hospitallers), whom he had thought to have put an end to, were reviving; for the fleet he sent against them was lost, and he himself died shortly after.[2]

A new Pope, who had been chosen and soon ab-

---

[1] Appendix, lxxviii.   [2] Bosio.—Vertot: iv. 14.

dicated, one perhaps too unworldly for this world, even during his short reign found time to praise the Hospitallers.[1] His learned and wily successor, letting himself go to the audacious temptation of what was partly offered to him by the not upright kings of Europe themselves, and the unhappy circumstances of the time, tried to erect a despotism both spiritual and temporal; but whatever he was to others, he imitated his predecessors in being kind to the order—"Claret devotione conspicua Ordo St. Johannis Hierosolimitani"—are the words in his brief to the King of Portugal;[2] and in another, to our Edward, not dissimilar, as also in Rymer.[3] And now Villiers died; yet not in 1296, as Vertot has, for a document shows Sir John Villiers was reigning in September, 1297.[4]

1294

1295
1297

That donations from private persons were still coming to the Hospitallers, and that, though the Teutonics had relinquished their name of German Hospitallers, they bore no ill-will to those they had left, is clear from the Hochsperg in the Appendix; where a father retired from the world, as dead to it from the moment he had joined the Teutonics,

---

[1] Cod. Dipl. Geros., ii., Num. iii.—Appendix, lxxix.
[2] Id. Id. iv.
[3] Id. Id. vii.
[4] Id. Id. x.

witnesses his son's confirmation of his own gift to the Hospital. Later it might be otherwise; but now they had known them too well and recently, not to esteem and love all three of the military orders.[1]

Villiers' successor was Sir Otho de Pins in 1298, a Provençal born, but descended from an illustrious Spanish family; and his stem still to be seen at Rhodes.[2] Yet Sir Otho might have been too old. He avoided deposition from his own knights by very wisely dying on his voyage to seek protection from Rome; and so the election took place of Sir William Villaret, of the langue of Provence,[3] and it is the first time I read of that term in the order, into which how, or when it obtained I cannot say; but regret it as implying not union but division, and which, if it bred emulation, did also discord; but what is certain is, that it does not come from the institution, and can at any time be without nicety expunged. Not having that patriarchal sanctity, it becomes a mere passing discipline, to be thrown aside as taken up.

1298

1300

In 1299, the head of the Tartars sent to Boniface VIII. to proclaim Jerusalem free, and all

---

[1] Appendix, lxxx.—Seb. Paoli: Osservazioni, ii. 524.
[2] Seb. Paoli: Serie, ii. 461.
[3] Seb. Paoli (Cod. Dipl. Geros.): Serie, ii. 461.

Europe; and that the Tartar had liberated it from the Mahometan yoke, and so that the Christians might come back to re-people their lands, and sent letters of the same tenor to the Grand Masters of the Hospitallers and Templars, inviting them to return, and enter into peaceful enjoyment of their former possessions.[1] Villaret was at the time Prior of St. Gilles, and there, nor did he come instantly to Cyprus on his election; but first visited various houses of the order in France, including that of the Hospitalleresses under his own sister. And if it be interesting, we may learn that the dress of these ladies consisted in a robe of scarlet cloth and a cross of white linen with eight points.[2]

Ever since the Polos had been at Acre, years before its destruction, even further back than St. Louis' crusade, Cyprus had heard of Tartary and of Christian propensities in the Tartars,[3] or at least their finest horde; so now a body of Hospitallers, horse, was sent in 1301, in furtherance of the league that had been proposed by Nicholas IV., and these with the Tartars advanced all over Palestine, and had even the comfort to enter Jerusalem, but found it, like all the other towns in those

[1] Treves Chron.—Bib. Crois., i. 331.
[2] Bosio.—Vertot: iv. 34.
[3] S. Bertin. Chron.—Bib. Crois., i. 419.—Appendix, ciii.

parts, lying quite open; the Saracens having razed everything like a fortification in them after taking Acre. And might then have visited *Emmaus*, alias *Nicopolis*, with an intention of taking up their poor abandoned garrison, but it was much too late; no Hospitallers to take—nothing but a ruin of some years, yet not by Saracens, but God, evidently by an earthquake or other natural subversion!

If the khan was, as is said, a person of extraordinary intelligence, and an assiduous reader of the Cyropediad, and the life of Alexander, and that those princes were his models, no wonder he preferred Christianity to Mahometanism; for he could not but observe that what is against Nature must be false. All beneficent natural changes are slow and gradual, as the corn, the tree, the human creature. With what invisible slowness does the flower produce the fruit, and this enlarge and ripen! The line of separation you can never find. As the oak is in the acorn, so the grown-up male or female is in the infant. It is but a fair, slow development, without any change of essence, and requires years. But unnatural things are, for the most part, sudden and violent, and, nearly always, wicked or disastrous, like earthquakes or hurricanes. From the creation, the imperceptible progress which has now produced Christianity, has been going on, and applies to your reason, which asks time for reflection; but the Koran or the sword admits none, but takes you by utter surprise.[1]

He and his were soon forced to return to their own country, in consequence of a civil war, and so the Hospitallers had to retreat as well, from evident inability to withstand the Sultan of Cairo, who was coming.[2]

In the meantime, Sir Gaudin, who had been made Grand Master of the Templars, after him killed at Acre, went with the King of Cyprus to make a diversion on the Syrian coast, and took Tortosa; but in 1302 it was won back by the Saracens, with the loss of one hundred and twenty of the Templars,[3] which being considered a great number, prepares us to disbelieve the exaggerations of times at hand.[4]

Not that the fusion of Hospitallers and Templars was in itself bad, but the design of depriving them of their independence for the benefit of a third, reminds you of the lawyer and two clients. And towards the end of 1304, when the two Grand Masters, of whom one was the glorious but un-

---

[1] Vertot: iv. 36.   [2] Id.: iv. 38.
[3] Seb. Paoli: Osservazioni, ii. 526.
[4] Condussevi la maggior parte del suo convento. Seb. Paoli: Osservazioni, ii. 526.

fortunate Molay, who had now succeeded to Gaudin, spoke to each other for the last time, the greatest difficulty was got over, it is said, by their mutual generosity. They were ready each, to abdicate, for the whole mixed body to elect their chief, who, as long as any of the existing Templars lived, was to be of their order, and, after them, that things were to be as before. But, though the two generous chiefs were agreed thus, not so their knights, whose ratification was quite necessary, and, therefore, the whole plan miscarried, and the substance of their argument was sent, in his own name, by Molay, afterwards, in his answer to the Pope, whether Molay dictated it, or availed himself of that prepared already by his immediate predecessor, Gaudin, who had been elected by the only ten Templars who got alive from Acre, and was succeeded by one of them, Molay.[1]

1305

"But my answer shall be simply that I cannot go till after I have settled respecting an island," replied the Hospitaller, on their second interview that same day; "and many islands being in these seas, no one knows which I mean. None, even of my own knights, except my brother, perhaps in case I should die. But as to you, I will make no secret of it, but present you another offer, since it

[1] Seb. Paoli: Osservazioni, ii. 462.

is no fault of yours, if you do not accept my former one. It is now two hundred years and more that our orders have uniformly been together, or if ever at all separated not for long; and often have we shared the greatest dangers, and fought and bled side by side. Even our rivalry, as some choose to call it, cannot but bind us close; I would have rather said emulation, for we have always had the same cause.[1] If there be any difference in our rule, it is very little. For me I love to think we form but one, and derive from the same stem; and believe you are of similar sentiments, so regret to see you no more. Wishing well to the Teutonics in Germany, their branching off was long before my time. But you and I have always been together, and have both spilled a little of our blood at Acre, and known noble Beaujeu and Claremont. I will tell you, therefore, the island in my mind's eye, is Rhodes,[2] so famous in ancient ages, and that shall become famous and opulent, and in every way a desirable residence in ours also. Now, with your assistance, we shall take that beautiful spot and strong, and we shall both reside there, as at Acre.

[1] *Nunquam assavit fieri cavalcata contro Saracenos.* Cod. Dipl. Geros., ii., Num. xv.

[2] The original has only *quœdam insulam,* to which a commentator, after the event, wrote in the margin *Rhodum*; but Vertot has chosen to join both; iv. 64.

Besides, our rule is, as I have said, essentially the same, and it is your duty, as well as mine, to fix ourselves as near Jerusalem as we can. Whereas, if you decide for Europe, I have dark forebodings. Your order, as well as mine, has many enemies, but yours worse; and gives greater food for envy. In Rhodes we should be, as it were, our own masters and have our own good swords to protect us. But in Europe are malicious tongues, stronger than the brightest courage—there called pride and pretension. There your fawning courtier is the hero, and nocturnal falsehood invents what triumphs over the best and bravest. Better in our island of roses, than in Paris with whatever splendour. Think on it well before giving me a refusal. You will reap honour, wherever you go. If riches, these will bring you flattery and ruin. Remember I told you so."—"We have both our duties," answered Molay, with pensive sadness, "and you must cleave to your knights, and I to mine. The Morea and the glories of Greece and Constantinople are the dreams of mine. Yet all you observe afflicts me. No doubt of wealth and honours; but what are they to produce? Farewell!"

And the generous pair never met again. He and his Templars embarked for the Piræus that very evening; and shortly after, he of the Hospital went reconnoitring several of the neighbouring islands.

During which came other letters from the new Pope; and that to the Grand Master of the Templars may have been a sort of duplicate of this. And if he of the Hospital was called only to hide the monstrous enormity, his disobedience was easily pardoned on Molay's being forwarded to Greece, and reaping full success; for the luckless nobleman obeyed, and went into the trap, Poitiers and Paris, —and was lost. Quickness and great secrecy were the Pope's injunctions; and writing in 1306 the earlier part of June, he says he would expect to hear their opinion on grave matters relative to the Holy Land, on the 15th of next November.[1]

But on his return from the islands, Sir William, finding his knights in ill humour, as ill-treated by the Court of Cyprus, and wishing to be in a home of their own, where they might attend to their duties and have to render an account to none but to their own superior and grand master alone, he thought it best to avail himself of the Pontifical orders, and go to Europe to try to organise a body to aid him in his projected invasion. More especially, seeing he was not to have the Templars,[2]

[1] Appendix, lxxx.—Cod. Dipl. Geros., ii., Num xvi.
[2] Sismondi : Repub. Ital., iv.—Appendix, cv.

and that Rhodes, which had once been Genoese, and was now Greek nominally, belonged in reality to Saracen pirates—a bold, fierce, and most lawless race, resembling the Malays of this day, their resistance was sure to be desperate; keeping his secret, and pretending it was a crusade, which, however small, would suffice for his views. But he died previous to his voyage, towards the end of 1306; and early in the next year the order chose another, Villaret,[1] who (his brother or not)[2] was at all events his near relation, and known to be acquainted with his secret. Sir Fulk de Villaret, the moment he was elected, sailed for France.[3] One year is of little importance, yet it is inexact. That letter of Clement was directed to Sir William; though it was Sir Fulk came to answer it in person, as required. Another brief to Sir Fulk himself, after his return from France, at Rhodes (against which he had advanced, but not as yet conquered, except in some little part), is dated August, 1307;[4] and from expressions in it, we cannot but perceive the Pope had recently spoken with the unconscious Fulk; who, however, heard nothing

1307

---

[1] Seb. Paoli: Serie, ii. 462.
[2] Seb. Paoli doubts—Vertot affirms it, iv.
[3] Bosio.—Vertot : iv. 64.
[4] Cod. Dipl. Geros., ii., Num. xviii.—Seb. Paoli (Cod. Dipl. Geros.): Serie, ii. 463.

to make him suspect the frightful truth, though abundant ill-will certainly met his ears; but having never had a personal interview with the hapless Molay, he might exert his prudence in the elevated dignity he was now clothed with, to avoid one; and be desirous of removing from that dangerous position as fast as he could, well aware that his own order was exposed to envy, as well as that of the guiltless Templars. Things were already running high, not perhaps publicly, but in the minds of the Pontifical and French Courts; for they captured Molay a very few weeks afterwards, of a Friday on the 13th of October, 1307, although his Holiness did not declare it till the year after; but it was equal to the capture (caperetur) in 1307. So we have two clear documentary proofs that Sir Fulk was Grand Master of the Hospital early in 1307.[1] In France he soon got what he wanted. A great crusade was impossible; but to gather a body of resolute individuals was easy. He might be in the greater hurry to return, that the courts had a gloomy aspect—though he knew that while the Hospitallers kept at a distance, and clear of inordinate show, their merit to Christendom and the Holy Land would be avowed; but that to be near

---

[1] Seb. Paoli: Osservazioni. ii., 526.--Appendix, lxxxii, and lxxxiii.

was dangerous. Gratitude was a reed not to be much relied on, happy if not converted into crime. Nor had he even a personal acquaintance with Molay. So Fulk ought not to be suspected; but it was better heave off, and he did so. The financial means were chiefly by a subscription of ladies, particularly those of Genoa, who sold their jewels for that purpose.[1] Some of these Genoese Amazons took the cross themselves, whose cuirasses, made small and with bulges to receive their breasts, were shown in the arsenal long after.[2] He had only to select the number of warriors he desired from several. Many of the most illustrious houses in Germany[3] took the white cross on that occasion. But he was so reserved, and perhaps severe a man, that not one of them dared to inquire where he was going to. So passing Rhodes, to lull any suspicion of the Saracens, he sailed to Cyprus, and there taking all his knights and their effects; sailed again to the astonishment of the King of Cyprus, and every one else. But when out of sight of Cyprus, Sir Fulk veered north-east, and keeping Syria on his right, instead of landing, went into a port on the coast of Asia Minor, and anchored. Immense

[1] Bosio.—Vertot: iv. 79.
[2] Michaud: Hist., v. 160.—Misson's Italy in 1702.
[3] Bosio.—Vertot: iv. 80.

was the wonder of his whole fleet; and not even his own choice knights but wondered where he could be bound for. Thence, however, he appears to have sent to the Emperor of Constantinople, asking him for the investiture of Rhodes, which pride and anti-Latin hate refused, though leave would have been only titular, for the expulsion of the Saracen pirates would not have been a whit the easier. If that the Greek Emperor gave Rhodes to the Hospitallers, ever got into the head of any one, he must now get it out of it; for the fact is not so. Were it, we should have it (as we have that of Charles V.), or some record of it, in these documents. A capitulation gave full time to get away the archives. Not as at Acre. Pirates seem to have been indeed at that time the only real inhabitants of the island,[1] the Venetians having all decamped long before, and most of the Greeks still earlier; later they returned. Nor did this refusal produce much effect on Sir Fulk, whose spies had already made their reports concerning island and capital; so that he had determined where he would disembark. Only it made him declare his project to his followers, unanimous in their approbation. So he let his allies think and call themselves crusaders; and such he called them, to gratify their vanity, and give them the pomp and

[1] Sismondi : Rep. Ital., i. 280.

circumstance of a crusade. His invasion succeeded at first, all the lesser islands and part of Rhodes itself yielding nearly without a struggle; but by little and little, the difficulties grew. The pirates who were at sea came back, and the war became long and bloody. In consequence, the crusaders went away one after another, and Sir Fulk had scarcely any one more than his own Hospitallers to support him, quite ineffectual, had they not paid troops. But to pay them? Yet so strenuous were his exertions, that he engaged the Florentine bankers to advance him a loan of money—a difficult matter in those times; and he had the ability to infuse his own spirit into his little army, resolution to conquer or die. Sanguinary in the highest degree were several attempts to take the city, into which the pirates had at last retreated, after a terrible resistance of four years. But take it he did in the end, what remained of the outlaws escaping by sea, being the first to proclaim their own defeat throughout the islands of the Archipelago, and along the coast of Lycia;[1] still at expense of a great number of his bravest Hospitallers, and one shout of admiration resounded through all Christendom[2] of *Knights of Rhodes*, a title that was to endure illustrious for above

---

[1] Bosio.—Vertot, iv. 89.   [2] Id.   Id. iv. 90.

two centuries.[1] A letter from one of our kings in 1309 (I suppose Edward II.), shows what has been already observed, that the order was still considered rather equestrian than naval.[2] Thus that glorious body of the select of all Christians on the edge of its orbit, or not far from it, wheeled its second course of more than another hundred years under seventeen grand masters.[3]

1309

---

[1] Werner : Chron.—Bib. Crois., i. 352.
[2] Cod. Dipl. Geros., ii., Num xxi.—Rymer.—Bib. Crois., ii., 882.—Appendix, civ.
[3] Appendix, cvii.

BOOK THE THIRD—RHODES.

CHAPTER I.

WHY a defence of the Templars, triumphantly defended and fully, long since? To go over the ground so nobly trod by Raynouard were at least superfluous. Whoever accuses them after that, it can only be to display his own erudition. Five centuries had not been able to prove their guilt, and now it is utterly disproved, however hard to prove a negative.[1] There is not a reasonable and well-informed man in Europe, who thinks them guilty of any one of the enormities imputed to them. They were perhaps somewhat haughty, and exaggerated their wealth,

---

[1] Michaud: Hist., v. 428.

accumulated (yet for how short a time, a few months!) in Greece; which was folly, but no crime— crime were a wicked misnomer. I will not say, not challenging disgrace the most opprobrious, and imprisonment, and tortures, faggots, death—for these make one shudder with horror and indignation; but not even the lightest and most mitigated chastisement. Quite the contrary, they merited high praise for their virtuous and valiant actions. Their true and only crime was, their much-overrated riches. But the Templars had faults! Indeed! What a discovery! How profound! Societies of mortals should have none! Whatever their faults, they were not to be mentioned the same day, with their most barbarous murder, but entirely disappear. Their rent-roll was great, no doubt; and now that Palestine was lost, its resolute defenders become resident in Europe, had no longer necessity for expenditure that invariably devoured their income. Far from hoarding money, they had been frequently obliged to borrow by selling, or mortgaging some of their property, or on many urgent occasions during the holy war, accept charity; not for themselves, but for the benefit of the entire body of Franks. If their estates were to be curtailed, could that not be done without such base, hideous, merciless ingratitude? Their amazing self-devotedness during the last dying struggle—Acre alone—death-rattle of Syria—might have spared them such palpable inventions; even had they fallen into material misdemeanors—which is not proved in law, but the very reverse, far more innocence than could have been expected from soldiers exposed to the numerous temptations of a martial life; nor may it be unfair to consider some indulgences a compensation nearly due to frequent distress and danger. Ascetic heroism is too rare a combination to require. But finally no discreet jury but would have acquitted the Templars. The question for any further trial could be only of what damages, for so slanderous an indictment. But open court, or fair defence, not an atom had they of either. How league with the very Saracens that slew them? Secret friends of who sawed them asunder? Of who hoped to annihilate their order at Acre, and were very near doing so? Had it depended on Philip le Bel, the Hospitallers had fared like the Templars. The Teutonics were safe in their native Germany. But the snare was evidently set for both the others. That ultimate conversation in Cyprus had been their crisis. So the Templars deciding for southern Europe, sealed their destiny, and Rhodes saved the Hospitallers. It is clear the Pope was far from inclined against the warriors he eulogised as they deserved, at the very moment he was inviting them into his clutches. From which I am far from deducing any malignity of intention in him, but a weak and ineffectual dislike of what he had promised; and therefore he hesitated for a whole year, from when Le Bel had all the Templars through his dominions thrown into prison as malefactors in one day in 1307, which creates a confusion of dates; some historians counting from that kingly, and others from the Papal condemnation. The Pope had weighty displeasure,[1] at what the king had done, seized on the Templars to burn them, and confiscate their property, in 1307; and only in 1308 his Holiness consented to condemn their entire order. Bsovius, Gurtler, and all the annalists of that unhappy body, are of one accord on this point. The miserable Pontiff made several attempts to free himself from his horrible promises; but they had been the price of his tiara, and his abject nature was too eaten up by ambition to descry any way but executing it. It seemed to him necessary; as if crime and injustice can ever be necessary. Not that Clement wished worse to the Templars, or better to the Hospitallers, but, as he condemned one, he would have condemned both—abandoned

---

[1] Cod. Dipl. Geros.—Seb. Paoli: Osservazioni, iv. 526.

both to the flames, if required. It might be partly age's feebleness; and piety leaveth to a dotard that not warrantable excuse, but unenviable palliation. At such fearful and extravagant iniquities imputed to his venerated order, well might unfortunate Molay, as full of wonder, make a great sign of the cross, and exclaim that such enormous inventors merited what is inflicted on liars and coiners among Saracens and Tartars. What punishment is that? To have their paunches ripped open, and their heads cut off.[1] They had read what purported to be his avowal, and was not. Even his had been constrained under tortures; sad tribute to the feebleness of human nature, and his imagination tried to relieve him from those horrible agonies of corporal pain; but still worse words had been forged afterwards, and feloniously inserted into that doleful cry; so he boldly denied the whole, retracting what he had pretended, and declaring those other fictions too grossly false ever to have occurred to his disordered brain, and utterly and extravagantly untrue, and invented by them-

[1] Prima e secunda Vita di Clemente V.—Vertot: iv. 132.—Muratori—Platina : iii. 179.—The Templars went by Sicily to Greece, says Bosio. Why that round-about? At all events, what time to get *ricchissimi* in Greece by their savings *d'ogni anno;* since they left Cyprus in 1306, and were in France in 1307? Bosio : par. ii., lib. 1.

selves. But they were the very men who owed him most gratitude in this world, and, far bitterer woe, unworthy chief ministers of that sacred creed for the defence of which he had devoted his whole life to exile and danger; he who wanted neither wealth nor rank, but had them both from birth, as of one of the richest and noblest families in Burgundy. And if he had now become Grand Master, was it a step higher? Had he not been born a prince? Or whither does the Grand Mastery direct him? And not Mahometans his execrable assailants, but Christians. And who will now deliver him to the flames, after all they could to force him to disgrace himself by a false confession, and, what is still worse, succeeded in a certain fashion! But turn from such abominations. Yet what historian whose lot bids his passing that way, but is in honour and conscience bound to fling his tribute of execration on the murdered creature's grisly cairn? How exaggerated had been their wealth and numbers, was soon shown; for though France was the head-quarters, and almost home to the Templars, they were found not thousands, but about seventeen score. Nor could it well be otherwise, since only ten got alive from Acre, and when, after a reinforcement from Europe, they lost one hundred and twenty in the Tartar war, it was held to be little less than extermination;[1] and the property all confiscated to the crown did not much enrich it. It was in almost that kingdom alone, that the truth was put to a proper test; for though a year later, the Templars over the whole world were condemned by the Pope, and their order abolished, yet their estates were variously disposed of, in each different country. Spain passed them over to the order of Calatrava. Many kings shared them between their nobility and clergy. Many confiscated them partly, and partly doled them out in gifts to crusaders. In Germany having who resolutely demanded a trial, they were tried and acquitted.[2]

Woe to the corrupted! Worse woes to the cowardly! That our wicked enemy triumphs is not from our want of strength, but from our arrant cowardice! As the Pope abolished the whole institution, what availed their being proved innocent, except saving those individuals from the flames? As to their estates there, they melted away. Those in Portugal were given to the order of Christ, created on purpose.[3] But no example that the persons of the Templars were subject to any capital punishment, except in France; nor their entire

[1] Seb. Paoli: Osservazioni, ii. 526.—Forsell: iii. 10.
[2] Vertot: iv. 163.
[3] Seb. Paoli: Osservazioni, ii. 533.

property confiscated to the crown, except in France. So much astute wickedness at the time renders it hard to affirm whether it was or not with Villaret's free consent; but certainly it has that appearance, and bears his name and signature in full, and those of divers of his chiefs, a power of attorney, with the vote of all the knights assembled in council by the sound of the bell at Rhodes, as is the custom, naming a commission to go to Europe and receive the goods of the Templars.[1] It was in the second sessions of the Council of Vienna, on the 3rd of April, 1312, that in the presence of the King of France and his brother Valois, and three royal sons, the order of the Templars was abolished, and their property decreed to the Hospitallers;[2] so that whatever occurred up to that moment, could have been but a temporary expedient and almost private transaction in comparison.[3] In England the order indeed was abrogated with a sigh; for England was Catholic, and what the Pope suppressed, it suppressed. But our king decided that their property should go to their natural

1312

1313

---

[1] Cod. Dipl. Geros., ii., Num. xxix.—Appendix, cix.
[2] Platina: iii. 190. Note M.— Bosio: par. ii., lib. i., anno 1312.
[3] Cod. Dipl. Geros., ii., Num. iii. Giun. Vatic. Secret.— Appendix, cliv.

heirs, and that it was for the parliament[1] and judges to declare who were such.[2] And so they did, for on an appeal from a family, one of whose ancestors in Ireland had left a considerable tenement to the Templars, and that family wishing to take it back, the full courts at London sentenced otherwise, and that the lands devolved to the Hospitallers, as in the case of a father who survives his son.[3] And in strict conformity with this is the English sovereign's command.[4] And it is a sign he had some entrails of pity in his composition, that he thought of allowing a daily allowance to the Templars; though it fills us with commiseration to think how gentlemen could exist on so wretched a pittance, and to what severe straits they must have been reduced to accept it. But it consoles a little, and has something I know not what, of sweet mercy, that of all Englishmen he selects the Prior of the Hospitallers for that charity, and ends by entreating him to execute his commission well; for that otherwise he should be much embarrassed to find another capable of easing his royal mind of future trouble re-

[1] Cod. Dipl. Geros., ii., Num. xxvi.—Rymer.—Appendix, cx.
[2] Id.   Id. xxx.   Id.   Id.   cxi.
[3] Lodge.—Sir William Betham.—Rot. Bi. :—Rolls and Records.
[4] Cod. Dipl. Geros., ii., Num. xxxi.—Rymer.—Appendix, Num. cxii.

garding those afflicted knights.[1] Elsewhere economy might have been one reason for killing them; for if they lived, could it have been on air? And they who were once so opulent, had now nothing; so that Molay had not threepence to fee a lawyer to defend him. The scoundrels gave him leave to have one, because they knew they had rendered him unable to avail himself of it.[2] While such were the nefarious transactions in Europe, Sir Fulk Villaret had been accomplishing the conquest of Rhodes, rather I should say the liberation of its native Christian population from their lawless tyrants, those Mahometan pirates. What became of the Colossus of Rhodes? Nothing of it was left, the rocks telling where its feet had stood. An earthquake threw it down, and its pieces remained on the beach for about a century, until in an incursion of Arabs, a Jew bought the fragments of brass, and carried them away, nine hundred camel loads. Objections that it would have fallen into the sea, savour of the hypercritical; for strange things are brought about by earthquakes.[3] The

[1] Cod. Dipl. Geros., ii., Num. xxxiv.—Rymer.—App., cxiii.
[2] Seb. Paoli: Osservazioni, ii. 532.—Bosio: par. ii., lib. i., anno 1307.—Vertot: iv. 126.
[3] Anciently, to be a Rhodian was a distinction, and some called themselves such who had not been born there. Bosio: par. ii., lib. i., anno 1309.

ancient tapestry of D'Aubuson showed terribly fierce assaults. More would be certain about the taking of Rhodes, were it not for the great fire in the archives there.[1] Next was to reduce, or rather visit (for that was enough) its dependencies, the islets of which there are several, the principal being the ancient Coos, country of Hypocrates and Apelles, since Lango, at present Stanchio, erected into a fief in favour of persons who had distinguished themselves in the last Rhodian war, not without commensurate obligations and charges regarding galleys and troops. At its conquest in 1314, it was confided in administration to the Langue of Provence, though afterwards, by the general chapter held[2] at Avignon, in 1356, opened to the whole order.[3] Nor is it not to be observed that this is the first time Langues are spoken of, and seem to have crept in clandestinely; for neither at Jerusalem, Acre, or even Cyprus, are they mentioned. Nor did they fail to produce bad crops from their very beginning, though only seven at first, while most dignities were common to the whole order, at least in 1318.

Calamo, renowned for its honey, had two ex-

[1] Seb. Paoli: Osservazioni, ii. 492.—Bosio: par. ii., lib. i.
[2] Id.: Notizie, ii. 498.
[3] Bosio: par. ii., lib. i., anno 1317.

cellent ports and abounded in fresh watersprings, and, to Villaret's surprise, showed a tolerable commercial town close to the ruins of a fine city. Calchi was fertile, with a strong castle to keep off corsairs. Lero gloried in its quarries of marble. The soil of several of those islets was rich. One was splendidly wooded. Another famous for wines. Another drove a good trade in sponges brought from the bottom of the sea by divers— nor could any youth be married, until he was able to remain a certain number of minutes deep under water. But chiefly one was prized for its ship-carpenters, who had the art of building light craft renowned for swiftness all over the Levant, sail, oar, or both ways. One of the smallest islets, though designated as magisterial, because considered more peculiarly assigned to the grand master, as forming part of his private domain, St. Nicholas del Cardo, is by Bosio called Palma, and in another place, Palmosa, and that is Patmos.[1] ("Patmos, now Palmosa, where St. John wrote his revelation.")[2] And if it be so, however sterile, it is interesting to a Christian. Or are there two islands of the name of Patmos—one near Stanchio, and one

1314

---

[1] Bosio: par. ii., lib. i., anno 1314. His words are clear; "Lisola del Patmo, modernamente detta Palmosa."
[2] Comp. Geogr., ii. 12.

close to Samos?[1] The question then is, which was of the writer of the Apocalypse? for that is the one which belonged to the Hospitallers.

Nizara (Porphyrus), famous through all the Levant for its mill and building stones, had been likewise noted for its hot baths, and for its delicious fruit of all sorts, soon became as it were a second Rhodes, having a beautiful town, oramented with marble columns and statues, in signal abundance; and afterwards a grand cross of the order resided there, and it rose to be a bishop's see, suffragan of the Rhodian Archbishopric.[2]

After which review, in the company of Anthony De Beck (who it is doubtful whether he was or was not a member of the order, but then Papal legate, and at one time Bishop of Durham),[1] Villaret returned to Rhodes eager to indulge in a life of luxury and repose from his devoirs. But that was not yet to be, and the pirates who had escaped, had roused their Mahometan brethren of Asia Minor— among whom a thriving Tartar horde, and it is possible with some Comnenian blood. Yet the celebrated Ottoman had to retreat; although the

As in Mr. Murray's recent Map to his "Handbook in the East."

[2] Seb. Paoli: Notiz. Geogr., ii. 502.

Cod. Dipl. Geros, ii., Num. xviii.—Seb. Paoli: Osservazioni, ii. 527.

knights were not given time to erect walls. New proof that valiant hearts and hands are the best of fortifications, and need none. But though Ottoman was driven from Rhodes, he attacked the other adjoining islets and ravaged them; and an obstinate and fierce war ensued, during which the knights are said to have received much assistance from Amadeo V. of Savoy, and that, to perpetuate the memory, his descendants have ever since worn the white cross; and, as device, the word *Fert* meaning *Fortitudo ejus Rhodum tenuit*. And why may it not be quite true?[1] To write devices by initials, was the custom then. As to the cross, indeed they bore it long before; probably from the first crusade; but they may have continued to bear it more exclusively, not using much any other, whether eagle or lion—the rather that they had become sovereign and independent princes, and wished to show it; and, as Menestrier observes truly, at that time amongst the Italians the cross in an escutcheon was a sign of freedom and independence, and hoisted by any municipality as a proclamation of liberty. It was the cap of liberty of the period.[2] Thus Florence had a cross half

[1] With some difference of date; but in the main Bosio agrees with the usual opinion about F. E. R. T.; par. ii., lib. vi. anno 1444.

[2] Art. de Blason, cap. vi.

white and half red, with the word *libertas*.[1] And the small town of Macerata having declared itself independent, displayed a cross and rebelled against its former government.[2] Undoubtedly since Amedeo was in England in 1309, and at Rome in 1310, he could not be at Rhodes in 1310; but he could very well be there in 1315, true date of his succour in question.[3] It is surely strange to find a vacancy in 1315. But so it is. In 1306 he is in Dauphiny, in 1307 at the royal marriage in London, in 1308 at Montmellan with his son and Beatrice of Savoy; in 1309, at the coronation of the King of England; in 1310 at Chambery, and with the emperor on his passage into Italy; in 1311 he is to be traced at Vercelli, Milan, Rome, until his return to Piedmont in 1313; in 1314 in Dauphiny; but there we would have a stop, if it were not that he was at Rhodes in 1315. These particulars, because other historians have decided that Amadeo's visits to London and Rome precluded the possibility of his Rhodian feats. But on the contrary, it is very near proof certain that this chronology is correct, since it coincides with the year he could be at

[1] Borghini : Dis., ii. 143.—Appendix, cxiv.
[2] Appendix, cxv.
[3] Buffier : Hist.—Nice foro Gregorio, vii.—Laonico Calcondela, 1.—Villani.—Appendix, cxv.

Rhodes; whereas, if it followed the vulgar error of placing the attack on the islets in 1310 (as for many other reasons no extremely attentive reader can), then indeed the whole ancient Piedmontese tradition were indubitably a fable. As to Amadeo's ancestors having worn the cross before him, that is no impediment to his having gone to Rhodes. Even the coin alleged may have been by the Louis, Baron of Vaud, who died in 1350; just as well as by his uncle of the same name, who died in 1301. And the *Fert* and the dog's collar on the tomb of the father of Amadeo V. prove nothing; for though very ancient, who knows when it was erected? If in the latter years of Amadeo V. himself, it would be a flattery to assign his device to his father. Such things are not uncommon in the fine arts. Virgil has several anachronisms. And in Raphael's great painting, the School of Athens, are there not cardinals and friars as auditors of Socrates, and companions of Plato? Therefore, registered as historic be what the learned diplomatist has high Piedmontese authority for, if his own were not more than sufficient. The knights *were* enabled by Amadeo V. in 1315, to expel the Ottoman invaders from the islets, so that Rhodes might leisurely rebuild itself and fortify. But a few months were enough for quiet and luxury to

1315

breed indiscipline. Villaret, blinded by his glory, was unable to withstand the temptation of success. Instead of giving good example to his young knights, quite the contrary. They had in him an excuse for every excess. And it appeared that valour and luck legitimated vice.

Langue was a word of division regarding the order, but of union between conspirators. If that was too harsh a term to be applied to those young knights then, it was quickly to suit their mutinous conduct. Nor were the riches, supposed flowing into the treasury from the downfal of their former companions-in-arms without offering a veil of sanction to every wild and ruinous expense. In vain one of the elder knights exhorted them to beware, that it was the very same turbulence and vanity that led the Templars to destruction; that their enemies desired nothing more than to be furnished with an excuse to ruin them; that it was not from love of Hospitallers that Philip le Bel burned the Templars; that if the Parliament of Paris[1], and even Rome herself, declared the Hospitallers were to possess all the property, yet that was only in show, to fling the odium on them, and the King of France in fact seized every stiver of it in his dominions for himself; and that the Pope

[1] Cod. Dipl. Geros., ii., Num. xxviii.—Appendix, cxvi.

well knew how, in despite of all his fine words, the different sovereigns and their greedy nobles would in some way or other contrive to get most of the rest of it; that no reason whatsoever to expect that the cardinals and Papal prelates would not do, as with their oily discourse they had always been in the habit of doing—namely, under various pretexts, wriggle themselves, they or their relatives, into the richest commanderies and other benefices of the order, and dispense graces to favourites at no allowance, and in substance pursue with ungrateful pertinacity their own best defenders; and even the worse ill-treat them, the more they are sure of their devotedness, and that they would submit to any injustice, rather than rise against their spiritual chief; that they ought not to close their eyes against what he had just received, this copy of the French king's letter to the Pope, by which it is evident he desired to extinguish the Hospital as well as the Temple, and he read to them his true expressions.[1]

"Now if by reform that same was purely meant, you know I should not object; but it is that I know he means reform such as he used with the Templars. Clement praised those unfortunate gentlemen to the last, until they were entrapped into destruction.

[1] Cod. Dipl. Geros., ii., Num. xxvii.—Appendix, cxvii.

Under pretence of reforming us, or uniting us to a new military order, the intention is to destroy us, and deprive us of all we have, and merge our name even (which has become too glorious for safety) in another from some unknown vocabulary, to serve its turn, and shortly be abolished. Yes, had our ancestors and we all acted less nobly well, we should not now be in so dangerous a predicament. Yet, at the very moment when prudence the most consummate is so requisite, you draw down the reproaches of censorial hypocrites. It is to ruin you and us all."

Yet what could be done, when Villaret, with his own debauchery, publicly warranted that of his subjects? This, and his monstrous favouritism, and occasional haughtiness and undue severity, and still more undue indulgence, caused tumults, which ripened into revolts, and even attacks upon his life. So that he had to throw himself on the Pope's protection; and we have Papal documents to this day of those disgraceful scenes. First, comes a letter of recommendation brought by a person who may have been a spy, *to console and advise*,[1] and next the brief. " We are sorry to know you have been assaulted, and obliged to fly from Rhodes by your own knights into a

1317

[1] Cod. Dipl. Geros., ii., Num. xlii.

fortress in another part of that island; and although their demeanour appears to have been most improper, yet you are accused of having partly occasioned it; so that we cite both them and you into our presence, to investigate the affair, and decide on due information." This parchment, like so many others, has just escaped out of its hiding-place, and appears in history for the first time.[1] Rumours went of one of Villaret's confidential menials having been bribed to poison, or otherwise murder his master, upon whose flight the rioters elected as *locum-tenens* the old knight Sir Maurice de Pagnac, who hardened them in their resistance to despotism; and that, little by little, such as Villaret would end by erecting an absolute tyranny instead of the order's primitive free institutions. To answer which, the Pontiff at the same time wrote a brief to Pagnac, calling him likewise to Avignon,[2] and another, naming a vicar of the order.[3] Assuredly a new Pope, whatever internal dissent he may have felt from his predecessor's policy, followed it in the main, not sorry at this opportunity for a reasonable intervention, under cover of which he could deprive the knights and their grand master

---

[1] Cod. Dipl. Geros., ii., Num. xliii.—Appendix, cxviii.
[2] Id., Id., Id. xliii.—Appendix, cxix.
[3] Id., Id., Id. xlv. and xlvi.—Appendix, cxx.

of all independence, and dispose of his dignity himself, which eminently agrees with the mysterious terms wherein he writes to the King of France,[1] as well as that appearance of pleading the Hospitallers' right to the property of the Templars in the bull to the King of Sicily; but finishes by approving of his Majesty's determination, though he could not but have known full well it was to confiscate the chief part of it to the Sicilian crown, as indeed he did.[2] Nor is not the same evil intention observable in the bull to the King of Spain, in which he assents to the formation of the Montese Concordat consigning the Moorish war to another to be chosen, and the Valencian property of the Templars to maintain that new knighthood, and the Arragonese property given to the Hospitallers, with the accompaniment of what was sure to eat it up, the united expenses of that entire operation.[3] Up to this date, it is clear that the commanders were mere administrators, removable at will upon the smallest sign, who retaining the value of their own dress and food, paid all the rest into the common treasure; and likewise it is laid down formally

1318

---

[1] Cod. Dipl. Geros., ii., and Num. xli.
[2] Id., Id. Num. xl., xlvii.—Appendix, cxxi.
[3] Cod. Dipl. Geros., ii. Num. xxxvii. and Num. xxxviii.

by Bosio, that the *supreme* tribunal of the order is the chapter-general, to which the grand master and his knights and clergy alike submit.[1]

So Villaret, and Pagnac, and some knights, went to Avignon, and Villaret was sentenced to accept a priory, but totally independent of any future grand master, and only responsible to the Holy See, which, to the guiltless order, was a double sacrifice, losing the rent of a priory, and paying a prior in no way obedient to it, and having a grand master either directly named by the Pope, or indirectly chosen under his influence. Nor did his Holiness deny himself the satisfaction of hurrying to direct a brief to the fallen grand master, wounding him more severely from the novelty, and showing him that he was no longer an independent sovereign, but miserably dependent, both in temporals and spirituals; for, after writing to Villaret as a king, and companion of kings, even so far on his journey as Naples,[2] he, within a few weeks, changes tone altogether, and does not give the fallen even the title of knight, as if he were not such any longer, but quite a private person, to whom he doles out a

[1] Bosio: par. ii., lib. i, anno 1321.
[2] Cod. Dipl. Geros., ii., Num. l. and li.—Arch. Vatic. Secr.—Appendix, cxxii.

priory, in charity, at another's expense.[1] How long Sir Fulk continued to vegetate, is scarce worth notice; yet he remained in that forgotten state for years, never stirring from a castle of his sister's, to which he had retired, near Montpellier, where he was buried.[2] But his station was instantly conferred on Sir Helion de Villannova,[3] by a few knights summoned to elect him in the Papal palace itself; which, if an honour, was such a one as induced the belief in many people, that he was not merely favoured by the Pontiff, as he was publicly, but that he altogether received the dignity from him, and not from the order. If so, he testified his gratitude in kind, by selling one of the order's estates to his Holiness, near his native Cahors, where, being sprung from a low family, he was proud to enrich it.[4] The pecuniary embarrassments of the order were real in proportion to its flushed expectations, when promised the exaggerated property of the Templars; but, in point of fact, only just so great as a usurer might wish, or perhaps

1319

---

[1] Cod. Dipl. Geros., ii., Num. liv. and lv.—Arch. Vatic. Secr. Appendix, cxxiii.

[2] Appendix, cxxiv.

[3] Bosio: par. ii., lib. ii, anno 1322.—Seb. Paoli: Serie, ii., 463.

[4] Bosio: par. ii., lib. ii, anno 1325.—Vertot: v. 185, affirms the said Pope was son of a cobbler.—Grandson of a private soldier, according to an annotator on Platina, iii. 196, Note A.

cause, in order to lend it ready money at an enormous interest, or purchase its lands cheap. The date having been objected to, Seb. Paoli thought it necessary to corroborate it by an unanswerable document—the letter of John XXII. himself, which the perspicacious Bosio had never seen (since coming from the Vatican), but had formed his opinion without it—letter in which Villannova is advised not to abdicate, but accept the place of grand master to which he had been called—letter containing the names of the knights at the election, and dated Avignon, 14th of the Calends of July, 1319.[1] Perhaps in Bosio's time, things were too fresh; but now what harm that we know the secrets of the drama at Avignon, and the name of all the actors, by a document detected in the most secret corner of the archives of the Vatican and labelled secret? Villannova's election was irregular, what of that? It serves only to steady an historian in his path to truth, and enables him to find his way through those remote labyrinthine antiquities. Earlier it might have served malignity, but at present only aids laborious and innocent investigation. What quantity of good or harm the French revolution did, may be matter of opinion,

[1] Cod. Dipl. Geros., ii., Num. vi.— Gi. Vatic.—Appendix, cxxx.

but that it opened the archives of the world cannot be doubted.

Nor did the vicar cease command at Rhodes; but continued there as the *locum-tenens* of Villannova, who delayed a long time in Europe, impeded by a severe malady, and visiting the establishments in France, where (at Montpellier) he held a general chapter.[1] There Sir John Builbrulx was turcopolier. Does Builbrulx sound like an English name? Yet English he certainly was, and could not but be, since turcopolier. If ever was an exception, it was not at such a period; for then, for the first time, the order was formally divided into languages. The three grand crosses which hitherto had by custom never failed to be conferred on Englishmen alone, Grand Prior of England, Bailly of the Eagle, Turcopolier, were in that chapter-general made the property of the English language. That Builbrulx was at the same time made one of the conventual baillies, is a proof he was esteemed singularly sagacious and upright; for such baillies were chiefs of their different languages, or nations, and obliged always to reside with the grand master.[2] The use had crept on by degrees, and been found convenient; yet did not become legal with unanimity. For

---

[1] Seb. Paoli: Serie, ii. 464.
[2] Bosio: par. ii., lib. ii., anno 1330.

though it was in a distant country, respecting Rhodes, and on treacherous ground, where it was requisite to weigh well every word; with the recent example of the Templars before their eyes *in terrorem*, and supported by high authority on the reasonable plea of equalising the commanderies; still there was no small minority against it, but nevertheless the majority made it a standing law. We for the future shall have to speak of Languages, for the present only seven,[1] exact conformity with Hallam, but soon eight, and of Inns belonging each to a Language. Consider them like what our own Inns of Court once were, European, not Eastern invention. No peculiarity of the order, which in that respect only kept clearly in the wake of custom; not merely for meals, but also for debating, each exclusively in its own language. That at the grand master's and in the chapters being Latin, French, or Italian, or a mixture of all three—a sort of Lingua Franca, varying according to time and place. "Unwilling am I," said a knight, "to find fault in this chapter general, with whatever is the practice. Yet are there many who like me prefer staying here at home in Europe, where there are many occasions of usefully exerting bravery and military skill—where our religious rites can be more

[1] Hallam: Lit of Europe, i.

solemnly performed, and whence there may chance to be a crusade—rather than drag a tepid existence in a small island so distant from Palestine, that it appears to several against both the letter and spirit of our profession—as it did to our choicest members at Cyprus—persisting to squander our time, wealth, and force in hostilities against pirates, on that unfaithful element to which we were unused (and worse if we become used to it), instead of backing our own good steeds on a wide continent, not shut up in a paltry ship, but established in some illustrious metropolis, where we can apply to our duty of exercising magnificent hospitality on an extended scale, and curing the infirm of every Christian nation, or advance to battle at the head of the armies of all Christendom. It is this vile Rhodian war that has reduced us to these present embarrassments of finance,[1] and the monstrous interest we have to pay to the Florentines. Thence a division in our order, as is proved by our holding this debate in land not our own, and our order shall dwindle away perhaps, until its very existence shall soon cease. A few may grumble; but here we have our grand master with us, and here let us remain."

And when riches were spoken of, and the great

[1] Cod. Dipl. Geros, ii., Num. liv., lvi. Vatic.—Consideratis oneribus dicti Hospitalis; magnum ejusdem prejudicium.

expenses to which Villaret had put the order by the conquest of Rhodes, it called up a rather aged knight: " Yet we should be rich (though probably for only moments) if the property of the Templars had been given us, as promised. It is not the Rhodian war (nobly employed money), nor was Villaret then other than a deserving hero, and as such his name will go down to posterity; but it was crafty politics that broke down his fine mind, and drove him on dissipation, which was artfully increased by the promises held out to him. I know I am trenching on perilous matters, but nevertheless I had rather say the truth, and be also burned alive, than remain silent before this august meeting of our own brethren, and seem by my silence to consent to throw a blot, through our late grand master, on our whole brave body and their exertions on so many days of glory, at the expense of so much blood, and the lives of so many of our renowned companions. Are not the papers in two mountains before us? And besides what we see, how much is unseen? It is easy to trick warriors. A million times rather tricked than trick. From this basest of wickedness, O Lord, deliver us! I despise their tricks far too deeply to envy them. Much better would it have been for us—a thousand times better—never to have been insulted with offer of any of the Templars' spoils. A base offer! but worse, a plot to ruin us.[1] Bulls misled us into expenses that indeed are ruinous; effeminate vices (not the Rhodian war) generated the consequent destructive and shameful debts, and were beneficial to none but villanous usurers. Behold the rolls of those royal and imperial folk[2]—whom I cannot much blame, since they possibly act in favour of their own dominions. Rely on those despots, who will! Few of them but take the Templars' property to themselves, under a thousand excuses. So we incur all the odium, and they have all the profit; even so, it is better for us not to have ill-gotten goods. It were a profanation, a desecration, an infamy never to be washed out. Besides I tell you what has been often told you by revered lips, that it is the work of infernal conspirators. Instead of vainly descanting on that, let us bend to necessity, and allow that there is a relaxation of discipline which ought to be amended by obliging all the commanders to leave off loitering in Europe, and remove to head quarters, wherever it be, for at least some years, under pain of losing their com-

[1] Cod. Dipl. Geros., ii, Num. xxii., xxiii., xxiv., xxxviii., xxxix., xl., xli., liv., lviii.—Giunt. Vatic., iii., iv.,v.—Appendix, cxxvi., cxxvii.
[2] Cod. Dipl. Geros., ii., Num. xxvii, xxx., xxxi., xxxii., xxxiii., xxxiv., xxxv., lvi.

manderies; and let such residence be a necessary qualification for any of the high employments. Rhodes will thus cease to be looked on as a place of exile; and idlers, by this removal from infection, may learn some probity and honour. Therefore, most venerated vicar, I beseech you not to think of me—though one of your most dutiful servants—but of what I have said; and allow me to propose a law of that nature to this assembly."

And so it was proposed and passed, and stands on the statute-books still. But was it executed? It is to be hoped it was, sometimes at least—however feebly.[1] That vicar, or *locum-tenens*, was the De Pins who had been made such in 1317, and still retained the situation, the grand master being absent. Never had the vicar the least pretension to be more, nor is he ever named anything else, in the documents.[2] Vertot has no excuse![3] Vertot is full of errors. Thus he talks of a bull of 1323, and upon no such thing being found, he is supposed to have meant that of 1322. Which is however to the King of England, and not to the

1325

---

[1] Bosio: par. ii., lib. ii., anno 1331.
[2] Cod. Dipl. Geros., ii., Num. lix.—Appendix, cxxvi.
[3] Seb. Paoli: Serie Chron., ii., 463.—Cod. Dipl. Geros., ii., Num. xlv.-Appendix, cxxv.

Hospitallers.[1] Or who is willing to believe what he tells us of De Pins (who had been vicar now above twelve years, during which the order went on acquiring naval customs and that vicar himself an able seaman) having put, under whatever plea of expediency, all the able-bodied but unarmed men of a colony to the sword, and permitted the rest and the women and children, to be carried into slavery?[2] Vertot cites no authority for the enormity he relates, and proud am I of my inability to discover any. That John XXII. kept a sharp look out, on at least his noblest spies, is evident from his secret letter to the order's prior at Pisa.[3] Sir Thomas Larchier, who was Prior of England in 1329 and had been for several years before, abdicated; and Sir Leonardus de Tybertis took his place. Why? Was it a single exception at the king's desire? But he might have been an Englishman, though then the order's ambassador at Venice.[4] At all events, Tybertis lived little.[5]

1327

Nor even when Villannova embarked at last in

[1] Cod. Dipl. Geros., ii., Num. lviii.
[2] Vertot: v. 184.
[3] Cod. Dipl. Geros., ii., Num. lx.—Giunt. Vatic. Secret. —Appendix, cxxxi.
[4] Cod. Dipl. Geros., ii., Num. lxi.—Seb. Paoli: Osservazioni, ii. 537.
[5] He was the twenty-second Prior of England. Appendix, xxx.

1332, was it without some difficulty on the score of his health, which was not yet strong enough to support so long a voyage, in the Pontifical opinion.[1] Nor did he find any difficulty to engage the vicar to deliver up the supreme power, nor had there not been transactions during that length of period, chiefly as to adding to the fortifications of the city of Rhodes itself, and the other chief towns of the island, as well as various strong towers and castles round all its coasts, not omitting several fortresses in the environing islets. The shipping too had considerably increased, and now merited the name of a fleet. Just previous to the arrival of Villannova, the King of Castile had attempted to create a new order, and endow it with the spoils of the Templars, but the Pope refused his consent; which did not make any essential change, since they went to Calatrava just the same, which could not but occasion discontent in the Spanish language at Rhodes.[2]

One of the first things which Villannova and his senate had to decide, was whether to enter into a league with France and Venice against the Turk, which that the order assented to

[1] Cod. Dipl. Geros., ii., Num. lxiii.—Vatic. Secret.
[2] Cod. Dipl. Geros., ii., Num. lxii.—Vatic. Secret.—Appendix, cxxxii.

is not curious; nor that Venetians soon left them in the lurch.[1] But what of Sir Deodate and the dragon? St. George and the dragon for a wager! It is about this time! What of that?—What? That it is a fable to be sure. Yet its being totally a fable (as following good authorities, I am prepared to affirm) were no sufficient reason for not relating it. Beyond doubt Livy knew, just as thoroughly as his modern readers, that many of the things he tells could not possibly be true. Yet he tells them nevertheless! For they showed what those times believed. When savages bored a traveller with some wonder of their idol, that he recounts it is no proof in the least that he believes it. No truth surely, in itself; but it is true in this, and thus far, that it demonstrates how over easy they are in credence. Why should the historian be taxed with the fictions he quotes? His business is to inform us how such a nation thought, not how he thinks. Describing a crime, is he for that criminal? But the story I refer to would give a false opinion of those times; as if it could have been entertained then, and I am quite persuaded it could not; but that it was the invention of posterity, when become too prone to accuse their ancestors. Superhuman, perhaps! But this was nothing superhuman, nor even pretended to be.

[1] Cod. Dipl. Geros., ii., Num. lxv.—Vatic. Secret.

People had the contrary before their eyes, and it accorded with their every-day experience to resort to facile means of instantly annihilating a hideous wild beast, without any personal exposure of coming to close quarters with it, which would have only been ridiculous in those distant days, as well as in our own. Regulus and his army in Africa, do not apply here. The Romans having but swords, lances, and arrows, how could they manage with a boa whose dried skin measured one hundred feet and more? But not only gunpowder was used a little by the Turks, in 1330; but was so ordinary at that time, that they made use of it invariably and profusely, at every little battle or siege, showed every person what sufficed, at once, to consume any scales, however thick. And, although the generous spirit of the knights might reject it against fellow-creatures; yet naturally they could not be scrupulous concerning a noxious serpent, which had already been fatal to some of their own companions. The Greek fire could be thrown either from the hand in the shape of a grenade, or from tubes, like a rocket, at any mark a considerable distance off; and what could melt and consume iron and brass, could the toughest hide. Or a ball or steel point, if shot from the zembourek, could pass through a stout cuirass of the best steel; and what greater resistance from a skin, however hard? So there would have been no necessity for a personal combat, on horseback—too pickering round and round as at a regular tourney. The warrior may have had his couple of bulldogs trained in Europe, to attack the belly, which is the weak point in most animals; and on that the whole story seems to have been raised, not by contemporaries, but in posterior ages. So it were doubly erroneous in me to enter into a prolix account of what is probably not only false, but tends to give a false opinion of the times in question.[1] Perhaps I have said too much about it as it is; but I thought it necessary to give substantial reasons for rejecting what cuts such a figure in Vertot, and is, indeed, in great part, an idle tale magnified into undue importance by himself.[2] As to the inscription on the tomb, " cy gist le vainqueur du dragon"—a more than dubious fact—that epitaph avails little, except

[1] Seb. Paoli: Serie Chron., ii. 464.
[2] Vertot: v. 194. Yet as I may have tickled curiosity, which was not my intention, here is the whole substance of the story, warning it dull enough. A dragon in the island of Rhodes, killed several people, and as many knights as went to attack him; so the grand master forbade any more. But Sir Deodate went to France, and returning with his dogs, slew the monster. Instead of praise, he was punished for disobedience; yet acquired the name of Champion, and it is said to have been written on his tomb.

you can tell who was the dragon. What is sure is, that the warrior was noted for his independent boldness of spirit, and that his order had much to exasperate their minds at that period; and even while a mere knight, he was looked upon by his brethren as their champion. They were too much occupied with a human dragon, to have leisure for an inferior class; threatened as the order were with that prodigious expense, the maintenance of the entire Christian fleet,[1] not voluntarily, but against their will, and clearly beyond their ability, in spite of their most oppressive self-taxation; *mortorio* and *vacante* being then first levied, as well as the plate and jewels of the dead, with whatever could be saved by a rigid limiting of the knights' table to one substantial dish, flesh or fish, and pursued by homilies severer than to the Templars, at the very moment those luckless gentlemen had been under sentence of dissolution and martyrdom, it might be expected a like destiny awaited themselves. While they were in a permanent state of war with the Turk, who never left them a moment's quiet— all their heroic efforts did not prevent European slanderers from converting the brightest trophy of their domestic politics, that not a poor man was in their dominions, into a cause of grave reproof; for

[1] Bosio: par. ii., lib. ii., anno 1344.

at this very date is it recorded, how under their wise government mendicancy had entirely disappeared, there being plenty of labour for every individual in health, and for the sick and invalid a magnificent hospital to retire to, where they found abundant comforts of all kinds spiritual and temporal;[1] confronting which, and the contented mediocrity of commerce and of social luxuries at that time in Rhodes, with the exuberance of wealth, mendicity, discontent and worse, and of colonies and manufactures at present in the most advanced nation in Europe, suggest an intricate question for wiser heads than mine. Yet was this their excellent example of real charity and true statesmanship, turned into an accusation of not giving alms, or rarely and but little. No wonder then, if their most inoffensive recreations were made sins of the blackest hue. Exiles, ascetics, cut off from the enjoyment of society, a sluggard called it criminal in them to have fine dogs and horses—as if it were a holier thing to indulge in curs and bone-setters, forgetting they were not mendicant friars, but soldiers of the noblest houses of Christendom, young barons and heirs to large fortunes, if they pleased.[2]

[1] Vertot: v. 192.
[2] Cod. Dipl. Geros., Num. lxix.—Appendix, cxxxiii.

Sir Philip de Thame was twenty-third Prior of England in 1342, and long before—and a great favourite of the then King (Edward III.), who 1343 with difficulty allows of his going to Rhodes, and requires his return quickly, for that his government cannot well go on without him; and that he was an Englishman, so not to quit the kingdom without leave, under a great fine.[1] A violent Turkish campaign rendered the year 1346 more full of fierce conflicts and dissensions than usual,[2] 1346 in which the Hospitallers of course took a prominent part; when, in the midst of such scenes, poor Villannova died, to the great grief of the Pope, as was to be expected.[3]

---

[1] Cod. Dipl. Geros., ii., Num. lxviii.—Seb. Paoli writes Thames; others, Thane.—Appendix, xxx.
[2] Cod. Dipl. Geros., ii., Num. lxxi.
[3] Seb. Paoli: Serie, ii. 464.

CHAPTER II.

SIR DEODATE DE GOZON the magnanimous, must have been elected before the latter days of June in 1346; since one of the documents found by Seb. Paoli in the secrets of the Vatican, is the Papal congratulation on his election to the grand mastery, dated the 4th of the Kalends of July, the fifth of his Pontificate.[1]

The story of that courageous and princely Provençal's choice of himself, is quite as fabulous as about the serpent; for Clement VI. in that confidential paper affirms he who was grand preceptor[2] hesitated whether he would accept the dignity of grand master unanimously offered to him, and only

---

[1] Cod. Dipl. Geros., ii., Num. viii. Vatic. Secret.—Appendix, cxxxiv.

[2] Bosio has Great Commander, by a slight error of the press, I suppose, or pen; and Bosio had never seen this Vatican document: par. ii., lib. iv., anno 1346.

accepted at length after mature reflection; which diffidence agrees with his two subsequent attempts at abdication,until dissuaded by the highest authority in those days. Yet during his short reign he did much, both as to the Turkish war, and domestic policy; and sent a circular to the Priors of Denmark, Sweden, and Norway, lamenting that they had never paid any responsions since the loss of Acre; yet could not but have learned the order was seated at Rhodes, so he cited them formally to send them yearly to the Receiver in Flanders.[1] Responsions were only a very easy head or quitrent on commanderies, leaving abundant sufficiency to the holders—a priory being the aggregate of several commanderies.

Sir Deodate won a sea-fight against the Turks near Lemnos, taking a hundred and twenty of their small vessels, and put to flight the thirty-two largest,[2] and while he kept the order neutral between Genoese and Venetians, when these latter over the former won a victory, celebrated through all that century,[3] he protesting he could not prevent individual knights from siding with either; and that individuals could not do much

[1] Cod. Dipl. Geros., ii., Num. lxxii.—Appendix, cxxxv.
[2] Bosio: par. ii., lib. ii., anno 1347.—Vertot: v. 224.
[3] Platina: iii. 226, Note H.

harm on either side, since they counterbalanced each other.[1] The order was in great esteem then both in Europe and the Levant, most of the chief captains in Spain and Italy being Knights of Rhodes; and as for the Pontifical States (at that time a principal Italian power) nearly all its governors of celebrity, including even the Duke of Spoleto, were of the same.[2] Sir Deodate finding many of his commanders so protected by the Pope and the Kings of France and Castile, Arragon, Portugal, England, and others, that he was unable to reduce them to obedience, he renewed his abdication in too urgent terms to be refused; and while consent (making itself precious) was coming, he employed his hours in the useful toil of adding to the fortifications of the city of Rhodes, when in December of 1353, he had a stroke of apoplexy, that at his great age was instant death.[3] His successor was Sir Peter de Cornillan, or Cormelian, a Provençal gentleman, Prior of St Gilles, and remarkable for the regularity of his life, and austere and ancient manners; as the new Pontiff well observes in his brief to the knights, approving highly of their choice,

1353

1354

[1] Bosio: par. ii., lib. ii., anno 1356.
[2] Id.: anno 1348.
[3] Seb. Paoli: Serie Chron., ii. 464.—Bosio: par. ii. lib. ii., anno 1353.

sweet as the perfumes of myrrh![1] In the very last days of 1354,[2] a ship with the Papal banner entered the harbour of Rhodes, and soon was it known that it bore an embassy, at the head of which was the Grand Prior of Castile, who, with the other two commanders, had a stately audience from the grand master almost immediately. " Not only with that letter, dated last August, and which orders me back to Avignon within February next, and if the first part of my voyage has been dilatory, the fault is of foul weather, and not mine; nor shall it be mine in the other half either, for I shall return on board as soon as I have a reply, this very day. But also I am charged by his Holiness to tell the grand master and council how continually he is receiving complaints[3] of the inaction and lethargy of the order; and that they are living too far from Palestine, where they ought to reside, and carry on war against the Turk, as the whole world knows they could; that even if they lived in Greece or Italy, it were better than in this little out-of-the-way island; that the fortifications you are erecting round Rhodes, are totaly useless and superfluous, and merely display your own ill-will, and determi-

[1] Cod. Dipl. Geros., ii., xi. Giunt. Vatic. Secret.
[2] Bosio: par. ii., lib. ii., anno 1354.
[3] Cod. Dipl. Geros., ii., Num. lxxiii.

nation to be of no utility to Christendom; that you ought to be giving battle to the Paynim in some part of the Continent, where success would be of real importance and extremely easy; that it is the public voice, it would be greatly preferable to create a new order, and cut you down as a withered tree, like the Templars; and that, finally, your Smyrna quota should not be allowed to fall into arrear, but be paid annually at Avignon, as treaties duly explained prescribe, and his Holiness commands peremptorily."[1] Which struck the poor old grand master mute, from astonishment and mortification; whence one of the grand crosses rose, and got leave to answer: "You, Heredia, of all men, should be the last to speak thus to him your sovereign, and us your brethren! Why are you Prior of Castile and Castellan of Emposta, one of the highest of our order, and some say the highest private dignity in Europe, and next to the grand-mastery itself? Why are you ambassador at Avignon? Is it not our goodness? Do you not owe it all to us? Why take the round by Avignon? It is with us must be sought what you probably desire! Will you never discern better? Do we not wink at your errors and continual absence? You are certainly

[1] Cod. Dipl. Geros., ii., Num. lxxiv.—Bosio: par. ii., lib. ii., anno 1359.

much oftener at Avignon than Rhodes, which ought not to be. Who avoids danger here? Why this is the very post of danger and honour! Reside in Palestine! we heartily wish we could. But could we? How? His Holiness says the whole world knows we could; but I for my part am entirely at a loss to imagine how, except all Christendom jumped up in arms like one man to assist us; but that is neither possible, nor perhaps desired by that Holy See which thinks European crusades far more necessary. The Smyrna quota with us has never been in arrear, nor please God ever shall. It shall be paid strictly, as the treaty says; but not to Avignon, to be eaten up by greedy churchmen; but directly to the furnishers of arms and stores for the Turkish war. The arrears are of the Papacy, that never has paid an obolo. Leave it to the infidels to call them devils, that most brave, most barbarously ill-treated garrison.[1] We entreat the Pontiff to pray for their souls; for unless Christian succours bestir themselves, the choice of our chivalry may every hour be cut to pieces—as indeed their profession inculcates—nor will they shrink from it! But should we calumniate or disregard them? Fortifications superfluous? Would they may not

---

[1] Diables enragos.—Chereffedin Ali.—Seb. Paoli: Osservazioni, ii. 539.

be found not strong enough! Why threats and reproofs towards such honest servants? New order is but the usual scarecrow. Glorious fools like us are not so easy to find. What are we, if not too devoted and too patient?"

Limited as were Sir Peter's days, he had a chapter holden at Rhodes, not living as long, as with his usual inexactitude, Vertot pretends, much less nine years as Foxans, but twenty-two months as Bosio,[1] or rather until about mid autumn of 1355, as Seb. Paoli decides.[2]

His successor was Sir Roger de Pins, likewise of the language of Provence, and related to that Sir Odo de Pins, who had been the twenty-third grand master in Cyprus. This Sir Roger held a chapter at Rhodes likewise, in which many excellent statutes were made for the administration of commanders, and forbidding servants-at-arms to wear exactly the same cross as the knights. Prince of the utmost courtesy and most merciful feelings, at the same time a rigid disciplinarian, and of generosity and propriety of conduct, he reigned candid during ten no candid or quiet years.[3] Of the most splendid devotedness was the conduct of the knights, at Smyrna, in universal opinion,

1355

[1] Bosio: par. ii., lib. ii., anno 1355.
[2] Seb. Paoli: Serie, ii. 464.   [3] Id.: Id., ii. 464.

including that of their declared enemies; yet did it draw down a reproach from him[1] in whose service they were dying with a heroism that the rest of the world celebrated. They had declared the post untenable, but when ordered to hold it, they died in the attempt. What more could mortals do? " Honore tamen super omnia preservato," says the describer of that siege.[2]   1358

This twenty-ninth grand master had the statutes, which were written in French in 1300, translated, the cream of them, into Latin, and with the conventual seal to them, sent a copy to each priory.[3] It was some compensation for the injustice, where least to be expected, that a tribute of grateful respect was paid by the north of Europe, by a donation to the order, from the Marquises of Brandenburgh and Lusatia, " High Chamberlains of the Holy Roman Empire," of a kind of island between the Elbe and the Weser, and comprising several districts once a bishopric, afterwards a principality, and modernly a part of Lower Saxony. Its date is Taengermunde and Vranckenvorde in die *beati Marcelli Martyris*, 1360.[4]   1360

[1] Cod. Dipl. Geros., ii., Num. lxxiv.
[2] Seb. Paoli: Osservazioni, ii. 540.—Beltramio, quond. Leonardi de Mignanellis, de Senis tunc in illis partibus commorantis. M.S. di Siena.
[3] Bosio: par. ii., lib. iii., anno 1357.
[4] Cod. Dipl. Geros., ii., Num. lxxv.

The thirtieth grand master, if by descent a Spaniard, was a Provençal by birth, in line from the Counts of Barcelona, sovereigns of Catalogna, certainly, and perhaps of Italy.[1] Whatever blaze of glory he inherited from his ancestors, Sir Raymond de Berenger showed his were qualifications to add to its lustre. After taking Alexandria by surprise, and burning the piratical fleet in its port,[2] a very bold and necessary exploit, though at the expense of one hundred knights killed, and a great loss of horses (for those pirates spread destruction throughout the Christian shores of the Mediterranean), his return to his island was instantly followed by a letter to the procurator general for all the receivers to be commanded forthwith to send in all the responsions, and arrears, and debts, they could possibly collect, with whatever they could get on credit, to enable the order to resist the invasion of Rhodes that was on the point of ensuing by the Sultan of Babylon, in league with the Turks;[3] so that in this most urgent danger the monies were absolutely requisite to its very existence, and this official note bearing the date of

1365

---

[1] Seb. Paoli: Serie, ii. 466.
[2] Bosio: par. ii., lib. iii., anno 1365.
[3] Id. :   Id., anno 1366.

the twentieth of March, 1365,[1] demonstrates how expeditious Sir Raymond was, to have planned and executed such a feat in two winter months. A few weeks later he wrote letters to the Pope, the Emperor, the Kings of France, Hungary, England, Scotland, Arragon, Dacia, Poland, the Queen of Naples, the two Archdukes of Austria, and the Doge of Venice, to each a separate letter in Latin, imploring their aid for Christendom.[2] But what did that noble commencement avail? The letters were unattended to, and worse still, the division into Languages began already to produce its dreadful effects. That between the Languages of Provence and of Italy had got high, so began his doubts of his own ability for the grand mastership, and that another of more skill would succeed better, and he wished to abdicate; but the Pope refused his consent.[3] Do not ask what the Pope had to do with it; for the Pope was their spiritual head, and then stood very high in the estimation of all men.

In 1366, some refugee Armenians were permitted to establish in the island of Samos, and we see what industrious Bosio could not have seen; a brief to

---

[1] Cod. Dipl. Geros., ii., Num. lxxvi.
[2] Bosio: par. ii., lib. iii., anno 1366.
[3] Id.: Id., anno 1373.

the emperor instigating him to assist the Hospitallers.[1] In the same 1366, the order sends to buy horses at Naples to take to Rhodes, where, also, a chapter general met, in which the turcopolier was a Sir William Middleton.[2] Fact is we find the grand master at Genoa, with Urban V., and the Admiral and Prior of Rhodes, and many knights of the order, all of them lodged in its house in that city, in 1367.[3] Not that Gregory XI. did not remove the Papal Court from Avignon, passing by Genova, a little later, but also Urban V. had done the same, but returned and died in France.[4] In the disputes between Provence and those of Italy, an appeal was made to his Holiness, who deputed two cardinals to hear and decide; so that Languages had too soon the result of trials out of the order,[5] and if followed up had superseded grand masters and general chapters altogether, and completly undermined the first basis of its independence. What was it but not to be governed by themselves, or representatives, but by another?

1366

1367

[1] Cod. Dipl. Geros., xii. — Giunt, ii. 405.—Appendix, cxxxvii.
[2] Bosio: par. ii., lib. iii., anno 1366.
[3] Seb. Paoli: Serie, ii. 465.—Bosio.—Petrarch.—Append., Num. cxxxvi.
[4] Platina: iii. 242.
[5] Bosio: par. ii., lib. 3, anno 1372.

CHAP. II.]   ST. JOHN OF JERUSALEM.   313

In 1373, Smyrna was again in the hands of the Christians, and threatened with a mighty invasion of Turks by sea and land, the then Pope writes to the Hospitallers to guard it well, since to their care it was confided.[1] This in February, but in June he begs the grand master not to assist the Genoese, who were going to attack Cyprus.[2] And at that very same day and place, but probably at a late hour, he receives and answers an embassy from the grand master, and blames his knights, and that Raymond himself ought to restrain their freedom of speech, and that besides this written brief, which he sends by a trusty ecclesiastic, there will also be another ecclesiastic, who will let him know the same, still more seriously, by word of mouth.[3]   1373

Early in 1374,[4] there was a chapter of the order holden at Avignon, at which Berenger did not attend, for "*his great age*,"[5] but in which, though its being not in Rhodes, but on a foreign shore, testified it lay under foreign influence, nothing improper

[1] Cod. Dipl. Geros., ii., Num. xiii.—Giunt. Vatic. Secret.
[2] Id.,   Id.,   Id., xiv. Id.   Id. —Appendix, cxxxviii.
[3] Cod. Dipl. Geros., ii., Num. xv.—Giunt. Vatic. Secret.—Appendix, cxxxix.
[4] Cod. Dipl. Geros., ii., Num. lxxxi.
[5] Seb. Puoli : Osservazioni, ii. 465.

or disagreeable to him was enacted, so that his death was preceded by a gleam of content. He expired in the spring of that year; for then he was succeeded by Sir Robert de Julliac, Grand Prior of France, elected in Rhodes, but at that time in his priory. So passing by, he did his homage to the Pope, from whom he received the charge of Smyrna, in the name of his order, with an assignment on the tithes of the kingdom of Cyprus of one thousand livres annually, to maintain the garrison.[1] Not, certainly, of the hardest, yet hard, at first sight, to find *Alis* for Hales— Sir Robert Hales, who became the twenty-fourth Prior of England, towards the close of Edward the Third's reign.[2] The Scotch as well as the Irish commanderies formed an integral part of the English Language, and its grand priory the grand priory of England. Only the first of the Irish commanders was indulged with title of prior, in courtesy. Scotland did not think an empty ambiguity worth having, though its kings squabbled about it.[3]

Julliac indubitably was alive in August, 1376,[4]

1374

---

[1] Seb. Paoli: Serie, ii. 466.
[2] Bosio: par. ii., lib. iii., anno 1376.—Appendix, xxx.
[3] Id. : Id., anno 1376.
[4] Cod. Dipl. Geros., ii., Num. lxxx.—Seb. Paoli: Serie, ii. 466.—Appendix, cxl.

since we have it under his own hand in the document inserted in the bull: so that at all events they are a little in error who sustain he died in the preceding June.[1] But be it permitted to add, for my own part, that he continued grand master some days after March, 1377, date of the bull which still calls Heredia Castellan d'Emposta; who, however, became elected to the grand mastery before the 21st of August next ensuing, of which he is the *fili Magister*.[2]

1376

1377

Gregory XI., as Vertot has it, with some not unusual want of exactitude[3] as to dates—to disdain which may in his time have passed for genius— sailed from Marseilles, reached Genoa on the 18th October, 1376, landed at Corneto, and spent the Christmas there, and entered the mouth of the Tiber early in January, when Heredia, then Grand Admiral of the order, Castellan d'Emposta, is decribed as a hale old man with a white beard, holding the ship's helm,[4] and, as ambassador of the order, bearing its standard—real Gonfalon of the Church—on the entrance into Rome on the 17th of

---

[1] Seb. Paoli: Serie, ii. 466.
[2] Cod. Dipl. Geros., ii., Num. lxxxi.—Seb. Paoli: Osservazioni, ii. 541.—Appendix, cxli.
[3] Vertot: v. 289.
[4] Seb. Paoli: Serie, ii. 466.—Appendix, cxlii.

January, in 1377.[1] His election in the next spring or summer at Rhodes made him instantly set out; for until then he had been a resident at the Papal Court as the order's ambassador, and Governor of Avignon and the contiguous country for the Pope. Also he went on extraordinary embassies to France, England, Spain, his native country; but however frequent, his usual residence was Rome.[2] If it were to convert an able dangerous opponent into a zealous friend, it was surely wise policy; since, though a knight of the order, he was at all times ready to sacrifice its interest to that of the Court he served; which being the central point of Christendom at that time, and he its prime minister, he had acquired the personal esteem of nearly every noted statesman in Europe; and having added great opulence to his elevated birth and mental qualifications, he was considered a personage of extreme distinction. The misfortunes of his latter years notwithstanding, the Knights of Rhodes chose well, and he will for ever be cited as one of the best and most worthy of their noble grand masters. That his brother was Grand Justiciary of Arragon, and their ancestry of the most illustrious of Spanish grandees, is little to what he was himself. Before

[1] Platina: iii. 251.—Muratori: Note D.
[2] Bosio: par. ii., lib. iii., anno 1376.

leaving Rome, he may have been given the bull LXXXI. to regulate his conduct at Rhodes; which he did not reach,[1] since on his way he aided the Venetians to take Patras, and afterwards in an incursion into the Morea[2] with the Christian army, he, near Corinth, fell into an ambush, and was made prisoner by the Turks; who, on his refusal to allow his knights to pay a considerable sum as they offered, with three priors as hostages for the payment, he, thanking them, opposed it as contrary to the statutes and injurious to the treasury, so that, if ransomed at all, it should be by his own family, not by the order; for that though it was by a stratagem, in no fair battle, yet in whatever way, a knight imprisoned is a knight dead. On which the infidels carried him into the Albanian mountains, where he underwent the harshest slavery,[3] not however for several years, as pretended; and his family must have sent his ransom the instant they heard it, since he had got to

[1] Seb. Paoli: Serie, ii. 467.
[2] Bosio: par. ii., lib. iii., anno 1378.
[3] Yet not improbable is Bosio's version, quoting Foxanus, that the grand master was at last persuaded to abide by the first agreement, and left three hostages while the money was coming from Rhodes, which it did immediately, and in every likelihood was repaid as soon as it could come from Spain. The hostages (who all three volunteered), were, the Prior of England, of St. Gilles, and of Rome. Bosio: par. ii., lib. iii., anno 1378.

1381 Rhodes before the 28th of March, 1381, which is the date of his letter to the order's captain general in Smyrna to take and try for high treason not a knight, but an officer in the pay of that town, and if found wholly or in part guilty, have the condign sentence put into execution instantly.[1] In a chapter general during his absence, it was ordained that the knight or servant-at-arms, who did not keep his horse and a man to groom him properly, and who had not his arms in order, and did not exercise himself frequently in shooting, should neither receive food from the order nor money.[2]

If a senex in 1377, what was Heredia four years older? Yet no doubt this command alone suffices to show he had the promptitude and decision of youth. He was moreover a fine example that a lofty mind does not become penurious from age; quite the contrary, as indeed should always naturally be, for the longer man lives, the more he sees how passing little is what can be bought with money, speaking merely of this world—nor love, nor friendship; nor anything of the honours worth having—much less wisdom or things truly valuable have their price in gold; fair fame, peace of mind,

---

[1] Cod. Dipl. Geros., ii., Num. lxxxii.—Appendix, cxliii.
[2] Bosio: par. ii., lib. 3, anno 1380.

one moment's tranquil sleep, can money buy them? What veritable dross then is money! Money-maker as he had been in his youth and manhood— even to upwards of fifty, and consequently enormously rich, and *crescit amor nummi quanto ipsa pecunia crescit*, he showed himself generous and splendid, the very reverse of avaricious, from the moment made grand master; as careful of the order's interests and privileges, as before neglectful of them; and parsimonious as to its treasury, was most liberal of his own; and his splendour and generosity always went on increasing to his last breath, and he ended by becoming remarkable for something not unlike prodigality! And so it is without the least wonder, as to the brightest-minded; because the longer they exist, the clearer they discern the petty value to be put on human wealth—what a trifling portion of happiness it can purchase, if any; how shallow, fleeting, utterly insignificant, are what the purse-proud term riches! But finding the majority of his order in favour of Urban VI. as legitimately Pope, however personally tyrannical and finally odious.[1] The great

[1] Very ferocious; accused of having had five of the suspected cardinals tied up in as many sacks, and thrown into the sea during his voyage from Naples to Genoa. — Bosio: par. ii. lib. iv, anno 1384.

schism beginning in 1379, Urban died, and other Popes too, but the schism went on and lasted forty years, with infinite evils to all Christendom, and doubts and disputes among the best men.[1] Naples, Savoy, France, Arragon, Castile, taking one side, and Germany, England, Hungary, Poland, and the greatest part of Italy, the other, Heredia resolved on going to Europe, to endeavour to restore peace; yet, before he left Rhodes, took an oath not to give any place or exert magisterial authority in any way or dispose of the public property, till back on the island, according to a statute made in the late chapter convened in his own name; and carried several of the chiefs of the order with him to observe his conduct, of which they could on no occasion disapprove, for it was always in the highest degree disinterested and eminently noble. What passed in his interior, none can say; but if he rather inclined to the country he was native of, and that in which he resided so many years, it was no marvel; and if he avoided exposure to the violence of party, his companions never objected to that prudence; and in retiring to Avignon and his old friends, he appears to have renounced politics entirely, and taken a resolution to keep exclusively in

---

[1] Bosio: par. ii., lib. iii., anno 1379.

private life. Never more do we hear of his meddling with the world's affairs. Others used his name indeed, but he remained perfectly passive. It is probable he abdicated about 1383, though we have no decided proof,[1] but he is said to have lived until 1399; and during those final years, sent two ships at his own expense for the Smyrnian war, as well as large gifts of money to the order's treasury several times, without inquiring what party reigned, or who governed at Rhodes. Farewell then, brave and glorious Heredia! Farewell, high-minded nobleman. If thou didst take the wrong side, yet so did also a large minority of thine order, eight cardinals, and many of the finest countries in Europe, including the whole of thy native country, Spain, and dear, lovely France! Hard for thee to decide!

Sir Richard Caracciolo, a Neapolitan gentleman, was made the thirty-third grand master; but appears never to have been at Rhodes. And all recounted of him is, that in 1391 he established a house of Hospitallers at Florence; nor could any of his acts have been of high worth, since they were

1383

---

[1] This is the critical date according to some, when the nomination to various dignities, which until then had been conferred by the chapters general, was allotted to the grand masters in council.—Bosio: par. ii., lib. iv., anno 1383.

all subsequently annulled and forgotten.[1] And as he was born in Italy, there too he died in 1395, as his sepulchre testifies on the Aventine.[2] Of Caracciolo's grand mastery no one has a right to demur, leaving him out, like Vertot; since the inscription had the authority of the Holy See *ipso facto* by permitting it, and a cardinal renewed it when almost worn out by time.[3]

Then Sir Bartlo Caraffa bore the title of *locum-tenens* for a few months, as his tomb—also on the Aventine—shows; of whom we know little, except that he was a lover of young lions, and two years before his death, had a letter from the Common Council of Florence excusing their not being able to send him any, the cubs having died that winter of the cold; but promising him the next litter, that republic having the breed.[4] Yet since not he, it must have been a *locum-tenens* of his, though under the name of grand master, who was at the unfortunate battle of Nicopolis, where Bajazet, previous to his conflict with Timour, had to withstand the united strength of France, Venice, Papacy, Hungary, Greece, Germany, and the Knights of

1395

---

[1] Cod. Dipl. Geros., ii., Num. lxxxiv.
[2] Seb. Paoli: Serie, ii. 467.
[3] Id., Id., ii. 467.
[4] Seb. Paoli: Osservazioni, ii. 542.—Gian. Villani: x. clxxxv.

his liberty, the fierce conqueror refused to accept his word not to make war on him, and with the utmost pride exclaimed: "On the contrary, the sooner the better; you will find me always prepared, and ready to win a second Nicopolis."[1] The Christians in truth lost the battle and twenty thousand men. In 1396 was thirty-fourth grand master, Sir Philip de Naillac, of Aquitain; and to reconcile all the extreme parties, it was then that Heredia died.[2]

1396

Naillac went to Rhodes, where his conciliating manners did much good; and thence sent trusty ambassadors and agents, and one of the ablest knights, to prepare a desperate defence against a more terrible than Bajazet; and the Tartar, not from fanaticism (for of no religion was he, whatever the Persian pretend), but from sheer despotism, and because he wished to domineer over every other sovereign, and could not bear that not only Greek Constantinople, but also a small island, was defended by the water from his authority, resolved to attack Smyrna, the rather that it had resisted the Turk triumphantly for years; and that a despotic punctilio was uppermost in Timour's mind is clear

---

[1] Bosio : par. ii., lib. iv., anno 1397.—Froissart.—Michaud : Hist., v. 213.
[2] Seb. Paoli : Serie, ii. 468.

from his declaring he would be contented if his banners were set on the hissar, or citadel, which is indeed the upper Smyrna. But the knight commanding there, could of course assent to no such thing.[1] So, subsequent to various attempts, Timour got on horseback, though it was the very depth of winter, and undertook the direction of the siege himself; he being a great captain, according to the Arabian Ali, and indeed an incomparable hero —at least equal to Cyrus, Alexander, or Cæsar, according to his French biographers;[2] and after divers mines had been ineffectual, a breach was effected in the ramparts, communication with the sea cut off, and the town taken by storm, and the hissar as well, with a tremendous slaughter of every human creature within its walls—many in the heat, more in cold blood—murdered, man, woman, child. Even razed the place itself, in a considerable degree. That those of the order who were there were slain, is not surprising, though mournful. To their devotions at daybreak, and ere noon corpses. They captivated their will to obedience unto the death, doubly their duty, both as soldiers and as knights. Most valiant to the last. They fell for their own honour, and the protection of Christendom. A

[1] Seb. Paoli: Osservazioni, ii. 539.
[2] Sainctyon: Hist. du Grand Tamerlan, ed. 1679.

statute of theirs expressly forbids them any sign of lamentation. Still their historians may complain of the apathy of the persons who left them in such straits. Those persons had the excuse of the communications cut off. But why did they wait for that? Shame on Europe's miserable parties and ingratitude! Yet the noble defence is said to have a little deferred Constantinople's evil day, and perhaps saved the rest of Christendom. The Turks were bad enough, but far worse the Tartars. Timour himself may in several things have been superior to his countrymen. The "iron cage" and all about it may be mere fable; but if it be true, as universally related, that he had Bajazet's favourite son butchered, did he not share their sanguinary disposition? A young man of no conspicuous family having entered by the dispense of one Pope, and being sent by another with an injunction to make him shield-bearer of the whole order, the knights did so, though grumbling at what they declared contrary to their statutes—growing pretensions, which, if they almost always allowed, it was always with remonstrances and regret. John of Perusia was a noble-hearted person, and well worthy of promotion, whatever his birth; for from the moment of their profession, all the knights were on complete equality, nor was it allowed even to recur to past proofs, and preceding rank was waived. His converse with the choicest spirits of Christendom, and to be accustomed to the best tastes and customs of the whole civilised world, soon put him quite at his ease with his companions. We are wrong in thinking there was no civilisation at that time, because so near to what are forsooth called the dark ages. There was, but restricted to a few. And who were those few, if not the highest-bred families in Europe, of which Rhodes contained the choice? Their aristocratic youth might surely lead the fashions, and practise whatever of civilisation existed. That they used table plate we have seen, and very costly foreign furs and embellishments for their houses, horses, arms, armour; and two centuries earlier, we find their grand master sending a courier from Jerusalem to Bohemia, with the keys of one of their fortified castles, to King Wratislau, in order that he and his might rest in it as long as they pleased, for that it stood on the road he had to pass from Asia Minor into Syria. Now what more splendid hospitality? Would it not be a grand thing at present from England to France? But then it was from south of Jordan to north of the Danube. If travelling enlighten the mind (as it does), who travelled more than those knights? Why, they were always travelling. Their head-quarters displayed the best of different customs, and had all the chief tongues then spoken in Europe, and others that are dead there, or were never living there. If gold forks were used by the fine ladies in Constantinople, let us recollect that at that exact time one of the knights was its emperor. Who had them, if not he? And the famous Frederick I. of Germany, did he not delight in saying he was their equal? And the royal houses of France and England, we may be quite sure there was nothing finer in either than with their near relatives, the Knights of Rhodes. If it be learning to be versant with all that remained of old Greece and Rome, and to be excellent in various sciences, but particularly such as relate to war, and not deficient in whatever of literature Europe or modern Greece offered, they had fairer opportunities than then existed anywhere else. If their table was reduced to a single dish, that was at a moment of great exertion, and even then related only to themselves, not to their guests; of whom they had generally more than one imperial or royal personage to maintain in beseeming grandeur. That they had young lions domesticated, hounds trained in France, hawks, and field sports, has been shown, and quite natural. Enough of their domestic architecture remains at Rhodes to shame even our present mansions; and their buildings were only a reminiscence of Palestine, a poor miniature; as Famagosta of Acre. They appear to have been no great writers; but that resort of nations was in itself an academy. Soldiers have occasionally plenty of leisure to study. But Perusia soon closed his career; for he was ordered to Smyrna, where, after that brilliant defence, he and the entire garrison perished to a man. Vertot mistakes the Persian, who only says some of the inhabitants escaped by swimming out to the ship as they did; but the sad truth is, the knights were all killed. Timour's black banner had been hung out; the first day's white meaning *surrender*; the second's red, *blood of a few*; the third's black, *universal destruction*. As to the heads, the difference between Christians and flat-nosed Tartars was patent. Total destruction was the delight of the Tartars. The description of the state in which they had left Hungary about this time makes one's blood curdle. "We began to visit those deserts so lately such populous districts; the steeples were all we found in part standing; so we plodded from steeple to steeple, our only landmarks; for leagues and leagues not a house; high weeds and brushwood everywhere; some remains of roots and onions, nothing else, in what had been the gardens of the peasantry, only food we could find, and glad to get it; but too generally we had to live on air. We never met a living soul for a long time; we had to sleep beneath no roof, for not one did we ever find; after eight days we entered what used to be a town, but there too, not a single living creature, but only bones and heads: at last the King of Hungary arrived with some knights of Rhodes, and then we were assured the Tartars were gone."[1]

Naillac in person led a party against the fort, held by some Tartars left stationed there by Timour when he returned to Samarcand; and, having exterminated them, built a new, very strong fortress on what is supposed by many to be the precise site of the ancient Halicarnassus, and called it St. Peter's of the Freed; and about 1399 it became the sole asylum for all enslaved Christians to escape to along that coast of Asia Minor. The knights kept there a famous race of very large watch-dogs, who learned to distinguish men, with an instinct at least equal to that of those of the Grand St. Bernard. A Christian refugee, having thrown himself into the bottom of

[1] Joannis Thurocz: Chron. Hungarium.—Bib. Crois., iii. 215.—Rogerii Hungari Chron.

a well, or rather cistern, to avoid the Turks, who pursued him, he must have died of hunger, but for one of those sagacious and faithful animals, who, during several days, threw him down the greater portion of the bread given to him every morning for his own nourishment; until the servant, who dealt out the breads, surprised to see the dog got leaner every day, set to find out what he did with his food, and discovered the truth to his astonishment. So the good mastiff acquired his niche in history; of which who shall deprive him?

This celebrated fort had seven lines of bastions and walls landward, and on that side might be really inexpugnable; whoever got within it, must have passed seven gates. Over the inmost, however, was inscribed an avowal that to keep it, required more than human ability: *Nisi Dominus custodierat, frustra vigilat qui custodit;* but towards the sea was the point of attack; yet to take it, you must first have taken Rhodes itself. *Saint Pierre de Libertini* was now its name, and its site was won the very same year that Smyrna fell—1399.[1]

Later, Naillac's wise policy preserved Cyprus

---

[1] Bosio: par. ii., lib. iv.—Seb. Paoli: Notiz. Geogr., ii. 499.—Appendix, cxlviii.

from a civil war, of which Venetians, Genoese, and French, were blowing the coals.[1]   1403

The despot of the Morea—a Porphyrogenitus—wishing to sell his dominions, got the stipulated sum from the order, partly in money, and partly in jewels; but the Spartans refused to be sold, or let the magisterial commissaries into the town at all. So the bargain had to be broken, and the value refunded; but the imperial swindler having spent or hidden the bulk of it, the order had much trouble to obtain back their own, and only by quotas and after years.[2]

Much praised then at Rhodes, chiefly in a peace between the emperor and other Christian powers, as the foremost of the pacific diplomatists, was a Sir Peter Holt, Turcopolier;[3] and eventually he became Prior of Ireland.[4]

Naillac returned to Europe for the Council of Pisa, in 1409, and the conclave there which he guarded.[5] The Papacy subsequently revoking

[1] Cod. Dipl. Geros., ii., Num. lxxxv.
[2] Id., ii., Num. lxxxvii. — Bosio: par. ii., lib. iii.
[3] Cod. Dipl. Geros., ii., Num. lxxxviii.—Appendix, cxi. —Bosio: par. ii., lib. iv.
[4] Bosio: par. ii., lib. iii. p. 82.
[5] Appendix, cxliv.—Platina: iii., 293, etc.—Bosio: par. ii., lib. iv, anno 1409.—Seb. Paoli: Serie, ii., 468. Y. Z.

much—perhaps as much as it conscientiously could—he undertook various long voyages and journeys, including to England, where the crown gives a safe-conduct for him, and a suite of a hundred persons, and their horses, goods, and harness, on the 8th of March, 1410; and finally at Ancona in Italy, in the last days of 1419, he pleaded the aforesaid revocations, and persuaded all he could assemble of his till then refractory knights, to recognise the reigning Pope (Martin V.), which put an end to the schism; and pardon was promulgated, and a seal on the past.[1] Back at Rhodes, after an absence of eleven years, he convened a chapter general there in 1420; where divers statutes of great moment were made, amongst which particularly deserving of notice are:—

1.—That no knight under what pretext soever can cite a companion before any other tribunals, ecclesiastical or civil, than those of his order alone.

2.—That none but a member can be present at its chapter general. And in three months after it he died in June, 1421.[2] Able prince as his diplomatic labours show, having been ambassador for

---

[1] Cod. Dipl. Geros., ii., Num. xcii.—Bosio: par. ii., lib. iv., anno 1420.—Appendix, cxlv.

[2] Seb. Paoli: Serie, ii. 468.—Statuti Tit. vii. 10, 41.—Bosio: par. ii., lib. iv. 138.—Vertot: vi. 377.

both the King of France and Duke of Burgundy in the Levant, and for the Papacy at the Courts of Paris and London;[1] and Naillac too it was that negociated the treaty of peace between Genova and Cyprus,[2] and brought to pass other laudable matters.[3]

END OF VOL. II.

---

[1] Cod. Dipl. Geros.
[2] Id., ii., Num. lxxxv.
[3] Id., ii., Num. lxxxvi.—Bosio: par. ii., lib. iv., anno 1414 and 1418.

Milton Keynes UK
Ingram Content Group UK Ltd.
UKHW021539101023
430299UK00016B/820

9 781783 313167